ROUTLEDGE LIBRARY EDITIONS:
FAMILY

Volume 16

I0130502

THE FAMILY IN ASIA

THE FAMILY IN ASIA

Edited by
MAN SINGH DAS
AND
PANOS D. BARDIS

Routledge
Taylor & Francis Group

LONDON AND NEW YORK

First published in Great Britain in 1979 by George Allen & Unwin

This edition first published in 2023
by Routledge
4 Park Square, Milton Park, Abingdon, Oxon OX14 4RN

and by Routledge
605 Third Avenue, New York, NY 10158

Routledge is an imprint of the Taylor & Francis Group, an informa business

British Library Cataloguing in Publication Data
A catalogue record for this book is available from the British Library

ISBN: 978-1-032-51072-9 (Set)
ISBN: 978-1-032-53944-7 (Volume 16) (hbk)
ISBN: 978-1-032-53946-1 (Volume 16) (pbk)
ISBN: 978-1-003-41443-8 (Volume 16) (ebk)

DOI: 10.4324/9781003414438

Publisher's Note
The publisher has gone to great lengths to ensure the quality of this reprint but points out that some imperfections in the original copies may be apparent.

Disclaimer
The publisher has made every effort to trace copyright holders and would welcome correspondence from those they have been unable to trace.

The Family in Asia

Edited by
Man Singh Das
Northern Illinois University
Panos D. Bardis
University of Toledo

London
GEORGE ALLEN & UNWIN
Boston   Sydney

First published in India in 1978
First published in Great Britain in 1979

GEORGE ALLEN & UNWIN LTD
40 Museum Street, London WC 1A 1LU

© Man Singh Das and Panos D. Bardis, 1979

British Library Cataloguing in Publication Data

The family in Asia.
1. Family—Asia
I. Das, Man Singh II. Bardis, Panos D
301.42'1'095   HQ663   78-40927

ISBN 0-04-301097-0

Printed in India

Editors' Introduction

The purpose of this book is to introduce the reader to the family structure and family relationships in various Asian nations. The nations discussed here are what Western scholars refer to as under-developed, emerging, developing, or Third World nations. "Third World" denotes that in terms of economic development, Asia, Africa and Latin America occupy a separate position from that of the West and the Communist block. In each chapter the respective author attempts to show the past, present and future characteristics of the particular nation which he has studied. The authors tend to focus on the traditional family systems, new and emerging family systems, the consequences of change for the societies and other more specific topics such as family planning. Each chapter is written by a social scientist who has spent a great deal of time "in the field" over a period of months or years gathering data on the Asian country about which he writes. Taken as a whole, the book can be viewed as a compilation of first-hand accounts that should aid the reader in determining the similarities and differences in the family structures of a wide variety of Asian nations.

LEVELS OF MODERNIZATION AND DEVELOPMENT

The nations of the world can be arranged on a continuum from the most highly developed on one end to the extremely underdeveloped on the other. Several different levels of development will now be discussed.

Highly Developed Nations
These nations are the highly industrialized and urbanized countries. They trade extensively and have many international contacts, they

have a well-developed system of internal communications and elaborate, much used transportation networks. They produce and consume a great deal of energy, and are highly productive economically. They value and strive for technological advances and have a large, well-respected scientific community. Health care facilities are generally good (except in the case of poor people in non-socialist countries), the infant mortality rates are low, and the average life span is quite long.

Developing Nations
These countries are making a determined attempt to reach the economic level of development attained in the highly industrialized nations, but have not progressed far enough to be included in the "highly developed" category. The national governments and political leaders of these countries are often instrumental in this push toward modernization, although they may face opposition from the more traditional familial and religious centers of power.

Less Developed Nations
These countries have the highest birth and death rates, the highest population densities, poor food supplies and little or no foreign trade. Their natural resources have been greatly exploited by both the capitalistic and communistic highly developed nations. Often Western corporation have used the natives of these lands as a source of cheap labor for extracting valuable raw materials. These nations are not technically advanced and possess very little scientific know how. Internal communications systems are developed and often totally inadequate. They do not produce or consume a great amount of energy. Medical facilities are generally quite poor, and high infant mortality rates and short average life spans prevail. The supply of food in these countries is limited, and hunger and malnutrition are quite common. Even in these underdeveloped nations there is a trend toward modernization and industrialization, although the obstacles in the way of achieving a Western standard of living in many cases seem insurmountable.

Of the countries discussed in this book, Japan is perhaps the most highly developed, having one of the most rapidly expanding and powerful economic structures in the world today. The Asian nations described here which fall under the category of developing nations would include India, Pakistan, Iran, China, South Korea and the Philippines. Thailand and Afghanistan are examples of underdeveloped nations. Both appear to be slow in accepting social and economic change.

TYPES OF FAMILY STRUCTURE

As nations become more modernized, the dominant family structure in turn approximates the nuclear family unit found in the highly developed nations. Briefly, the major types of family structure are as follows:

The Extended Family

One of the most common generalizations in social science is that agricultural or underdeveloped societies contain extended family structures. The extended family ideally includes multiple nuclear families and any unmarried or dependent kin, usually under the rubric of paternal leadership. An example of an extended family might be a middle-aged father with his spouse, their married sons and wives and children, their parents, and perhaps brothers and their wives and offspring, along with unmarried brothers and sisters. The combinations differ, depending on the particular nation and area in question. An extended family may have as many as thirty or forty members living in attached dwellings and working on commonly held land. The traditional extended family is very often a distinct social system, meeting the social, political and economic needs of its members.

The Limited Extended Family

In certain emerging or developing nations, the family structure is in a state of transition from the traditional extended family to the modern nuclear family. Here the extended families tend to be more compact and smaller in number, without the all-encompassing quality of the traditional extended family. For instance, a son and his wife may live with his parents until he is financially able to establish his own household, but the important fact is that eventually he seeks to assert his independence. Although the limited extended family may contain more than just the husband, wife and their offspring, it is not necessarily the center of all social, political and economic activity for the family. In many developing nations the urban areas tend to approach the nuclear family structure, while the rural areas exhibit family units that are closer to the extended family ideal type.

The Nuclear Family
This type of family consists only of a single set of parents and their immediate offspring. It is the most common family form found in the highly developed nations, although it is also found to a lesser degree in the developing and underdeveloped nations. The nuclear family is an independently operating social unit that is more or less residentially and socially separated from other family units and parental families. We should keep in mind that both the nuclear and extended families are ideal types, while many actual families contain elements of both types. But the distinction is useful for theoretical and analytical purpose.

SOME DISTINCTIONS BETWEEN FAMILY STRUCTURE IS LESS DEVELOPED AND HIGHLY DEVELOPED NATIONS

In this section an attempt is made to contrast the family structure in many less developed countries with that of the highly developed, technologically advanced nations. Once again, we are dealing with ideal type notions to which there may be several exceptions. The idea of a structural continuum is also applicable to each of the contrasts here.

Less Developed Countries	*Highly Developed Countries*
The family is more likely to be extended.	The nuclear family predominates.
Households tend to be located in rural or agricultural areas.	Urban areas contain a high percentage of the total number of dwelling units.
Social control is handled within the family unit. The family itself enforces behavioral norms.	Outside agencies and institutions, such as the police and the courts, are a major factor in the enforcement of formal laws and regulations.
The families are often totally controlled and dominated by a male leader or leaders. Women are expected to abide by the judg-	There is a tendency toward equalitarian decision-making in the family. Women are now moving into many previously male-domi-

ments of the males, and in many cases to be subservient to the wishes of the males.

nated roles. (Although sexual equality is a long way off even in the highly developed nations, the United States being a prime example!)

The family or kinship group takes precedence over the individual. The individual is expected to sacrifice personal desires and needs if they conflict with the overall goals of the family unit. The individual is taught to be dependent on the family unit for emotional and physical support.

Individualism and independence are encouraged. The child is taught to think of his own future and to value personal satisfaction above all else. Parents often sacrifice so that children may reach a higher socio-economic level.

Religion and religious beliefs often play a major part in the day to day lives of family members. The family quite frequently participates in religious activities as a unit. Religious leaders are held in high esteem.

Secular institutions compete with religion for the devotion and attention of the people. Athletes, entertainers, and charismatic political leaders are all "worshipped" in varying degrees. Religion tends to be at best a one day a week activity, rather than a way of life.

The family fulfills many basic social functions. It is the chief economic unit for its individual members, with the household and surrounding fields as the center for economic activity. Socialization, education, religious training, and health needs are all included within the basic family unit.

Major societal functions are delegated to several different major social institutions. The family no longer plays an important part in the economic system, educational training, political decision-making, and health care. Mass media may influence the socialization process every bit as much as parental input.

Not a lot of value is placed on formal education, since it is not of direct value to the family as a group.

Education is viewed as a prerequisite for economic and in many cases social success. Education is a primary means of achieving social mobility.

Elders are respected and revered, they are looked to for words of wisdom and experience.

Old people are often seen as a nuisance, and in many cases spend their final years in loneliness and silence. Instead of having a respected place in the household, they are often shuffled off to nursing homes and retirement centres where they live solely with other old people.

A rigid caste-like social structure

A class system of some type exists,

may preclude any attempts or even the thought of achieving upward social mobility. The individual is born into a set of ascribed roles that he can do little to alter.

but there are at least some opportunities for social mobility. There is also the possibility of downward mobility, as in the case of American families that are economically destroyed by the cost of a prolonged, serious illness to a family member.

Very little family planning and birth control. This topic will be discussed further in a later section of this chapter.

Family planning and birth control are much more in evidence in the highly developed countries.

The divorce rate is generally much lower.

The divorce rate is generally much higher.

Mate selection and marriages are often totally arranged by the parents, without even seeking the consent and approval of the potential mates.

Much more emphasis is placed on romantic love as a prerequisite to marriage. Potential mates are introduced to one another through the dating process. There is much more informal interaction between the sexes, which is taboo in many less developed countries (particularly in countries where the Islamic faith predominates).

Sexual intercourse is performed first and foremost for the purpose of procreation.

Sex is highly eroticized, procreation is often explicitly avoided, and intercourse is enjoyed as a pleasureable act in itself.

Although polygyny is rarely found in most cultural settings today, when it is found it is mostly in the less developed nations. (But monogamy seems to be the dominant marital form in almost every society, regardless of level of development.)

Serial monogamy seems to be the dominant marital form of in every highly developed nation.

Once again, we should emphasize that the characteristics described above do not hold true in every instance, as the reader will discover when he reads the individual chapters on the various Asian family structures. These are merely some rough generalities that are presented in this introductory chapter as food for thought.

THE DEMOGRAPHIC TRANSITION

The movement of a population from a condition of high birth rates and high death rates to one of high birth rate and low death rates, and finally to one of low birth rates and low death rates has been referred to as the "demographic transition." To date, the transition from slow growth to rapid growth to slower growth has followed the sequence in all industrialized countries. In the underdeveloped or Third World nations, improved sanitary and medical techniques have reduced the death rate drastically in the past few years, while the advent of birth control has come slowly, if at all, to many of these countries. The result is a continuing high birth rate, which, coupled with the lower death rate, has created the "population explosion" that many social scientists feel may lead to widespread famine in some Third World countries in the very near future. Third World countries are being forced through the demographic transition in a much shorter time period than was the case with most of the Western industrialized nations. There is a feeling that the birth rate must be reduced drastically in these developing nations, and as the articles in this book point out, many of the governments involved are actively advocating family planning and birth control, in some cases going against centuries-old traditions of such practices.

OBSTACLES TO POPULATION CONTROL IN LESS DEVELOPED NATIONS

There are several reasons why population control in Third World countries has not kept pace with the decelerating death rate. Here is a list of possible explanations:

1) Children tend to marry at an early age, often shortly after reaching puberty. Thus, several additional childbearing years are added to the marriage.

2) The traditional family system has stimulated birth rates through its emphasis on male verility, as demonstrated through procreation and female worth, as demonstrated through early and consistent childbearing.

3) Religion is often cited as an obstacle to population control in the developing nations, although this is probably not a major factor in most of the Asian countries discussed in this book. (It is an important obstacle in countries where Catholicism is the dominant religion, as is the case in Latin America.)

4) The ideal family size in Third World areas, even where more or less autonomous nuclear families are concerned, remains at substantially high levels.

5) Along with a traditional indifference to family planning comes a profound ignorance of basic sexual physiology. Birth control information and education are sorely needed.

PRELUDE OF WHAT IS TO COME

The family structures of the following countries are discussed individually in the remaining chapters of this book: Thailand, Afghanistan, India, Pakistan, Iran, China (Taiwan), South Korea, Philippines and Japan. Each chapter focuses on the traditional family forms in the specific nation in question, and then goes on to emphasize the changes that have taken place in the family structure and the consequences of these changes for the society in general. The family is seen as a dynamic, constantly evolving and emerging entity, and not as a static, unchanging, monolithic societal force, although the family is often slower to change than other social institutions, such as the economy. It will be seen that the family in Asia is moving slowly toward the Western nuclear family model, but retaining certain structural forms and traditional values and incorporating these within the modern family structure. It is hoped that this book will contribute to the organization and development of a systematically organized body of theory and research on the Asian family.

MAN SINGH DAS
DeKalb, Illinois
PANOS D. BARDIS
Toledo, Ohio

Contributors

PANOS D. BARDIS (Ph.D., Sociology, Purdue University) is Professor of Sociology at the University of Toledo, USA.

DAE HONG CHANG (Ph.D., Sociology, Michigan State University) relinquished his post as Chairman of the Department of Sociology-Anthropology at the University of Wisconsin-Whitewater to devote himself to research and teaching at Wiehita State University, Kansas.

MAN SINGH DAS (Ph.D., Sociology Oklahome State University) is presently an Associate Professor of Sociology at Northern Illinois University.

GIRI RAJ GUPTA (Ph.D., Sociology, University of Rajasthan) is Professor of Sociology at Western Illinois University, USA.

M. JAMIL HANIFI (Ph.D., Anthropology, Southern Illinois University) is Associate Professor of Anthropology at Northern Illinois University, USA.

GLORIA V. JAVILLONAR (Ph.D., Sociology, University of Nebraska-Lincoln) Assistant Professor of Sociology at the University of South Alabama, USA.

PROMILLA KAPUR (Ph.D., Sociology, Agra University) is Senior Research Fellow of the Indian Council of Social Science Research, New Delhi.

J. HENRY KORSON (Ph.D., Sociology, Yale University) is currently a Consultant to H.E.W. for a family planning research project at the University of Karachi.

ROBERT J. LAZAR (Ph.D., Sociology, University of Minnesota) is currently affiliated with Roosevelt University, USA.

MINAKO KUROKAWA MAYKOVICH (Ph.D., Sociology, University of California) is Associate Professor of Sociology at California State University at Sacramento, USA.

HAROLD E. SMITH (Ph.D., Cornell University) is Professor of Sociology at Northern Illinois University, USA.

JACQUILINE RUDOLPH TOUBA (Ph.D., Sociology, Purdue University) is Associate Professor of Sociology and Head of the section of Comparative Sociology at the Institute for Social Sciences and Research, College of Social Sciences and Cooperative Studies, University of Tehran, Iran.

ALINE K. WONG (Ph.D., Sociology, University of California) is Lecturer in Sociology at the University of Singapore.

Contents

I Asian Family and Society—A   ROBERT J. LAZAR
   Theoretical Overview

II The Thai Rural Family   HAROLD E. SMITH   16

III The Family in Afghanistan   M. JAMIL HANIFI   47

IV The Family in India
   1 *The Joint Family*   GIRI RAJ GUPTA   72
   2 *Touchable-Untouchable
      Intercaste Marriage*   MAN SINGH DAS   88
   3 *Christian and Non-
      Christian Interreligious*   MAN SINGH DAS   98
      Marriages
   4 *Women in Modern India*   PROMILA KAPUR   108
   5 *Abortion Attitudes Among*   PANOS D. BARDIS   148
      *University Students in
      India*

V Modernization and Social   J. HENRY KORSON   169
   Change—the Family in
   Pakistan

VI Marriage and the Family in   JACQUILINE
   Iran   RUDOLPH-TOUBA   208

VII The Modern Chinese Family   ALINE K. WONG   245
   —Ideology, Revolution and
   Residues

VIII   The Korean Family   DAE H. CHANG   277
       Modernization and Birth
       Control—An International
       Survey of Attitudes Toward
       Oral Contraception   PANOS D. BARDIS   320

  IX   The Filipino Family   GLORIA V.
                                      JAVILLONAR   344

   X   The Japanese Family   MINAKO KUROKAWA
                                      MAYKOVICH   381

  XI   Summary and Conclusions   MAN SINGH DAS
                                      PANOS D. BARDIS   411

       Index   421

CHAPTER I

Asian Family and Society—A Theoretical Overview

ROBERT J. LAZAR

This chapter is formed as a theoretical outline of issues which are critical in the analysis of the interrelationship between Asian society and family social systems. While no specific hypotheses are formulated or tested, this essay is intended to form the basis for the development of such hypotheses. The general strategy of formulating large-scale theoretical hypotheses involving only a few variables but not testing them is supported by Levy *et al.* (1965). The specific strategy followed in this essay has also been followed by Inkeles (1969: 615-632).

BASIC CONCEPTS

Prior to sketching the analytic framework employed in this essay, definitions of some basic concepts appear to be required; such concepts are society, family, and Asian. For purposes of this essay, following Parsons, a society is defined as a large-scale relatively self-contained social system, with the capacity of existing longer than the longest living individual participant. According to Murdock (1949: 1), a family is defined as "a group characterized by common residence, economic cooperation and reproduction. It includes adults of both sexes, at least two of whom maintain a socially approved sexual relationship, and one or more of their children of their own or adopted by the sexually cohabiting adults." The concept Asian as employed in this essay is defined in an indexical fashion by pointing to common features of socio-cultural existence in China, Japan, India, and Thailand.

Since this essay is organized around a comparison of the traditional and modern forms of the Asian family and society, definitions of the concepts of traditional and modern are also required. A traditional society is one characterized by a relatively slow rate of social change, while a modern society is characterized by a relatively rapid rate of social change. Many other less general characteristics may be envisaged as useful in the differentiation of traditional and modern societies. In demographic terms, the traditional society is one which has a relatively high birth rate along with a relatively high death rate. The modern society is one which has a relatively low birth rate and a relatively low death rate. In economic terms, the traditional society is organized around agriculture, while the modern society is organized around the distribution and consumption of a large and endlessly varying range of mass-produced goods and services. In terms of social stratification, the traditional society is characterized as having a limited range of statuses and roles, allocated on a primarily ascriptive basis; traditional social systems feature great social distances between various strata and limited individual and group social mobility. In contrast, the modern society is characterized as having a large and varied range of statuses and roles, allocated on a primarily achievement basis. Modern societies feature limited social distances between strata, and high potential for major individual and group social mobility.

However rigid or flexible societies or families are in their usual manner of according members statuses and roles, these social systems also vary in the extent to which they may be characterized by stability or by relatively rapid social change. There is no firm relationship between rate (and magnitude) of social change and the extent of stress experienced by members of various social systems. While Inkeles (1969:616) notes in illustrative fashion the case of individual and systemic stress which accompanied rapid social change in the course of the Industrial Revolution in Western nations, he fails to note the extent to which individuals and groups in traditional stable social systems may experience intense or prolonged stress and therefore find substantial difficulty in achieving the tasks facing them. Moreover, a distinction should be drawn between the normative or ideal moral standards and behavioral aspects of family and social life. The argument here is that intense or prolonged stress should lead to changes in ideal norms or behaviors, or both norms and behaviors. In our discussion of the Asian family as a social system, the conventional division of the life cycle as found in the human development literature is adopted here. Reference is made to the stages of 1) infancy and childhood; 2) youth; 3) the middle years; and 4) old age. For the family as a social unit, reference is made to the stages of 1) formation; 2) maturity; and 3) disintegration. Justification for a theory of Asian societies is provided by Jacobs (1971: 525-530).

ANALYTICAL FRAMEWORK

In this effort to describe the general relationship between family and society, for traditional and modern families and societies, society is taken as the independent variable and family as the dependent variable. Several general aspects of communal life are held to insure systematic, though not complete, coverage of all of the complexities inherent in the family-society relationship. The dimensions to be considered are (Inkeles, 1969: 618):

1) *Ecological:* here we note the size, density, physical distribution, and social composition of the population; its relationship to its resource base, and to surrounding populations.

2) *Economic:* this has special reference to the social forms for defining, producing, and distributing goods end services. The type and amount of material resources available in a given society are also important. Economic and ecological elements may be intimately interrelated.

3) *Political:* the political subsystem encompasses the structure of power: its distribution, forms, and application, along with the institutional arrangements for generating, legitimating, and exercising it.

4) *System of values:* economic and political institutions of course embody values, but many important values which guide socialization efforts are not most visible or effective in their institutionalized forms. In addition, a large part of socialization consists in the simple effort to inculcate values.

These dimensions are of different types. The ecological dimension represents the biological basis of all human social systems. The system of values dimension represents culture. The economic and political dimensions refer to essential functions which must be accomplished within the family unit, but refer to essential functions as well as to specific institutional formations regarding society. For example, the economic dimension helps call our attention to economic activities within the family as a self-contained economic system. In contrast, the economic dimension of society helps call our attention to the economic aspects of the social units contained within a society, including the specific organizations and institutions formed around economic activity.

Thus, members of a factory organization may be able to produce what is required of them, however much they might dislike one another. If they are not able to achieve the economic goals, the organization may not long survive. In contrast, low income through a poor crop or job loss does not necessarily lead to family disintegration; such disintegration is likely if the members of a family can no longer be comfortable in the presence of one another.

While the dimensions under analysis (ecological, economical, political, and system of values) vary together for societies and families in both Western and Asian cultures, under traditional and modern circumstances, the central thrust of this essay is directed at highlighting the social changes which qualitatively distinguish the two cultures.

TRADITIONAL ASIAN SOCIETY

The right to authority was determined by the intrinsic merit of age, only slightly qualified by moral and intellectual considerations. This right to authority was validated by provision of customary services to the population. The terms of service, as well as initial rights to authority, could not be set by a self-proclaimed elite. Moreover, this elite could not claim the right to authority by demonstration of a superior ability to resolve socio-political conflicts; thus Asian mythology frequently celebrates the rise of a young man of appropriate moral and intellectual qualities to a leadership position after a heroic deed.

The dominant principle of economic rationally was communal

service; while the principle of profit-making was not looked down upon, wealth had to be directed toward serving the community. Even Karl Wittfogel (1957) in his work on hydraulic despotism and total power recognized a minimal level of public service, below which even the greediest despot could not operate.

The dominant activity in the countryside was labor-intensive agriculture, while retail trade and handicraft production were dominant economic activities in towns and cities. In both cases, profit-making was secondary to communal service. This observation is supported by the development of guilds and trade unions in the post-feudal West and their absence, until recent times, in Asian cultures.

In the division of labor, activities performed by persons of appropriate age and intellectual and moral qualification were highly valued and highly rewarded; activities performed by others were limited in value and reward. In contrast, in Western industrial cultures, all forms of work were held to be of equal moral value however differently various labors were rewarded.

In the order of social stratification, only those of the proper age and intellectual and moral qualifications had their interests recognized in law. Others had no right to seek protection of the legal order. In contrast, Western legal traditions display an extensive development of the principle of universal protection of all under law.

Maintenance of the extended family structure, combined with an increasing ability to produce larger food quantities on limited parcels of land, led to families of increasing size. The principle of descent favored an equal division of resources among all legitimate heirs. Individual members of each generation obtained less in each division of resources than was the case for members of any previous generation. In Western cultures, the problem of inheritance was resolved through the separation of property and status or the selection of persons in a single status as inheritors.

The central focus of Asian theology was adjustment to an existing social order; in such an order, the rules were determined by members of the intellectual and moral elite, who rewarded adjustment and punished deviation. In contrast, Western theology has been dominated by an otherwordly concern; men were to find individual solace and contentment in the hereafter. In the post second world war decades, since 1945, the otherworldly concern of

Western theology has been minimized and concern for change in the secular order has been developed. Western theology retains a concept of man as essentially active, while Asian theology largely regards man as passive.

TRADITIONAL ASIAN FAMILY

The traditional Asian family, under ideal conditions, was limited to members of a single extended multi-generational family. Through the device of fictive kinship, otherwise unrelated adults could be included in a household, thereby sharing in the economic and social psychological security, as well as the conflicts and anxieties of other family members. Members of both sexes and all age groups were usually present in the household.

The right to authority in the family was limited to those having the ascriptive qualification of the oldest married male. In part, age was held to have intrinsic merit and, in part, because men were held to have appropriate moral qualifications, family authority was limited to older married men. The elderly were venerated as repositories of communal and family wisdom. Reaching old age was a rare event for members of a family. During their lifetimes, the elderly had experienced nearly the entire range of natural and communal crises and their experience could therefore be depended upon as a source of reliable guidance in any present crisis. This restriction of the right to authority on the part of the eldest male family member was a constant source of stress in the traditional Asian family, because family responsibilities had to be carried out by both the younger men and the women of the family.

Since the family household was large, appreciably large resources and incomes were required. This was not problematic, since many people could work for its economic survival. Economic opportunity outside the family was limited. While individual wealth could be achieved, one was expected to devote such wealth to the support of one's family. Relatives and their families always had a valid claim to the economic resources of one's own family in time of n eed. In a subsistence economy, this possibility of extended claims to resources already stretched thin was a constant source of stress. Moral obligation conflicted with economic scarcity.

In the division of labor within the traditional Asian family, everyone was expected to work, but work done by older family members was considered of greater moral worth than that done by younger family members, and work done by men was considered of greater moral worth than that done by women.

On the ecological dimension, the high birth rates and high death rates typical of traditional Asian societies meant that members of traditional Asian families would have regular and intimate exposure to the events of birth and death. The constant presence of adults and young people of various ages and both sexes meant that infants and young children would be socialized by many people rather than just the mother and perhaps a few siblings. If the mother were unable to perform her child-rearing tasks, numerous substitutes for her would be available. In any event, this meant that the relationship between the mother (and her associates in child-rearing) and the child would involve less intense interaction between the mother and child than would be the case in the smaller nuclear family. Few problems would result if those charged with child-raising responsibilities were consistent in their activities, but marked inconsistencies could produce serious problems for both adults and children in the family.

Economic resources available to a family have a clear influence on child-socialization practices within the family. Under ideal normative conditions in the traditional Asian family, children would be exposed to the full range of age and sex graded work responsibilities. Since traditional Asian families shared homogeneity of economic circumstances, child-rearing practices would be similarly limited in variability.

The political system of traditional Asian societies might be characterized as rigidly authoritarian; thus children in traditional Asian families might be treated by adults in an authoritarian fashion. There is, however, equal merit in the argument positing reactions in the family contrary to the predominant tendencies in the political system outside it.

The values of the surrounding society will be impressed upon the child in an indirect manner prior to the development of language and related experience. Thus, for example, the prevailing sense of time is impressed upon the child through feeding schedules, toilet training, play and sleeping arrangements, and in many other ways. In traditional Asian society and in the traditional Asian family, the sense of time was flexible rather than rigid. Therefore, infants and young children were allowed to develop at their own pace rather than being faced with time schedules in feeding and rigid developmental schedules.

The restriction of young people to activities within their family household and the high proportion of adults within that household increased the extent of adult control and decreased the basis for opposition to parental desires. The extent and strength of the control of young people by adults is suggested by the lengthy historic endurance of the practice of arranged marriages in the traditional Asian family.

The control of adults over young people, as well as the control of the oldest male over other members of the family, was enhanced by a more or less total control over scarce economic resources. Moreover, occupational training took place through working along-side the adult members of one's own family or through apprentice-ship-adoption to another family. Limitation of activity to the family circle meant that young people could not become active in politics as individuals or organize groups to do so effectively. While the values of a traditional Asian society and the traditional Asian family do not change rapidly, every other adult attempts to provide the youth with a proper sense of values for right living. Even if the maxims formed a completely consistent doctrine, differences might be observed between the ideal normative value and actual behavior. Young people, even in a traditional Asian family, would be constantly forced to make choices or retreat into passivity.

During the period of youth, young people in the traditional Asian family were involved in the process of family formation; they were valued for bringing their own children into the family, a future economic resource and a guarantee of family continuity. As young people reached positions of adult responsibility, the extended family reached a stage of maturity; newcomers were not likely. The family would undergo no further growth. Members of traditional Asian families, in common with members of traditional family structures in other societies, are faced with the problems of a prolonged period of time in a sub-adult status; members of such families may meet the responsibilities of adults but lack the full share of the social honor accorded to adults.

During the stage of disintegration in the traditional Asian family, numerous unrelated adults live in the family household. While members of the family continue to share economic responsibilities, they no longer live under the same roof. The dominant pattern is one of individual nuclear family residences located in the close proximity of a family compound. The central problem of life during the adult years is maintenance of pacific relationships in the family. While the years of old age are dominated by a gradual decline of physical capacity, the elderly retain positions of power and command of economic resources of the family.

MODERN ASIAN SOCIETY

The model of modern Asian society and the model of the modern Asian family following it are drawn from materials on Japan (Cole, 1971; Sano, 1958; Nakane, 1970), China (Yang, 1965), Taiwan (Wolf, 1968), India (Kurian, 1961), and Thailand (Wit, 1968).

The right to authority is determined primarily by moral and intellectual qualifications monopolized by a self-proclaimed elite. Though the command of wealth, military power, and educational resources enables members of the elite to demonstrate a superior ability to solve problems of the existing order, their primary claim to authority rests on a perceived obligation to serve society.

The economy of modern Asian societies remains directed at communal service. Profit-making becomes an important principle of economic rationality, but profits are not more important than communal solidarity. The dominant activity in the economy of the countryside remains labor intensive agriculture on small family plots, but the extent of labor required has decreased compared with the requirements of traditional agriculture. Light manufacturing is now found in the countryside, along with heavier investments in social overhead areas, such as schools, hospitals, and transportation. Electricity and modern sanitation are becoming more widespread in the rural areas, along with extensions in the mass media. Individuals and entire families in modern Asian societies, unlike their traditional counterparts, now migrate to urban centers in appreciable numbers.

The dominant activity in urban economic life is labor for salaries and wages in large industrial organizations. Even in the most industrialized of all the Asian countries, Japan, employment relationship is viewed as a lifetime relationship between the employee and the company. The concept is that of the company as a surrogate family, providing the security of constant employment, as well as a broad range of social welfare benefits, such as child care, housing, and medical care. The massive development of trade unionism in Japan is of recent origin (since 1945). While the unions favor mobility from corporation to corporation, the unions themselves take on the qualities of the family surrogate.

In the division of labor, there is a tendency for all forms of work to be accorded equal moral worth, but rewards for white-collar work tends to be greater than that for manual or machine work. Work done by men tends to be more highly rewarded than work done by women, but there is a tendency for an increasing proportion of the women in modern Asian societies to be employed outside the home. Recruitment to positions of leadership in industry, government, and the military tends to be, in both ideal normative and behavioral senses, on the basis of particularistic qualifications of family and school ties rather than on the basis of universalistic qualifications of demonstrated past performance or educational training.

In the system of stratification, the legal order is not directed at the protection of the interests of a traditional intellectual and moral elite, but is instead directed at allowing all to present valid and sometimes competing claims for communal recognition and protection of their rights.

The principle of inheritance in modern Asian societies has shifted from the traditional form of inheritance by all legitimate heirs to a more modern form of inheritance by a more limited set of heirs. In the countryside, inheritance is by ultimogeniture or inheritance by the last born child. In the city, inheritance is limited largely to the wife and children. Thus, regardless of city or rural residence, those who inherit wealth and property obtain individual shares not seriously diminished from the holdings of the previous generation.

In the area of theology, concern remains directed at a man's adjustment to an existing social order, but there is a significant concern directed at the promotion of what are considered as proper changes in that order. Over time, fewer and fewer religious festivals are observed; this holds for both observances in the home and in the local temple. Only a few of the most significant festivals are communally observed. The single outstanding quality of religious practice in modern Asian societies is the similarity to religious practice in modern Western societies, that is, a quality of ethnic identification rather than a quality of genuine participation in a religious community.

MODERN ASIAN FAMILY

In some Asian countries, such as Japan, both birth and death rates are low. In most Asian nations, however, the introduction of public health measures has reduced only the death rate, while birth rates remain relatively high. Regardless of whether the population size tends towards stability (Japan) or growth (China), the traditional extended family living in a single residence has declined in favor of smaller nuclear family households.

Because the family circle is smaller, the intensity of interaction between mother and child is likely to be much greater than in the traditional Asian family. In the countryside, nuclear family residences along with residences of unrelated household members are likely to be located in the close proximity of a family compound; this leads to a slight reduction in the number of adults supervising the care of infants and young children. In the nuclear family household of urban areas, the number of adults per household who take care of children is small. In both urban and rural areas, as economic opportunities outside the family multiply for both men and women, infants and young children are likely to be supervised by non-family adults. Thus, the reduction in the number of supervisors and the reduction of time spent with children both serve to increase the intensity of interaction with children in the family.

In urban areas such as those of China and Japan, there is an increasing level of personal income, widespread modern as well as traditional social welfare practices, more leisure time, and above all, common work involvement in large organizations. Thus, urban child-rearing practices in Asian countries are likely to become more homogeneous. At the same time, in the Asian rural areas, increasing number of persons find non-family employment. To the extent that non-agricultural employment opportunities develop in the rural areas, diversification in child-rearing practices in those areas is likely.

While the dominance of adults over children in the modern Asian family is complete, the political system outside the family is of some influence in shaping the form and content of the socialization

of children. Both traditional and modern Asian political systems
show strains of authoritarian patterns. Further research and theoretical concern are required on the question of consistency or
opposition between the political system outside the family and the
nature of the adult-child relationships within the family.

Since the value system of any culture is impressed upon infants
and young children in an indirect fashion, one can only plead ambivalence in the case of the modern Asian family. Thus, as industrialization becomes stronger in Asian countries, one should find
more emphasis toward precise uses of time; therefore, child-
rearing should become more rigid (demand feeding schedules and
strict developmental requirements). As a scientific outlook becomes
dominant, expert opinion rather than family opinion (based on
traditional experience) should dominate child care.

In the modern Asian family, the power of youth is enhanced in
two ways: first, the household is small and fewer adults are present;
and second, the youth are free to associate with others in opposition
to parental desires.

Young people in both urban and rural areas spend more of their
time in non-family institutions. Extended periods of education and
occupational training are required in industrializing or already
industrialized societies. The division of labor is extremely complex, and work training in the family or through apprenticeship is
no longer sufficient. Young people therefore represent cost rather
than income in their own families. They are, at this point in their
lives, socialized by non-family adults who relate to them in an
impersonal fashion. In the case of Japan, the development of technical schools and colleges served to reduce the frustration of many
young people who could not gain entrance to the few highly valued
university programs. In most Asian countries, however, the central
problem with young people in the modern Asian family is one of
handling youth discontent. Aspirations concerning economic participation or style of consumption rise on the basis of participation
in educational institutions or attention to mass media, yet, for rural
youth, little opportunity may exist for the realization of these
expectations.

Young people in modern Asian societies are increasingly able to
represent effectively their own political interests. The Red Guards
of China and the youth movement of Japan demonstrate this. The
values and actions of the older generation are no longer acceptable

to the youth. The stimulus for the youth movement in politics appears to be related to conditions of rapid technological and social change, combined with revolutionary leadership. Thus, youth movements in politics appeared in Japan after the second world war (1945), and China after the Communist revolution.

The system of values in the modern Asian society and in the modern Asian family is in a state of flux. The resulting values are neither traditional Asian nor modern Western. Conflict and ambivalence are found among both adults and youth concerning appropriate values to guide them in handling the problems of living.

For example, in the traditional Asian family, concern for security was focused on the entire family; in the modern Asian family, this has been reduced to concern for individual security.

Arranged marriages are no longer acceptable to young people, who favor the principle of romantic love. Nonetheless, formal family introductions and the ritual of the go-between are maintained even where much of their original substance has been lost.

While the adult is to fit his place and perform appropriately in a changing social order, the order person is no longer highly valued. The cultural world for which his wisdom and experience were of importance no longer exists. If the power of adults in the modern Asian family is problematic, older persons have no power at all. The time perspective in the socialization of older persons tends to be short-term rather than long-term; they have little to look forward to.

CONCLUSIONS

This paper has focused on issues related to socialization to highlight the nature of the relationship between family and society.

Socialization is a requirement of organized social life; hence, every organization is a producer of socialization. Some organizations, such as armies or factories, have other primary goals; thus, they rely on prior socialization of their potential members by other organizations. The family is the most universal and the most important organization for general socialization.

Socialization is a lifelong process; an individual is never completely and finally socialized. Organizations other than the family play an important role in socialization at different points in the life cycle.

While socialization is ordinarily associated with continuity and
stability, socialization may also serve as a stimulus for major social
change. Further research and theory construction in the area of the
modern Asian family require an adequate model of modern Asian
society, as well as a model of the modern Asian family, in addition
to specialized, practical family studies. This essay was intended as
a modest contribution in that direction.

Modern Asian societies have retained the principle of elite rule,
though authority is claimed on the basis of non-traditional values.
Economic activity remains organized around communal service.
Recruitment to leadership positions in military, industrial, and
government bureaucracies is on the basis of particularistic rather
than universalistic qualifications. Large organizations are viewed as
surrogate families for their participants; thus the Weberian criterion of efficiency is minimized in favour of communal service,
though all of the elements of formal bureaucratic structure are
present. The legal order of modern Asian societies tends toward
universalism.

Modern Asian families tend toward small nuclear family households in both urban and rural areas. In the rural areas, the nuclear
family residences of family members are clustered around a family
compound, often including households of non-related adults. Young
people are more powerful within the family circle because there
are fewer adults in the family household and because the young
people are now free to associate with others. The traditional value
of concern for the security of the entire family has been reduced
to concern for individual security. While young people favor the
principle of romantic love in finding mates, the traditional ritual of
the go-between is often retained.

In modern Asia, the traditional structural forms and values have
been modified rather than left behind entirely. The theories and
concepts of Western sociology should not be blindly applied to
studies of modern Asian societies and modern Asian families.

A special theory of the Asian society and of the Asian family is
required. As Jacobs put the issue (Jacobs, 1971: 529):

But we do suggest that there may have to be a drastic overhaul
of much of the intellectual baggage of western sociology, which,
contrary to its claim of universalism, is ethnocentric not only in
its concepts but also in the kinds of questions it brings to the

study of non-Western societies. Otherwise one can but fear that sociology will not measure up to the formidable challenge of being both valid and useful to the study, formulation, and prosecution of social action programs in such non-western societies.

REFERENCES

Cole, Robert
   1971   *Japanese Blue Collar: The Changing Tradition.* Berkeley: University of California Press.

Inkeles, Alex
   1969   "Social Structure and Socialization" in David A. Goslin (ed.), *Handbook of Socialization Theory and Research.* Chicago: Rand McNally. Pp. 615-632.

Jacobs, Norman
   1971   "Max Weber, The Theory of Asian Society, and the Study of Thailand." *The Sociological Quarterly,* 12 (Autumn). Pp. 525-530.

Kurian, George
   1961   *The Indian Family in Transition: A Case Study of Kerala Syrian Christians.* The Hague, The Netherlands: Mouton and Company.

Levy, Marion J., Jr., and others
   1965   *Aspects of the Analysis of Family Structure.* Princeton, N.J.: Princeton University Press.

Murdock, George Peter
   1949   *Social Structure.* New York: Macmillan.

Nakane, Chie
   1970   *Japanese Society.* Berkeley: University of California Press.

Sano, Chiye
   1958   *Changing Values of the Japanese Family.* Washington, D.C.: Catholic University of America Press.

Wit, Daniel
   1968   *Thailand: Another Vietnam?* New York: Charles Scribner's Sons.

Wittfogel, Karl August
   1957   *Oriental Despotism, A Comparative Study of Total Power.* New Haven: Yale University Press.

Wolf, Margery
   1968   *The House of Lim: A Study of a Chinese Farm Family.* New York: Appleton Century Crofts.

Yang, C.K.
   1965   *Chinese Communist Society: The Family and the Village.* Cambridge, Mass.: M.I.T. Press.

CHAPTER II

The Thai Rural Family

HAROLD E. SMITH

INTRODUCTION

The following presentation on the family in Thailand is based
chiefly on a review of the literature but also includes findings from
an empirical study in which the author participated. The topics
treated include something of the economic, demographic, and
religious aspects of the Thai nation; an overview of the structure
of Thai society; the roles of men, women, children, and elders; a
typology of families; mate selection and marriage; getting the newly
married couple established in their household; family conflict and
its dissolution; child-rearing; family planning policies and activities;
and brief comments on other Thai family systems. Finally, a brief
discussion is offered concerning social changes in Thailand and in
the Thai family with some speculations regarding its future. In the
treatment of the topic, an attempt is made to get at the norms
defining expected behavior using a comparative sociological
approach. The major focus will be on the rural family of central
Thailand.

Background

Thailand, a nation-state of more than 40,000,000 people,
is centrally located on the mainland of southeast Asia. Its

economy, based chiefly upon agriculture, has recently begun to diversify, but manufacturing is slow to develop, Bangkok, the nation's capital, and Thonburi, its twin city, constitute a metropolis of approximately 4,000,000 persons. The Thais have a long history of political independence and have never been a colony of a European power. Following the rule for 700 years by an absolute monarch, a revolution in 1932 ushered in a government by a council of ministers and a parliament with powers defined more or less by a constitution. The king of Thailand remains with titular powers. On several occasions in the past three decades, the parliament or the council has been dissolved or replaced in a *coup d'etat* with new leaders assuming power. Until recently, the top leadership in the council was composed chiefly of former military officers. In the past one hundred years, modernization has occurred gradually in Thailand with accelerated change taking place in Bangkok, the capital, and in a number of smaller cities. The rural areas which account for four-fifths of the Thai population are gradually changing also, although much more slowly than the urban centers.

The people of Thailand reflect some diversity in their ethnic background and local dialect. The Thai predominate and constitute more than 80 per cent of the total population. The Chinese-Thai are the largest minority, followed in size by the Malay-Thai. There are, however, a number of regional subgroupings within the category referred to as Thai. These include the Thai of the central area, the Thai Khorat, the Thai Yuan in the northern area, and the Thai-Lao in the northeast part of the country. Each of the foregoing has a distinctive dialect, with that of the central area and Bangkok having the most prestige. Such differences are minor compared to similarities.

While the people of Thailand are nominally Buddhists, their religion is permeated with animism. Hence spirit worship and propitiation of the spirits are prominent, especially in a time of sickness or crisis. From Brahminism, the Thai have adopted notions of the heavens and hells, as well as certain ceremonies and ideas about their political system. Much energy, money, and manpower are involved in the conduct of Thai Buddhism. Almost every population center has its temple-affiliated buildings and staff of local monks. In the life of rural people of Thailand, the Buddhist monk has the most respected social role. There are status gradations within the organization (the Sangha) of which the monks are a part, and monks are at the top of the hierarchical system in rural communities. While every male is supposed to spend at least one rainy season living the ascetic life of a monk, probably no more than one-half actually do. However, such religious achievement has traditionally been valued above wealth and political power. In addition, the area near the temple is often a social center for local residents and the site of certain local ceremonies, most of which have a religious accent.

A Hierarchical Society

The predominance of vertical social relationships over others is an interesting and important characteristic of Thai society in both urban and rural areas. When this writer along with faculty members of a Thai university in 1965 were on a field trip, the official who accompanied and led the project paid for the food and provided transportation. This "largess" did not just happen—it is an expected Thai pattern that a "patron" cares for and distributes material resources to his "clients" who in turn provide services and loyalty to him (Piker, n.d.: 155-159).

These vertical relationships are characterized by inequality and deference of inferiors toward superiors. Phillips (1965: 32-34) illuminates this point when he discusses "respect patterns":

These patterns are based, in the first instance, on the status inequalities that exists in almost all social relationships: within the family, usually in terms of the relative ages of people; elsewhere in terms of age, wealth, power, knowledge, and religious or governmental role. Secondly, they are based on the assumption that every individual, regardless of his position in the hierarchy, deserves respect.

The older-younger pattern guides relationships so that younger members in their greetings and in other ways show respect for their elders. Status differences are reflected in conversation since the pronouns used vary with the rank of the speaker and with that of the person spoken to (Cooke, 1968). Parents are solicitous in caring for their children. Older children take pride in having to look after a sibling, and the latter in turn performs the tasks requested of him. The family is thus a training ground for the superior-inferior patterns appropriate with relatives, teachers, monks, government officials, and others.

Rural Social Organization

The rural people of Thailand, as well as other Asian societies, characteristically live in small hamlets or villages. These are sometimes called agricultural villages reflecting the predominance of farming enterprises as sources of income and subsistence. Three principal types of Thai villages have been identified by de Young (1955: 8-12). These are 1) a cluster settlement of dwellings which are surrounded by rice fields, with a road for outside connections; 2) numerous houses lining one or both sides of a river or canal which provides outside access; and 3) isolated homesteads or small groups of houses relatively isolated but in the midst of rice fields with a tiny canal connecting to a larger canal or river. Villages vary in size from about 50 to 200 homes with an average size of about 100 dwellings and comprising 400 to 500 persons. The villages are not necessarily discrete social units, however; Piker (n.d.: 83-84) points out that a large part of the social interactions of some residents of one village may be with certain residents of another village. The village has been a convenient locus for the research of social scientists. Larger villages were identified as communities by Kaufman (1960), Moerman (1966), and Keyes (1966).

The village is often considered a social unit from the viewpoint of ecological and societal structure. As residents of a specific village, individuals and families relate in certain ways to local, provincial, and national government. For paying taxes, reporting of births, marriages, deaths, etc., villagers are administered or represented for governmental affairs through, or by, the village headman.

The most prominent element in the social organization of Thai rural society is the family household which together with the kindred is treated below (see TYPES OF FAMILY SYSTEMS). Before offering that explanation, some aspects of the agricultural situation will be discussed briefly. There are three principal ways that villagers are related to land in rural Thailand: 1) mostly, farmlands are owned and operated by family-household units. The average household of five or six persons can normally provide all of the labor needed to farm up to eight acres of rice. Family households which own or operate acreages larger than this typically secure additional labor (see below). 2) Some lands are held by urban residents as an investment and are farmed on a rental or sharecropping basis. Absentee ownership is most prevalent in the rice lands of central Thailand. 3) From one-third to one-half of all family households neither own nor rent agricultural land and are referred to here as landless families (Piker, 1972: 6-9). Among the factors thought to be related to landlessness are: i) the relatively high cost and limited supply of farmland; and ii) the scarcity of suitable uncleared land which might be homesteaded. The principal means of support of landless families have been 1) agricultural wage labor with payment either in cash or in kind or both; 2) home crafts such as hatmaking and basketware; and 3) non-farm wage labor.

Rice Farming and Village Labor Exchange

Wet-rice farming, which is the predominant type of agriculture in Thailand, requires careful timing regarding the various steps of the production process. This is one reason why family households that own or operate more than eight acres normally employ or secure additional labor. Preparation of the fields and seedbeds involves plowing, harrowing, drainage, irrigation, uprooting, and transplanting, any or all of which require high labor inputs. A certain amount of water is essential for each operation in rice farming, except harvesting. However, too much water may make these tasks impossible and preclude use of a rice paddy until the next season. Hence there are real time limits to be met by rice farmers as the water level rises during the rainy season.

The seasonal nature of labor requirements of wet-rice agriculture offers an interesting study of the intertwining of economic and familial roles. Four ways of meeting the need for extra labor are indicated. Traditionally, the single family household obtained additional workers in periods of peak labor through the communal work group (Soontornpasuch, 1963: 44-55). In the pattern, which is disappearing, the head of the family solicited assistance from relatives and neighbors by promising to help them later when they had the same sort of need. The problem of extra labor was also met through the kindred which is explained below. Hired labor at prevailing wage rates constitutes another answer, and this pattern has increased in recent years. Taking the landless family into your household either on a quasi-kin or patron-client arrangement, with compensation in housing, food and wages is still another method (Piker, n.d.: 156). A particular family household might rely on but one of the foregoing methods, or may utilize two or more of them in combination.

For comparative purposes, some observations about Thai society's integration are offered. Typically, in Western societies, there is considerable autonomy in institutions or societal parts as is implied in the use of expressions such as the economy, the church, the school, etc. In Thai rural society, on the other hand, there is a high degree of integration with the family and kinship providing an organizing role. Economic, religious, educational, and other elements acquire relevance as they are brought into the life cycle activities of the family household. Such elements have an existence as part of the larger operation of the family and kin groups in an agricultural way of life, which is in step with the seasons of the year and which has been traditional. To some extent the orientation of villagers regarding economic behavior is influenced by religious values which are taught or exemplified by local Buddhist practitioners or monks.

One research team (Blanchard, 1957:5, 13) contends that "the Thai consist of a homogeneous spiritual community, sharing the same language (in spite of dialect differences) and religion, agreeing upon the fundamental questions of morality and torn by no debates on what it means to be a Thai . . . . Every citizens know his country has a king, and his king is to be respected and revered, honored and obeyed. . . . His picture of the world would be incomplete without the king's image in the center, for the king embodies the values of national unity. His (the king's) person—all that it symbolizes—molds the society of villages into a nation sharing common values and moving toward a common destiny."

TYPES OF FAMILY SYSTEMS

The Family Household

The term family household (or simply family) is used here in an inclusive sense to designate the kin group members who live together in a single dwelling or in adjacent dwellings, who share a single hearth, and who act as a unit in economic, familial, and in other affairs. The household contains typically a nuclear family and may also include a parent or siblings of one of the spouses. In addition, two or more nuclear families may join in a single household. This group acts together in providing food, shelter, and the like, in rearing children, and in religious observances and ritual occasions.

Income, Consumption, and Family Size

Some idea of the economic characteristics of the family household in rural Thailand is provided by a study of Smith and others (1917: 17-26) which involved a sample survey of more than 900 rural families in 1963-64. Except in the rubber growing areas of south Thailand, income was derived chiefly from production of rice (40 per cent) with the remainder coming in approximately equal amounts from livestock and poultry, outside labor and home industry, and fruits and other crops. Food purchased was the largest item of expense, taking about half (53 per cent) of home consumption funds. Clothing and home repairs together accounted for one-fourth (24 per cent) of home expense with the remainder somewhat equally divided among medicine, equipment and furnishings, and other items. The above data are biased by the study's deficiencies in that household expenditures for ceremonies, recreation, travel, and charities were not obtained.

The average household size in rural Thailand is generally reported between five and six persons with a range from one to thirteen persons (*Thailand Population Census*, 1960). From their survey data Smith and others (1971:32-33) found relationships between size of household and 1) annual money income; and 2) annual household expenditures. They reported that the larger the household, the larger the income of the family household. If this finding is true, it may simply indicate that a larger family means more workers, the ability to farm more land, and hence more income. They also reported that the larger the household, the larger the family expenditures. This second inference would seem to depend on the previous one. In other words, if income goes up with size of family, then household expenditures can be expected to go up also.

Thai Rural Families—A Typology of Forms

Marriages in rural Thailand are almost entirely monogamous.

However, polygyny has been known to occur in both rural and urban areas, albeit chiefly in the latter (Smith, 1973b). Three family household forms that are typical of rural Thai society and one residual category have been identified. These are 1) the nuclear family, which predominates; 2) the limited extended family; 3) the extended family; and 4) others. Each will now be described and explained in turn.

Nuclear family. The prominence of this family form has been indicated by Sharp *et al.* (1953) and Wijewardene (1967), both of whom refer to the nuclear family as an ideal in Thai rural society. Further confirmation is provided by the research of Smith (1973a) and Piker (n.d.). Husband, wife, and offspring typically compose this type of family. However, variations are possible and include the married couple only or either parent and children only. Occasionally, a dependent parent or relative of the husband or wife may be present also. This form accounts for 50 to 60 per cent of all family households.

Limited extended family. In this pattern the family may be extended beyond the nuclear in either of two ways. First, a married daughter (or son) and spouse (recently married) are present with her (his) parents and possibly grandchildren. An in-marrying husband is expected to become a part of the household work group. In another arrangement, parents in their old age continue to live with the youngest daughter (or son if no daughter is available) and her husband, who typically inherit the house and compound on the death of the parents. A highlight of this family form is its role as a launching platform for the young and as a haven for the retired. When a second child wishes to marry and bring her (his) spouse into the parental home, the older married sibling should be ready to move out and set up her (his) own independent household. When the previously married offspring is not prepared financially to become independent, the marriage of the next sibling may be postponed or other housing arrangements may be made. This same pattern applies when a third sibling plans to marry. There is a Thai belief that misfortune would occur should two married siblings both reside in the parental home simultaneously with their parents.

Incidence of married siblings residing with their parents has been reported by Madge (1955:43-55), who referred to this family form as the "two-tier" family. The limited extended family form was initially identified by Janlekha in his report on Bang Chan (1955). The view that membership in a limited extended family is a temporary situation which corresponds to a certain stage in the family life cycle is indicated by Soontornpasuch (1963:41).

Extended family. The extended family pattern refers to situations where two or more married siblings are part of a single family household either by themselves or with parents or other relatives. This pattern also typically reflects two or more residences in an area that are adjacent so that food preparation can be at a single hearth. In their study, Smith *et al.* (1971:33-35) reported numerous family households where members occupied several dwellings that were adjacent to one another, thus forming a kind of cluster. These clusters varied in size from three to twelve sub-units of the household with an average of four to five per cluster. Since great grandchildren were reported frequently, it would appear that in some of the extended families there were four generations present. The approximate percentage distribution of the foregoing family forms was nuclear, 64 per cent; limited extended, 7 per cent; and extended, 29 per cent.

Other family systems. This is a residual category needed to include family households which do not fit the previously delineated types, such as one person households or a situation in which a man is living with his nephew, or that of two related women living together, etc.

Polygyny. References to Thai polygyny in the literature are at best brief. However, it appears that plural marriage which existed in Thailand in ancient times still occurs today among some well-to-do males. The extent of polygyny is suggested in the 1953 study of Bang Chan (Phillips, 1965:41), where such marriages were reported by 2.7 per cent of the family heads. Similarly, in a recent survey of fertility of the Malay-Thai in south Thailand, polygynous marriages were reported by only 2.6 per cent of the sample population (Goldstein, 1970:335). It has been customary for the man seeking a second wife to secure the approval of his first (primary) wife, who enjoyed a status somewhat superior to subsequent or secondary wives. The law in Thailand permits a man to register any child regardless of who the mother is, so that a secondary wife's child enjoys privileges similar to those available to the offspring of the primary wife. That polygyny has been chiefly an urban phenomenon in Thailand is asserted by Smith (1973b), although it has been practiced by a small percentage of well-to-do farmers also. A movement in opposition to polygyny developed in the present century and led eventually to legal reform. In 1935, a new family law was enacted which required that marriages to be fully legal must be registered and that "neither party (getting married) is already the spouse of another person" (The Civil and Commercial Code of Thailand, Book V). It was thought that the new law would cause polygyny to die out since it reduced secondary wives to lower status. However, there was no penalty for not registering one's marriage. It appears that the extent of polygyny has been very little, if at all, affected by the Marriage Registration Law. Nevertheless, this legal provision is a large step toward orderly marriage and divorce records.

The Kindred

A second unit of social organization commonly found in rural Thailand is the "kindred," which Murdock (1960:3-5) defined as "the only important grouping of kinsmen other than the dominant small family unit." There is not complete agreement among scholars regarding Thai kinship terminology. The usage here is close to that of Piker (n.d.:102 ff.) and Soontornpasuch (1963: 87-92). An illuminating account of kindred in a central Thai village is provided by Piker (n.d.:102 off.), who found that about two-thirds of the village families belonged to at least one kindred.[1] In addition to relationship (cognate and affinal) with some degree of sentiment, the exchange principle and mutual reciprocity were fundamental in the kindred group. On the basis of an understanding among family heads, two or more family households would look to one another for exchanges of resources and labor, such as assistance with farming tasks, loans of food and farming tools, and loans of money. Piker also indicated that landowning families were much more likely to be kindred members than landless families. Perhaps this contrast is related to the emphasis on the exchange-of-goods-and-services function of kindred plus the fact that landless families have few resources to exchange and do not need the labor of

[1]The research of Piker was conducted in Banoi and nearby hamlets in 1962-63 and again in 1967-68, which are near the city of Ayudhya.

others. Piker (n.d.:105-107) found it useful to distinguish between hierarchical and sibling kindred. The former consisted of a parent household joined in a kindred with one or more married offspring households, while the latter was composed of two or more married sibling households.

A view of the kindred has been reported by Soontornpasuch (1963:87-92), who defines kindred in a slightly more inclusive manner when he states, "this category includes...(cognates)...affines and other non-kindred such as farm laborers, friends and neighbors...(it) exists at times when it congregates itself around a given individual for certain purposes, very often on the occasion of an individual's rite of passage, or in any communal works, e.g., transplanting, harvesting, etc....Although these obligations are reciprocal rather than compulsory in nature, the groupings tend to provide a continuing network of relationship from which further similar groupings may arise." Soontornpasuch (1963:92) further comments: "The concept of kindred, thus, has a vital role in the operation of the Thai social system. A man's kindred provides a field with alternatives in which he can move or choose any means suitable in fulfilling his social and economic needs." Compared to the previous usage, here the relatives are central in the kindred membership which is made up of persons who somehow select each other and who expect to assist one another in farming and other tasks, but who also join with contributions or assistance as appropriate for rites of passage. Presumably, the continuity of kindred associations depends on exchanges of goods and services being made with trust and confidence and when this is lost so is the kindred relationship. This view of the kindred by Soontornpasuch reflects similarities with the "personal alliances" identified in rural Philippine society by Hollensteiner (1963: 63-67).

A frequent explanation for kindred formation is the desire of parents or older siblings to share resources in exchange for services of offspring or younger siblings. A more general rationale for the kindred in rural Thailand follows from a recognition that there are no voluntary associations or interest groups generally. Neither are there large-scale corporate groupings such as clans or lineages. Hence the kindred serves the need of family members for a larger entity with which they can identify and relate themselves. This is important in the sense of physical protection and as a cushion against misfortune. Kindred groups seldom last longer than a generation or two, which is understandable in view of their tendency to organize around specific individuals.

Mate Selection and Marriage

The Thai youth of marriageable age seeks a bride among the young women that he already knows. This is likely to be a large group since there are many opportunities for heterosexual contacts resulting from association among young people in school, in village ceremonies, in work exchanges, and in other affairs. While young men are relatively free in their social contracts, young ladies are kept under surveillance by their parents at all times. The parents of the girl prefer that courting takes place at their home. The young man may seek chances to see the young woman by offering to help her or her parents in the evening after his own work is done. Semi-private visits and courting on the girl's house veranda are a common pattern.

The young Thai generally secures the approval of parents before marriage occurs. This is obviously necessary when the newly married couples are generally dependent economically on one set of parents in the early part of the marriage. If the parents agree with their son's marriage desires, they make an approach to the girl's parents. They may do this themselves or through a go-between. The boy's parents may disapprove of his marriage plans when they: 1) need the son's labor at home; or 2) feel that he should become a monk before marriage; or 3) disapprove of the girl; or 4) cannot afford the necessary financial arrangements for the marriage.

As in other societies, there are bargaining aspects to mate selection in Thailand. Following the approach initiated by the boy's parents to the girl's parents, financial matters are taken up if interest on both sides continues. Bargaining centers on the amount of the boy's gift to the girl (*khongman*) and his gift to the girl's parents (*sin sord*). It may also deal with property arrangements in regard to farming and residence after marriage. It is usual for the young woman's parents to ask for a higher price than they expect to receive. When the man or his parents cannot make an adequate offer, the match is precluded. If both sides reach agreement, preparations go forward for the marriage, or, if this is not immediately feasible, an engagement is arranged, the main purpose of which is to delay the wedding date until such time as both sets of parents can get ready for the occasion (Soontornpasuch, 1963:126-130).

The *khongman*, as mentioned previously, is presented by the man or his party. Traditionally, it is a piece of gold. However, it may be a necklace, bracelet, belt or diamond ring. Land and working animals are also used to secure the agreement. At the same event, an amount of cash may be given to the girl's party as a reward by the man, since the girl has agreed to marry him. In central Thailand, this can amount to a sum of money between 3,000 baht ($150.00) and 15,000 baht ($750.00). It is likely to be larger in well-to-do families and smaller in low income families. This gift may be used by the young woman's family in preparing for the wedding that will take place in her home, or it may be given to the young couple. Marital choices of parents, and therefore of Thai youth, tend to reflect economic values. Thai villagers frequently encourage their children to marry into a family which has an economic standing in the community similar to their own or slightly higher. Piker (n.d.: 135-137) observed that the in-marrying man obtains rights in the property of his bride's family in exchange for the "bride price" which he pays.

Generally, a young man and young woman are considered married after they have performed marriage ceremonies as prescribed by local custom and tradition. Assuming that an agreement has been reached between the persons involved, marriage simply consists of certain rituals, properly performed. To this event, parents, kindred, and friends are invited as witnesses. In turn, they give their approval and blessing to the new couple by pouring sacred water upon them. The wedding event also symbolizes the agreements arrived at through negotiation and bargaining between the parents of each young man and young woman on their behalf. Thus the approval of the parents occurs prior to the wedding, which provides an opportunity for recognition and approval by a wider circle of relatives and friends.

In comparing Thai and Western societies in regard to marriage, Chandruang (1940) observed: "Our marriage is purely a personal agreement with social sanctions, but their (Western) marriage is a religious and legal contract." In Thailand, marriage norms and expectations are maintained by public opinion and social pressures. Exceptions to this can be found in elopements and common law type marriages among persons who are more or less without any family connections.

On the basis of his research in Banoi village, Piker (n.d.: 131-134) made the following observations in regard to the meaning of marriage (summarized by the author): 1) mutual affection does have a part in the movement of Thai young people toward marriage. However, since parental selection of the spouse may render personal preferences irrelevant, expediency became paramount. 2) The young woman is likely to be concerned about the prospective reliability of the husband as a provider. When parents select and the husband turns out to be a ne'er-do-well, the bride can always blame her parents. 3) The young man also seeks economic security and has such expectations resulting from involvement in the enterprises of the bride's family. Along with other men he acknowledges the advantages of the steady hand of a wife who manages the household and family finances. 4) The set of parents who assume the major role in establishing the new family (usually the bride's) hope for one or more prosperous offspring on whom they can be dependent in their old age.

Marriage registration. As indicated above (p. 25), a 1935 family law directed the registration of marriages. The extent of such registration was investigated in 1963-64 as part of a larger survey employing a quota sample of Thai rural households (Smith, 1973b). Findings indicated that about one-half of the family heads had registered their marriages and the remainder had not registered, since there was no penalty. The following variables were found to be directly associated with the rate of marriage registration: 1) size of family; 2) amount of money income; 3) number of children in the family; and 4) age of the family head. It would appear that tradition rather than the law has had the greater influence in marriage and family patterns as far as the rural areas are concerned.

Establishing the New Family Household

The large majority of newly married couples start their married life as part of the parental household, and this pattern reflects both economic and traditional elements. At least two different economic influences are reflected thereby. On the one hand, this facilitates the accumulation by the young couple of farming experience and also the cash and other necessities for starting a farm operation of

their own. Secondly, the parents' farm and household may need
the services of either the husband or wife or both. When a son or
daughter brings his or her spouse to live with the family, it becomes
a limited extended family as described above. The young couple
may have a room in the parents' house or a separate dwelling in
the same compound. In either case, meals are taken together with
the parents, siblings, and other family members and are served
from a single kitchen. The labor of the new in-law, son or daughter,
is contributed to the household unit of which he or she becomes an
integral part. If this residence is temporary, the new couple is
generally assisted in accumlating the capital necessary for beginning its own household later. The couple may be allowed to farm
a portion of the parents' land, either free of charge or with a nominal rent. Instead of this, the young people may be given the rice
crop from a certain portion of the parents' land. In other cases,
the couple is given annually a certain quantity of rice up to 200
tang or an amount of cash. After finishing their work for the household, the young people may find outside employment also.

The set of parents with whom the new couple resides after
marriage is of basic interest to students of marriage and kinship.
If a general pattern can be observed, it may indicate one or more
traits of the Thai kinship structure according to Kemp (1970:73-
85). It was found by Janlekha (1955:86) in Bang Chan village and
by de Young (1963:64-65) in San Pong village that no marked preference was shown for either the wife's or husband's parents in the
matter of initial residence. However, nearly all of the newly
married couples in Pa-ao village (Madge, 1955:44) and more than
three-fourths similarly in Banoi (Piker, 1972:141-144) took up
residence following marriage initially with the wife's parents
or relatives of the wife. The latter reflects a matrilocal kinship
pattern.

There is a widespread practice in rural Thailand for the youngest daughter (or youngest son if there is no daughter), when she
is married, to bring her husband to live with her parents. This is a
functional pattern in that it is intended to ensure care of the
parents in their declining years. The youngest daughter in this case
would typically inherit the parents' house, compound, and equipment. The son-in-law becomes head of the household, of course,
when his father-in-law dies or retires.

Adult Roles: Men, Women, and Elders

The Thai husband has a ritual superiority derived largely from Theravada Buddhism. The wife shows respect for her husband in certain symbolic ways and should not suggest her own superiority in either actions or speech. There are tendencies toward equality of the sexes in Thai culture also, and only a few tasks in the agricultural village show a clear division of labor. The heavy physical farm labor is typically done by men and cleaning after meals is usually left to the women. Most tasks can be performed by either men or women and the division of labor between the sexes is flexible generally. There is apparently no attention paid when a man does a woman's job and *vice versa*. For example, a woman may do plowing and a man may be a midwife. There is a male-female distinction in religious affairs since the role of Buddhist monk (*bhikku*) is available only to men. However, women are much more active than men in providing food and other needs of the monks who may be residing at the local religious center (*wat*).

To some extent, husband-wife relationships reflect a division of labor of convenience. While each has control in certain areas, consultation occurs regarding the ongoing family affairs. The husband is the traditional leader in farming, securing and repairing property and equipment. However, the wife has charge of the regular household activities and care of the children. She controls the purse in regard to expenditures for food, clothing, and home furnishings. Milling the rice, when done by hand, is usually a female task. The role of women in marketing is a distinctive Thai pattern. Regularly, women sell the home-produced fruits, vegetables, and other items. Thai women and farm produce are a familiar sight in the waterways and market stalls of the towns. Merchandizing activities are likely to be seen by men as less prestigious than the traditional role of the farmer.

Leadership in village affairs is typically a male function. The village headman is always a man, since one duty is protection and the maintenance of law and order. The hamlet committee and temple committees are composed of men. Occasionally, women perform leadership roles also, but with much less frequency than men.

While sex differentiation is minimal, it is still present. Hanks and Hanks (1963:439), in their view of Thai culture, speak of hardness, self-centeredness, and power as masculine qualities and softness, pity, and nourishment as female characteristics. While men bring "food from the fields" and make contacts with the outer world, women nourish the family and hold the hearth group together. Aggressiveness and loudness in speech are not condoned for either sex. However, men are permitted more indulgence than women in these matters. It has been a tradition for a man to serve for a period of time as a monk. This experience makes a man learned and brings him to maturity. Monkhood also marks the male's entry into adult life and increases his prospects for a good marriage. There is no direct parallel of monkhood in the life of the woman. The nearest indication of her achieving adulthood occurs at the time of the birth of her first child. In some cases, marriage may mark this transition also.

The traditions of status and respect in Thailand accord deference to older persons. At house blessing ceremonies, funerals, and other social occasions, the older people are seated in positions of honor. At weddings the elders are first in recognizing and blessing the newlyweds. It was observed in Bang Chan (Sharp, 1953:83) that respect for elders was based partly on wealth, knowledge or sanctity, as well as on age. In other cases, deference for an older person may depend on his position in a specific relationship, such as father-son or pupil-teacher. However, a young person with very desirable qualities may be held in higher regard than an older one who lacks such attributes.

The strongest indications of deference to elders are found in the kinship system. An elaborate terminology to designate kin as either younger or older is used according to Benedict (1943:168). From birth onward, all Thai are trained to give respect to family members in the generation above, as well as those of one's own generation who are older than the speaker. Older members in the village are generally addressed as grandfather or grandmother regardless of biological relationship. These behaviors are largely symbolic and suggest a general idealization of seniority and age. To live a long time is considered a blessing and an indication of much earned religious merit. There is a tendency for village old people to be more active than others in religious observances and in participation in *wat* (religious center) activities and responsibilities. This interest and attention to Buddhism on their part brings to them a high regard from community members. A few old men who are dependent and who lack status from wealth or close kin may re-enter the priesthood and retire to the *wat*. Similarly, old dependent women may become nuns. It has been observed that old people are not supposed to take advantage of their preferred status (Sharp, 1953: 87). They are supposed to live modestly regarding the consumption of food, clothing, and adornment. They should keep in the background when others are active in the home, especially when the younger generation has visitors of its own age.

It was also observed in Bang Chan that it was the middle-aged men, both priest and lay, who actually determined policy and ran the *wat* (Sharp, 1953-85). In Ku Daeng (Kingshill, 1965:71), age was less important than several other factors in determining the prestige rating of village leaders. One active young monk, aged forty-two years, rated very high. The average age of these leaders was forty-seven years. Older men did not have the physical stamina for such cooperative tasks as building roads, repairing canals, and other active roles.

Socialization of the Child

One study of the Thai rural family (Piker, 1964:152-271) throws considerable light on parent-child relationships and the following discussion is based on this research.[2] While the preferences for male children is perhaps stronger than for female offspring, Thai villagers actually want both. Piker treated parental ambivalence regarding the desirability of having children as integrally related to their conceptions of the ideal son and the ideal daughter. The characteristics of the ideal son will be mentioned briefly and then those of the ideal daughter will be discussed.

Pre-school male children, though indulged by family members, should show ample signs of compliance and devotion. The son should be diligent in primary school and do well in order to advance through enough education to qualify for a civil service position, with its job security. Furthermore, he should not incline overmuch to typical male tendencies for irresponsibility such as drinking and

[2]Piker's study was conducted in Banoi, a small village in central Thailand, in 1962-63. Data regarding socialization were obtained from observations of seven families having at least four children which were visited frequently, and from extensive interviews of thirty-six mothers and fifteen fathers.

gambling or fighting. At age twenty he should become a Buddhist monk for one summer season, as this would yield great religious benefit to him as well as to his parents. After this he would assume an economically secure position and be able to devote attention as needed to his parents. The ideal daughter shows loyalty and com‑ pliance. As early as she is able she assists her mother with house‑ hold chores and the care of younger siblings. While she should be diligent in school, this goal is subordinate to her need for close parental guidance until she marries. Parents are anxious that her virtue be protected so that she would attract as a marriage partner a son‑in‑law with a reputation for diligence and reliability. The married daughter and her family will provide support for her parents in their old age.

Ambivalence of parents in regard to having children is derived from the prospect of positive feelings about success in producing children who come close to the ideal and from the prospect of negative feelings when they are seriously disappointed in the be‑ havior of their offspring. Concerns expressed by villagers regarding parenthood included 1) having children is trouble; 2) a feeling that they may be unable to give their children an adequate start in life; and 3) anxiety concerning character development. Characteris‑ tic behaviors that were socialized by the pre‑weaning, post‑wean‑ ing, and later stages are now discussed.

In the pre‑weaning period, the infant experiences from parents and other relatives a high level of oral and affectional indulgence, especially in feeding and placating the child's desires. The father plays with and enjoys his offspring, but expects his wife to handle infant crises and trauma. Toward the end of the pre‑weaning period, threats, punishment, and unfulfilled promises are also used by the mother to supplement indulgence as control devices. A mother usually weaned a nursing infant within several months after she incurred a new pregnancy. The length of time a child was nursed was shorter for mothers engaged in wage labor than for others. Weaning after a period of nursing by the mother means removal of the breast accompanied by the child's frustrations. In this period the child experiences a sharp reduction in the pattern of indulgence both in amount of maternal attention and in oral satisfaction. The new state of affairs is accompanied by some degree of rejection by the chief agent of attention, the mother.

Piker (1964:209-214) identified in his Banoi research recurrent patterns of children's roles: 1) the youngest sibling has a privileged position; 2) the second youngest sibling adjusts to his loss of favored status initially with aggressive behavior and hostility toward the new rival and toward the mother; 3) his attempts to recoup his lost primacy are met with failure and in fact are often ignored, and the aggression is regarded placidly by the parent; 4) the next older siblings, having given up hope of regaining the privileged position, have begun to take on adult behaviors and frequently imitate the mother's approach to the baby. Proto-adult behaviors are much more characteristic of girls than boys until the latter are strong enough to assist with work in the fields; 5) intersibling aggression is consistently discouraged by parents who use a wide range of control techniques, including threats and physical punishment.

While Thai rural parents idealize gentleness and tolerance in interpersonal relations, they practice a mixture of indulgence and threats or punishment in child socialization. Overactivity is seen as a nuisance and is discouraged. At five to ten years of age and beyond, children learn gradually how to care for themselves, that is, bathing, eating, dressing, and going to bed. Parents also attempt to control a "wanderlust" in growing children, and this reflects an anxiety that offspring might reject their immediate family or develop characteristics of the ne'er-do-well son or wayward daughter. Children are strongly guided to be diligent in school and deferent toward adults and superiors. After age ten, girls are urged to play only with other girls as part of parental concern with female virtue. Boys of this age, even more than girls, face strenuous parental pressure to avoid unnecessary "wandering," since it might lead to fights and interpersonal animosity in which the parents could become involved. Other undesirable behaviors often associated with "wandering" included stealing and gambling.

Other socialization by Thai rural parents of children is chiefly unintentional and less explicit. Fear of parents is felt to be an aid in obtaining obedience when indulgence and affection do not seem adequate. Physical punishment is the principal means of instilling this fear and is widely used by parents. Sons are frequently punished physically more than daughters since they are more "obstinate." There was a notable lack of consistency in parental enforcement of obedience/compliance upon children. There is but minimal direct teaching of children about sexuality. Only a few adolescent girls are told about menstruation by their mothers. Most have a knowledge of pregnancy and childbirth, having observed the latter in their parental home. In a more recent paper, Piker (1972:11) discussed the effects of socialization on adult personality. He called attention to the conditioning of young girls (aged five to six years) in task-oriented roles in the family home as a sequel to the role of second youngest sibling and its high order of neglect and frustration. Boys by contrast have little or no structured alternatives until several years later. Piker finds in this differential handling of the sexes a basis for the greater ego strength of village women over village men.

As boys and girls grow up in the village family, they are taught by parents the numerous tasks required of life on the farm. By the age of fifteen years they have gained experience in all of the various kinds of farm and home work. In addition, their labor is usually essential to the success of the farm operation. In this way they acquire a number of skills that will prove useful in their later adult life. In the rice village, these skills include: preparation of the paddy, irrigation, sowing and transplanting, harvesting, caring for livestock, fishing, and preparing food for meals. In addition, several heavy work skills are learned by young Thai males. Another large task of the first few offspring in the family is the caring for their younger siblings. The observation of adult roles and apprenticeship by Thai youth is a distinctive feature of the traditional Thai family.

It can be seen that rural Thai youth are generally dependent on their parents and kinsmen for training in the basic skills and folk knowledge that is essential to making a living on the farm. The village school does have compulsory education through the fourth grade, and in some areas through the seventh grade. However, the curriculum is very general and makes no contribution to the technology of farming and homemaking. While the children provide labor which is central in the farm and home operation, they are compensated, not in money, but in the necessities of life, including food, clothing, and shelter.

Family Conflict and Dissolution

Little is known about the extent of separation of spouses and family dissolution among Thai rural families. The lack of family stability was suggested in the Bang Chan study. Phillips (1965:26) reported that 20 per cent of a group of interviewed families had dissolved within a period of four months. It is possible that at least part of this may have occurred just after the rice harvest when many husbands are temporarily absent in wage employment. Soontornpasuch (1963:160-163), a Thai scholar, on the other hand, points out the security of the marriage bond in Thai rural communities. He cites the aid of parents and relatives in mediating difficulties that may arise between a husband and wife. However, he further indicates that separations and marriage dissolutions do sometimes occur and that two common causes are the serious negligence of either spouse in performing his role in marriage and adultery on the part of the wife.

As indicated previously, the pattern of marriage and dissolution among Thai rural families is largely a matter of traditional social norms and is also a personal matter. Hence, if one is dissatisfied with his marriage, ending that relationship is also a personal affair. Further, marriage is not a value in the Buddhist religion. On the contrary, Buddhism encourages a person to make merit as an escape from a life of suffering. Cases where a man may leave his family to enter a *wat* (religious center) and become a monk are well known. In fact this is often considered a laudable act, and little or no disapproval is to be found. A wife and children who are greatly dependent economically on the husband-father may be scattered by his entering the monkhood.

The coming of registered marriages has added an element to the marriage dissolution process. If the marriage is registered, it cannot be ended legally without the approval of the district officer. However, such consent can be obtained when evidence of mutual agreement of the spouses to separate is provided. In this case the action is known as a divorce. However, one-sided family break-ups may be impeded by the marriage registration requirement. When mutual agreement to separate is lacking and suit for divorce is brought by one spouse, each case is handled on its own merits (see Marriage registration, p. 29, above).

THE THAI URBAN FAMILY

Only a sketchy treatment of the Thai middle class family in Bangkok can be attempted here, in the absence of research reports on the topic. However, brief mention of the Thai urban family has been made in other reports which have been drawn upon, along with the author's observation during two years' residence in Bangkok. Compared with Thailand as a whole, Bangkok is largely Westernized. Blanchard (1957:486-487) observed that increased Westernization is seen by the Thai as a means to improve social status. However, the contrary notion of maintaining and strengthening Thai culture also has been observed. Evidence of Westernization is widespread, including the use of English and other European languages and the presence of numerous United Nations and other international and national agencies in Bangkok which make it a regional world capital. Many leaders of government, which is highly centralized in Bangkok, have sought deliberately to modernize and Westernize. One evidence of this is the greater value placed on European and North American college degrees compared with those of Thai universities. However, many rural social values have been exemplified in the city, such as regard for religion, personal habits, and respect for superiors and elders.

In contrast to the peasant orientation that largely characterizes life in the agricultural village, a middle class style of life is descriptive of much of the urban population in the nation's capital. This reflects the existence of a high proportion of families with the following: middle incomes, either a secondary or higher education, and employment in government or business. In the rural family, work is performed typically in the home or in fields nearby and often with the participation of other family members. In contrast to this, the urban family organization reflects a separation between occupation and family. Accompanying this separation is considerable differentiation of sex roles similar to that in other urban settings. Much more than in the village, the family is dependent upon the school in Bangkok for the socialization of youth and for the preparation for adulthood. Education often involves separation also since the city youngster typically completes more schooling than his rural counterpart and often must travel long distances to reach the school. Opportunities for urban youth to work with adults as apprentices, as in the village, are extremely limited except possibly for young women who assist their mothers. However, there is a widespread pattern among high income and secure middle income families to employ a maid for cooking and laundry work, which largely frees other family members from such homemaking duties. This also permits time for leisure pursuits and family centered activities.

With regard to family formation, there is in the city, as compared to the village, more opportunity and more freedom for social interaction between single young men and women (Thamavit and Golden, 1954:382) and fewer restrictions. With the wide availability of motion pictures, there is increasing acceptance of going to morning or afternoon shows together. Couple dancing is also practiced to a growing degree particularly among those young people who have been to Western countries for educational or other reasons. However, among the more traditionally oriented, proper social contacts of men and women are made at the home of the latter when others are present. Marriage rites in the city are generally compressed into a shorter time frame although in other respects they resemble the traditional rural marriage. In addition, the group ceremonies may take place in a public building or restaurant rather than in the home of the bride's parents. Finding housing for the newly married pair is a critical problem in Bangkok with the result that the couple may reside with in-laws for a considerable period of time.

FAMILY PLANNING IN THAILAND

Reservations and obstacles to effective family planning are found in nearly all societies and Thailand is no exception. In early 1970, an antinatalist policy was announced by the Thai government and the principle of family planning was given public approval at the highest level. However, efforts toward population control and family limitation prior to this were quietly under way and resulted in important advances in the middle and latter 1960s. Principal responsibility for setting up and administering family planning in clinics, the distribution of advice and supplies, and the training of personnel has been located in the Thai Ministry of Public Health. In addition, one Bangkok University hospital and several private clinics have made important contributions to family planning. Thomlinson (1971:101) has indicated: "by the beginning of 1970 approximately one-tenth of Thailand's married women aged 15-44 were using some effective form of contraception (including sterilization of themselves or their husbands." Thomlinson also predicted that Thai expenditures for family planning in the 1970s would show a sizeable increase and that the rate of annual population growth would be lowered by possibly one-fourth by 1980 (1971:106-107). Two interesting ideas for family planners emanate from the Thailand experience. One of these is a programed-instruction manual developed for a self-instruction course in family planning methods for midwives and nurses. The other idea applicable to countries suffering a shortage of physicians is the Thai practice of permitting midwives to prescribe oral contraceptives. After a period of instruction, the midwife is prepared to deal with "patients" by asking a series of questions about health and to conduct a simple external examination. If she found it advisable, the midwife could then give the woman a supply of pills for contraception control. One factor in the rapid progress of family planning in Thailand was the decision of a number of influential Thai physicians that birth control was needed. They then proceeded to install family planning into place alongside previously established activities in the Ministry of Public Health under the guise of being research on family health. The other factor was assistance to family planning from two foreign agencies. One of these was the U.S. Agency for International Development and the other the Population Council (Thomlinson, 1971:98-99).

The receptivity of the Thai public regarding family planning was the subject of six interview surveys completed during the period 1964-68. Three of these were in a central province, one each in a northern and a southern province and one in Bangkok, the nation's capital. The principal results were, according to Thomlinson (1971:101), that "most multi-parous Thai women were ready for birth control." While the women expressed generally a desire for a limited number or no more children, they were largely unaware of ways to achieve this goal. Presumably, they would take advantage of a program that provides knowledge and supplies of a type already available to more educated and affluent persons.

THE THAI RURAL FAMILY AND THE FUTURE

Relative to Western societies, the tempo of social change in rural Thailand is a very gradual one. Modernization of the country began in the second half of the 19th century under the leadership of the Thai kings. The commercialization of agriculture, particularly rice, began to accelerate and reached a high level soon after the beginning of the 20th century. Further impetus to change was associated with the coming to power in Thailand of a council of ministers—parliament type of government. Transportation and communication have improved considerably especially in the last twenty-five years. To some extent education is increasingly seen as the route to a better position and increased wealth, although this is reflected more in the behavior of well-to-do urban families than among the rural villagers. While most of the changes in Thai culture may be referred to as "Westernization," the Thai have been rather successful in adapting new elements so that they fit into the Thai scheme of things. Of direct impact on the rural population adjacent to Bangkok and other urban areas has been the expansion of the urban job market and the increased reliance on money as a medium of exchange. The non-farming aspects of Thai society have become better known to villagers as a result of the ease of travel and the increased use of radios. These bring into the rural villages information from government agencies about opportunities for better living associated with agricultural services, health services, etc.

The Thai rural population has grown very rapidly. The growth of the total population was recently estimated at 3.2 per cent per year and a doubling in only about twenty-two years (Thomlinson, 1971:1). Land suitable for agriculture that might be cleared and available for new settlement is very limited. Along with the foregoing elements, population pressure on agricultural land has resulted from the commercialization of agriculture, which has been accompanied by absentee landlordism. There has also been an increase in the number of landless rural families, according to Piker (1972:6-9; n.d.:176-187), who investigated one community where at least half of the village families were landless. However, these families, which neither owned nor entered farmland, were able to subsist on wage labor or by providing services for their landed neighbors. This reflected the considerable prosperity of the landowners. During previous decades there was considerable out-migration of villagers also, according to Piker. The foregoing changes appear to be associated with certain changes in rural family structure. For one thing, there has been kindred fragmentation associated with out-migration of rural villagers. That landlessness leads to kindred dissolution was mentioned above since kindred groups depend largely on exchanges of resources and services. Since the landless villagers have little if any resources to exchange, compared to the landed villagers, they are not likely to participate in such kindred groups. This can have important results in view of the value of the kindred as a refuge or haven in time of crisis. Economic security for landless villagers depends on their establishing arrangements with landowners who will employ them for specific tasks or for specific periods of time and on their finding nonagricultural wage labor or establishing services that others will purchase.

Piker (1972:10-11) entertains the prospect that memory of landownership will gradually fade in the life pattern of landless Thai families. This possible change, along with developments associated with differential access to land or to kindred alliances, could lead to enduring patterns of social status differentiation. Briefly, membership in an extended kin group and ownership of land might in the future be a recognized social distinction in the agricultural village between the two statuses—landowner and landless persons.

Piker (1972:11) also offered an interpretation of possible changes in child-rearing practices. To some extent, moneymaking opportunities have opened up in the village for women. In addition to growing fruits and vegetables for the market, some women provide a service, sell food, or make marketable craft products. Such activities are perhaps characteristic of more economically oriented persons and so far constitute a small minority of women. However, it appears that these women use child-rearing patterns modified from that presented above (p. 27) chiefly in the direction of diminished indulgence in the treatment of the youngest child. The mothers do this by using more older sibling care and more bottled milk in lieu of nursing the infant, and by giving less total attention to the child's demands. Piker (1972:11) points to possible beneficial consequences if this child-rearing change catches on widely. It suggests the possible reduction or perhaps elimination of the near traumatic rejection and neglect experienced by the second youngest child under traditional socialization patterns and also improved maturation of the child. On the other hand, the development of an active mastery orientation (previously absent) would be enhanced.

SUMMARY

This essay on the Thai rural family is based on a review of the literature together with the author's own field experience. Thailand is very largely a rural society, as about 85 per cent of the population resides in small villages where economic activities are centered on agriculture. Bangkok-Dhonburi, the nation's capital and only metropolis, is an expanding commercial center in which considerable Westernization is evident. The superiority of things urban and governmental and the inferiority of "ruralness" apply in Thailand as in many other societies.

Kinship and marriage units predominate in the Thai rural social structure and provide a wide variety of functions. In other words, families whatever their form, are organizing centers of rural life. Thus, it is the family which is the source of identity, provides shelter and sustenance for members, cares for the aging until their death, and trains the young for careers in farming and homemaking and launches them after they marry. The family has large financial obligations for marriages of offspring, cremation of the dead, and other ceremonies. In comparative perspective, nearly all aspects of life in Thai rural society are relatively fused through family and kinship units. This characteristic is in contrast to the relative autonomy of politics, the economy, religion, the family, and the school in urban industrial societies.

The typology of the Thai family includes the following five patterns listed in order of the frequency of their occurrence: 1) the nuclear family, regarded as the ideal form; 2) the extended family; 3) the limited extended family, which is unique in that it consists typically of two subfamilies united in a parent-son or parent-daughter relationship; and 4) other, which refers to one-person households and unusual groupings; 5) polygyny, which is chiefly an urban phenomenon and practiced by less than 2 per cent of Thai adult men. After families, kindred groups are second in importance in Thai rural society. Such groups bring together in an operating unit two or three families or similarly sized groups of kinsmen who exchange resources and services, utilizing the principle of mutual reciprocity. Labor, tools, loans of money, and foodstuffs are examples of items exchanged by kindred groups.

Thai young people generally choose their marriage partners subject to the approval of their parents, who bargain relative to

economic considerations. Marriage is essentially a personal agreement involving social sanctions. While Thai men have a ritual
superiority, there are also tendencies toward male-female equality.
For only a few village tasks is there a clear division of labor. The
roles of men and women are largely interchangeable. The traditions of respect and social status in Thailand accord deference to
older persons.

The attitudes of parents in regard to having children and rearing them show a mix of anticipation of success and apprehension
that they may be disappointed. While the father indulges his offspring when they are very young, the mother has the chief role in
child-rearing. She uses threats and punishment to supplement indulgence as means of control. One researcher of Thai child socialization points to the trauma of the second youngest sibling at the
time the new baby arrives. He asserts a relationship of this period
of frustration and the nature of adult personality.

Family planning activities have gone forward in Thailand since
the mid-1960s. One demographer has estimated that one-tenth of
the married women aged fifteen to forty-four were using some type
of contraceptive in 1970. If use of contraceptive increases, it may
well reduce the 3 per cent annual growth rate that has for long
characterized Thailand's population.

One possible influence for change in rural Thailand is the persistence and gradual increase in a landless families. Another indicator is the out-migration from villages of population which tends
to fragment kin groups. Landlessness may well be associated with the
dissolution of kindred groups, since the landless villagers have few
if any resources to exchange. They are less likely than their landed
neighbors to participate in such groups. This change is of importance in view of the value of the kindred as a haven in time of
crisis.

REFERENCES

Benedict, Paul
    1943   "Study in Thai Kinship Terminology." *Journal of American Ori-
           ental Society*, 63.
Blanchard, Wendell (Ed.).
    1958   *Thailand: Its People, Its Society, Its Culture.* New Haven, Conn.:
           HRAF Press.

Central Statistical Office
1962 *Thailand Population Census: 1960.* Bangkok, Thailand.

Chandruang, Kumut
1940 *My Boyhood in Siam.* New York: F.A. Praeger.

Civil and Commercial Code of Thailand
1965 Book V (as amended to 1953) of Books I-VI. Bangkok: Aksornsasn Press.

Cooke, Joseph
1968 *Pronomial Reference in Thai, Burmese, and Vietnamese.* Berkeley: University of California Press.

de Young, John E.
1955 *Village Life in Modern Thailand.* Berkeley: University of California Press.

Goldstein, Sidney
1970 "Religious Fertility Differentials in Thailand." *Population Studies,* 24 (November).

Hamburger, Ludwig
1965 "Fragmentietre Gesellschaft: Die Struktur Der Thai Familie." *Koelner Zeitschrift Fur Soziologie und Sozial Psychologie,* 17.

Hanks, Lucien M. Jr., and Jane R. Hanks
1963 "Thailand: Equality Between the Sexes" in Barbara E. Ward (ed.), *Women in the New Asia.* Paris: UNESCO.

Hollensteiner, Mary
1963 *The Dynamics of Power in a Philippine Municipality.* Quezon City: University of the Philippines.

Janlekha, Kamol
1955 "The Economy of a Rice Growing Village In Central Thailand." Doctoral dissertation. Ithaca, N.Y.: Cornell University.

Kauffman, Howard
1960 *Bangkhuad: A Community Study in Thailand.* Locust Valley, N.Y.: J.J. Augustin, Inc.

Kemp, Jeremiah
1970 "Initial Marriage Residence in Rural Thailand" *In Memoriam. Phya Anuman Rajadhon.* Bangkok: The Siam Society.

Keyes, Charles F.
1966 "Peasant and Nation: A Thai-Lao Village in A Thai State." Doctoral dissertation. Seattle: University of Washington.

Kingsbill, Konrad
1965 *Kudaeng: The Red Tomb, A Village Study in Northern Thailand.* Bangkok: Bangkok Christian College.

Madge, Charles
1955 *Village Communities in Northeast Thailand.* Bangkok: United Nations Technical Assistance Board.

Moerman, Michael
1966 "Ban Ping's Temple: The Center of a Loosely Structured Society"

in Anthropological Studies of Theravade Buddhism, *Yale University Southeast Asia Cultural Report*, No. 13.

Phillips, Herbert
  1965 *The Thai Peasant Personality*. Berkeley: University of California Press.

Piker, Steven
  1964 "An Examination of Character and Socialization in a Thai Peasant Community." Doctoral dissertation. Seattle: University of Washington.
  1972 "The Post-Peasant Village in Central Plains Thai Society." Paper presented at the annual meetings of the Association for Asian Studies in New York, N.Y.
  No date. "A Peasant Community in Changing Thailand." Unpublished manuscript.

Sharp, Lauriston, *et al.*
  1953 *Siamese Rice Village: A Preliminary Study of Bang Chan 1948-49*. Bangkok: Cornell Research Center.

Smith, Harold
  1973a "The Thai Family: Nuclear or Extended." *Journal of Marriage and the Family*, 35 (February).
  1973b "Polygyny and Marriage Registration in Thailand." *Southeast Asia: An International Quarterly*, 2, No. 3 (Summer).

Smith, Harold, *et al.*
  1971 *Rural Thai Families: A Sociologic and Economic Survey*. Washington, D.C.: The Clearinghouse for Sociological Literature. NCR microcard editions.

Soontornpasuch, Suthep
  1963 *The Thai Family: A Study of Kinship and Marriage Among the Central Thai Peasantry*. A Masters thesis. The University of London School of Oriental Studies.

Thamavit, V., and R. Golden
  1954 "The Family in Thailand." *Marriage and Family Living*, 16 (November).

Thomlinson, Ralph
  1971 *Thailand's Population: Facts, Trends, Problems and Policies*. Bangkok: The Thai Watana Panich Press Co., Ltd.

Wijeyewardene, G.
  1967 "Some Aspects of Rural Life in Thailand" in T. Silcock (ed.), *Thailand: Social and Economic Studies in Development*. Durham: Duke University Press.

CHAPTER III

The Family in Afghanistan

M. Jamil Hanifi

Of all the Central Asian Muslim countries, Afghanistan has the most diverse social organization. Afghanistan is a country created by political consideration and not by socio-cultural cohesion, and is made up of a number of different ethnic groups which do not form an integrated socio-cultural unit.

The groups living in Afghanistan recognize a great many cultural differences among themselves. One of the well known cultural and social divisions is that between Pushtuns and non-Pushtuns, including Tajiks, Persian-speaking minorities, Uzbeks, Kirghises, Kafirs (Nuristanis), and Turkomans. Geographically, this division corresponds to the physical layout of the Hindu Kush mountains, running from northeast to southwest. Roughly, those people to the south and east of the mountain are Pushtuns, those to the north and northwest are non-Pushtuns. Despite the vast socio-cultural diversity, similar principles of organization appear in the various family systems, partly as a consequence of a common Islamic cultural tradition, and partly due to a long and continuous intranational cultural contact.

Afghan society is overwhelmingly rural-agricultural. A very small fraction of an estimated 16,000,000 population live in cities. Thus, the portrayal here of the Afghan family refers primarily to the preponderant rural sector. Only when necessary, reference will be made to the family structure and organization in urban settings.

With increasing Westernization the traditional Afghan family and kinship groups are becoming less significant in the ordering of daily life, in both quality and quantity. Urban areas exhibit the greatest degree of change, while rural villages most often cling to traditional notions of the structure and function of kinship groups.

Ecological factors such as the high birth rate and the eventual reduction in the size of farm holdings will create economic pressures on the continued existence of the traditional Afghan-Islamic extended family. However, situations change faster than the cultural values which give them meaning; the result is individual and group conflict. Even in the few large cities and towns, the legal and social relationships prescribed by legislation are inoperative due to lack of support by an appropriate system of cultural values. Urban residents retain a sense of belonging to a group of wider kin than the immediate family. This retention discourages the formation of groups which cut across blood lines, and the traditional mistrust of strangers and nonkinsmen inhibits cooperation between unacquainted or unrelated individuals.

All of these values and modes of behavior inhibit the rapid development of modernization and technological advancement which require, among other things, the acceptance of the priority of nonkin relationships over, or at least equal to, kinship bonds.

The fundamental unit of the Afghan society is the extended family. The cultural traditions which regulate the structure and functions of the family originated among the pastoral nomads who, centuries before the rise of Islam, roamed throughout Central Asia. The Afghan-Islamic society maintained most of these traditions related to the family and gradually accepted them as part of the Islamic tradition, largely settled and organized around agriculture. That cultural tradition, which penetrates the entire Afghan social structure, emphasizes the importance of the individual's complete loyalty to his family and gives the familial unit a vital role in social, economic, and political matters. Traditionally, a person learns from earliest childhood to defer to the opinions of the family elders and to place family well-being before all personal wishes and desires. Marriages are often contracted for reasons of family unity and welfare. Political loyalties remain unaltered throughout a family's successive generations.

Continuities in the Afghan extended family structure and functions are most evident in villages and towns and among the nomadic Kochis. In larger towns and cities, where contact with Western cultural traditions are profound, alterations in the traditional social structure are observable, and functions once performed by the traditional extended family are being fulfilled by the government and other formal institutions. Urbanites still identify themselves with their individual families, but the role and the influence of the family in personal matters are gradually decreasing. The traditional Afghan family comprises more than just the nuclear family of the husband, the wife, and their unmarried children. The individual's basic familial unit is his extended family, consisting of parents, children, and patrilineal relatives to the third level, such as aunts, uncles, and cousins. The traditional household includes a man and his wife or wives, unmarried children, and married sons and their wives and children. Additional members may include a man's unmarried, widowed, or divorced sisters, his parents, childless and elderly aunts and uncles, patrilateral first cousins, and his brother's orphaned children.

The extended family is the most important basic unit in the Afghan social structure, but the smaller familial unit of husband and wife (wives) also exists. Among the Kochis, where kinship ties are strongest, several closely related families which claim a common ancestor are grouped together into larger kinship units resembling a patrilineage. The members of the lineage work in the same vicinity within their tribe, and generally pitch their tents within a contiguous area.

The extended family is patrilocal. On marriage, a son customarily brings his wife into his father's house. If the house is too crowded, additional rooms are built or a smaller house is constructed nearby. In villages and towns, families of the same patrilineage are likely to live in particular sections. Economic unity is the most fundamental characteristic of the Afghan extended family or household. Only through membership in a household does an individual take part in the economic life of the village. Household membership also provides the most definitive identification of individuals *vis-a-vis* the rest of the village. In another sense, the Afghan village relies on a household to produce offspring with the basic characteristics that provide village continuity. Hence, authority and responsibility within the village are primarily household matters. A man is in charge of his wife, children, and their dependents, and responsible for their good conduct.

The numerical preponderance of simple households is not necessarily inconsistent with the acceptance of the three-generation extended household as the ideal. Even under stable demographic conditions, less than half of the households would meet the ideal. If a life expectancy of sixty years for men is assumed, and an average gap between father and son of twenty-five years, it is evident that an average household head would have to spend fifteen years after his father died before his grandson would be born, and then he would experience ten full years as head of an extended household before his own death.

Even under ideal conditions, then, the proportion of extended families in a village at any one time would be relatively small. In fact, achieving an extended family is even more difficult under real conditions. Adult Afghan men often die prematurely, leaving unmarried children. The infant mortality rate in Afghanistan is high, as is the rate of infertility and miscarriage among women. Innumerable conditions join forces to reduce the possibility of the formation of the ideal Afghan household.

In cities, such as Kabul, and in large towns, the proportion of extended families is less because of the nonagricultural economy and the greater prevalence of Western cultural values pertaining to family life. In villages, and in rural areas, however, the traditional Afghan values of family organization have persisted.

Although land is individually owned, household members pool their resources and exploit them cooperatively. The main resources are land, animals, and able-bodied plowmen, and efficient production depends on a correct balance among them. Roughly eight to ten acres a year can be plowed by one man and one team of oxen, and for maximum production, land, stock, and manpower must increase in proportion.

In short, the extended family is practically the only organized economic unit in Afghan rural society, sharing production and consumption. It shares all resources belonging to members; it distributes the total production and income among its members according to need and social position. Increasingly, modern farms are becoming primary economic units in terms of production, but this phenomenon is still restricted to certain areas, such as the eastern and northern villages where there is not much dependency on irrigation.

The Afghan extended family is also the primary social unit. Individuals are identified primarily by the family to which they belong. Enculturation and socialization take place primarily within the household; children learn the roles that they will perform as children, adolescents, and adults (see section on child-rearing). When an occasion prescribed formal visiting, households are usually the visiting and visited units. Thus, the Afghan extended families are the basic social units through which individuals interact with the larger socio-cultural environment.

The Afghan family is patricentric. Within the extended family the contrast between males and females is emphasized in every possible way. This distinction is especially clear in the division of labor. Men do the heavy fieldwork, control major household resources, make all major decisions, conduct all relations with the outside world, and defend the household and its honor. Women carry out all domestic tasks, do light work in the fields, at least outwardly, and submit to the will of their men.

The mutual separateness and dependence of men and women are factors that hold the household together. Neither men nor women can live outside the household because of the strict division of labor. Since most of the women in the household are related only through marriage to the rest of the members, they are bound to one another by their relationships to men. It is the husband-son who bridges the gap between mother-in-law and daughter-in-law, and the brothers who bind the wives together. Conversely, one of the main factors that unite the male core of a household is the collective duty to safeguard the honor of the Afghan women.

Age, or generation, is also a primary consideration in the structural division of the Afghan extended family. For both males and females, generational seniority confers authority and prestige. Young girls are expected to be deferential to older women, to wait upon them, and to listen until asked to speak. Likewise, boys and young men defer to and obey older males. But generational distinctions do not override those based on sex. Afghan brothers do not group themselves with their sisters against their parents, nor husbands with their wives against their children. Thus, even though Afghan mothers command their small children, male and female, adult sons command their mothers.

The possible paired relationships within an extended family are numerous. But the more common and important ones are husband-wife, father-son, father-daughter, mother-son, mother-daughter, brother-brother, sister-sister, brother-sister, brothers' wives, and female-male in-laws. The first eight can be present in all Afghan households, extended or otherwise, while the latter two are peculiar to households with more than one married couple.

A woman is outwardly required to submit to the will of her husband, but she is an indispensable part of the household. Much household activity is outside the concern of husbands and this guarantees a wife autonomy to manage these affairs. The wife, like all women, accepts her overall inferiority as part of the Afghan social order, but her immersion in her own affairs greatly mitigates this sense of inferiority. Beneath the outward submissiveness is a realization and understanding of the indispensability of her own household activities.

A household is based on the relationship of husband and wife for the procreation of children. Marriage is a well-defined and heavily sanctioned institution which serves to perpetuate the extended family and the village cultural tradition.

Authority Structure Within the Family

Afghan husbands wield all of the legitimate authority, while wives exercise constrained influence over decisions. If a husband is unreasonable, the only real recourse for his wife is to return to her parents or other close relatives. In cases where a wife seems to dominate her husband, or exercise inordinate influence on him, he is certain to lose his respect and honor in the eyes of his friends, relatives, and other villagers.

Companionship is not valued in the relationship between a man and his wife or wives. A man must never show affection for his wife in front of anyone else, and it is assumed that there are few common grounds for conversation between an Afghan husband and wife. The relationship is confined primarily to economic cooperation and sexual intimacy. Such a relationship does not preclude affection, but the only permitted public manifestations of it are economic cooperation and procreation of children.

This allows for a viable household to be established and maintained around almost any suitable couple that can achieve a minimal level of cooperation in the face of misfortune and misunderstandings. A successful marriage is not measured in the context of personal relations; the main criterion of success is the existence of healthy sons.

A father's authority over his sons is absolute; sons are expected to obey their father, and they most often do. Apart from formal education, fathers are almost alone in the role of educating their sons in culturally acceptable behavior, and essential farming skills. Sons begin to help their fathers from around the age of eight, and by the age of twelve they are expected to know how to handle a plow.

As a son reaches middle age and his father becomes too old for heavy work, control of household affairs may pass to the son. But formal respect and acknowledgement of the father's authority is never lessened and he remains the nominal household head. Even in old age, a father almost always arranges and finances his son's marriage(s), and he continues to give advice which is expected to be followed.

Son's generally inherit their father's land. When asked about inheritance of land, a rural Afghan will generally draw a quadrangle in the dust and divide it by lines down the middle, insisting that land is divided equally among the sons. In reality, no single consistent body of rules governs inheritance. Islamic prescription, tradition, and local custom are followed. Which rules are obeyed and how they are applied depends on the state of family affairs, especially the relations and interests of the close kin.

A girl lives in her parents' home for the first thirteen to seventeen years of her life. Thus, the relationship with her father is not only attenuated by the traditional segregation of the sexes, but is also cut short early in her life. Fathers are disappointed at the birth of a daughter, and they usually bemoan the trouble of bringing up daughters only to see them pass to someone else as soon as they become useful. Often, when asked how many children he has, an Afghan father will omit his daughters from the count.

This intimacy is suddenly interrupted by the girl's marriage, which normally takes place between the ages of thirteen and seventeen. Marriage is a time of severe grief for the bride's mother, and no attempt to conceal the emotional pain is made. After marriage, a girl still seeks advice, help, and comfort from her mother, and she visits as often as is feasible. If the distance is great, then a daughter will try to visit for a month or so once a year; if not, the visits are frequent and casual. In any event, the emotional bond of mother and daughter is maintained throughout their lives.

Relations Between Siblings

Afghan brothers, more than any other kin, are brought close together by the social system. Generally, they are bound by a common generational level, and by common interests in inheritance and duties to their parents, sisters, and brothers. These impel brothers, especially if they are close in age, to develop a mutual intimacy which progresses from childhood to the neighborly cooperation and mutual dependence of adulthood.

Because they are within the same generation, brothers freely associate with one another. Certainly, seniority confers authority, but the relationship is primarily one of mutual equality. Brothers normally share or attend the same room, help one another in harvest, stand by one another in sickness, and generally assist one another in any way possible. Many Afghan men spend a good deal more time in the company of their brothers than of their wives.

Normally, brothers are expected to separate from their father's household soon after his death. But in some cases, the attachment of brother for brother delays the separation indefinitely, and sometimes permanently. Even when brothers do separate, they generally reside as neighbors and continue their close relationship.

Before marriage Afghan sisters are just as close to one another as brothers are to brothers. They grow up together, and learn from and with one another the tasks which they will be expected to perform as married women. Again, age confers respect and authority, though the exercise of authority among sisters is usually flexible and relaxed.

However, after marriage these close ties generally do not persist as they do among brothers. This is due to physical separation and not to any loss of emotional attachment. Sisters may marry into households in different villages or into mutually antagonistic households, in which cases their relationship would be curtailed. If they marry into the same household, or two very closely related ones, or even if they live in the same village, they will normally continue close association throughout their life cycle.

As small children, brothers and sisters play together and help one another, but early in childhood, separation in play according to sex becomes pronounced, and little Afghan boys tend more and more to go with their fathers and little girls with their mothers. By the age of nine or ten, a boy will begin to assert his male preroga-

tives. It is not unusual to see a boy of this age giving orders to his
fourteen or fifteen year old sister, which she will carry out without
any parental intervention.

Brothers and sisters grow apart as they grow older. When the
sister marries and leaves her parents' household, her brother has
even less contract with her, and because she is married his interests
in her and obligations towards her have been partially preempted
by her husband. Brothers retain concern for their sisters, but it is
without intimacy and grounds for seeking one another's company.
From the sister's point of view, her brothers succeed her father
as the source of refuge and defense against her husband and his
kin. If no such needs arise, a woman will have little to do with her
brothers.

Marriage and Sex Roles

In a very real sense, a woman's relationship with her mother-in-
law is far more crucial for the stability of her marriage than is her
relationship with her husband. A bride comes into a household as
a relative stranger, and the establishment of rapport with her
mother-in-law, under whose direction she will work, is a critical
factor in her acceptance into the household.

The Afghan bride is expected to subordinate herself to her
mother-in-law, wait on her, and perform all the more menial household tasks. However, her role is not far removed from that of
daughters. Outwardly and formally, she is expected to act toward
her mother-in-law as she did towards her own mother.

The stability of the relationship is based, however, on inward
and informal factors. Most often, a warm sense of intimacy and
cooperation develops, although quarrels and tensions are fairly
frequent. Such contingent factors as personality, the relative social
standing of natal and marital households, and the degree of difference of ethnicity and custom of the two household affect the
relationship.

Every Afghan girl knows that she will almost inevitably be with
a household with a mother-in-law, and she is enculturated in the
proper respect for her. Both sides are rewarded with success and
penalized for failure, so that both the mother-in-law and her son's
wife have a stake in the marriage.

Every woman marries into a household and is put into daily

contact with her husband's father and brothers. Afghan women are generally deferential and distant and even stilted with their husband's father. To her husband's brothers, respect is due and help is expected. The principle of levirate is operative upon the death of the husband. In many ways, a woman's relationship with her brother-in-law is similar to that of her husband. She owes him respect and deference as a male-in-law, and he in turn takes care of her in her husband's absence, and can marry her in case of her husband's death. Thus, a brother would be a perfectly respectable person to take a man's wife to town, or to the doctor, or on some long journey. Each honorably carries out his and her reciprocal duties although in terms of friendly restraint.

An Afghan girl, even after marriage, is responsible to her father and brothers for her moral conduct. Afghans strongly value pre-marital chastity in women, and an unmarried girl, discovered unchaste, is severely punished. Only among a few Kochi tribes, however, is death still imposed for such an infraction. Sexual offenses on the part of a married woman are punishable by her male relatives and her husband. The sexual conduct of Afghan men is not subject to the same social controls and is seldom questioned.

Women, although they are traditionally considered subordinate to men, have certain rights within Afghan society. A childless widow inherits one-fourth of her husband's property. A widow with children receives only one-eighth of the estate, her children inheriting the remainder. Daughters and sisters also have inheritance rights. The inherited share of a son is twice that of his sister. A woman may leave her husband if he fails to support her adequately, and men are enjoined to respect a woman's honor and are forbidden to harm her or her personal property. Also, the 1963 constitution of Afghanistan provides for universal suffrage of women.

Marriage, both as a relationship and as an event, is a most important element of Afghan life. As a relationship, the basic unit of Afghan social structure—the household—is founded directly upon it, as are all intra-household relationships.

As an event, marriage is the most conspicuous, expensive, elaborate ceremony in rural and urban life. It serves as almost the only form of organized merrymaking, involving many kin of the couple and much careful planning. The cost of a wedding may equal nearly the entire annual income of a household, matching the social and ritual importance of this central institution.

Only the incest rules of a Islam formally restrict the choice of marriage partners. These prohibit to a man his lineal descendants and ascendants, his parents' sisters, his own sisters, his nieces, and grand-nieces, his father's wives and widows, their stepdaughters, his wife's mother and son's wife, and his living wife's sisters. Beyond this, it is quite common for a man to marry his patrilateral and matrilateral cross-cousins. Marriage among parallel cousins occurs. but rarely. Although there is no Islamic prohibition against parallel cousin marriage, the cultural affinity of Afghanistan with traditional Central Asia is the likely explanation for this rarity.

However, certain informal factors are considered when a prospective bride is sought. Parents of the boy, especially the father, theoretically controls the selection of the bride, yet the boy exercises considerable influence over the choice. The primary qualities sought in a bride are honor and efficiency, the former being more explicitly important. Any obvious interest in the opposite sex, let alone outright contact with a boy or man, results in the loss of a girl's honor and substantially diminishes her chances of finding a suitable mate. Her efficiency is evaluated in terms of skills, ability, and desire to work hard, physical health, and personality traits, such as good nature, beauty, and submissiveness. A prospective groom is evaluated primarily in terms of status—his family tradition and current family position, all measured against the marital expectations of the prospective bride.

A close kinswoman (e.g., a cross-cousin) is often preferred, not only because she is easier to find and requiring a lesser bride price, but also because she will most likely fit into the household more easily, since she already has established relationships with household members, especially with her new mother-in-law, which reduces the degree of dislocation for the bride.

No two wedding ceremonies are exactly alike. They vary with the social standing of the parties involved, with the area in which they live, and with the cultural tradition operative. The desired season for weddings is the winter, either early or late, in order to avoid the most severe weather. Summer weddings are few in number, limited in scale, and usually restricted to secondary marriages—those involving a widow or widower, a divorcee, or a polygynous union.

Supposedly, the Afghan mother can only suggest and advise, and the young people have no say at all. In practice, the young people make known their wishes, and mothers, whose main interest is marriage, in fact play a major role in the decision. Although there are always exceptions, a boy usually marries between the ages of sixteen and twenty-two, while girls ordinarily marry three to four years earlier.

Once a father selects his prospective daughter-in-law, he goes with, or sends, two close kin and a respected older man to serve as negotiators and pay a formal visit to the girl's home. They are greeted by a similarly constituted group and negotiations through the intermediaries are begun. If the union is satisfactory to both sides, an initial statement of the bride price is agreed upon, with a first installment sometimes expected.

The betrothal and its waiting period precede the actual marriage. The ceremony marking the formal betrothal, which takes place a month or so after the initial meeting, is entirely a woman's affair. A group of the boy's female relatives, including his mother, visits the girl's home, and is received by her close female relatives. Two or three days of reciprocally provided meals and dancing follow, strictly without men. Presents, usually including gold or silver ornaments, are also given to the bride.

The betrothal may last anywhere from a week or two to a year or two. But several months is considered a respectable time. During this period, the betrothed are not supposed to see each other. They normally, however, do meet with the connivance of the girl's household. These meetings are not viewed as illicit, but simply as an implicitly acceptable deviation from the ideal norm. If an engagement is broken during this period, a girl's honor is said to be diminished because of her close contact with her betrothed.

The actual wedding ceremony begins at the groom's house from three to four days before consummation. Males and females celebrate separately at first, dancing, singing, telling stories, and doing almost anything that reflects the happiness of the occasion. At the girl's home, the public ceremony is usually restricted to several nights of dancing by a close circle of female kin and neighbors.

On the day of consummation, or the night before, a group of seven or eight women, relatives and neighbors of the groom, is selected to be escorted by a party of men to the bride's home. When they arrive, the men and women are entertained and dined separately. Then, amid much fanfare and weeping, the bride leaves in a procession with her new neighbors and relations to her future home. Ideally, she should make the trip mounted on a horse, but in reality she may leave on a horse-drawn cart, on a donkey, in a car, in a taxi, in a truck, or on foot. The final ceremony at the threshold of the new household varies, but it always serves to· end the festivities.

Before this final day, an exchange of wealth between the two households take place. The bride's household is responsible for providing the trousseau, usually containing such things as mattresses and bedding, rugs, a supply of clothing for the bride, and presents of clothing for all members of the bridegroom's household and close kin, especially the bridegroom himself.

The bride price paid by the groom's household varies in worth, depending upon the wealth of the respective households and the value of the bride's trousseau. In urban settings it is usually paid in cash and gold or silver ornaments, while in the countryside it consists of sheep, camels, and sometimes ornaments of silver or gold. The bride price does not constitute a sale in the strict sense of the principle. It is really regarded as *quid pro quo* for the trousseau, with which it is most often systematically evaluated and compared. In addition, according to Islamic principles, an Afghan groom must commit a variable amount of wealth (*mahar*) to the bride. Although the bride rarely has actual possession of this wealth, in cases of the husband's death, or if she is divorced, she can claim it.

The actual marriage ceremony is presided upon by a mullah, (a Muslim religious functionary). The groom is present, and so is the bride, who is normally represented by her father or oldest brother. All marriages must be officiated by the mullah. Afghanistan has not, so far, provided institutions for civil marriages.

Divorce

According to traditional Islamic law, a man may divorce his wife by pronouncing any words of dismissal three times before two witnesses. Once a woman is divorced, the Quran provides that if the woman is pregnant, she should wait three months before marrying again. Also, it is suggested that a man cannot marry his divorced wife until she has been married to another person and divorced or widowed. The father may remarry at any time, and he must support all his children. If the husband divorces his wife on grounds of her unfaithfulness, then he is not required to pay her *mahar*. Actually, Islamic law is loosely followed. A man may formally dismiss his wife only to realize that he cannot get on without her, and he will not hesitate in recalling her.

There is no social disgrace attached to a woman who has been honorably divorced. She may remarry, provided that she is not pregnant by her previous husband (but she must wait three months to find this out). Older children of a divorced couple remain in the father's custody; young children should be returned to the husband once they are weaned. But ordinarily, they stay in the mother's care until age seven for boys and age nine for girls.

If a woman desires a divorce, she will usually leave her husband's household and return to that of her nearest living male relative. In such a case, the Islamic law does not recognize the divorce, but if reasons are satisfactory, the community sanctions it. In fact, a prolonged separation of a man and his wife, initiated by either for whatever reasons, tends to be synonymous, in meaning and consequences, with divorce. The primary cause of divorce initiated by Afghan men is sterility of the wife and inability to bear male children. For those initiated by women, maltreatment on the part of the husband and bad feeling between the wife's and husband's kin groups are two chief reasons.

Child-Rearing Patterns Among Pushtuns of Afghanistan[1]

This paper will examine the structure and function of the traditional Afghan extended family, and some modifications within this sociological cell due to increasing modernization, urbanization and marriage. Although the child-rearing patterns discussed in Appendix I reflect the Pushtun society, they also accurately describe the general features of child's role in learning among other ethnic groups within Afghanistan.

The family occupies a central place in almost every aspect of Pushtun life, and concern for the family is one of the central values in the Muslim Pushtun culture. Pregnancy, childbirth, and infant care are therefore of greatest importance. A wife without children, or even one without male children, is pitied by her friends and

[1]Reprinted with permission from the *International Journal of Sociology of the Family*, 1 March 1971, pp. 53-57.

often threatened by divorce. The attitude of the Pushtun mother reflects this generalized emphasis on being fruitful and multiplying. Social scientists who have studied the Pushtan society have all stressed the importance of the family as the basic unit of the social structure.

The traditional Pushtun family is extended, patrilineal, patrilocal, patriarchal, endogamous, and occasionally polygynous (Wilbur, 1962). It is extended in that a household normally consists of the patriarch and his wife or wives, his unmarried children, and his married sons and their children. It is patrilineal in that the descent is through the paternal side and family loyalty is to the paternal descent line. The married daughter of a family transfers complete allegiance to her husband's family. It is patrilocal in that the married sons live in the father's household rather than depart to establish homes of their own. It is patriarchal in that the eldest male possesses complete authority over the extended family. The family is endogamous to the extent that there is a preference for marriages within the extended family (parallel cousins) or with relations of near degree. The family may be polygynous in that the male has religious Muslim sanction to marry four wives; in practice most men have a single wife, and very few have more than two.

At the present time, nuclear families, particularly in urban settings, have separate households, but patrilocality predominates. The husband chooses a dwelling place near his own father and brothers. Thus, members of an extended family often lived in close proximity. Extended families usually live in the same part of the village or the city, so that they constitute a distinct geographical unit. When we add to this the fact that members of a given lineage are usually of the same religious sect (Shia or Sunni) and that there is some tendency for villages made up of persons of a given sect, we can understand why Barth (1969) calls the in-group identification of the Pushtuns a series of concentric spheres with the individual at the centre.

The manifestations of modernization in Pushtun family life, arising primarily from urban contact, have been alluded to in some recent studies of the predominantly traditional Pushtun culture, but little work has been done on the changes occurring in such specific areas as that of the enculturative processes. Group comparisons have been made only in the most impressionistic and general fashion. Yet a comparison of specific practices in relatively traditional and modern groups might yield important data on the direction and rate of change in those practices.

In view of the key place of the family in Pushtun society and the changing nature of that society, the study of children and child-rearing in various groups, traditional and modern, urban and rural, would appear to be one of the most valuable contributions which anthropological research could render to the study of Pushtuns and other groupings of similar cultural patterns. The present paper, however, deals with the traditional, rural Pushtun family.

Pushtuns parents, mothers and fathers alike, are eager to have children and pleased at every pregnancy. The delight is particularly great when the couple is childless or when it has no son. The newborn child is received with warmth and treated with indulgence. He is breast-fed from birth, usually on demand, and picked up whenever he cries. He is swaddled for several months, which usually makes it possible for his mother to keep him at her side day and night. Most mothers spend much time with the child, fondling the infant and playing with it.

Indulgence for most infants begins to decrease as they approach the first birthday. Weaning takes place abruptly, either late in the second year or early in the third, and is often accompanied by emotional upset (Spain, 1963). Toilet training usually begins before the first birthday, and training techniques are severe. Nevertheless, training is not usually completed until late in the second year (Wilbur, 1962).

Mothers oppose all manifestations of aggressive behavior by children. Most Pushtun mothers do not want a child to fight, even in self-defense. Aggression against parents is most severely frowned upon. The "good" child is thought of as one who is obedient and polite, though this ideal seems to be achieved rarely. There is little permissiveness for making noise, fighting, or even playing in the home, but neither is there much expectation that the child of five will carry out constructive household tasks. The Pushtun mothers seem to aim at coping, or enduring, rather than molding.

Corporal punishment and threats of punishment, rather than praise or reward seem to be the prescribed techniques of behavioral control. Mothers who wish to reward their children often give them something to eat, and food occupies an important place in the thoughts of the children. Perhaps because of this, feeding problems are not common.

The attitude toward sex is generally repressive. Nudity is generally taboo from infancy. A slight degree of permissiveness for nudity in males is allowed. Most children receive no sex instruction. Masturbation in them is denied by Pushtun mothers, and any occurrence is punished promptly on discovery.

By about age five there is a tendency for a child to identify to some degree with the like-sexed parent, thus demonstrating that the sex role is being learned. In describing their hopes for the future of their children, mothers will speak of marriage for the girls and of education and employment for the boys (Smith *et al.*, 1969). Parental roles seem well defined, with responsibility for the child and household resting on the mother. The mothers ordinarily discipline the children, and they will approve of the father's disciplinary actions even if they judge him to be severe.

Most Pushtun mothers permit dependency in children and sometimes even encourage it, but some look upon it as a nuisance (Caroe, 1958:203). For neither group, however, is dependency so serious a problem as in some other cultures. Pushtun mothers generally expect the child to behave independently at a fairly early age. This expectation may be an outgrowth of the mother's tendancy to focus attention on infants and to expect siblings to care for the younger children and for themselves. If the psychological explanation of an "achieving society" were granted, we might thus be able to explain the enterprising, individualistic, and achieving nature of the Pushtuns, as shown in such matters as relatively higher degree of innovative and entrepreneurial behavior as an outgrowth of this early training in independence.

One of the earliest experiences of the Pushtun infant is that of being wrapped in swaddling clothes. Strips of cloth, new or used, are wrapped around the child until he or she is snug and relatively immobile. In some instances the child's arms are wrapped at the side. This custom has historical-cultural depth, and is till quite prevalent in traditional Central and southwest Asia (Grangvist, 1950), including Afghanistan. It is often sufficiently prolonged to bring about a change in the head shape of the infant. Some writers have suggested that prolonged swaddling might also produce significant personality effects (Child and Whiting, 1953). Even where it is not prolonged, it is one of the major aspects of child care in the earliest months.

The weaning techniques used among Pushtuns are similar to those found in most societies in Central Asia. The child is given some early experience in eating soft foods. He or she may be given some bread mixed with sweetened milk or warm tea, perhaps by smearing it on a finger and letting him or her suck it off. Or the infant may be allowed to suck a piece of tough bread that has been soaked in milk. When the time for weaning arrives, the process is fairly abrupt. Quinine or other bitter and repellent substances may be dabbed on the mother's nipples. In some cases the child is turned over to a relative for a few days. Ordinarily, the relative is a grandmother or aunt, or another person familiar to the child.

The infants often respond violently to this abrupt treatment. On the average, the babies experience a great deal of upset.

The problem of weaning upset has long been of major interest to psychologists. Since Freud's early work pointed to the importance of gratification, students of child psychology and some cultural anthropologists have paid particular attention to this, one of the great emotional crises of infancy. Research on the problem in America has indicated that the amount of emotional upset is related to three aspects of training (Sears, 1957:92). How long the baby is nursed before weaning, how severe the weaning methods that are used, and how decisive the mother is, should provide the board framework for future research in order to determine the answers to these questions among Pushtuns, and eventually relate their answers to the Pushtun personality type.

Another area in the process of enculturation, in which some data are available, is that of bowel control. Toilet training, like weaning, has been the subject of a considerable amount of speculation and research by persons interested in child-rearing. Because of the close quarters, or because the small child is so often with the mother, the Pushtuns begin toilet training early. They begin earlier on the average than do other groupings in the area who have been rated as beginning the process early (Child and Whiting, 1953:74). The median age at the beginning is at eight or nine months. In general, the Pushtun mothers who start toilet training early, use severe training methods fairly often, but complete the training process late.

Freudians have suggested that strict and early toilet training may produce an "anal character." Such a person is not only concerned with cleanliness. He also exhibits a miserly frugality, a petulant obstinacy, and a compulsiveness that expresses itself in "orderliness," "tidiness," "punctuality," "meticulousness," and "propriety." To those who know Pushtuns, or who have read studies of them, this list is startling in its in appropriateness. Perhaps some evidence could be adduced for emphasis on tidiness and on propriety, but most students of Pushtun culture, including this author, have borne out the impressions that the Pushtuns are generous within their means (in a culturally determined fashion), flexible to the point of inconsistency, and noncompulsive to the point of fatalism. "Anal character" would indeed be a poor way to describe the Pushtun personality.

Under the impact of the writings of Freud and his followers, psychologists and anthropologists have given a tremendous amount of attention to the development of sexual and affectionate behavioral patterns in children. There seems to be general agreement that all children have sexual needs, more or less broadly defines, and that these needs develop with the child's experiences. There seems to be agreement also that a healthy development occurs when a child is neither excessively inhibited nor excessively indulged at any stage of his development, with the definitions of "inhibition" and "indulgence" determined, in most cases at least, by the norms of the culture. In the process of development of affectional needs and acquiring sex goals the child acquires a sex role. That is, he or she learns to act in a manner appropriate to members of his or her sex, for such learning is rewarded in numerous ways. On this much, at least, there is consensus. Within this general framework, however, there are many questions unanswered. Indeed, almost any specific question about child-rearing practices that relate to sex behavior or sex typing might produce different answers if posed to different experts. Here, too, there is need for research to match the abundance of views.

In terms of sex discipline, when the father does the disciplining, it is more likely to be a boy than a girl that he disciplines. A stereotype of the Pushtun family life is that of the compassionate mother shielding the child against the stern father. There may be many Pushtun families in which the stereotype holds, but such families are not the majority.

The Pushtun father's main role concerns matters outside the

home. Disciplining of the child, executions of household tasks, making decisions about the child—all of these are the responsibility of the mother. Only matters not relating directly to the children are in the father's hands. There is some evidence that the father plays a slightly dominant role in the more traditional homes, and that the mother plays a more dominant role in the less traditional families. In general, the home is a woman's place (Caroe, 1958). The Pushtun mother is closer to her children than the father. Her interests being centered in the home and family, she is able to devote more time, attention, and sympathy to her offspring. Consequently, it is usually to the mother that the son or daughter turns for support when he or she encounters personal problems.

Relations between brothers are tempered by age differences. A brother much older is remote as a person; respect is due him and there is little occasion for companionship. Boys tend to play with cousins or other boys of their own age, rather than with older or younger brothers, and as they grow older, a latent feeling of rivalry seems to develop among the brothers, who are potential heirs to the family property, and younger brothers may resent the eldest brother who will become head of the family upon the father's death.

The brother-sister bond, on the other hand, is a very close one. After the death of the father, the brother looks after the welfare of his sisters. The happy relationship between brother and sister, and between brothers' and sisters' children, is traditional among Pushtuns.

The limited insights provided in this paper regarding the form and content of the traditional Pushtun family and into the patterns of child-rearing and child behavior would appear to justify the belief that there is a great deal of room for the application of research techniques of child psychology in Central Asia in general and among Pushtuns in particular and, more profitably, in a cross-cultural perspective. Not only have we touched upon something significant about Pushtun families in this paper, but have also provided some insights into the child-rearing patterns and behavior among Pushtuns. This paper is only a first step, however, and the gaps within it point to much needed research in this respect among Central Asian cultural groupings. Only after the accumulation of far more data will we be able to make, with my confidence, the necessary comparisons so sorely needed by those concerned with enculturation processes in a cross-cultural context. In view of the certainty that such material will be called for, and given, on a basis of the fragmentary knowledge now available, the demand for further research appears acute.

In light of the current data regarding child-rearing among Pushtuns, and the other groupings in that area, it can be seen that the field is "white unto the harvest." The first task concerning the social scientist (with a cross-cultural perspective) who wishes to serve as harvester is the selection of an area or areas of concentration. No one person can hope to do an adequate job over the whole field. Therefore, the author would like to pose a few questions as guides in the delineation of the area of investigation. These studies should seek information of use to behavioral scientists in attempting to answer three broad questions, or groups of questions:

1) Are there relationships among elements of child behavior which are found among Pushtuns as well as other cultures? More specifically, are there correlations among those behavior variables which hold among Pushtuns as well as among other socio-cultural systems?

2) Are there general norms of child-rearing among Pushtuns which can be related meaningfully to general norms of child (or even of adult) behavior, so that we can speak of consistency between cultural norms of child-rearing and Pushtun personality type(s)? Some cultural anthropologists have argued that cultures form more or less integrated wholes, configuration, or Gestalten. They believe that, if a culture is to maintain its integration, it must produce, at least in part by the training of its children, personalities which fit into the culture. Thus, child-rearing is important as a mechanism for the transmission of culture, and the study of child-rearing is important to provide clues to the configurations or Gestalten which characterize the Pushtun culture.

3) Do the group differences which have been found in Western studies, particularly the American, of parent-child behavior, exist in a dissimilar society—in this case, a Central Asian cultural variety, the Pushtuns?

Changes in the Traditional Pattern

Family patterns in urban areas are generally characteristic of the direction in which rural patterns are changing. There are still significant differences between the two, but they are gradually lessening. The scope and significance of kinship ties in the cities are considerably less than in the Afghan villages. Friendship, neighbor, and business relations are more functional and relevant to urban life. Kin become relatively dispersed and new relationships, such as employer-employee, operate in circumstances which either do not exist or which are covered by kinship relations in rural areas.

Nuclear family households are the most common household form in the cities and large towns. Economic specialization, which sends each male (and sometimes female) on his separate way, does not require an extended family unit to provide for the needs of its members. Nevertheless, variations on the extended family still exist in small numbers in urban areas, although they are rarely fully extended.

Because of this, relationships within the household are generally limited to those of husband-wife, father-children, mother-children, and children-children. Those relationships are not greatly different from those in rural Afghanistan, although the changes in the urban woman's status have affected them. Finally, there is an increasing number of civil codes with respect to marriage and divorce in the making and adherence to them is on the rise in urban areas. Despite attempts on the part of the national government to propose and at times to enact civil codes, one clearly notices something of a resurgence of religious ceremonies in the urban areas, with only token cognizance of the few existing civil codes.

REFERENCES

Bacon, Elizabeth E.
  1958   *Obok: A Study of Social Structure in Eurasia.* New York: Viking Fund Publications in Anthropology, No. 25.
Barth, Fredrik
  1965   *Political Leadership Among Swat Pathans.* New York: Humanities Press.

1969   "Pathan Identity and its Maintenance," in Fredrik Barth (ed.),
        Ethnic Groups and Boundaries. Boston: Little Brown.
Bellow, Henry Walter
   1891   *An Inquiry into the Ethnography of Afghanistan.* Woking, England:
           Oriental Institute.
Caroe, Sir Olaf
   1958   *The Pathans.* London: Macmillan.
Child, Irvin L., and John Whiting
   1953   *Child Training and Personality.* New Haven: Yale University Press.
Dupree, Louis
   1974   *Afghanistan.* Princeton, NJ: Princeton University Press.
           Gaudefroy-Demonbynes, Maurice.
   1950   *Muslim Institutions.* London: Allen and Unwin.
Granqvist, Helma
   1950   *Child Problems Among the Arabs.* Helsingfors, Finland: Soder-
           strom Company.
Hanifi, M. Jamil
   1971   "Child Rearing Patterns Among Pushtuns of Afghanistan,"
           International Journal of Sociology of the Family (March). Pp.
           53-57.
   1974   *Islam and the Transformation of Culture.* New York: Asia.
   1976   *Historical and Cultural Dictionary of Afghanistan.* Metuchen,
           NJ: The Scraecrow Press.
Pehrson, Robert
   1966   *The Social Organisation of the Marri Baluch.* Chicago: Aldine.
Schurmann, H.F.
   1962   *The Mongols of Afghanistan.* The Hague: Mouton.
Sears, R.R.
   1957   *Patterns of Child Training.* New York: Peterson and Company.
Smith, Harvey H., *et al.*
   1969   *Area Handbook of Afghanistan.* Washington, D.C.: United States
           Government Printing Office.
Spain, James W.
   1963   *The People of the Khyber.* New York: Frederik A. Praeger.
Wilbur, Donald N.
   1962   *Afghanistan: Its People, its Society, its Culture.* New Haven:
           Human Relations Area Files.

CHAPTER IV

The Family in India

India is a vast country with about 600,000,000 people of different ethnic, cultural, and religious backgrounds. It would be impossible for one author to include all the various types of marriage and family institutions in a single chapter. Therefore, the editors have requested several Indian scholars to write about various aspects of family life in India.

This chapter attempts to explore the following: The joint family, caste-Hindu-untouchable intercaste marriages, interclass and interreligious marriages, women in India, and premarital sex attitudes among university students in India.

THE BACKGROUND[1]

In order to understand the family in India, it may be relevant to discuss a few aspects such as demographic structure, economy, polity, religion, and social structure.

The subcontinent of India is situated in the southwestern section of Asia. It encompasses an area of 1,261,597 square miles (3,267,536.23 square kilometers). This region is occupied by 600,000,000 people. India claims second place in the world population index. About 60 to 75 per cent of these inhabitants are dependent on agriculture, the economy being predominantly

[1]Most of the facts reported in this paper are oversimplified for a student who does not have a fair knowledge of the Indian culture. However, it is suggested that for a much better understanding one may look up some of these original works, particularly ethnographic studies.

agrarian.

As for the political sphere, India attained its political independence from the British in 1947 after a long struggle. A parliamentary government was formed with sixteen states and seven union territories composing the federal repub¹ic of India.

India has been the birthplace of two major religions: Hinduism and Buddhism. Among several religions prevalent in India Hinduism, Islam, Christianity, Sikhism, and Jainism are most popular. The population following Buddhism and Zoroastrianism embodies less than 0.1 of 1 per cent of the population.

The social structure is also diversified. Hindu society is composed of a hierarchical system of a multitude of *jatis* (castes) which also includes the untouchables. These *jatis* possess specific historical, mythical, economic, political, religious, and cultural associations. Theoretically, one is placed in a certain occupational category according to one's birth; however, this does not preclude a person's chances for social and economic mobility. Who possesses power in a village hinges upon one's economic and political resources and to some extent *jati* affiliation. Each *jati* practices its unique religious rituals. Each worships at its own temples and shrines. However, visitation to a temple is sometimes restricted by caste rank. In modern India, such prohibitions have been outlawed. Certain social norms are observed by all members of the *jati*. The *jati* also determines with whom one may eat, from whom to take food, and how to dress.

The above are just a few of the social stipulations permeating the Indian life style. Thus, we see the hereditary class system as a very real form of social control. The rigidity which marks the *jati* system of India is very similar to the black-white social interaction in America, yet its basis is not only the racial differences among the people but several historical, religious, and cultural variables.

It is our objective in this discussion to present insight into the Indian family life style. We will focus on socialization processes, family patterns, types of marriages, mate selection, intermarriage, divorce, changes in the family structure, and the future status of the family in a few regions of India. After this, each topic will then be generally delineated. References to studies are cited whenever possible.

1. THE JOINT FAMILY—*Giri Raj Gupta*[2]

The Nature of the Joint Family

The main textbook of the Hindu law, *Mitakshara,* states that there should exist common ownership of property. Although this law does not obligate brothers to live together in their parents' home, to share a common kitchen, to participate in religious services, to give deference to their parents, to work together, to realize one's role in the family, to aid one another, and to bring one's wife to this same residence, it assumes this life style. Thus, this pattern of joint living is customary and viewed as the ideal way of life. It is believed to be a sound convention that will remain in the family of orientation while the parents are living.

This family pattern is very helpful to the newly married who will be joining this family life style. They are young and lacking material as well as psychological readiness to be independent. This joint family arrangement provides them with economic support and warm interactions among members. A large, harmonious family carries a good reputation and status in the village. To achieve these qualities by persons on their own would prove to be a more difficult task.

With so many people gathered in one household, who is vested with the authority to rule so many? The eldest male is acknowledged by the family members as possessing authority over the household. Loyalty, submissiveness, respect, and deference are bestowed on him. These attributes also encompass other relationships in the family, such as children to their parents, a wife to her husband, and younger brothers to their older brothers. In a general way, restraint permeates social relations in the joint family.

After the parents pass away, a varied amount of time elapses before the brothers divide the property and separate. Usually, the brothers wait until all their younger brothers and sisters are educated and married. This separation is inevitable, considering the physical conditions of so many living together, and often the jointness of the family works against its own ideals. Unless the brothers have joint economic enterprises, the nature of their employment usually prevents the physical unity of the joint family.

[2]The author is grateful to Aileen Smith, who has helped him in the preparation of this paper. However, the author is personally responsible for the content of this chapter.

Disputes related to sharing of work and many kinds of quarrels among brothers' wives are unavoidable. This separation is merely physical. Mutual aid and fraternal solidarity still remain to be shared by all brothers.

Thus, the brothers begin their own families, which are nuclear family types initially; but soon they develop into a joint family, maintaining the cyclical family pattern: joint family—nuclear family—joint family. Hence, this new nuclear family type does not really exist as a separate entity, but as a sector of the continuous extended family arrangement.

Are there socio-economic differences in this country's family patterns? Family forms are affected by family occupations. For example, Brahmins, a priestly- caste, who do not cultivate the land themselves, retain for a long duration both the strong authoritarian eldest male role and the joint family life style. Since land is the sole pecuniary source and is held jointly, it would not be economically viable for a son to leave the joint family after marrying.

Besides socio-economic differences, are there rural-urban variations in Indian family patterns? The weakening of joint families is supposed to be conspicuously present in the city environment. In Calcutta, a study of 100 families from a poor area and 101 from a wealthier sector was performed; and the above were employed as the sample. This project exhibited that 80 per cent of the latter area were joint family oriented, while 57 per cent of the former area were the same. In the town of Navsari, 57 per cent of a sample of 246 families were joint in organization (Kapadia, 1956: 112-115).

Mandlebaum (1970) contends that the joint family is of rural affiliation. Dube reported about two decades ago that the extended family is urban in character. However, in his study of Shamirpet, a village, the joint family characterizes the family structure (Dube, 1955:36). Hence, the joint family pattern, as it exists in India, is apparently and ideal an a common life style.

Cast? and the Joint Family

Pauline M. Kolenda, who has done extensive research on the family in India since 1949, inquired as to whether joint families are more characteristic of higher castes or lower castes. She concludes from her data that "joint families are least characteristic of Untouchables and more characteristic of Sanskritised castes" (Kolenda, 1968:390).

74

74 *Family in Asia*

Among the Chamars, a laboring caste, of Senapur, a village near Benaras in north India, a son lives a few years in his family of orientation after marriage. After these few years, he takes his family and moves into his own house. He works independently of his father and brothers, thus being neither obedient to, nor econo- mically dependent on, the former. The Adi Dravida women are more self-reliant, both economically and socially, than are the Brahmin females. The former can earn cash wages by working in the fields. Socially, they obtain divorces and widow remarriages do take place. Hence, these economically independent women are not much oriented toward the extended family system.

The Chamars of Senapur are leather workers, the majority being landless laborers. The Thakurs possess a joint family pattern of living. However, they are not capable of realizing their aspirations, due to the poverty which encompasses their lives and produces various repercussions. This low level of income results in short life spans; consequently, the probability of three generations living in one household is slim. Also, the Chamar wives do not reinforce filial or brotherly cohesion. Like the Adi Dravida women, they are financially better off than their husbands and, therefore, have no monetary reasons to remain with their spouses.

These three studies support the generalizations that landowners (Brahmins, in this case) maintain the multicouple life style for a long time. Noncultivating landowners (Adi Dravidas) retain this family pattern for a shorter period. Finally, landless laborers (Chamars) tend to maintain the extended family system for at least a short time despite the hindrance of early mortality and indepen- dent wives (Cohn, 1961:1051-1055; Gough, 1956:827).

THE SOCIALIZATION PROCESS

The life cycle of a person is composed of a series of ceremonies beginning with the bathing and naming of the infant. If the baby is a boy, he also enjoys rituals at the time of his first haircut and entering into school. The child is given his way by the family until he reaches the age of about six. Duties to be performed by both sexes follow. Boys help to herd the cattle, while girls help with the housework and watch over their younger siblings. During this period they become more responsible for their roles.

After the couple marry and have children, how will they raise their offspring? After the child is born, both the mother and baby remain in a room, separated, due to impureness, from the rest of the members of the household. Approximately six days after the birth, the infant is named and the house is cleaned.

During the learning years, the child is constantly in the company of the grandparents. The grandparents fondle, cuddle, toilet train, and rear the youngster. Only when the child cries, is the mother called to give the breast to soothe the infant. This is the only time one will see mother-child interaction in the presence of elders. Out of respect for elders, tenderness and affection are never expressed between spouses or between parents and children. In the latter case, the parent explains: "I don't like to fondle him, even when we are alone in our room; if I did, he might get into the habit of running to my knee in the bazaar, and that would not look right." This was stated by a father in the village of Deoli, who had a son eighteen months old (Carstairs, 1958:68).

From five on, the child becomes cognizant of the importance placed on physical cleanliness after defecation and imitates his parents in this behavior. In addition, children learn the principles by which physical distance is determined along the members of various castes.

There is no childhood stage formally defined in the Indian culture. Children are found right alongside adults in almost all activities. They do not take afternoon naps, have early bedtimes, or baby-sitters to take care of them while their parents attend adult events.

What is the father's role in the inculcating process? The father-child relationship can be described as marked with deference, and an element of formality is generally found in actions and speech. To give an example, a youth in India will uniformly speak to his father and elder brother employing *Ap* which denotes honor and deference; thus, it is from the father that the male child learns repression of emotions, such as anger, crying, and other masculine characteristics. This socialization process is identified with the sanskritized castes of the village of Deoli.

Rajput mothers demonstrate a socialization process unique in India (Minturn and Lambert, 1964:230-232, 235, 237-238). A sample of Rajput family life styles was observed in Khalapur, which is approximately 100 miles (160 kilometres) north of Delhi.

Affection for Rajput children is conspicuously absent. The infant is placed on a cot, wrapped in a thick quilt, and left alone. He is not fondled, cuddled, or entertained by children or adults. When he cries, food is supplied. Impatience is exhibited by Rajput mothers when the youngster desires attention, fusses, or whines. As the child grows older, he is reprimanded for crying. Also, children are never praised to their face. This is justified by the rationalization that the child might think too much of himself, and not accept a subordinate status in the joint family. This latter quality is imperative for the harmonious functioning of the extended family organization.

Why do a lack of warmth and emotional repressiveness by these mothers permeate the life of a Rajput child? One explanation is that Rajput women are all living together, confined to a courtyard with their children. If affection or favoritism were to be demonstrated, jealousies may ensue. Thus, coldness towards all children precludes disputes.

Besides a lack of warm mother-child relations, a lack of learning responsibility and self-reliance is present in the family life of Khalapur. Children do not have to do chores, dress themselves, and the like, since the Rajput caste is high and servants are employed to perform menial tasks.

Another interesting aspect of the Rajput child-rearing process is the condemning of fighting among peers because this upsets the peace that has to prevail in a household where so many interact in a confined sphere. This is because when the boy enters into the men's world, aggression and physical dominance are aspired to, as they are virility symbols. The Rajputs, traditionally a warrior caste, emphasize obedience and peace so as to live harmoniously in the joint family. However, parent-child relationships are usually dominated by affection, respect, and compassion; and sentimental bonds and the personal sacrifices incurred play a cohesive role in maintaining the unity of the family. This is indeed appropriate to the warrior caste life style.

Marriage is one of the most important events in an individual's life. Generally, at the rural level, girls marry at ages twelve and thirteen and boys at fourteen and fifteen. Arranged marriage is common. The marital process is composed of a series of observances lasting two to three years (Gupta, 1974: 54-77).

Marriage gives full adult status to males and females. Parenthood, especially giving birth to a boy, is important. Marriages are arranged through a matchmaker. Marital transactions are economically and socially oriented. The latter provide new relationships and the maintenance of existing bonds. The wedding lasts for two to three days and certain rites are spread over a couple of weeks. The question again arises: are there marriage stipulations in existence? Yes. These are norms about residence; a four-clan rule of avoidance; other personal, racial, moral, physical, and economic characteristics; caste endogamy; and village exogamy.

Though modernization has influenced family organization, yet traditional norms are followed, that is, arranged marriages, village exogamy, caste endogamy, extensive ceremonies, and week-long weddings.

Rampur, a village in northern India, as located 15 miles (24 kilometers) west of Delhi, the capital of the Republic of India. Despite its proximity to urban influences, Rampur remains similar to other Punjab villages. Jats, who are mainly landowners and farmers, dominate this area. Thus, farming is the principal form of livelihood.

Given this agriculturally oriented life style, does the joint family system naturally follow? The data gave the following results: there were sixty-seven nuclear households, eighty-one extended families, and two households were composed of widows or widowers living alone (Lewis, 1958:17). Thus, the majority were a part of the joint family type of organization.

In the completion of the life cycle, ceremonies also characterize death of a person in Rampur. The sons and brothers shave their head and mustache, don special clothing, sleep on a cot, and perform several purification rituals on the death of their father or brother. At present, most of these elements remain, while the rest of them have been abandoned.

Some of these patterns are a complex of wedding ceremonies, arranged marriages for young children, and restrictions related to the selection of a marital partner.

Lewis notes that Rampur villagers prefer their agrarian life style to the occupational and educational opportunities of the city. In the last fifty years, two families have left the village.

Ramkheri, a village in the heart of central India, lies 7 miles (11.2 kilometers) from Dewas, a town of 27,000 people in Madhya Pradesh State. Agriculture is the main occupation in this part of India.

In contrast to the common household type encountered in the northern parts of India, the nuclear family was found to predominate (139 households) over the extended family (46 households). Although most families live separately, they farm the land jointly (Mayer, 1960:181).

Ramkheri is normally able to meet most of its needs at the local and regional levels. Generally, one would find it difficult to expect drastic changes in the family life style of this central Indian village.

Gopalpur is a small southern village which lies 15 miles (24 kilometers) east of the town of Yadgiri, a government center; 15 miles (24 kilometers) west is the town of Narayanpet, where selling surplus grain and purchasing clothes and items of day-to-day use occur between Gopalpur and this town.

Of the households in Gopalpur, most include parents and children and are nuclear families. Usually, though, they are located next to their kin so as to reap the benefits of the extended joint family system. Living within this family type, the child spends his first year in a wooden cradle. When he cries, he is nursed. As the child grows older, his surroundings are viewed first from the hip of his older sister and then from the playground. In the latter, he interacts with children, playing adult roles. Formal training is not required. What is conspicuous about Gopalpur child play is the absence of physical aggression. Disciplining a child demands withdrawing of services to the child. The child is told time and again that if he does not behave his mother would not love him and would become indifferent to his interests.

All men and women are obligated to be married in this village. If divorce or death should occur, another person of equal status should be sought promptly. Marriage is important for economic and social benefits because it prompts more kinship ties and inter-village relations. Marriage is arranged by an agreed go-between. Child marriages are practiced in Gopalpur. The bride is customarily nine or ten years old and the groom between fifteen and twenty-five (Beals, 1967:19, 30-31).

MATE SELECTION

What type of marriages take place in India? Hindu couples planning to marry are obligated to belong to the same caste and subcaste.

Subcaste refers to a further subdivision of castes into endogamous categories which, for all practical purposes, are themselves independent castes. A bride cannot belong to the same clan as the groom; the usual span of prohibition is four clan groupings. Such endogamy facilitates the bride's adjustment. Ideally speaking, intercaste marriage is prohibited; but recently, due to freer caste interactions, intermarriages do occur on a small scale.

In addition to caste and subcaste endogamy and clan exogamy, village exogamy also appears to be of common practice. This custom leads to joint family solidarity by abating intravillage quarrels. But in village marriages do occur. A prerequisite is a highly populated village composed of many different castes.

Monogamy seems to permeate the marital relations among the inhabitants of India. Formerly, polygamy was legal. This has subsequently been outlawed. When it was legal, though, it was practiced only on a small scale.

Even though castes are socially exclusive, they are economically interdependent. Each group performs an occupational function in the village or town which cannot be encroached upon by the others except farming, which can be pursued by all.

But how are mates selected? It is the parents' responsibility to see that children are properly married. The parents, in selecting a potential bride or groom, consider his or her attributes, the main ones being clan exogamy, wealth, education, and political affiliation.

In the selection of a spouse, astrological considerations are important. In southern India, among the lower and middle castes, astrology is not considered significant in this respect. It is also being abandoned by the literate and urban populations.

Another interesting aspect of mate selection is the positive correlation between caste rank and the distance between brides' and grooms' residences (Gupta, 1974:66-68). In the village of Faizabad district (UP), 37.5 miles (60 kilometers) is the average distance for higher castes and 6.4 miles (10.24 kilometers) for lower castes (Gould, 1960:486).

It is obvious that economic factors play an important role in mate selection. Thus, one views marriages as economically oriented, as indeed the wedding is.

Arranged marriages are still greatly adhered to and supported with modifications. Families of prospective spouses exchange pictures, thereby allowing them to form an idea about the latter. Sometimes a formal meeting of the future bride and groom is arranged in the presence of their elders. Rarely does a secret date between the two take place. In cases of older subjects, consent by the man to marry the chosen woman is sought by the parents. Courtship involving romantic love does not exist before marriage. Social interactions between the two sexes are at a minimum. Even in higher edcation, sexual separation exists.

Marriage arrangements follow a definite system. If one has something to gain, one deliberates, manipulates, and is scrupulous in order to obtain the most profitable economic and social transaction. This process is typical of the higher castes. If one has little to gain, precedings are brief and matters are settled promptly. This arrangement is usually followed by the lower castes. A good mate selection is viewed as one in which both sides feel they have advanced both economically and socially.

If these arranged marriages are not viable, what remains? Divorces are alien to the Sanskritized castes because of their religious beliefs and rituals. Marriage is a sacrament, a sacred bond, unalterable, and unbreakable. This belief is emphasized by religiously oriented marriage ceremonies and yearly ritual cycles. On the other hand, among the lower castes, divorce is a customary practice due to the civil orientation of the marriage ceremony. Thus, one's marital problems and divorce are influenced by one's caste rank.

THE CHANGING SCENE

Let us now turn to the effects of modernization of family life in India. An interesting study was conducted by Margaret Cormack (1961: 61-63). She distributed questionnaires and conducted interviews among 500 college students throughout India. She wished to explore their attitudes towards social change in India.

In order to evaluate attitudes toward Indian family changes, Cormack (1961) asked questions which would yield insight into past and present features and future developments. The following are examples:

Things permitted to me as a child	
As a child up to about the age of 12, I was permitted to:	
Play. with children of any castes	79%
Play with children of the opposite sex	76%
Go outside unaccompanied	69%
Freedom in adolescence	
This freedom was:	
More than my parents had	53%
About the same	39%
Less than they had	14%
I hope to raise my children:	
With more freedom	47%
As I was raised	39%
With less freedom	3%

One of the conclusions was "that freedom of children is greater than in the past—and less than the future" (Cormack, 1961:61-63).

The author claims that: 1) "There are a lot of myths about the Indian family. Despite its sanctity it has always had its dark side and does now." 2) "Authority clashes are increasing and are likely to increase still more." "My parents don't want me to become an army officer, but I shall insist." 3) "The Indian family is increasingly failing as a social security system. Individuals and other institutions take over much of this function." 4) "The Indian family is increasingly failing as an emotional security system, though it may regain this function" (Cormack, 1961:86-87).

A respondent said: "I won't accept a bride chosen by my parents. I don't care what caste my wife is, but she must be educated!" Another student vehemently opposed the idea of the dowry. He proceeded to tell the story of a father who was poor and in endeavoring to marry off his eldest daughter, "he was not able to meet the inordinate demands of the groom. He found his younger daughter (twelve years old) hanging from a tree with a note saying she hoped her suicide would remove the obstacles in the way of her elder sister's marriage." A Calcutta student exclaimed, "I know eleven cases personally in my family where marriages were arranged. It is a sad fact that in only two cases were the marriages happy." Thus, it is in the area of Indian marriage where the students are most critical. Their views have changed from the traditional ways. Research on women suggests that the majority (75 per cent) felt that women should have the opportunity to be educated. Again, 85 per cent held the belief that women should be encouraged to attend college. When asked about the most important function of a woman, 90 per cent mentioned being a good wife and mother. Only 38 per cent believed that she should be free to develop her own talents. Again, giving priority to the family, 56 per cent said that women should be gainfully employed only if their families are not neglected. Then, 47 per cent stated that if wives wish to work, they should be allowed to.

As for modernity, how does industrialization affect family organization in India?

Milton Singer (1968:435-439, 447), in studying the Indian joint family in an industrial environment, followed a genealogical or family history approach. He interviewed nineteen outstanding families in Madras City and thus examined intergenerational change. There was definite residential mobility, change in household types, and educational advancement within the generations. All subjects were born in either a village or a small town and all migrated to the city. Twelve out of the total of nineteen constituted nuclear households. Fourteen had members with some college education, most of whom had specialized in engineering and science.

Seven families belonged to large joint households. Sons, when they left the family of orientation, built a house nearby Kinship contacts were thus maintained. There was a passage from "older modern" to "newer modern" occupations between the generations. So one may ask is there structural change or structural persistence within these industrial families? Singer believes that these two elements are occuring simultaneously. As proof, he cites the following adaptive processes: *compartmentalization*, that is, the home is an area of religious practices and traditional norms, the office and factory, areas of business and modern values; *vicarious ritualization*, that is, rituals and ceremonies are contracted under a professional priest; *separation of ownership and control*, that is, a joint household is operated like an industrial organization. Singer adds that the joint family oriented industrial business can be destroyed. This may occur through lack of cooperation, lack of talent, a lax policy and therefore not sufficient funds for initiating or expanding the business, and the nationalization of private companies.

M.S. Gore (1965:209-210), in his discussion on "The traditional Indian family," states that one might find strains in the extended family system. Such debilitation is due to a partially industrialized economy, urban areas dissolving the bonds between the occupational and kinship systems, different economic pursuits within families, and the liberalizing influence of education.

Dube (1955:220-223) agrees with Gore and contends that there have been some recent changes in the village of Samirpet due to modernization and the introduction of Western technology. These alterations are in the area of dress; food; daily articles, such as alarm clocks, fountain pens, razors, and bicycles; advanced medicine; and mass communication, especially cinema and newspapers.

City influences, the development of industrialization, and assimilation of Western ideas have diminished family togetherness. Most people prefer moving to the city rather than remaining in their native communities. Traditional values are thus declining considerably. For instance, among the Aggarwals of Delhi, filial solidarity is gaining at the expense of the conservative idea of fraternal cohesion. Closer bonds between spouses are also becoming more prevalent. Women are further acquiring a higher status in the family (Gore, 1968:109, 235).

Another study of Bangalore, a southern city of about 1,000,000 inhabitants, is the setting for obtaining insight into the effect of industrialization and urbanization on family organization. Urban middle and upper classes were selected due to their urban outlook. The following discussion deals with the factors which maintain the extended family and those which hinder stability in the urban environment.

India is geographically separated from Europe and the effects of the industrial revolution. There is less movement from rural to urban environments due to the following traditional ways of life: the caste system, early marriages, traditional laws of inheritance, a multitude of languages and cultural patterns, and lack of education, which inhibit migration. However, industrial and urbanization processes are now changing all this.

Factors conducive to the decline of the joint family are family feuds and property divisions, the Income Tax Law and the New Estate Duty, individualism, a better standard of living, and higher education for women. The expense of weddings and religious ceremonies, dowries, and higher education force people to seek employment in the city. Due to these changing conditions the children enjoy new freedoms and considerable independence (Ross, 1961:24-26).

The mother is the chief agent of socialization in the urban setting. In this process, she is assisted by pediatricians and nursery schools. As children grow older, girls aid their mothers with the housework and boys run errands and do the shopping. Due to educational opportunities for the youths in the city, college becomes an important goal. Adjustment to college life, however, is difficult due to the conflict between traditional and Western ideals.

The changes, however, are slow and ossasionally indicate a conflict between parental wishes and the aspiration of the adolescents. The boys are beginning to assert their wishes in mate selection while the girls have not yet started openly questioning parental decisions. Educated middle class urban men and women are especially interested in a free choice of mate. Below are two typical comments: "I have told my parents that I will absolutely not have an arranged marriage." "I will never tolerate the old-fashioned way of arranging marriages. Boys and girls should have sufficient opportunity to know each other well before they enter into the sacred union of marriage" (Ross, 1961:254-255).

Also, more liberal views are held by these college educated subjects concerning caste, race, religious endogamy, and dowries. They thus suggest less expensive weddings and new leisure activities are ideas upheld by these young people. The latter usually involve fellow students rather than kinsmen. Most of the respondents stated that they employ their free time reading, chatting, entertaining members of the same sex, and playing musical instruments. A few mentioned movies, restaurants, and dancing when "dating" members of the opposite sex (Ross, 1961:238-239, 241).

One more aspect of Indian marriage should be explored. This is the working woman. Indian women are changing their traditional role in society. They are no longer thinking of themselves as child-bearing machines and serfs of their homes. They are now moving out of the house. Opportunities for modern education and geographical and occupational mobility have created new social and economic patterns. Careers are chosen in lieu of marriage and a wife now is also a working member of society. Many wives have to work out of financial necessity, others simply to raise their standard of living, and some for psychological, social, and intellectual reasons.

The changing roles of Indian women have created problems of adjustment in married life. They expect more satisfaction of their individual needs. This is the subject of Promilla Kapur's study, who sampled 300 female white-collar workers, teachers, and doctors. She concludes that a "wife's employment, as such, does not affect marital adjustment favorably or adversely." She adds that it is other elements linked with employment that create strains in marital relationships. The factors conducive to marital dissatisfaction were found to be similar in both groups—those who were maladjusted before employment and those who were dissatisfied after obtaining work (Kapur, 1970:399).

Hence, we find that most studies suggest a weakening in the traditional ways because of industrialization and Westernization.

Modernization is also affecting the caste system. In the past, a way to raise one's caste status was to emulate a member of a higher caste.

In the village of Madhopur live the Thakurs, landowners of high caste rank, and the Chamars, leather workers and farm laborers of low caste status. The Chamars have attempted to raise their status by assimilating traditional high caste customs. The authority and power wielded by the father have become stronger, while the wife has been secluded and restricted more extensively. Religious and food observances have been sanskritized. The Thakurs, however, are being influenced by recent social changes, such as geographic mobility, higher educational opportunities, and Western ideas. In lieu of their former ways, they prefer weaker kinship bonds. The emphasis placed on clan and village prominence has been diminished. Rigid restrictions between husband and wife have been lifted. Less honor and formality are bestowed on the father. Thus, the Chamars are trying to raise their status within the existing system (Cohn, 1955:67-68).

As prominent members of a caste increase their wealth, they attempt to gain a still higher status. A way to achieve this is to adopt ostentatious mannerisms. A case in point is the Yadavas, a cattle-keeping subcaste. They have renounced such low caste customs as the eating of meat, drinking of liquor, elaborate weddings, child marriages, and large dowries. They also wear the sacred thread, obtain new names, donate to educational causes, and support intercaste marriage.

Recently, due to political reforms, one is able to raise one's status outside the caste system. One's dominant status is that of a citizen, not of a caste member. Through political participation and achieved status, rather than sanskritization and ascribed status, one realizes one's place in society. Hence, one would believe that social restrictions are no longer operational, but they do exist dormantly.

Thus, by industrialization and Westernization, the traditional Indian values have been greatly modified. So, too, through social and political reforms, the caste system has been weakened. Predictably, these systems will continue to change to keep pace with modern standards and life styles.

REFERENCES

Beals, Alan R.
1967 *Gopalpur: A South India Village*. New York: Holt, Rinehart, and Winston.

Carstairs, Morris G.
1958 *The Twice-Born: A Study of a Community of High Caste Hindus*. Bloomington: Indiana University Press

Chauhan, B.R.
1967 *A Rajasthan Village*. New Delhi: Vir Publishing House.

Chekki, D.A.
1968 "Mate Selection, Age at Marriage, and Propinquity Among the Lingayats of India." *Journal of Marriage and the Family*, 30 (November). Pp. 707-711.

Cohn, Bernard S.
1955 "The Changing Status of a Depressed Caste" in M. Marriott (ed.), *Village India*. Chicago: University of Chicago Press. Pp. 53-77.
1961 "Chamar Family in a North Indian Village." *The Economic Weekly*, 13. Pp. 1051-1055.

Cormack, Margaret L.
1961 *She Who Rides a Peacock*. New York: Frederick A. Praeger.

Desai, I.P.
1964 *Some Aspects of Family in Mahuva*. Bombay: Asia Publishing House.

Desai, Kumud
1964 *Indian Law of Marriage and Divorce*. Bombay: Popular Prakashan.

Dube S.C.
1955 *Indian Village*. London: Routledge and Kegan Paul.

Dumont, Louis
1959 "Dowry in Hindu Marriage as a Social Scientist Sees It." *The Economic Weekly*, 11. Pp. 519-520.
1961 "Marriage in India: The Present State of the Question." *Contributions to Indian Sociology*, 5. Pp. 75-99.

Gist, Noel P.
1953 "Mate Selection and Mass Communication in India." *Public Opinion Quarterly*, 17. Pp. 481-495.

Gore, M.S.
1965 "The Traditional Indian Family" in M.F. Nimkoff (ed.), *in Comparative Family Systems*. Boston: Houghton-Mifflin. Pp. 209-231.
1968 *Urbanization and Family Change*. Bombay: Popular Prakashan.

Gough, K.
1956 "Brahmin Kinship in a Tamil Village." *American Anthropologist*, 58. Pp.784-853.

Gould, Harold A.
1960b "The Micro-Demography of Marriages in a North Indian Area," *South Western Journal of Anthropology*, 16. Pp. 476-491.

Gupta, Giri Raj
1974 *Marriage, Religion and Society: Pattern of Change in an Indian Village*. New York: John Wiley and Sons.

Kannan, C.T.
 1961 "Intercaste Marriages in Bombay." *Sociological Bulletin*, 10 (September). Pp. 53-68
 1963 *Intercaste and Inter-Community Marriages in India*. Bombay: Allied.
Kapadia, K.M.
 1956 *Marriage and Family in India*. Second edition. London: Oxford University Press.
Kapur, Promilla
 1970 *Marriage and the Working Woman in India*. New Delhi: Vikas Publishing House.
Karve, Irawati
 1965 *Kinship Organization in India*. Second revised edition. Bombay: Asia Publishing House.
Kolenda, Pauline
 1968 "Region, Caste and Family Structure: A Comparative Study of the Indian, Joint Family" in M. Singer and B.S. Cohn (ed.), *Structure and Change in Indian Society*. Chicago: Aldine. Pp. 339-398.
Kuppuswamy, B.
 1957 *A Study of Opinion Regarding Marriage and Divorce*. Bombay: Asia Publishing House.
Lambert, William H. and Leigh Minturn
 1964 *Mothers of Six Cultures*. New York: John Wiley and Sons.
Lewis, Oscar
 1958 *Village Life in Northern India*. Urbana: University of Illinois Press.
Madan, T.N.
 1965 *Family and Kinship: A Study of the Pandits of Rural Kashmir*. Bombay: Asia Publishing House.
 1962 "The Hindu Joint Family." *Man*, 62. Pp. 88-89.
Mandelbaum. David G.
 1948 "The Family in India." *Southwestern Journal of Anthropology*, 4. Pp. 123-239.
 1970a *Society in India: Continuity and Change*, Volume I. Berkeley: California University Press.
 1970b *Society in India: Change and Continuity*, Volume II. Berkeley: California University Press.
Marriott, McKim
 1955 "Little Communities in an Indigenous Civilization" in M. Marriott (ed.). *Village India*. Chicago: University of Chicago Press. Pp. 171-222.
Mayer, Adrian C.
 1960 *Caste and Kinship in Central India*. Berkeley: University of California Press.
Nimkoff, M.F. (Ed.)
 1965 *Comparative Family Systems*. Boston: Houghton-Mifflin.
Patel, Tara and Vimal Shah
 1969 "Family in India" in Jefferey K. Hadden and Marie I. Borgatta (ed.). *Marriage and the Family*. Itaska, Illinois: F.E. Peacock. Pp. 81-92.
Ross, Aileen
 1961 *The Hindu Family in its Urban Setting*. Toronto: University of Toronto Press.

Shah, A.M.
  1974   *The Household Dimension of the Family in India.* Berkeley:
         University of California Press.
Singer, Milton
  1968   "The Indian Joint Family in Modern Industry" in Milton Singer
         and B.S. Cohn (ed.), *Structure and Change in Indian Society.*
         Chicago: Aldine.

2. TOUCHABLE-UNTOUCHABLE INTERCASTE MARRIAGE—*Man Singh Das*

The subject of intercaste marriage has, in recent years, attracted national as well as international attention. Not only have Indian sociologists discussed intermarriage (Kapadia, 1954a: 61-87; 1954b: 131-157; 1955:161-192; 1968; Ross,1961:270-273; Kannan,1961:53-68; 1963), but American students of the family have been and remain engaged in empirical studies of the Negro-White intermarriage in the United States (Golden, 1954:144-147; Barnett, 1963a:424-427; 1963b:105-107; Burma, 1963:156-165; Pavela, 1964:209-211). Kapadia's (1954a:61-87; 1954b:131-157; 1955:161-192; 1968) studies reflect the views and attitudes of university graduates with respect to marriage and family relationships in the Hindu community. These opinion surveys suggest that a large proportion of those interviewed in the Bombay area favoured intercaste marriages and expressed their readiness to allow their children to enter into such marriages. In addition, Kannan (1961:53-68; 1963), in analyzing the nature of intercaste marriages in Bombay, arrives at two main conclusions: 1) The majority of marriages took place between subcastes of a major caste group (i.e., Brahmins). 2) The remaining marriages were largely between various high caste (touchable) groups (i.e., Brahmins, Kshatriyas, and Vaishyas).

Intercaste marriage in India is generally understood to mean not only marriage between subcastes of a major caste group (as between Brahmin subcastes, Kapadia, 1968:124), but also marriage between two major castes (as between Brahmins and Vaishyas or any other castes, Kannan, 1961:53-68). These approaches[3] to the study of intercaste marriages are in fact ambiguous, and a clearer definition of intercaste marriage is needed.

[3]According to this writer, marriage between subcastes of a major caste group (as between Brahmin subcastes) could be defined as "intracaste" marriage, and marriage between two major castes (as between Brahmins and Vaishyas or any other castes) could be defined as "intercaste."

The present study is primarily concerned with intercaste marriages between high (touchable) and low (untouchable) castes in India, and not the marriages between subcastes of a larger caste group. The latter marriages are on the increase, but empirical studies of the few marriages that take place outside the bounds of a large caste group are still lacking.

This study seeks to answer the following questions: What is the predominant type of union between high and low caste persons? Is it a union of low caste men and high caste women, or the reverse? Between which couples is intermarriage most frequent? What is the general pattern in intercaste marriage? Why do people enter into such marriages? The present study may contribute to the understanding of status ascription and achievement as these considerations operate in the context of mate selection outside the bounds of one's endogamous group. It may be assumed that males and females try to choose the marriage partner from a status higher than their own. A male whose ascribed status is lower will tend to marry a female whose ascribed status is higher. Similarly, a female whose achievement level is lower will tend to marry a male whose achievement level is higher than hers. This means that the most frequent type of intercaste marriage would occur between low caste males of high achievement and high caste females of low achievement.

METHODS AND PROCEDURES

The sample consisted of both male and female partners in twenty-one marriages in which caste differences were present. These couples resided in various parts of north India, mostly Lucknow, Allahabad, Kanpur, and Delhi. The names and addresses were obtained through referral or the "snowball" technique. In the selection of these couples, the process of randomization was not employed. The data were obtained through intensive interviews with these couples. Interviews were conducted between 1963 and 1968. Of the twenty-three couples, only twenty-one could be interviewed, as the other two had moved away.

FINDINGS

The predominant pattern of intercaste marriage involved a low caste husband and a high caste wife. Table 1 indicates that nineteen

TABLE 1. Castes of married couples

A. High caste husband and low caste wife

Brahmin husband-low caste wife			Kshatriya husband-low caste wife			Vaishya husband-low caste wife			Total
Brahmin husband-Sweeper wife	Brahmin husband-Chamar wife	Brahmin husband-Dhobi wife	Kshatriya husband-Sweeper wife	Kshatriya husband-Chamar wife	Kshatriya husband-Dhobi wife	Vaishya husband-Sweeper wife	Vaishya husband-Chamar wife	Vaishya husband-Dhobi wife	
0	1	0	0	1	0	0	0	0	2

B. Low caste husband and high caste wife

Sweeper husband-high caste wife			Chamar husband-high caste wife			Dhobi husband-high caste wife			Total
Sweeper husband-Brahmin wife	Sweeper husband-Kshatriya wife	Sweeper husband-Vaishya wife	Chamar husband-Brahmin wife	Chamar husband-Kshatriya wife	Chamar husband-Vaishya wife	Dhobi husband-Brahmin wife	Dhobi husband-Kshatriya wife	Dhobi husband-Vaishya wife	
1	1	2	4	3	2	0	4	2	19

low caste males married high caste females, and in only two cases high caste males had married low caste females.

When the occupational levels of intercaste married couples were compared, it was found that the most frequent type of marriage was between the professional male of low caste group and the nonprofessional female of high caste group. Nineteen couples fell in this category (see Table 2). In two cases, husbands of high caste group were nonprofessional and their wives, who belonged to the low caste, were professional. Marriage between a high caste male who was also a professional and a low caste female who was also a nonprofessional was absent, as was marriage between a nonprofessional male of low caste group and a professional female of the high caste group (see Table 2).

TABLE 2. *Professional and nonprofessional levels of intercaste married couples*[4]

Caste	Professional husband-nonprofessional wife	Nonprofessional husband-professional wife	Total
High caste husdand-low caste wife	0	2	2
Low caste husband-high caste wife	19	0	19
Total	19	2	21

With regard to the rural-urban background of these couples, the general pattern of marriage involved the urban male of low caste group and the urban female of high caste group. Nineteen couples fell in this classification (see Table 3). In two cases, high caste males from the rural area had married low caste females of urban background.

Table 4 shows the age differentials of the couples. Where the marriage involved a low caste male and high caste female, fifteen of these couples were of the same age, and in the other four cases husbands were younger than their wives. In two cases, where the

[4]The professional group included: college professors, lawyers, doctors, dentists, scientists, engineers, and school teachers. The nonprofessional group consisted of clerks, kindred workers, skilled and semi-skilled workers, and unemployed.

marriage was between high caste males and low caste females, the husbands were older than their wives.

TABLE 3. *Rural-urban background of intercaste married couples*

Caste	Urban husband-rural wife	Urban husband-urban wife	Rural husband-urban wife	Rural husband-rural wife	Total
High caste husband-low caste wife	0	0	2	0	2
Low caste husband-high caste wife	0	19	0	0	19
Total	0	19	2	0	21

TABLE 4. *Age differentials in intercaste married couples*[5]

Caste	Husband younger than wife	Husband and wife of same age	Husband older than wife	Total
High caste husband-low caste wife	0	0	2	2
Low caste husband-high caste wife	4	15	0	19
Total	4	15	2	21

SUMMARY AND DISCUSSION

The data characterize most minority dominant marriages in India. The most frequent type of intercaste marriage involves a low caste male of high achievement and a high caste female of low achievement (nineteen out of twenty-one couples). Conversely, the minor

[5]Age difference of one year or more has been considered here as either younger or older. If the difference between the ages of husband and wife is less than one year the age has been considered the same.

trend in marriage is between high caste males of low achievement and low caste females of high achievement (two out of twenty-one cases).

The findings seem to suggest that a higher ascription status may be attained when low caste males marry high caste females. Similarly, the achieved status of high caste females tends to be raised by marrying low caste males with high achievement. The pattern of gaining higher social mobility is also evident in marriages between high caste males of low achievement and low caste females with high achievement.

In two cases, where high caste males had married low caste females, one male belonged to the Brahmin caste and the other represented the Kshatriya caste. Conversely, their wives came from the Chamar caste. Though Chamars represent a low caste, they are not considered as unclean as sweepers. Some Chamars in India work with leather and others are farmers. In both cases, women's parents' owned farmland. Through sanskritization[6] these low caste families have been able to raise their hierarchical position in the Hindu community. Though theoretically it has been forbidden by Brahmins, in recent years low castes have begun to adopt the customs and practices of high caste people (Bailey, 1959:227).

The high caste group may not be opposed to one of their men marrying a low caste woman, because from their viewpoint it is permissable for them to keep mistresses from the low caste. They resent the idea of their women marrying low caste men. In India a woman of Brahmin caste living as a mistress of a man of the same caste would not be condemned and ostracized so much as a woman who married a Sudra. Hindu religious laws forbid marriages between high and low castes. However, the laws of Manu generally approve a marriage with a person of the same *varna*, but do not entirely forbid a marriage outside the *varna*, as later writers have done (Ketkar, 1909:143-145). Conversely, the state laws and secular norms in India permit intercaste or mixed marriages.

[6]By sanskritization is meant that a low caste is able, in a generation or two, to rise to a higher position in the hierarchy by adopting vegetarianism and teetotalism, and a higher caste's ritual and pantheon. In other words, a low caste person adopts the customs, rites, and beliefs of the Brahmins, and also leads a Brahmanic way of life (Srinivas, 1959).

It is interesting to note that low caste males and high caste females have a tendency to raise their ascription or achievement level through intercaste marriage. It was pointed out by most of the high caste female informants who had married low caste males, that since in most cases marriages are still arranged by parents, it is difficult for them to find suitable young men in their own caste, for such men may prefer to marry women of the same socio-economic background. (In this case, the couples met each other individually and also through newspaper advertisements and not through the traditional method of arrangement by parents.) This would mean that high caste females would marry low caste males only if they were unable to find husbands of a higher socio-economic level in their own caste. However, high caste women insisted that they did not believe in the traditional caste system. They would marry men from any caste as long as they had a good education and high aspirations and also if they were in love with them.

It is difficult for high caste people of a lower socio-economic stratum to send their children beyond high school because college education is very expensive. Conversely, it is easier for low caste people (though most of them come from a lower socio-economic background) to give their children a high school or college education because of the special provision that the Indian Constitution makes for the "scheduled" or "backward" castes. In the agencies of central and state governments one post in eight of those filled by competitive examination is reserved for scheduled castes. Standards and age limits are adjusted to their poorer education. Government scholarships are likewise reserved for students from these communities. This would suggest that socio-economic mobility is easier for low caste people than for high caste persons.

The data on rural-urban background of married couples and the adoption of residence after their marriage show a distinct pattern in intercaste marriage. In all the twenty-one cases couples were living in cities after their wedding (see Table 3). This suggests that intercaste marriage is likely to take place in the *Gesellschaft* type of societies where old Hindu religious norms are giving way to secular norms. In the *Gemeinschaft* type of communities (small, rural, and agrarian) intercaste marriage is difficult because relatively rigid religious norms are still prevalent. Touchable-untouchable caste married couples would probably encounter little or no opposition in cities even if their castes were known. However, they would face mass resentment and opposition in villages. In all cases the pattern of residence was neolocal (couples had to break away from the traditional joint family system).

The touchable-untouchable caste marriages in India are becoming possible especially in cities because, although the old religious norms of the "ideal caste" call for a stable caste hierarchy, the Constitution of India and the secular norms oppose the old religious ideas. Therefore, in practice (or the "actual caste"), the caste system has become unstable, especially in the cities, with secular norms opposing and replacing older Hindu religious precepts (Das and Acuff, 1970:48-54).

In conclusion, it may be said that as India gradually moves toward industrialization and urbanization, the traditional caste system will increasingly become unstable with secular norms opposing and replacing older Hindu religious ideals. This anticipated social change in India, it is believed, will also bring about change in the rigid attitude and behavior of people toward touchable-untouchable intercaste marriages. It is suggested that intercaste marriages would help break down the traditional caste system. They will also help wipe out caste distinctions and untouchability.

Marriages which are increasingly common in India, especially in urban and industrial areas, are not between high and low caste people but between the members of various subcastes within a large caste group (as between Brahmin subcastes). At present, many of the modern-minded and liberal people in India believe that intercaste marriages should be accepted (legally such marriages are permitted). But they are not always willing to contract such unions, especially if suitable marriage partners can be found within their own caste or subcaste. A very strong emotional bond, a determination to revolt against mores, customs, family and religious practices, or some practical gain in the form of wealth or social position seem necessary to overcome these difficulties (Ross, 1961:273).

It is apparent from the intercaste marriages included in this study that most of these unions took place in civil courts, were based on romantic love, and were against the wishes of the parents. In most cases, married couples had been opposed by their families at the time of marriage, but reconciliation usually occurred later on, especially after the birth of the first child.

The importance of intercaste marriage is increasing, and the general attitude of the members of the castes involved in such unions is one of non-opposition, tolerance, or indifference. Those who oppose intercaste marriages do so out of their ignorance, prejudice, or ethnocentrism. Some point out that couples who enter into touchable-untouchable caste marriages would find it difficult to adjust to other caste customs and practices. Others suggest that if the marriage is not successful, the parents of the woman would find it very difficult to take their daughter back, especially if she needs the financial security of her parents. Also, the children of intercaste marriages may suffer, as do their parents, the restrictions and deprivations of the untouchable castes, particularly if the parents are living in small rural communities.

One thing is apparent from the analysis of intercaste marriages in India, that they characterize mostly low caste dominant marriage. Men can raise their status by achievement, women mainly by marriage. Men of low ascribed status can marry women of higher ascribed status if men bring higher achieved status than women could readily get in their ascribed status group. For both men and women in India the pattern of intercaste marriage strongly suggests that persons of low status ascription with high achievement tend to marry persons of high status ascription with low achievement. Evidently, all people value both kinds of status and seek them, either as personal characteristics or through marriage.

CONCLUSION

In a study of intermarriage in India between high (touchable) and low (untouchable) castes, twenty-one couples were intensively interviewed. Their names were obtained by referral or "snowball" technique. This study may further the understanding of status ascription and achievement as these considerations operate in the context of mate selection outside the bounds of one's endogamous group. The dominant pattern in intercaste marriage is between low caste males of high achievement and high caste females of low achievement. Nineteen out of twenty-one couples fell in this classification. Conversely, the minor trend (two out of twenty-one couples) is between high caste males of low achievement and low caste females with high achievement. For both men and women in India the pattern of intercaste marriage suggests that persons of low status ascription with high achievement tend to marry persons of high status ascription with low achievement.

LIMITATIONS OF THE STUDY

1) The sample was very small, so one cannot safely generalize from these findings. But we must realize that marriages between high (touchable) and low (untouchable) castes are relatively rare. Conversely, there is no single authoritative and reliable source from which information could be obtained, as all such marriages may not take place in civil courts.

2) The study was limited to just a few large urban and industrial areas in north India, thus the ideal description of intercaste marriages cannot be applied equally to all segments of Indian society as considerable regional, ethnic, rural and urban, as well as socio-economic status differences in family relations in the Hindu community are known to exist.

3) The sample used in this study was based on the referral or "snowball" technique, so it cannot be considered a probability sample. The only source from which a probability sample could have been drawn would have been court records. Even these records may not have made it possible to locate the intercaste married couples, who might have moved to some other place. Since the process of randomization was not employed in selecting the subjects, one must be cautious in drawing generalizations.

4) This is an exploratory study, since not much has been done in this area. Thus, one cannot make comparisons with previous studies.

REFERENCES

Bailey, F.
  1959 *Caste and the Economic Frontier.* Manchester: Manchester University Press.
Barnett, L.
  1963a "Interracial Marriage in California." *Marriage and Family Living,* 25 (November). Pp. 424-427.
  1963b "Research on International and Interracial Marriages." *Marriage and Family Living,* 25 (February). Pp. 105-107.

98 *Family in Asia*

Burma, J.
1963 "Interethnic Marriages in Los Angeles, 1948-1959." *Social Forces*, 42 (December). Pp. 156-165.

Das, M. and F. Acuff
1970 "The Caste Controversy in Comparative Perspective: India and the United States." *International Journal of Comparative Sociology*, 11 (March). Pp. 48-54.

Golden, J.
1954 "Patterns of Negro-White Intermarriage." *American Sociological Review*, 19 (April). Pp. 144-147.

Kannan, C.
1961 "Intercaste Marriage in Bombay." *Sociological Bulletin*, 10 (September). Pp. 53-68.
1963 *Intercaste and Intercommunity Marriages in India*. Bombay: Allied.

Kapadia, K.
1954a "Changing Patterns of Hindu Marriage and Family." *Sociological Bulletin*, 3 (March). Pp. 61-87.
1954b "Changing Patterns of Hindu Marriage and Family." *Sociological Bulletin*, 3 (September). Pp. 131-157.
1955 "Changing Patterns of Hindu Marriage and Family." *Sociological Bulletin*, 4 (September). Pp. 162-192.
1968 *Marriage and Family in India*. London: Oxford University Press.

Ketkar, S.
1909 The History of Caste in India, Volume I. New York: Taylor and Carpenter, Booksellers and Publishers.

Pavela, T.
1964 "An Exploratory Study of Negro-White Intermarriage in Indiana." *Journal of Marriage and the Family*, 25 (May). Pp. 209-211.

Ross, A.
1961 *The Hindu Family in its Urban Setting*. Toronto: University of Toronto Press.

Srinivas, M.N.
1959 "Note on Sanskritization and Westernization" in Introduction to the *Civilization of India*. Chicago: University of Chicago Press.

3. CHRISTIAN AND NON-CHRISTIAN INTERRELIGIOUS MARRIAGES—*Man Singh Das*

The subject of interreligious marriage has, in recent years, attracted national as well as international attention. Not only have Indian sociologists discussed interreligious marriage (Kapadia, 1954; 1955; 1968; Ross, 1961; Kannan, 1961; 1963), but the religious community in all facets of life has become gravely and empirically concerned over this issue (*Indian Witness*, 16 and 30 April 1970). Opinion surveys suggest that a large proportion of those interviewed in the Bombay area favored some type of interreligious marriage and were actively engaged in advocating its practice. In addition, Das (1971), in analyzing the nature of interreligious marriage, arrived at these basic conclusions: 1) The majority of marriages took place between non-Christian husbands and Christian wives. 2) The remaining marriages consisted of Christian husbands and non-Christian wives.

Interreligious marriage in India is basically understood to mean marriage between Christians and non-Christian Hindu or Muslim persons. The present study was primarily concerned with interreligious marriages involving Christians, all of whom were Protestants, and their non-Christian Hindu or Muslim partners. The study sought to answer the following questions: What is the predominant type of interreligious marriage? Is the marriage union between Christian husband and non-Christian wife, or the reverse? What couples tend to have interreligious marriages? What is the general pattern of interreligious marriage? Why do people enter into such marriages? The present study attempts to facilitate an understanding of various factors that contribute to mate selection outside the bounds

TABLE 5. *Christian and non-Christian interreligious marriages in India*

Christian husband and non-Christian wife		Non-Christian husband and Christian wife	
Christian husband-Hindu wife	Christian husband-Muslim wife	Hindu husband-Christian wife	Muslim husband-Christian wife
11	2	29	17
For 9 Christian husbands, first marriage; and for 2, second marriage. For 6 Hindu wives, first marriage; and for 5, second marriage.	In both cases husbands and wives were previously married (second marriage).	For 27 Christian women, first marriage; and for 2, second marriage. For 19 men, first marriage; and for 10, second marriage	For 12 men, first marriage; and for 5, second marriage. For 15 women, first marriage; and for 2 second marriage.

N = 59 couples.
All Christians were Protestants.

of one's religious group. It may be assumed that the predominant type of relationship is between non-Christian Hindu husbands and Christian wives, and non-Christian Muslim husbands and Christian wives.

SAMPLE AND METHOD

The sample consisted of both male and female partners in fifty-nine marriages in which religious differences were present. These couples resided in various parts of north India, mostly Lucknow, Allahabad, Kanpur, and Delhi. The names and addresses were obtained through referral or the "snowball" technique. In the selection of these couples, the process of randomization was not employed. The data were obtained through intensive interviews, which were conducted between 1966 and 1973.

FINDINGS

The predominant pattern of interreligious marriage involved a non-Christian husband with a Christian wife. Table 5 shows that twenty-nine non-Christian Hindu men married Christian women, and seventeen non-Christian Muslim husbands had Christian wives. The remaining thirteen cases indicated that eleven Christian husbands had non-Christian Hindu wives, and two couples were of the Christian husband and Muslim wife type.

With regard to age differentials, where the marriage involved a non-Christian Hindu husband and a Christian wife, the husband was older in twenty-one cases; the spouses were of equal age in seven cases, and in one case the husband was younger. Where the marriage consisted of a non-Christian Muslim husband and a Christian wife, twelve cases involved an older husband, while in four cases the partners were of equal age, and in one case the husband was younger. In thirteen cases involving Christian husbands and non-Christian wives, four cases included a Christian husband and a Hindu wife, the former being older; in six cases the spouses were of equal age; and in one case the husband was younger. Marriages between a Christian husband and a Muslim wife (two cases) indicated no age difference.

TABLE 6. *Age differentials in Christian and non-Christian interreligious marriages in India**

Age differentials	Christian husband and non-Christian wife		Non-Christian husband and Christian wife	
	Christian husband- Hindu wife	Christian husband- Muslim wife	Hindu husband- Christian wife	Muslim husband- Christian wife
Husband older	4	0	21	12
Husband and wife equal	6	2	7	4
Husband younger	1	0	1	1
Total	11	2	29	17

*Age difference of one year or more has been considered here as either younger or older. If the difference between the ages of husband and wife is less than one year, the age has been considered equal.

In twenty-three of the twenty-nine marriages which involved a non-Christian Hindu husband and a Christian wife, the husband was more educated than his wife; in five cases, the spouses' education was equal; and in one, the wife was more educated. In fourteen of the seventeen cases involving a non-Christian Muslim husband and a Christian wife, the husband was more educated than his wife, and in three cases, the partners were equally educated. The minor trend (thirteen cases) involving a Christian husband and a non-Christian Hindu wife included seven cases with more education for the husband, and four with equal education. The two remaining cases involving Christian husbands and non-Christian Muslim wives included one couple with more education for the husband and one with no educational difference.

When the major fields of specialization were compared among Christian and non-Christian husbands, it was found that a Hindu[7] husband (twenty-nine cases) was involved in these major categories: thirteen were in engineering, two were in the humanities, five in the medical sciences, eight in the physical life sciences, and one in the social sciences. Of seventeen Muslim husbands, nine were in

[7]Hereafter, Hindus or Muslims will be understood to mean non-Christians.

engineering, one in the humanities, three in the medical sciences, and four in the physical life sciences. Similarly, in the remaining cases involving Christian husbands having Hindu wives (eleven cases), two men were in engineering, one in the humanities, two in the medical sciences, five in the physical life sciences, and one in the social sciences. The two Christian husbands having Muslim wives were in the physical sciences.

TABLE 7. *Educational differences in Christian and non-Christian interreligious marriages in India*

Educational differences	Christian husband and non-Christian wife		Non-Christian husband and Christian wife	
	Christian husband-Hindu wife	Christian husband Muslim wife	Hindu husband Christian wife	Muslim husband Christian wife
Husband more educated	7	1	23	14
Equal	4	1	5	3
Wife more educated	0	0	1	0
Total	11	2	29	17

Table 9 shows the place of origin, rural or urban, of these couples. The pattern of marriage is non-Christian husband and Christian wife (forty-six cases), with fourteen urban husbands and five suburban. The suburban husbands had chosen and married nineteen women from an urban area and eight from the suburbs. The Christian husband-non-Christian wife marriages (thirteen cases) show that the urban husbands had married eight women from an urban area, and two from suburbia. The suburban Christian husbands (three cases) had urban wives. In all fifty-nine cases, not one person had come from a rural area.

TABLE 8. *Major fields of specialization of Christian and non-Christian husbands in India*

Field of specialization*	Christian husband and non-Christian wife		Non-Christian husband and Christian wife	
	Christian husband-Hindu wife	Christian husband-Muslim wife	Hindu husband-Christian wife	Muslim husband-Christian wife
Engineering	2	0	13	9
Humanities	1	0	2	1
Medical sciences	2	0	5	3
Physical and life sciences	5	2	8	4
Social sciences	1	0	1	0
Total	11	2	29	17

*Engineering includes chemical, civil, electrical, industrial, mechanical, and others.

Humanities include architecture, creative arts, languages, literature, liberal arts, and others.

Medical sciences include dentistry, medicine, and others.

Physical and life sciences include biological sciences, chemistry, geosciences, mathematics, physics, and astronomy.

Social sciences include economics, history, home economics, international relations, law, psychology, and sociology.

TABLE 9. *Place of origin of Christian and non-Christian husbands and wives in India*

Christian husband and non-Christian wife								
Urban husband			Suburban husband			Rural husband		
Urban wife	Suburban wife	Rural wife	Urban wife	Suburban wife	Rural wife	Urban wife	Suburban wife	Rural wife
8	2	0	3	0	0	0	0	0

Non-Christian husband and Christian wife								
Urban husband			Suburban husband			Rural husband		
Urban wife	Suburban wife	Rural wife	Urban wife	Suburban wife	Rural wife	Urban wife	Suburban wife	Rural wife
14	5	0	19	8	0	0	0	0

The couples' religious participation indicates that when the non-Christian husband is most active, the Christian wife is not active at all; when the husband is active, the wife is also active (two cases); in one case, the wife is least active. When the non-Christian husband is least active, in five cases the wife is most active, in nine active, and in twenty-nine least active. The most active Christian husband has a wife who is not actively involved. Of the two active Christian husbands' wives, one is active and the other least active. Of the least active Christian husbands' wives, two are active and nine least active. Only in non-Christian husband marriages where the male partner is least active can one find a significant number of wives (five cases) actively involved in religion. In this category, one also finds the least active wives (twenty-nine) of non-Christian husbands.

TABLE 10. *Religious participation of Christian and non-Christian husbands and wives in India*

Christian husband and non-Christian wife								
Husband most active			Husband active			Husband least active		
Wife most active	Wife active	Wife least active	Wife most active	Wife active	Wife least active	Wife most active	Wife active	Wife least active
0	0	0	0	1	1	0	2	0

Non-Christian husband and Christian wife								
Husband most active			Husband active			Husband least active		
Wife most active	Wife active	Wife least active	Wife most active	Wife active	Wife least active	Wife most active	Wife active	Wife least active
0	0	0	0	2	1	5	9	29

As for the number of children born to these inter and intrareligious marriages the seventeen Muslim husband-Christian wife couples had thirty-six children; the twenty-nine Hindu husband-Christian wife cases had fifty-six, the eleven Christian husband-Hindu wife couples had nineteen; and the three Christian husband-Muslim wife marriages had three. In all thirty Hindu cases, ninety-one children were born, while the sixteen Muslim couples had sixty children. These data strongly indicate the Hindus' emphasis on prolific reproduction.

TABLE 11. *Number of children born to inter and intrareligious marriages in India*

$N=11$	$N=2$	$N=29$	$N=17$	$N=30$	$N=16$
Christian husband-Hindu wife	Christian husband-Muslim wife	Hindu husband-Christian wife	Muslim husband-Christian wife	Hindu couples	Muslim couples
19	3	57	36	9	60

SUMMARY AND DISCUSSION

The data characterize most minority dominant interreligious marriages in north India. The most frequent type of interreligious marriage involves a non-Christian husband and a Christian wife (twenty-nine Hindu husbands and seventeen Muslim husbands, a total of forty-six couples out of fifty-nine cases). Conversely, the minor trend in interreligious marriage is between a Christian man and a non-Christian woman (eleven Hindu and two Muslim wives, a total of thirteen couples out of fifty-nine cases).

The findings seem to suggest that higher ascription may be attained when Christian women marry non-Christian men. Similarly, the position of Christians, who are basically considered low in status, tends to improve by marrying Hindu persons, who seem to enjoy higher status. This is evident in educational differences and fields of specialization, where the Hindus reflect a significant influence in high status areas.

Interreligious marriage in India has recently emerged as a highly controversial issue. An article written by the Reverend Jones (*Indian Witness*, 22 January 1970) on Christian and non-Christian mixed marriages elicited numerous comments for and against this type of union. Jones advocated interreligious marriage on a moral and ecclesiastical level. He proposed that alienation by the mixed couple from the church might occur if the church refuses to bless the marriage. He expressed deep concern for accepting such marriages on the premise that the Christian faith is strong enough to welcome non-Christians of good will into its social and worshipping fellowship. He also proposed that the constitution of the church of north India should be amended to allow solemnization of mixed marriages at the discretion of the bishop and the will of the couple involved.

Responses of Jones's article indicated non-opposition, tolerance, or indifference *(Indian Witness,* 30 April 1970). Those who did oppose interreligious marriage did so because they felt that such unions would eventually lead to some alienation from the Christian faith, since only one partner would be somewhat active religiously. The finding concerning this pattern generally reflected this attitude, and it was indicated, that most of the couples were either inactive or least active religiously.

The data on rural-urban background of these married couples show a distinct pattern. In all fifty-nine cases, the couples were living in cities or in nearby suburban areas, and after their marriage, continued to live there. This suggests that interreligious marriage is likely to take place in the *Gesellschaft* type of society, where old religious ideas are giving way to secular norms. In the smaller *Gemeinschaft* type of community (rural and agrarian), interreligious marriage is difficult because of relatively rigid norms which are still prevalent. Therefore, in practice, the actual religious customs are becoming unstable, with secular norms opposing and replacing older Hindu religious ideas (Das and Acuff, 1970).

In conclusion, it may be said that as India gradually moves towards industrialization and urbanization, the traditional caste and religious systems will increasingly become unstable with secular norms opposing and replacing older religious practices. This anticipated social change in India, it is believed, will also bring about change in the rigid attitude and behavior of people toward interreligious marriages. It is suggested that interreligious marriages would help break down the traditional religious system.

At present, many of the modern-minded and liberal people in India believe that interreligious marriages should be accepted, but they are not always willing to pioneer, especially if suitable marriage partners can be found within their own religion. A very strong emotional bond, a determination to revolt against mores, customs, family and religious practices, or some practical gain in the form of wealth or social position, seem necessary to overcome these difficulties (Ross, 1961).

Many factors that are apparent from the analysis of interreligious marriage characterize mostly non-Christian husband-Christian wife unions. Christians usually raise their status by marrying non-Christian persons. The Hindu counterpart, especially the husband, seems to have a high educational status. Evidently, mate selection is most desirable when a Christian male or female marries a non-Christian, that is, a Hindu or Muslim.

LIMITATIONS OF THE STUDY

1) Since the sample is very small, one cannot safely generalize from the findings. But we must realize that marriages between Christians and non-Christians are relatively rare. Conversely, there is no single authoritative and reliable source from which information could be obtained, as all such marriages may take place in civil courts.

2) The study was limited to just a few large urban and industrial areas in north India. Thus, the ideal description of interreligious marriage cannot be applied equally to all segments of Indian society, as considerable regional, ethnic, rural, urban, social, and economic differences exist.

3) The sample, based on the "referral" or "snowball" technique, cannot be considered a probability sample. The only source from which such a sample could have been drawn would have been court records. Even these records, however, may not have made it possible to locate interreligious marriages, since couples might have moved to some other place. Because the process of randomization was not employed in selecting the subjects, one must be cautious in drawing generalizations.

4) This is an exploratory study and one cannot make comparisons with previous studies.

REFERENCES

Bailey, F.
    1959 *Caste and the Economic Frontier.* Manchester: Manchester University Press.

Das, Man S.
  1971 "A Cross Cultural Study of Intercaste Marriage in India and the
        United States." *International Journal of Sociology of the Family*,
        1 (May). Pp. 25-33.
Das, M. and F. Acuff
  1970 "The Caste Controversy in Comparatiye Perspective: India and
        the United States." *International Journal of Comparative Sociology*,
        11 (March). Pp. 48-54.
Indian Witness
  1970 "Mixed Marriage." 22 January, 16 and 30 April.
Kannan, C.
  1961 "Intercaste Marriage in Bombay." *Sociological Bulletin*, 10
        (September). Pp. 53-68.
  1963 *Intercaste and Intercommunity Marriages in India*. Bombay:
        Allied.
Kapadia, K.
  1954a "Changing Patterns of Hindu Marriage and Family." *Sociological
        Bulletin*, 3 (March). Pp. 61-87.
  1954b "Changing Patterns of Hindu Marriage and Family." *Sociological
        Bulletin*, 3 (September). Pp. 131-157.
  1955 "Changing Patterns of Hindu Marriage and Family." *Sociological
        Bulletin*, 4 (September). Pp. 162-192.
  1968 *Marriage and Family in India*. London: Oxford University Press.
Ketkar, S.
  1909 *The History of Caste in India*, Volume 1. New York: Taylor and
        Carpenter, Booksellers and Publishers.
Ross, A.
  1961 *The Hindu Family in its Urban Setting*. Toronto: University of
        Toronto Press.
Srinivas, M.N.
  1959 "Note on Sanskritization and Westernization" in Introduction to
        the *Civilization of India*. Chicago: University of Chicago Press.

4. WOMEN IN MODERN INDIA—*Promilla Kapur*

At first glance, it may appear rather out of place to have a chapter on "Women in Modern India" in the section on "The Family in India." But, since woman is the pivot of the family and the basic unit of psychological change in any society, and since she is one of the first socializing agents for the upcoming generations and the psychic factor in all cultures and civilizations, her role and status in a particular society play a very significant part in molding the social system, including the family and family relationships. Moreover, since woman's role is very important in teaching the new human entrants to this world the first lessons of life, and making them accept values which later affect their ways of thinking, feeling, and acting, and since women are the arbiters of social change, it is very essential to know about them—their rights and privileges, their thoughts, feelings, and behavior, and also their movement from traditional values to modern ideas. This knowledge will enable us to understand the past, present, and future of the family in India.

In a society as large and culturally diverse, complex and even contradictory as India, changes take place at different speeds and in different directions at different levels of the various sections of the population. As such, the directions and patterns of change among women tend to vary not only among different segments of society, but also in different kinds of family organizations which vary considerably both structurally and functionally. Owing to practical considerations and other constraints, the author, while discussing women in modern India, will delimit the discussion to the patrilineal Hindu society which is its dominant section. Under the existing cultural complexity, striking contrasts, and variation of the changing contemporary Indian scene, it is very difficult to make unqualified generalizations regarding the role and status of women in modern India. Thus, only an attempt is being made to present a general and broad all-India picture of women in relation to the family.

"Women in Modern India" can imply two perspectives. One may refer to women belonging to that section of society in India which is termed "modern"—progressive, rational, liberal, flexible, and open to change—whereas the other may refer to the changing position of women in India since about the end of the 18th or beginning of the 19th century till the present time, which is considered to be the modern era. The author proposes to discuss women in modern India in both of these perspectives. Though there are two views about women in India—the classical text view and the empirical view—here the emphasis will be on the empirical view of the role and status of women in modern India.

First, women will be discussed as they have been viewed and as they have been viewing themselves since about the end of the 18th century till the present time, that is, in the modern era, and then women of the progressive and "modern" section of India will be taken up. But since the present is always related to the past and many of the contemporary attitudes towards women are rooted in old ideas, a very brief historical survey of woman's changing status becomes necessary in order to understand women in modern India. This would be centered mainly around marriage and the family.

WOMAN'S POSITION FROM VEDIC TIMES TO THE END OF THE 18TH CENTURY

According to the studies of many Indologist and scholars of Hindu social organizations and of woman's status in ancient India (Cormack, 1953; Prabhu, 1954; Indra, 1955; Kapadia, 1958; Mookerji, 1958; Altekar, 1962; Shastri, 1962), in Vedic times women had absolute equality with men in the realm of religion. They had a respectable position both in the family and society. In the family woman was respected as a daughter, as a wife, and as a mother. The birth of a female child was welcomed and she was later given the same education as sons, was married at the age of sixteen or seventeen years, had voice in the selection of her life partner and in other family matters, and enjoyed considerable freedom of movement. A number of women took part in public life with men and entered the teaching profession. Ordinarily, monogamy was the rule, families were joint in nature, widows were not looked down upon and not many restrictions were forced on them; they were allowed even to remarry, but this was usually done within the family. Divorce was permitted. In the drama of family life, woman's place was, on the whole, as high as that of a man's and man and woman were regarded as having equally important status in social life. According to most authorities, women by and large enjoyed a high status equal to that of men at home and in society till 300 B.C.

Due to various socio-cultural and political factors that prevailed after 300 B.C., the status of women began to decline gradually. Girls' education was discontinued and they ceased to have any voice in the choice of mate, as their age at marriage was also reduced to below eight or nine years and their marriages were arranged by their parents even without their consent or merely with their formal consent. The theory of perpetual tutelage for women was formulated by Manu, the Hindu law-giver, according to whom woman has to depend on her father in her childhood, on her husband in her young age, and on her sons in her old age. He had set up the double standard of morality according to which a man had all the freedom and privileges, whereas a woman was considered inferior in every respect. In fact, the dictum that a wife ought to respect her husband as a god and serve him faithfully even though he were vicious and void of any merit was accepted as applicable to all women (Kapadia, 1958: 169-170; Altekar, 1962).

On account of various factors, by A.D. 700 the practice of sati—a widow's self-immolation on the funeral pyre of her husband or being burnt along with the body of her dead husband—female infanticide, the purdah custom, prohibition of widow remarriage and ill-treatment of widows, abolition of divorce requested by women and remarriage of divorcees became prevalent. Thus, the position of a woman was now much lower and her socialization diminished her individuality. She was completely subservient to, and dependent on, men for everything (Indra, 1955:30-31; Kapadia, 1958:169-170; Altekar, 1962).

Woman's status in India continued to decline till 1800 by which time she had become like a puppet moving when someone else pulls the strings (Dube, 1963:189). She was denied all rights and was kept in state of utter subjection (Desai, 1957:29). She was virtually a slave or chattel, her only function being "to minister to man's physical pleasures and wants; she was considered incapable of developing any of those higher mental qualities which would make her more worthy of consideration and also more capable of playing a useful part in life" (Dubois and Beauchamp, 1906:336). Thus socially, legally, ideologically, and morally, woman was almost a nonentity.

Complete neglect of woman's education, coupled with the practice of child marriage and the customs of polygyny, seclusion, purdah, and sati, with no provision for divorce and remarriage for widows, brought about tremendous degradation in the status of woman (Kuppuswamy, 1972:81; Narain, 1967:26). Most of the disabilities mentioned above were by and large prevalent among women of the upper caste rural families or of the traditional urban families. Women of the lower caste rural families, however, though they had no education and had to face child marriage, polygyny, and other restrictions, could ask for a divorce, and a widow could remarry, such freedoms being due to women's participation in agriculture and their husbands' work. Still, even among them, the divorced and remarried women were looked down upon as somewhat unworthy.

Intercaste marriage was also condemned severely (Kuppuswamy, 1972:181).

POSITION OF WOMAN FROM THE BEGINNING OF THE 19TH CENTURY TILL INDEPENDENCE

The position of women in India, especially among the middle and upper classes, began to improve in the beginning of the 19th century, owing to a variety of social, cultural, political, and economic factors. The untiring efforts of the social reformers and religious leaders, and of other enlightened and progressive men and women of India and other countries, contributed a great deal to such improvement. These liberal-minded leaders felt convinced that national development and progress were not possible without the education and emancipation of women, and believed that a nation which did not respect its women could never become or remain great. They realized that for the liberation of the country, as well as for its progress, the active participation of women was a *sine qua non*. They all stood for the principle of woman's emancipation and equality of the sexes.

Legal Privileges

Owing to the pressures of various movements and organizations initiated by the reformers and other liberal-minded men and women, such as Ram Mohan Roy, Iswarchandra Vidya Sagar, Ranade, Keshab Chandra Sen, Gokhale, Dayanand Saraswati, Annie Besant, Margaret Cousin, Sister Vivedita, Sarojini Naidu, Rama Bai Pandita, Vivekananda, and Mahatma Gandhi, certain laws were adopted during the British rule for removing the disabilities from which women had been suffering for more than 2,000 years and for ensuring them more freedom and privileges. The acts passed during this period were the Sati Abolition Act of 1829, the Widow Remarriage Act of 1856, the Child Marriage Abolition Act of 1860, and the Civil Marriage Act of 1872, which secularized marriage, raised the age of marriage for girls to fourteen years, permitted widow remarriage, and intercaste marriage, and enforced monogamy. The married woman's Property Act of 1874 widened the scope of *streedhana* by including in it a woman's own earnings, and thus encouraged women to engage in remunerative work. The Age of Consent Act of 1881 abolished, at least by law, marriage of girls below twelve years of age. The Child Marriage Restraint Act of 1929 made it punishable to marry a boy under eighteen or a girl under fifteen years of age. By the Hindu Marriage Disabilities Removal Act of 1946, marriage within the same *gotra* was validated.

Education

Apart from the various laws mentioned above, another significant measure that was introduced in the 19th century towards raising the status of women was the education of girls. It was Raja Ram Mohan Roy, rightly known as the Father of Modern India and the first important champion of the cause of women's education, who tried to convince the conservative people that the education of women was in keeping with the ancient religious traditions and beliefs in India. The American Misson was the first, however, to establish a school for girls in 1824. Such schools were later opened by the Indian Society in 1851. Thus, in the first half of the 19th century, it was through the efforts of foreign missionaries and Indian voluntary organizations that primary schools for girls were opened in Bombay, Bengal, and Madras states. But in the second half of the 19th century, great progress was made in women's education, owing to the efforts of the British rulers. The Woods Dispatch of 1854 on education declared that it was the responsibility of the government to promote primary education, particularly for girls. The establishment of Local Fund Committees in 1870 provided facilities for opening special schools for young women. The introduction of training colleges for women in 1870, and the setting up of the Education Commission in 1882, which made several recommendations for the opening of schools for girls and for employing women as inspectors of girl's schools and for giving special stipends to widows who came for teacher's training, went a long way in spreading girls' education.

Women's employment

In the latter part of the 19th century, another significant factor which improved the situation of women in India was their entering into the professions. Because of the opening of women's training colleges and new schools for nursing and medicine, and because of the recommendations of the Education Commission in 1882, women started entering the teaching and medical professions by the end of the 19th century. In the first half of the 20th century, the two world wars, particularly the second world war, brought about various socio-ecomomic changes and women were thus compelled to seek employment. In order to earn better salaries, they needed better education, which later helped them secure better jobs. These two factors—education of girls and their entry into the professions—suggest a marked change in the attitude of men and women towards women's education and employment, and constitute a definite revolution in Indian society.

Political Awakening and Privileges

The 20th century is of great significance in the history of the progress of women in India because their political awakening began in the early 1920's side by side with their participation in the national movement. Actually, feminism was introduced as early as 1917 under the leadership of women like Annie Besant, Sister Vivedita, and Margaret Cousin. A deputation of Indian women under the leadership of Sarojini Naidu made representation to the British parliament and demanded their right to sufferage on the basis of equality with men. Through the efforts of educated and enlightened men and women who all stood for equal rights for women, this goal was achieved within a short period of thirty years. The women of the West had to struggle more and took longer to attain this privilege. The success of Indian women was mainly due to the movement that had begun in 19th century with the demand for women's education, which necessitated many social reforms and had the support and encouragement of most leading men of India. It received a great impetus from Mahatma Gandhi, who inspired thousands of women of all classes to come out of their homes and participate in this movement and finally in the freedom struggle.

The women's organizations, like the Women's Indian Association, All India Women's Conference, National Council of Women, and the Young Women's Christian Association, played a very important and pioneering role in improving the status of women by using the resources of the women themselves. But as Panikkar

(1963: 107) has pointed out, it was not before Mahatma Gandhi entered the political scene that the women of India came to participate
in the national movement in large numbers, which lent great momen-
tum to their own cause. Gandhi's unique contribution, as Asthana
(1974: 59) rightly points out, "was the awakening of the immense
untapped power in Indian womanhood and its utilization for the
progress of the national movement." It was Gandhi who infused
political awakening among women and prepared the ground for
their emancipation. Thus, it was the active participation of women
in the political movement and freedom struggle of the nation that
helped them in bringing about radical changes in their status with
hardly any resistance from men. Large contingents of women
delegates started attending the Congress sessions, which evidences
the political awakening of the Indian women at that time. Yet,
another landmark of such political awakening and prestige could
be seen in their increasing numbers in the legislatures of the
country. By 1940, there were as many as eighty women legislators,
which placed India third among the nations of the world in this
respect.

POST-INDEPENDENCE ERA

The movement of women's emancipation gathered great momen-
tum and the pace of change in the socio-economic and political
spheres was greatly accelerated after Independence. The Constitution of free India stressed equality of the sexes. According to
the fundamental rights of the Indian Constitution, "The State
shall not deny any person equality before the Law or the equal
protection of the laws within the territory of India" (Article 14);
"the state shall not discriminate against any citizen on grounds
only of religion, race, caste, place of birth or any of them"
(Article 15); and, as given in Article 16, "there shall be equality
of opportunity for all citizens in matters relating to employment
or appointment to any office under the state," and "no citizen
shall on grounds of religion, race, caste, sex, descent or place of
birth be ineligible for or discriminated against in respect of employment in any office under the state" (Chakravarty, 1948: 75;
Wasi, 1958: 161). These provisions legally guarntee the educational,
political, and social equality of women with men. They thus enjoy

the same right as men to vote and contest elections, to seek and
to hold public office.

In the Political Sphere

In the first general elections of 1952, women participated with
enthusiasm and there as many as 120 of them who were either
elected or nominated to the state or central legislatures. This
number increased to 245 in 1957. Today there are women ministers, members of parliament, and ambassadors. India is one of
the first major countries in the world to have a woman as the head
of its government.

In rural India also political and economic consciousness has
greatly increased due to the five-year plans and community
development programmes. Women do participate in the various
village development projects and organizations.

In the Educational Sphere

The education of girls received great encouragement and attention after Independence and several special schools for girls were
established in the course of the first ten years after Independence.
According to the 1971 Census of India, the literacy rate for women
was as low as 6.0 per cent. Within ten years, it rose to 7.8 per cent,
and by 1961 it became 12.9 per cent, whereas in 1971 it was
approximately 18.5 per cent. The enrollment of girls in primary
and secondary schools increased considerably following Independence. But the greatest change has occurred in the enrollment
of women in the universities. Even during the period between
1950 and 1953, the number of women attending Indian universities doubled. Their enrollment in colleges increased almost ten
times from 1950 to 1965 (Report of Education Commission,
1964-66).

The progress in the field of professional education has been
even more spectacular—from 5,000 girls in 1950-51 to around
50,000 in 1965-66 (Kuppuswamy, 1972: 196; Report of Education
Commission, 1964-66; Wasi, 1971: 39). Thus, women have been
allowed to exercise their equal right of access to all educational
opportunities and they are in increasing numbers receiving
education in a variety of faculties, for example, engineer-

ing, architecture, accounting, business management, which were the preserves of the male.

In the Legal Sphere

Another significant development is women's new legal rights with regard to marriage and family issues. The Special Marriage Act of 1954 and the Hindu Marriage Act of 1955 have enforced monogamy, prohibited polygamy, legalized intercaste and inter-religious marriages through registration, and conferred equal rights of divorce and alimony to men and women. The Hindu Succession Act of 1956 provides for daughters the same right to inherit property as that of sons. Under this act, the daughter, the widow, and the mother all inherit the property of the deceased. The Hindu Adoption and Maintenance Bill of 1956 provides for the legal adoption of a female child by any male Hindu, subject to the consent of his wife. This act also provides for the adoption of a child by an unmarried woman, a divorcee, a widow, or one whose husband is of unsound mind or has renounced the world. The act also makes it obligatory for a Hindu male or female to maintain during his or her lifetime his or her minor legitimate and illegitimate children, as well as the aged and infirm parents and unmarried or widowed daughters, if they are unable to support themselves.

The Suppression of Immoral Traffic in Women and Girls Act of 1956, which came into force in 1958, deals with the problems of concubinage and prostitution and provides protection to girls and women against the pressures of the interested parties on them to become prostitutes or to be in that profession (Desai, 1957; Chakravarty, 1958:80-81; Narain, 1967:25). The Dowry Bill of 1960 legally prohibits the giving or accepting of dowry. The latest act—the Medical Termination of Pregnancy Act of 1971—legalizes abortion under prescribed circumstances. This new act is one of the most liberal laws of its kind in the world, as failure of contraception has been legally accepted as a valid ground for abortion (Mankekar, 1973: 65-69).

Thus, after India's independence, through the efforts of leaders like Jawahar Lal Nehru—a great champion of the cause of women's emancipation—the women of India have been legally and politically emancipated by virtue of various acts and statutes.

In Employment

Another factor of great importance affecting the family is the employment of women. Various studies (Hate, 1930. 1948, 1969; Desai, 1957; Sengupta, 1958, 1960; Kapur, 1970, 1974) have noted that one of the major consequences of the varied processes of change operating in free India has been the emergence of middle and upper class women from the seclusion and tradition-bound ethos of their homes and their entry into various gainful occupations and professions which had been largely the preserves of men. Women from the lower strata have all along been working by the side of their men in the fields and at crafts to help them in agriculture and cottage industries. And for about seven decades they have been working even for wages in the factories, mines, and plantations, and as menial servants. But, before the second world war, it was considered a disgrace for women of middle and upper class families, particularly for married ones, to secure outside gainful employment. However, increasing opportunities for education, the emergence of new socio-economic patterns, occupational mobility, and the economic tensions and strains which have particularly escalated after the partition of the country, have brought about the emerging middle class of working women.

The partition of free India dislocated many middle and upper class families whose members became refugees, and out of gross economic necessity the daughters, wives, or daughters-in-law of these families had to seek gainful employment. The most spectacular increase in such employment has been among the women of the middle classes, who are working in various capacities and at all levels. According to the Census figures, there has been a great increase in the recruitment of women in the services. "With the 1910 figures as 100, it has been found that it rose up to 143 in 1931, to 158 in 1951, and to 189 in 1961. Thus the number employed in these services is nearly double in 60 years" (Kuppuswamy, 1972: 198). During the period 1961 to 1971, opportunities for education, as well as for employment, for women have widened to a considerable extent and the number of the educated working women has increased sharply.

The various factors acting and interacting simultaneously have been both the causes and the effects of the changed attitudes and lives of the middle class educated women in India. Women have begun to realize that the mission of their lives does not end merely with becoming good wives and wise mothers, and that they have other important objectives in life as well (Hate, 1969; Desai, 1957; Kapur, 1970, 1974).

A change has come in the attitudes not only of the educated women but also of their family members, even of the older generation, and of society towards the gainful employment of the daughters and daughters-in-law of middle and upper class families. The studies of various scholars (Desai, 1957; Kapadia, 1959; Sengupta, 1960; Ross, 1961; Cormack, 1961; Arora *et al.*, 1963; Hate, 1969; Ramanamma, 1969; Jauhari, 1970; Kapur, 1970; Ranade and Ramachandran, 1970: 7; Ramanujam, 1972; Goldstein, 1972:112-113) have pointed out that today husbands, relatives, parents, or parents-in-law approve of the educated daughter's, wife's, or daughter-in-law's working and rather encourage them to help the family by supplementing its income. Dube (1963:202) has rightly noted that even the traditional conception regarding the place and role of women is changing in contemporary Indian society.

With the change in the attitude of the educated women and that of society towards the married woman's gainful employment, their number of educated and employed women has multiplied and they now constitute a class by themselves. Educated women are gradually realizing that work is not just a necessary evil, but a way of living, a full life, and provides a possibility for self-realization.

More and more of these women are developing a new outlook towards their employment and, instead of regarding it as a mere instrument of earning money, they derive self-confidence and pride from it. Now they do not get into paid occupations and professions only when hard-pressed by gross economic necessity, but also when they are motivated to satisfy their various socio-psychological needs and desires, such as attaining a better standard of living, having an independent income and individual status of their own, pursuing a profession or career, and being able to express themselves, utilize their education and leisure time creatively, and diminish loneliness, boredom, or unpleasantness at home (Hate, 1969; Desai, 1957; Kapur, 1960, 1970, 1973, 1974; Arora *et al.*, 1963; Verma, 1974; Narula, 1967:4-5; Vasanthakumar, 1964:12-13; Goode, 1965:76; Srivastava, 1972:186; Dhingra, 1972; Goldstein, 1972:106-197). Thus, economic necessity, as well as the changing concepts of sex roles, motivate women to secure gainful employment in increasing numbers. Thus, educated women in modern India are occupying positions at various levels, positions which were formerly the monopoly of men. And there is scarcely any avenue of employment which women have not entered in increasing numbers.

The educated married woman has to play simultaneously two roles—that of a working woman along with her traditional role of wife and mother. And this tends to create strains and tensions within her, mainly owing to the role conflict (Mahajan, 1966; Kapur, 1969; Kapur, 1970; Kaul, 1973). The speculative threat that the educated married women's gainful employment might affect her marital and family adjustment adversely has been to a considerable extent removed by the pioneer empirical researches carried out in this area by the author (Kapur, 1970), and later by other researchers like Dhingra (1972) and Barot (1972). The studies mentioned above strongly suggest that the educated woman's gainful employment does not in itself affect her marital and family relationships adversely.

In her study (1970), the author found that there has been a change in the educated working woman's attitudes, expectations, and her actual performance in relation to her husband's and her own roles and status in the family (Rao and Rao, 1973:175). This necessitates a readjustment in the already existing complex of role-set in each person's traditionally ascribed status-set. The working wife experiences marital tension and frustration if the members of her role-set do not simultaneously make necessary modifications in their expectations. The modern woman, who is the backbone of the family, is faced with multiple roles—housewife, mother, socialite, careerist, and satisfying companion and sex partner to the husband—some of which tend to be incompatible. In order to have an integrated personal existence in this situation, she has to renounce, subordinate, or merge some of her roles. And this tends to generate conflict, confusion, and contradictions.

The operation of the developments mentioned above in the status of women has brought about certain changes in the 1) patterns of marriage and marital relationship; 2) patterns of family and family relationships; and 3) size of family. The socio-economic and politico-cultural changes that have taken place in modern India, though they have affected women all over the country to a lesser or greater degree, have had greatest effect on the lives and marriage and family structure of the women of the middle and upper middle classes (Ward, 1963:63). Most of the empirical studies on women's attitudes and their marital and family relationships have also been carried out on middle and upper class women. And, above all and most significantly, family change as noted by Kirkpatrick (1963:144) and others is indicated at the levels of middle and upper classes from where it percolates into, and accelerates, the process of social change in the other strata of the social system. As such, the author of this study would concentrate mainly on the attitudinal and behavioral changes with regard to marriage and family among the women of the middle and upper classes in order to indicate the present as well as future trends in marriage and the family in India. "The importance of the middle classes arises from the fact that they radiate all the significant values and manners in all sections around them" (Mukerji, 1954:66).

A number of studies (Hate, 1930, 1946, 1969; Merchant, 1935; Kapadia, 1954-55, 1958-59; Desai, 1945; 1957; Tandon, 1959; Dube, 1963; Kannan, 1963; Fonseca, 1966; Krishnamurthy, 1970; Tripathi, 1967; Kapur, 1960, 1968, 1970, 1973, 1974) have found that the attitudes of educated women, more so of the educated working women, of modern India have considerably changed with regard to their role and status in the family and society and also with regard to the various aspects of marriage and the family. And the changes in their status and attitudes are in turn bringing about changes in the patterns of, and role-relationships within, marriage and the family in India. The changes brought about by the combination of women's political and legal rights and privileges, and their education and economic independence, in the covert and overt behavior of educated urban women with regard to the structure of, and relationships in, marriage and the family, have been noted by many scholars (Kuppuswamy, 1957; Cormack, 1961; Ross, 1961; Gore, 1968) besides the ones mentioned above.

PATTERN OF MARRIAGE AND MARITAL RELATIONSHIP

Concept of Marriage

As indicated by several studies (Coomaraswamy, 1924:86; Vivekananda, 1946:409-410; Ghurye, 1955:92, Kapadia, 1958:169; Altekar, 1962:32-34; Goode, 1963:208), the traditional Hindu concept of marriage is that of a sacrament which enables one to fulfill *dharma* (religious as well as social obligations towards the family, commu- nity, and society), *praja* (progeny), and *rati* (pleasure). According to this concept, the principle of familism is supreme and primary and must be followed, while the individual's interests, needs, and happiness are considered secondary to the interests of the family and community as a whole. The author found in her study (Kapur, 1973) of changing attitudes that among the educated, and more so among the educated working women, the number of such females who believed in the concept that marriage was a sacrament solem- nized primarily for the fulfillment of one's religious and social duty and for the good of the family was descreasing. On the other hand, the number of such women who believed that marriage was a social contract which is entered into primarily for the good of the indivi- dual and for his or her personal happiness and satisfaction was found to be increasing. This trend of emphasizing the "personal concept of marriage" and weakening the idea of sacrament started from the third decade of the 20th century, as is revealed by the studies carried out at that time (Hate, 1930, 1946; Merchant, 1935; Desai, 1945), and it is gaining ground among the educated women of the middle and upper classes.

Necessity of and Motivation for Marriage

Closely related to the concept of marriage are the ideas regard- ing the necessity of, and motivation for, marriage. Increasing numbers of the educated working women now think that marriage is a necessity, not because of the need to fulfil sacred and social duties or because it is a tradition and culture to which they must adhere, nor because of financial and social dependence, but because they believe that marriage is necessary for the satisfaction of their physical, emotional, and social needs, their social status and personal convenience and gains, and for material comforts.

Expectations from Marriage

The young educated urban women's expectations from marriage are gaining new dimensions. More of these women now expect marriage to meet, not only their basic needs, but also all the other needs of their lives—resolution of their psychological and emotional

problems, possession of husband, home, and children, companionship, love, sentiments, interests, values, understanding, social life,
and intellectual and sexual pleasures. Expectations of satisfaction of
their individual needs and of personal happiness from marriage are
mounting (Baig, 1958; Kirpalani, 1971; Kapadia, 1959; Barot, 1972;
Kapur, 1960, 1970, 1973, 1974). Another indication of their multiple expectations from marriage is seen in the analysis of their various
desires and aspirations with regard to the type of husband they would
like to have. More and more educated women want to have a mate
who is economically well placed, educated, intelligent, liberal, affectionate, and understanding. The difference that education makes is
also brought out in the studies (Prashar, 1970; Mitro, 1968; Mehta,
1969) which show that educated girls even in rural areas want well-
qualified husbands. Increasing importance is being attached to the
notion of marital satisfaction and happiness. Naturally, if so much
is expected from a single relationship and institution like marriage,
anything falling short of it is liable to create tension, discontent,
and frustration (Kapur, 1970, 1974; Barot, 1972).

Type of Marriage and Mate Selection

According to the traditional Hindu concept, marriage was an
alliance between two families rather than between two young people,
entered into primarily for the welfare of the family. As such, in traditional Hindu families, marriages of children were arranged by their
parents who were morally obliged to find mates for their children
who in turn were obliged to accept their parents' choice. Since
marriage was arranged by the families, without or with merely
formal consent of the prospective mates, and since their individual
interests were subordinate to the family ends, love was not a necessary basis for mate selection. Love between husband and wife was
supposed to be the result of marriage rather than a prelude to it
(Tagore, 1920). There was hardly any freedom of choice in the
selection of mates.

The attitude of the educated women of middle class families
began to change with regard to the type of marriage and the procedure of mate selection. The empirical studies carried out after
the second decade of the 20th century, like those of Hate (1930,
1946), Merchant (1935), Kapadia (1954, 1955), and Desai (1957),
do indicate a preference for marriage by choice among the middle

class educated youth. The samples of youth studied by Kapadia (1954:70-71), Desai (1957), Kapur (1960), Ross (1961:252), and Shah (1962) had exercised choice and initiative in the selection of their spouses and the number of love marriages and marriages by choice was found to have increased. In Shah's study (1962) of university students, almost all of them considered marriage a personal affair between two individuals in which it was their voice that should prevail. In a study by Fonseca (1966:137-138), 56 per cent of the educated non-students and women office clerks reported that they would prefer to choose their marriage partners themselves. But even this attitude was found to be changing. Various studies of college and university students in India, like those of Cormack (1961), Mathew (1966), and Sharayubal and Vanarase (1966), found that a large majority of college students preferred marriages arranged by parents with the wholehearted consent of the prospective mates. Whether marriage is arranged or not, most of them valued parental consent and support as highly essential and desirable (Sharayubal and Vanarase, 1966). Mehta's study (1970) of Western educated women also points towards similar findings.

In Gore's study (1968) of the Aggarwal families of Delhi, who are supposed to be quite orthodox and traditional, 42 per cent of the respondents were found to hold the view that, while marriage should be arranged by the elders, the parties to the marriage should also be consulted. His data clearly bring out a relationship between the levels of education and the preference for consultation of the boy and girl in the choice of spouse in arranging the marriage— the more educated a woman is, the more likely she is to consider it important that the boy or girl concerned be consulted regarding marriage (Gore, 1968:207-209).

In most of the studies mentioned above, there is an ambivalence in the attitudes of the educated middle class women towards the criteria of mate selection. On one hand, more of them now approve of mate selection by personal choice, whereas, on the other hand, a greater number of them also approve of having the advice and wholehearted consent of the parents or guardians. Mahajan's study (1965) also indicates a similar ambivalence in the attitudes of women students of Punjab University. But the stress on knowing the prospective mate well, as found by Mathew (1966), Mahajan (1965), and others, is a departure from the traditional criteria of mate selection and signifies that the educated girls in modern India no longer wish to play a passive role in the arrangement of their marriage. This is even more true of the young educated working women, as indicated in the author's studies (1970, 1973).

In the author's study (Kapur, 1973) of the changing attitudes of the educated working women, it was found that even within ten years—the time after which the author had studied the attitudes again—the number of such women who preferred arranged marriage but the wholehearted consent of the marriage partners had increased. At the same time, the number of those women who preferred love marriage with the wholehearted consent of the parents had also increased. Educated working women were found, in increasing numbers, to disapprove of "purely arranged marriages," as well as of "purely love marriages." More of them are now approving of the "modern type of arranged marriages" and the "rational type of love marriages." The study shows their increasing preference for a sort of quasi-traditional kind of marriage and mate selection where the willing consent of the prospective marriage partners and parents is considered desirable, whether the marriage be "arranged" or "love."

Age at Marriage and Age Difference Between Spouses

Traditionally, it was considered necessary to have the girl married before she had attained puberty, say, by the age of thirteen with a man who was nearly ten years or more senior to her in age. With regard to the attitude towards the suitable age of marriage for a woman, and the age difference between spouses, changes have been noticed. In Merchant's study (1935), on an average, the young educated women favored marriage at the age of 19.7 years. In 1959—during the first phase of the author's study (1973)—the majority of the educated working women thought that the most suitable age for a girl to get married was between twenty and twenty-four years, whereas in 1969—the second phase of the same study—the corresponding figures were eighteen and twenty-two. Ross (1961) found that in her sample, consisting primarily of the educated Brabmin families living in Bangalore, none of the unmarried women wanted to be married before the age of nineteen. The university students in Mathew's study (1966:47) regarded any age between twenty-two and twenty-four as the most suitable for a woman to marry, while the most frequently chosen lower and upper age limits were twenty and twenty-five years in Goldstein's study (1972:93).

There was a direct relationship in Gore's study (1968:203) between the education of the respondent and the age of marriage given for boys and girls—the more educated respondents tended to suggest higher ages. Women on the same level of education as men, by and large, specified higher ages than men did. How education makes a difference in the attitudes is also borne out by the fact that in many studies of the rural population (Mitro, 1968; Mehta, 1969; Prashar, 1970), the educated girls preferred the marriageable age for females to be between twenty and twenty-three. With this change in attitude, there has been a rise in the age of marriage, as a result of which the number of unmarried girls in the family has increased. And this change indicates an alteration in the traditional family structure in which there were hardly any unmarried young girls, as they used to get married before the age of thirteen, or fourteen.

However, a more pronounced change was discerned in the subjects' attitudes with regard to the upper age limit. In other words, such attitudes have become much more liberal within ten years (Kapur, 1973). This fact is evidenced by a much greater number of educated working women in the sample who stated ten years later that "any age" after eighteen is suitable for a girl to be married, depending on her feelings and the availability of a man of her choice. Similarly, with regard to the age difference between marriage partners, there was a marked change in attitudes on two scores. Firstly, increasing numbers of educated working women preferred a lower age difference between marriage partners—the husband should be one to seven years older than the wife. Secondly, more and more of them had started thinking that age difference is immaterial, and that it matters very little whether the man is two to twelve years older or younger than the girl, provided they approved of each other. This points towards a trend in the liberalization of their attitudes towards age difference between spouses, and more so towards the less traditional marriage between a younger man and an older woman (Kapur, 1973).

Intercaste, Interprovincial, Interreligious, and Interracial Marriages

The traditional Hindu marriage pattern is endogamous, involving persons of the same caste or subcaste, the same province, and the same religion. The attitudes of educated urban middle and upper class women are changing in this respect, and more and more of them are now approving of, and entering into, intercaste, interprovincial, and even interfaith marriages. The observations and studies of many scholars (Merchant, 1935; Desai, 1945:48-49;Ghurye, 1950:178-185; Kapadia, 1954a:61-87; 1254b:131-157; 1955:191-192; 1958:119; Cormack 1961:87; Kannan, 1963:203-211; Das, 1971:25; Sheth, 1972; Kapur, 1973:150-152) point towards this trend. Such liberal attitudes were also discerned among the young urban educated working women (Kapur, 1973).

Style of Marriage Ceremony

Desai reported in her study (1957) that out of the literate middle class women interviewed, 63 per cent preferred the traditional Vedic marriage to the modern civil marriage. In the author's study (1973) of attitudes carried out at two points of time with an interval of ten years, it was found that at both times, though a majority of the educated working women preferred marriages celebrated according to Vedic rites with, of course, fewer old religious customs, ten years later there was a much higher number of women who approved equally of marriages celebrated with simplified Vedic rites, civil marriages, or a combination of the two. A study of the attitudes of college girls in Bombay has given similar findings. It has disclosed that the greatest preference was given to a neo-Vedic marriage, followed in order of preference by the old Vedic and civil ceremonies (Sharayubal and Vanarase, 1966:27). In Cormack's study (1961:87), a majority of female university students reported that they were in favor of the traditional marriage ceremony. All the college girls in Mathew's study (1969:48) desired to have their marriages conducted in the traditional style.

Pattern of Husband-Wife Relationship

In the social structure of the tradition-oriented family, the typical pattern of husband-wife relationships is male dominance and female dependence. According to the traditional norms, the husband is an authoritarian figure whose will should always dominate the domestic scene. The wife is his subordinate and is expected to regard him as her master and serve him faithfully (Dube, 1955:141-145; 1963:190). Moreover, the ideal of *pativrata*, that is, being devoted to the male partner alone, nor only "implied fidelity to the husband but made service to the husband the only duty of the wife and her only purpose in life" (Kapadia, 1958:169-170). She had to adhere to a set pattern of roles laid down for her by tradition (Srinivas, 1942:195; Indra, 1955). In the social background provided by the authoritarian joint family there was hardly any recognition of individual interests or aspirations in the relationship between husband and wife. The latter's only concern was to see that she performed properly all the services needed by her husband, whose satisfaction was her joy in life (Kapadia, 1958: 169).

As pointed out by many (Kapadia, 1958:182-184; 1959:99; Dube, 1963:195-202; Kapur, 1970, 1973, 1974; Rao and Rao, 1973:169), women's education and employment have affected their attitudes towards, and even actual behavior with regard to, the traditional role relationships between spouses. The educated modern woman is no longer willing to accept the dominance of her husband. Desai's study (1945) indicates that many wives are consciously or unconsciously now wielding more authority. The material from interviews in the study conducted by Ross (1961:108) corroborates Desai's findings. The author has also found (1970, 1973, 1974) that more and more of the educated working women prefer to have a relationship of copartnership rather than inequality, the husband being the dominant spouse. Though they do not mind assuming a subordinate position, they strongly feel that the wife's position should be like that of a respected subordinate with a personality of her own and there should be satisfying companionship with the husband. In doing so, they go back to the Vedic ideal embodied in the *sattapadi* formula: "I take thee to be my companion in life" (Kapadia, 1958:184).

In the family, women are increasingly asserting their rights and privileges (Dube, 1963:194; Kapur, 1970; Barot, 1972; Rao and Rao, 1973:175-176). They are becoming effective members of the family and companions of their husbands, not merely their slaves. In the sexual relationship within marriage, educated women increasingly are challenging the passive role of the wife. They feel that, like other areas of marital relationships, sex should be a shared experience indulged in with mutual desire and for mutual gratification. More and more of them are questioning the typical one-sided sexual relationship between spouses in which sex is indulged only at the wish and will of the husband who alone is entitled to demand it from the wife. They now prefer mutual participation and copartnership rather than the husband's superiority and exclusive role in sex relations (Kapur, 1970, 1973; Barot, 1972). In the absence of other family members who provide companionship in a joint family milieu, both husband and wife depend on each other for all kinds of sharings and satisfactions (Narain, 1967; Ross, 1961). The author's studies reveal an increasing consciousness among the educated middle and upper middle class women of their right to attain sexual gratification within marriage, and of the view that a satisfactory sex relation is of great importance in making marriage happy and successful.

Women's high education, professional employment, and occupational status have contributed considerably towards changing the role of the married woman from that of a housekeeper and obedient servant to the master of the house to that of a companion to her husband, sharing with him the problems and experiences of professional work, while he, to an increasing extent, is helping with the work in the household. More and more of the husbands, though the number is increasing very slowly and gradually, living in nuclear families are sharing with the working wife the responsibilities of looking after children and of carrying out other household chores. The study of the employed mother in India by Rao and Rao (1973:175) concludes that "the traditional asymmetric husband-dominated family is changing towards a more symmetric or syncretic type of family where the mother is employed, indicating a major role-conflict resulting in a chain of consequences." There is much more give and take among different members of the family, especially in the educated urban working-wife families, where the role relationship is becoming more symmetrical and reciprocal (Dube, 1963:194; Kapur, 1970; Joshi, 1972: Rao and Rao, 1973), though not so much as educated women expect and desire (Kapur, 1970; Joshi, 1972).

Divorce and Remarriage of Divorced Women

According to the traditional thinking, marriage is a sacrament which is indissoluble and irrevocable. But, due to various changing situations and factors, the attitudes of educated women in modern India towards this aspect of marriage have also undergone a change. In various studies (Desai, 1945; Hate, 1948; Kuppuswamy, 1957) nearly 50 per cent of the females studied asserted woman's right to divorce her husband and favored dissolution of marriage. The author (Kapur, 1973) found that even while the number of edu- cated working women approving of woman's divorcing her husband had not increased much, the range of circumstances under which they justified, or accepted, woman's divorcing her husband or her remarrying after divorce had widened considerably. Though a majority of these women still felt that divorce should be a last resort, more and more of them have started approving of woman's dissolving her marriage even under such circumstances as "husband and wife not being compatible," "spouses not being able to pull on well together," or "spouses being completely dissatisfied with each other." The author's findings corroborate those of Kapadia (1958:182), in whose study of graduates 50 per cent of the subjects were for divorce on grounds of proven incompatibility. Since a greater number of young educated women feel that divorce should be granted if their marriage fails to meet their expectations, the rate of divorce is also increasing among educated women in large urban centers. And this is liable to disrupt the sanctity of marriage and to affect the family adversely (*Encyclopaedia of Social Work in India:* 324).

With regard to the remarriage of divorced women, educated females in modern India feel in increasing numbers that a divorced woman could marry again at any age and stage of her life, if she found it necessary and could find a person of her choice as her life partner (Kapur, 1973:155-156).

Education has been found to be directly related to the accep- tance of divorce, and education and women's employment have been the most important variables affecting attitudes towards divorce (Gore, 1968:215; Ross, 1961:274; Kuppuswamy, 1957; Kapur, 1970, 1973, 1974).

Widow Remarriage

It was found in various studies (Hate, 1948, 1969; Desai, 1957; Kapadia, 1957:48; Gore, 1968:216; Kapur, 1973:157) that a large majority of the people studied approved of widow remarriage. But, apart from finding approval of widow remarriage in increasing numbers of educated working women, the author's study (1973: 157) reveals that their attitudes have become liberalized with regard to this issue. More of them now feel that a widow could marry at any age if she found it necessary owing to various emotional and physical needs, even if it was not a case of economic necessity for her to marry. With this change in attitudes, the status of educated widows is also changing. This further indicates an alteration in the traditional family structure in which a widow was discarded and relegated to a shameful position in the family (Goode, 1963:268).

The thinking, beliefs, arguments, and behavior as revealed by various studies mentioned above further strengthen the conviction that, among educated urban women in modern India, marriage is now entered into less and less with the idea of spiritual, societal, altruistic, and familial gains, and more and more for the satisfaction of the individual's material, socio-psychological and sensual needs.

TYPE OF FAMILY AND FAMILY RELATIONSHIPS

The enactment and enforcement of new laws giving women legal equality with men, education at all levels, and gainful employment, along with other socio-economic changes, have considerably affected the attitudes and behavior of urban educated women in modern India, and to a lesser degree those of men and other members of the family. This has undoubtedly influenced their views with regard to their preferences for the type of family and role relationships within and outside the family. And thus, in turn, has necessarily brought about changes in the traditional patterns and formal structure of the family. Various empirical studies (Hate, 1930:107; 1946:79; Merchant, 1935:128; Desai, 1945, 1957; Kapur, 1960) reveal that the two old pillars of Hindu society—sacramental marriage and the joint family—which constitute traditional patterns, started weakening since the third decade of the 20th century. In these studies, a majority of the educated middle class women did not favor the traditional joint family and preferred the nuclear family, mainly because of their developing individualistic concepts of marriage and family life. The general trend appears to be that the percentage of those who are in favor of the nuclear family increases as the level of education rises (Gore, 1968:116). Gore's data (1968:235) suggest that in the urban areas and among the more educated people in modern India the fraternal joint family tends to find less favor than the lineal joint family. This is also supported by Kapadia's work (1955:184-185) on graduates, Ross's data (1961) on middle class families in Bangalore, and Desai's study (1964) of families in Mahuwa.

The social security program of the traditional joint family is undermined by the shift from a kin-oriented outlook to an interest-oriented philosophy, which has been accelerated by formal education, economic depression, financial independence, self-reliance. Western individualism, and other socio-psychological factors that have changed the position of women in the middle and upper classes (Devanandan and Thomas, 1960:42; Panikkar, 1955:3). These changes, especially women's education and the need for supplementing the family income by women's gainful employment, as well as western values, have contributed to the disruption of older family types and have stimulated the movement in the direction of natural families (Mukerji, 1954:67-68). As pointed out by Rao and Rao, all structures are interrelated, but the family and occupational systems are particularly interdependent. The mother's participation in the world of work has brought about structural and functional alterations in the family. This has been suggested by many studies (Rao and Rao, 1973:169).

As a result of education and economic independence, women have been particularly more expressive in their demands for individual families and it is mainly women who are in opposition to the traditional fraternal joint family (Merchant, 1935:123; Kapadia, 1955:170-174; Sharma, 1951:53-55; Gore, 1968:127), For example, Kapadia, in his study of graduates (1955), found that, though a large majority of male graduates were not discontented with the joint family, many of them felt unhappy mainly because their wives felt embarrassed and repressed in the joint family environment. The studies of family change also indicate a tendency among educated women, more than among men, to give preference to nuclear family living (Cormack, 1961; Gore, 1968). The findings of a study by Ross (1961) support other studies in suggesting that young educated modern women in India desire to have separate homes or to live in nuclear families more than men do. The more sophisticated ones are now more anxious to marry men who either live away from their families or else can afford to set up separate households after getting married. There is an increasing desire among young educated women to live separately from their in-laws (Ross, 1961:50, 182; Kapur, 1970). It has also been found (Kapur, 1970) that wherever and whenever the educated working women's efforts were successful, they left their joint families or in-laws and went to live separately with their husbands and children. This is so mainly because woman's lot is the hardest in the traditional joint family owing to the ill-treatment by and supreme authority of the mother-in-law over the daughter-in-law, who experiences humiliation and interference in her personal life. The difficulties experienced by women in joint families have been noted by many authors (Kapadia, 1959: 94; Ross, 1961:174; Cormack, 1953:130; Kapur, 1970; Barot, 1972). Because of the changed situation of educated people, more so of the educated working daughter-in law, the latter is less likely to tolerate ill-treatment from or domination by her in-laws, which in turn makes joint-family living more difficult and results in her preference for the nuclear family. This is why she does not wish to live in the traditional joint family and makes an effort to move towards the modern individual family.

Family Relationships

The traditional norms of relationships within the family are neither symmetrical nor equalitarian. Here authority lies in the head of the family, the eldest male member and older people, whereas the younger members are expected to obey the commands of their elders and carry out their wishes without question. Today, however, young people are democratically minded, as a result of education and economic independence. They now demand "reorientation of the relationship between the head and other elderly members of the family on the one hand, and the young men and women on the other, in a way that will provide full scope for the proper and healthy development of the individuality of the young" (Kapadia, 1958:171).

Along with the change in the structure of the family—from the traditional joint to the developing nuclear form—role relationships and authority are also changing. In place of superior-inferior and dominance-submission, the norms of interpersonal relationships within the family are increasingly becoming symmetrical and syncretical. They are gradually equalitarian and reciprocal overtones (Dube, 1933:194; Ross, 1961:121). This is more true of the educated working wife or working mother families of the middle and upper middle classes (Rao and Rao, 1973; Kapur, 1970; Joshi, 1972; Barot, 1972), where there is more give and take among different members of the family.

The affectional relationships within the family are also changing from being diffused over a large group of people in the traditional joint family to becoming concentrated on very few people in the nuclear family. In place of familiar relationships, the marriage relationship is becoming pivotal and familism is giving way to individualism (Ross, 1961:283-288; Kapur, 1970). As Gore rightly observes (1968:235), "many more women than men give primacy to the conjugal over the filial relationship." And this disparity between the attitudes of men and women does tend to give rise to problems in family life (Gore, 1968:235; Kapur, 1970).

Size of Family

The changing socio-economic status of women in modern India and the family planning program and facilities have helped the educated urban woman to plan her family. Thus, the birth rate among such families is also decreasing. Actually, a definite positive correlation has been found between the improved status of women and the low rate of fertility. For example, women's education, gainful employment, decision-making power, and interspouse communication, which are some of the most important indicators of the improved status of women, have been found to be related to the size of the family or fertility rate among women. Education has been found by the National Sample Survey to be negatively related to the fertility rate—the higher the education, the lower the fertility rate (Husain, 1972:261-270). Studies conducted on attitudes towards family planning also reveal that educated people desire to have about three children and adopt family planning on their own, whereas the illiterate wish to have four or five or more children (Mukherjee, 1974b).

The age of marriage which is related to education, has also been found in a recent study by Agarwala (1972) to be associated with the birth rate. The study shows, on the basis of demographic surveys and statistical analysis, that if the average age of marriage for females rises to nineteen there will be a decline in the birth rate to between 35 and 50 per cent over a period of twenty years. Decision-making power and interspouse communication have been found by studies like that of Mukherjee (1974a, 1974b) to be positively correlated with the adoption of family planning. These studies point out that a woman's becoming a decision-making partner with her husband in household affairs favors adoption of family planning practices, which reduce the fertility rate. They also indicate that the higher the frequency of interspouse communication, the greater the likelihood of the adoption of the family planning methods.

Studies like those by Dubey and Bardhan (1971) and Kapur (1970, 1973, 1974) indicate that fertility declines as married women secure gainful employment. Thus, modern women in India are having fewer children and modernism is found to be positively related to the preference for a small family (Mukherjee, 1974a).

GAP BETWEEN THEORY AND REALITY WITH REGARD TO THE STATUS OF WOMEN

"Reducing the birth rate depends not so much on new technologies as upon social and cultural change to break the crust of custom in family relations, so as to make India's women, in dignity and privacy, free at least to choose whether and when to have another child" (Tobias, 1970:4).

Woman in modern India has been legally and politically emancipated from her tradition-bound ethos. She has as many rights as men to education, employment, franchise, inheritance, property, marriage at a mature age, divorce, and remarriage, in addition to being her husband's only legal wife at a given time. Thus, theoretically, the equality of woman has been established. Yet, in spite of all these social, legal, and political changes in the position of woman in the last hundred years, particularly since Independence, there is a very wide gulf between the rights and privileges that have been guaranteed to woman in theory and what she enjoys in practice. And there are striking contrasts between the socio-economic status of a few modern women and that of the masses of women in India.

As many scholars have observed, a male is still considered qualitatively superior to, and more desirable than, a female. The dominant value systems, religious mores, and the institution of the patriarchal family are still authoritarian and promale. Thus, a woman in real life still suffers from many social disabilities and her position is still far from equal to that of a man (Hate, 1930, 1948, 1969; Desai, 1945, 1957; Dube, 1955, 1963; Sengupta, 1960, 1973; Ross, 1961; Cormack, 1953; Kapur, 1970; Mehta, 1970). She does not enjoy the same freedom as man. The double standard of morality —one set of social and moral norms governing the male and another governing the female—still prevails, defames, and degrades women, but not men, for the same acts (Roy, 1950; Patai, 1967). Even today, by and large, a woman is socially considered a vehicle for continuing the race and for gratifying and looking after man's needs and desires.

Thus, for the masses of women there is a big gap between theory and practice as far as their rights and privileges are concerned. But, viewed in the perspective of "women in the modern, progressive, and Westernized section of society in India," this gap has been narrowed. Women belonging to this section enjoy considerable and almost equal freedom and opportunities to move about and mix with people, to have an education, to secure employment, to select a mate, to combine marriage with a career, and even to dissolve marriage and to remarry after divorce or after the death of the mate. As Kapadia (1958:182) points out, the modern woman is no longer prepared to accept a social code which recognizes the dominance of the male.

The author has found that the attitudes of modern educated working women toward sex and the double standard have been liberalized. There is also a trend towards radicalism with regard to sex. This was evidenced in the statements of a small minority of women who expressed the views that premarital or extramarital sex indulgence needs little or no justification when two consenting and willing mature adults are involved (Kapur, 1973: 210-227). These newly emerging trends point towards a significant change in

sexual attitudes and mores among modern educated urban women
in India.

Yet, in spite of all the advancement in the position of modern
women in India, at the attitudinal and behavioral levels, the double
standard of morality continues even in the modern section of
society. This is evidenced by the fact that a modern woman, who
in reality enjoys equal rights and privileges of sexual freedom, of
dissolving marriage, and so on, is not very much respected and is
still a subject of severe social ostracism even among the so-called
modern men and women. In a tradition-oriented and male-domi-
nated society like India, the hold of traditional norms is still quite
strong.

However, in spite of the persistence of tradition, radical tendencies among women are slowly developing. The modern woman
is gradually breaking through the shell of a narrow existence and
rigid traditionalism. New horizons are opening up for woman in
modern India. The changes are, no doubt, most apparent today at
the level of the sophisticated urban elite, but gradually women of
older sections are also being affected by this trend. The transition
cannot naturally be rapid in a society that has been tradition-
directed for several centuries. But the resistence of orthodoxy is
gradually weakening (Dube, 1963:203).

Coexistence of Tradition and Modernity

It is necessary to emphasize that in India tradition and progress
co-exist peacefully in many aspect of life. There is a peculiar
mixture of tradition and modernity in the attitudes and behavior
of even the educated modern urban women with regard to sex,
marriage, and the family. For example, though there is increasing
permissiveness among them with regard to their attitudes towards,
and behavior in relation to sex, the findings of various studies
have shown that even educated modern women by and large do
not approve of premarital and extramarital sex for women (Kapur,
1970, 1973; Mehta, 1970; Fonseca, 1966:153-155; Hallen, 1966:9-10).

With regard to marriage, though an emerging trend was
evidenced in the thinking of a small minority of educated working
women who feel that the "institution of marriage is outdated and
redundant" and that there should be "no conventional marriage but

a free love relationship" (Kapur, 1973), it is strongly indicated by
various studies that these ideas have not come to stay. Indeed,
despite the newly emerging trends, marriage is considered by an
increasing number of educated women to be much more a necessity now than before and is very much more in vogue now than
even ten years earlier (Kapur, 1973). In spite of their education
and economic independence, marriage reigns supreme in their
lives and is the ultimate aim of life in a large majority of cases
(Arora, *et al.*, 1963; Jauhari, 1970; Tripathi, 1967; Cormack,
1961), though they have increasingly begun to believe that marriage
is not their only aim and sole source of satisfaction and happiness.
That is why more of them now want to combine marriage with a
job or profession in order to have an individual status and independent income and to satisfy their other various socio-psychological
needs.

Even while there is an increasing accent among educated women
on the freedom of choice in the selection of their mate and on
knowing the prospective mate well before marriage, there is, at
the same time, more and more emphasis now on parents or
guardians selecting or suggesting the prospective mate and on the
wholehearted consent of the parents even in cases where the
prospective mates are in love with each other and anxious to get
married. That is, the tendency is towards neoarranged marriage
rather than towards marriage purely by choice (Kapur, 1973). In
most urban middle class families, marriage continues to be regarded as the responsibility of the parents or guardians and is treated
mainly as an alliance between families whose status and reputation
are regarded as two of the most important factors, rather than an
alliance between individuals (Narain, 1967:35; Kapadia, 1958:136-
137). Similarly, even while more educated women approve or do
not mind intercaste, interprovincial, or even interreligious marriages, a large majority of them continue to prefer a marriage
celebrated in the traditional style (Cormack, 1961; Mathew, 1966;
Sharayubal and Vanarase, 1966; Kapur, 1973), though in a simplified manner.

In the author's study (1973), a small minority of educated working women presented unusual ideas. They criticized monogamous
marriage itself, labeling it as monotonous, unsatisfying, and inadequate for the complete fulfillment of the entire personalities of the
marriage partners. They even supported the concepts of "group

marriage" and "trial marriage" as alternative forms. Yet, a large majority of educated working women were found to be strongly approving of, and preferring, monogamous marriage. In the same way, though personal happiness and satisfaction in marriage are gaining importance and the concept of contract is slowly evolving, by and large, educated women still view marriage as a sacred and social bond which should be broken only under unbearable circumstances (Kapur, 1970, 1973; Barot, 1972; Kuppuswamy, 1957). They also give years of thoughtful consideration before taking up the bold step of dissolving the marriage.

With regard to the family pattern, there has also been a limited change in the attitudes and behavior of middle and upper middle class urban people (Kapadia, 1958:264-265; Ross, 1961; Gore, 1968:231-232). At present, because of economic necessities or personal reasons, there is a tendency to break away from the husband's parental home and to establish nuclear units. But the attitude of the younger generation towards the joint family is ambivalent. Young people do feel the need to belong to the joint family for the security that it provides, but at the same time they do not want to be in the joint family because of the social obligations and sacrifices that living in the joint family entails (Ramanujam, 1972: 25). Even educated working women have an ambivalent attitude towards breaking away from the joint family. On the one hand, they emphasize living in an individual family away from in-laws, while on the other they would very much like to be in a joint family or have some elderly members of the husband's parental family living with them who could help in looking after the children and home, especially when the women are away to work or elsewhere (Kapur, 1970). It is revealing that the sentiments in favor of the joint family appear to be on the increase (Merchant, 1935; Kapadia, 1955, 1956; Desai, 1964), and that "there is a strong feeling for the joint family in the generation that is coming up" (Desai, 1956).

Because of the factors mentioned above, there seems to be an emergence of a new type of family which could not be classified according to any simple typology. It is neither like the Western nuclear family nor the Indian traditional joint family. It is something like neo-nuclear or neo-joint family—having the wife's parents-in-law or widow mother-in-law or aunt or even dependent sisters-in-law and brothers-in-law living with the couple and their children. Studies suggest that the small joint family or a new nuclear or individual family with adhesion is now the typical form among the middle and upper middle classes in India (Ross, 1961: 49). Gore points out that everyone, particularly young educated people, want limited change in the family (Gore, 1968:232).

Thus, it has been observed by many scholars that the Indian joint family is changing rather than breaking. Indeed, even where the traditional joint family system breaks into nuclear units, it has given rise to a modified or new type of joint-family system. It merely breaks structurally, whereas functionally and sentimentally, individual units continue to form part of the joint family and all members maintain jointness in terms of family loyalty. While its appearance or structure is changing, the family unit continues to be a very stable one with its values, by and large, being basically unaffected. This is evidenced by various studies (Kapadia, 1958: 272; Cormack, 1961; Dube, 1955; Devanandan and Thomas, 1960) which indicate that there is a strong emotional involvement in, and sentimental attachment to, the family or origin even after separating from it to set up individual units.

It has been observed that, on special or ceremonial occasions, such as marriage, religious functions, festivals, and death, the whole family gets together. In times of stress and calamity, or in the hour of need, the members of the original family or parent family are expected to support one another and mutual consultations with regard to all major issues and decisions are regarded as desirable. As Mukerji (1954:73) observes, "in India the rich traditional training in familial relationships persists amidst change." The new family, like the traditional joint family, is expected to provide social security to all its members, including its present head and his wife in their old age. On the sentimental level, the only difference between the old and the new types of family is that one's own children and grandchildren are probably dearer to one than ones brothers or 'collaterals'. And it is this intensity of feelings towards the members of one's own immediate family that makes the new family different from the conventional one (Kapadia, 1958:265). Otherwise, it appears that the joint family remains as strong as ever at the sentimental and functional levels.

The process of educational, industrial, and urban development has, no doubt, created new situations and problems and has upset certain traditional mores and values. Yet, the family institution continues to be the core of Indian society and has not experienced a general disintegration (Goode, 1963:268-269).

On the basis of all the relevant literature and studies mentioned above, it becomes apparent that new opportunities for education and employment for women and new legal and political rights and equality for females, along with other socio-economic changes, are gradually changing the traditional conceptions of the role and status of women in India, at least in urban centers among the middle classes. And this has necessarily implied changes in the patterns of marriage and the family.

Yet, in spite of all the recent changes, marriage and the family continue to be very significant and meaningful institutions in woman's life. Though structural changes are taking place in marriage and the family, and some new emerging trends are appearing, less change is observed at the functional and emotional levels, and the new family type continues to be a mixture of tradition and modernity (Hallen and Theodorson, 1961:51-59; 1963:105-110).

It is interesting to note that, even while the ideas about the sanctity, permanence, and purpose of marriage have assumed new dimensions, the need for marriage and the family is being increasingly felt among women in India, including those with modern beliefs. Since woman is the pivot of the family, it is strongly felt that there will not be a general disintegration of the family in India in the foreseeable future, and that this institution will continue to be a stable unit and core of Indian society.

REFERENCES

Agarwala, S.N.
  1972 *India's Population Problem.* New Delhi: Tata McGraw-Hill.
Altekar, A.S.
  1962 *The Position of Women in Hindu Civilization.* Third edition. Varanasi: Motilal Banarsidas.
Anand, Kulwant
  1970 "Impact of the changing status of women on Population Growth." Ph D. thesis. Chandigarh: Punjab University.
Arora, K.K., *et al.*
  1963 "Women and Career." A Group Project Report. Bombay: Tata Institute of Social Sciences.

Asthana, Pratima
1974   *Women's Movement in India.* Delhi: Vikas Publishing House.
Baig, Tara Ali (ed.)
1958   *Women of India.* Delhi: Government of India Publications.
Barot, Jyoti
1972   "Modern Trends in Marital Relations" in *The Indian Family in the change and challenge of the Seventies.* New Delhi: Sterling Publishers Pvt. Ltd. Pp 60-68.
Chakravarty, Renu
1958   "The Law as it affects Women" in Tara Ali Baig (ed.), *Women of India.* Delhi: Government of India Publications.
1963   "The Working Woman." Seminar, 52 (December).
Chandrasekhar, S.
1972   *Infant Mortality, Population Growth and Family Planning in India.* London: Allen & Unwin.
Cormack, Margaret L.
1953   *The Hindu Woman.* New York: Columbia University Press.
1961   *She Who Rides a Peacock.* Bombay: Asia Publishing House.
Das, Man Singh
1971   "A Cross-Cultural Study of Intercaste Marriage in India and the United States." *International Journal of Sociology of the Family,* (May). Pp. 25-33.
Desai, G.B.
1945   "Women in Modern Gujerati Life." Unpublished Master's thesis. Bombay: University of Bombay.
Desai, I.P.
1956   "The Joint Family in India—An Analysis." *Sociological Bulletin,* 5 (September).
1964   *Some Aspects of Family in Mahuwa.* Bombay: Asia Publishing House.
Desai, Neera A.
1957   *Woman in Modern India.* Bombay: Vora.
Devanandan, P.D., and M.M. Thomas (eds.)
1960   *The Changing Pattern of Family in India.* Bangalore: The Christian Institute for the Study of Religion and Society.
Dhingra, O.P.
1972   "Women in Employment." Report. New Delhi: Shri Ram Centre for Industrial Relations and Human Resources.
Dube, S.C.
1955   *Indian Village.* London: Routledge and Kegan Paul.
1963   "Men's and Women's Roles in India" in Barbara E. Ward (ed.), *Women in the New Asia.* Paris: UNESCO. Pp. 174-203.
Dubay, D.C., and A. Bardhan
1971   *Social and Political Considerations for Family Planning Programme.* New Delhi: National Institute of Family Planning.

Dubois, A.J.A. and H.K. Beauchamp
  1906 *Hindu Manners, Customs and Ceremonies.* Oxford: Clarendon
        Press.
Encyclopaedia of Social Work in India
  1968 Delhi: Government of India Press.
Fonseca, Mabel
  1966 *Counselling for Marital Happiness.* Bombay: Manaktalas.
Ghurye, G.S.
  1950 *Caste and Class in India.* Bombay: Popular Book Depot.
Goldstein, Rhoda L.
  1972 *Indian Women in Transition.* Metuchen, N.J.: The Scarecrow Press,
        Inc.
Goode, William J.
  1963 *World Revolution and Family Patterns.* London: The Free Press of
        Glencoe.
  1965 *The Family.* New Delhi: Prentice-Hall.
Gore, M.S.
  1968 *Urbanization and Family Change.* Bombay: Popular Prakashan.
Hate, C.A.
  1930 *The Socio-Economic Conditions of Educated Women in Bombay City.*
        Bombay University: School of Economics and Sociology.
  1946 *The Social Position of Hindu Woman.* Bombay University: School
        of Economics and Sociology.
  1948 *Hindu Woman and Her Future.* Bombay: New Book Company.
  1969 *Changing Status of Woman in Post Independence India.* Bombay:
        Allied.
Hallen, G.C.
  1966 "Attitudes of Educated Youth Toward Marriage." *Social Welfare,*
        12 (February). Pp. 9-10.
Hallen, G.C., and G.A. Theodorson
  1961 "Change and Traditionalism in Indian Family." *The Indian Journal
        of Social Research,* 2(2). Pp. 51-59.
  1963 "Change and Traditionalism in Indian Family." *The Indian Journal
        of Social Research,* 4(1). Pp. 105-110.
Husain, I.Z.
  1972 "Educational Status and Differential Fertility in India" in I.Z.
        Husain (ed.), *Population Analysis and Studies.* Bombay: Somaiya.
        Pp. 261-270.
Indra, M.A.
  1955 *The Status of Women in Ancient India.* Second revised edition.
        Benaras: Oriental.
Jauhari, Prema
  1970 "Status of Working Women." Ph.D. thesis. Lucknow: University
        of Lucknow.

144 *Family in Asia*

Joshi, Rama J.
1972 "Contemporary Change in the Socio-Economic Role of Women in India: Its Impact on Family Life" in Kamla Bhasin (ed.), *The Position of Women in India.* Bombay: Leslie Sawhney Programme of Training for Democracy. Pp. 50-59.

Kannan, C.T.
1963 *Inter-Caste and Inter-Community Marriages in India.* Bombay: Allied.

Kapadia, K.M.
1954a "Changinging Patterns of Hindu Marriage and Family." *Sociological Bulletin,* 3 (March). Pp. 61-87
1954b "Changing Patterns of Hindu Marriage and Family." *Sociological Bulletin,* 3 (September). Pp. 131-157.
1955 "Changing Patterns of Hindu Marriage and Family." *Sociological Bulletin,* 4 (September). Pp. 191-192.
1956 "Rural Family Patterns." *Sociological Bulletin,* 5 (September). Pp. 111-126.
1957 "A Perspective Necessary for the Study of Social Change in India." *Sociological Bulletin,* 6 (March).
1958 *Marriage and Family in India.* Second edition. Bombay: Oxford University Press.
1959 "The Family in Transition." *Sociological Bulletin,* 8 (September).

Kapur, Promilla
1960 "Socio-psychological Study of the Change in the Attitudes of Educated Earning Hindu Women." Ph.D. thesis. Agra: University of Agra.
1968 "The Study of Marital Adjustment of Educated Working Women in India." D.Litt. thesis. Agra: University of Agra.
1970 *Marriage and the Working Woman in India.* Delhi: Vikas Publishing House.
1973 *Love, Marriage and Sex.* Delhi: Vikas Publishing House.
1974 *The Changing Status of the Working Woman in India.* Delhi: Vikas Publishing House.

Kapur, Rama
1969 "Role Conflict Among Employed Housewives." *Indian Journal of Industrial Relations,* 5 (July). Pp. 39-76.

Kaul, Beena
1973 "The Study of Adjustment of Women in Employment." Ph.D. thesis. Allahabad: University of Allahabad.

Kirkpatrick, Clifford
1963 The Family as Process and Institution. Second edition. New York: Ronald Press.

Kirpalani, Rajika
1971 "The Modern Woman " *Femina,* (2 August). Pp. 44-45.

Krishnamurthy, N.S.R.
1970 "The Emerging Young Woman in India." *Journal of Family Welfare,* 16 (June). Pp. 33-38.

Kuppuswamy, B.
1957 *Opinion Regarding Marriage and Divorce*, Bombay: Asia Publishing House.
1972 *Social Change in India.* Delhi: Vikas Publishing House.

Mahajan, Amarjit
1965 "A Study of Attitudes of Women Students Towards Mate-Selection." *Journal of Family Welfare*, 12 (September). Pp. 1-4.
1966 "Women's Two Roles: A Study of Role Conflict." *The Indian Journal of Social Work*, 26 (January). Pp. 377-380.

Mathew, A.
1966 "Expectations of College Students Regarding Their Marriage." *Journal of Family Welfare*, 12 (March). Pp. 46-52.

Mankekar, Kamla
1973 *Abortion.* Delhi: Vikas Publishing House.

Mehta, Anjana
1969 "A Study of the Opinions of School Going Youth on Certain Aspects of Family's Culture." Master's dissertation. Delhi: University of Delhi.

Mehta, Rama
1970 *The Western Educated Hindu Woman.* Bombay: Asia Publishing House.

Merchant, K.T.
1935 *Changing Views on Marriage and the Family.* Madras: B.G. Paul and Company.

Ministry of Education
1964-65 *Report of Education Commission.* Delhi: Government of India Publications.

Mitroo, Pushpa
1968 "A Comparative Study of Aspirations of Schoolgoing and Non-Schoolgoing Girls in Selected Rural Areas." Master's dissertation. Delhi: University of Delhi.

Mookerji, Radhakumud
1958 "Women in Ancient India" in Tara Ali Baig (ed.), *Women of India.* Delhi: Government of India Publications. Pp. 1-8.

Mukerji, D.P.
1954 "Indian Women and the Modern Family" in A. Appadorai (ed.), *Status of Women in South Asia.* Bombay: Orient Longmans. Pp. 65-73.

Mukherjee, B.N.
1974a "Status of Women and Family Planning: An Empirical Study." *Social Change*, 4 (September).
1974b "A Comparison of the Results of Family Planning KAP Surveys in Haryana and Tamil Nadu, India." *Studies in Family Planning*, 5 (September).

Narain, Vatsala
1967 "India" in Raphael Patai (ed.), *Women in the Modern World.* New York: Collier-Macmillan Limited. Pp. 21-40.

Pahikkar, K.M.
1955 *Hindu Society at Cross-Roads.* Bombay: Asia Publishing House.
1963 *The Foundation of New India.* London:

Patai, Raphael (ed.)
1967 *Women in the Modern World.* New York: Collier-Macmillan Limited.

Prabhu, Pandhari Nath
1954 Hindu Social Organization. New revised edition. Bombay: Popular Book Depot.

Prashar, Mridula
1970 "Conservatism and Non-Conservatism in Attitudes to Selected Social Issues of Two Generations in a Village Near Delhi. Master's dissertation. Delhi: University of Delhi.

Rajagopal, T.S.
1936 *Indian Women in the New Age.* Mysore: Jaya Stores.

Ramanamma, Angara
1969 "Position of Women in India With Special Reference to Poona." Ph.D. thesis. Poona: University of Poona.

Ramanujam, B.K.
1972 "The Indian Family in Transition: Changing Roles and Relationship." *Social Action,* 22 (January). Pp. 16-25.

Ranade, S.N., and P. Ramchandran
1970 *Women and Employment.* Bomhay: Tata Institute of Social Sciences.

Rao, V. Nandini, and V.V. Prakasa Rao
1973 "An Analysis of the Employed Mother in India." *International Journal of Sociology of the Family,* 3 (September). Pp. 169-178.

Report of Education Commission
1964-66 Delhi: Government of India Publications.

Ross, Aileen D.
1961 *The Hindu Family in its Urban Setting.* Bombay: Oxford University Press.

Roy, M.N.
1950 *The Ideal of Indian Womanhood in Crime and Karma: Cats and Women.* Bombay: Renaissance.

Sengupta, Padmini
1958 "In Trades and Professions" in Tara Ali Baig (ed.), *Women of India.* Delhi: Government of India Publications. Pp. 240-264.
1950 *Women Workers in India.* Bombay: Asia Publishing House.
1973 *The Story of Women in India.* Bombay: Indian Book Company.

Shah, B.V.
1962 "Gujarat College Students and Selection of Bride." *Sociological Bulletin,* 11.

Sharma, J.M.
1951 "Formal and Informal Relations in the Hindu Joint Household of Bengal." *Man in India*, (April-June). Pp. 53-55.
Sharayubal, and S.J. Vanarase
1966 "Attitude of College Girls Towards Marriage." *Journal of S.N.D.T. Women's University*, 1 (January). Pp. 19-31.
Shastri, Shakuntala Rao
1962 *Women in the Vedic Age*. Bombay: Bhartiya Vidya Bhavan.
Sheth, Jyotsna
1972 "A Matter of Arrangement." *The Times of India*. (12 March).
Shipstone, Eva I.
1972 "Educating the Indian Adolescent" in *The Indian Family in the Change and Challenge of the Seventies*. New Delhi: Sterling. Pp. 98-113.
Srinivas, M.N.
1942 *Marriage and Family in Mysore*. Bombay: New Book Company.
Srivastava, Vinita
1972 "Employment of Educated Married Women, its Causes and Consequences: With Reference to Chandigarh." Ph.D. thesis. Chandigarh: Punjab University.
Tagore, Rabindranath
1920 "The Indian Ideal of Marriage" in Herman Keyserling (ed.), *The Book of Marriage*. New York: Blue Ribbon Books.
Tandon. S.D.
1959 "Changing Attitudes and Culture Patterns Among Educated Earning Women in U.P." Ph.D. thesis. Agra: Agra University.
Tobias, George
1970 *Human Resources Utilization and Development in the Seventies*. New Delhi: The Ford Foundation.
Tripathi, Harsha J.
1967 "Changing Attitudes of Women in Post-Independence India." *Journal of Gujarat Research Society*, 29 (April). Pp. 92-97.
Vasanthakumar, Kaula
1964 "Her Emotional Problems." *Social Welfare*, 2 (May). Pp. 12-13.
Verma, Malika
1960 "The Study of the Middle Class Working Women in Kanpur." *The Indian Journal of Social Work*, 21 (December). Pp. 283-286.
Ward, Barbara E.
1963 "Men, Women and Change: An Essay in Understanding Social Roles in South and South-East Asia" in Barbara E. Ward (ed.), *Women in the New Asia*. Paris: UNESCO Publications. Pp. 25-99.
Wasi, Muriel (ed.)
1971 *The Educated Women in Indian Society Today*. Bombay-New Delhi: Tata McGraw-Hill.

5. ABORTION ATTITUDES AMONG UNIVERSITY
   STUDENTS IN INDIA—*Panos D. Bardis*

"For destroying the embryo...he must perform the
same penance"—*Laws of Manu*, XI, 88.

INTRODUCTION

Overpopulation. On 1 April 1971, India's population was 547,949,
809, or 15.3 per cent of the population of our entire planet. "The
increase from 1951 to 1961 was 108.8 million, at a rate for the
decade of 24.7%. In that decade the people of India added to their
number the equivalent of the population of Japan (the seventh
most populous nation in the world) with some four million to
spare." On the average, "more than one million lives are added to
India's numbers every month, and so the very considerable increases
in agricultural and industrial production since Independence have
not benefited the average Indian in similar proportion" (Mandelbaum, 1974:2; Lader, 1970:138).

Between 1965 and 1970, the number of live births per 1,000
persons, or crude birth rate, was 42.8 (the corresponding figure
for the USA in 1972 was 15.6). In 1958-59, the fertility rate was
136.7 per 1,000 people (the 1971 value for the USA was 59.3). On
the other hand, the crude death rate for 1965-70 was only 16.7 per
1,000 persons, excluding stillbirths, the 1971 rate for the USA
being 9.3 (United States Bureau of the Census, 1973:806; United
Nations, 1974:81-85). The rapid decline in India's death rate is
partly explained by the use of DDT and the resulting virtual
disappearance of malaria—an Indian leader has observed that
nowadays, if you wish to meet a mosquito, you must go to a zoo!

For India, an average diet of 2,250 calories per day has been
considered minimally adequate (the U.S. average is 3,110). In
1968-69, however, 50 per cent of the urban population and 40 per
cent of those living in villages had fewer calories per day (Mandelbaum, 1974:3).

Family planning. In view of these problems, India has attempted
to adopt family planning. Unfortunately, its "avowed commitment
to birth control has been so timid and perfunctory that the government can be accused of almost toying with the crisis until the
country was buried by it" (Lader, 1970:136). Of course, the influen-

tial Hindu classics have emphasized celibacy, which supposedly
leads to spiritual and physical strength. Such religious ideals, which
the Muslims have rejected, and which even the Hindus are beginning to question, were popularized and supported by both Gandhi
and Nehru. Indeed, Mahatma Gandhi "believed that birth control
would weaken the moral fibre of his people, and expected them to
follow his own unique idealism, limiting their families by self-
restraint. Later, Nehru's contraception campaigns not only lacked
force and adequate financial support; they were run by a spinster
Health Minister, who was decidedly unenthusiastic about the
subject" (Lader, 1970:137). In fact, in 1951, when India's activists
demanded a strong family planning program, Prime Minister Nehru
replied that economic underdevelopment, not overpopulation, was
his country's problem (Norman, 1965:406-407). It is no wonder,
then, that early after Independence the only genuine birth control
measures, such as urban clinics and motorized clinics for the
provinces, were introduced by private organizations (Lader,
1970:137).

In any event, family planning, whose symbol is a red triangle
with the apex down, was introduced by the first five-year plan of
1951-56 (Mandelbaum, 1974:6). The authorized annual national
budget for 1967 was $60,000,000, or $12 per capita (Berelson, 1969:
358). For 1968-69, it was Rs 370,000,000, or about $50,000,000. A
U.N. study further revealed that, in 1969, family planning encom-
passed 70,000 employees, including 6,100 physicians and 35,500
paramedical workers (Mandelbaum,1974:6; Simmons, 1971). In brief,
this program "has been officially promoted, especially research and
experimental work, ever since the first five-year plan. Naturally
enough there is, on the whole, readier acceptance of the ideas of
family planning in the cities where even the poorer groups rapidly
become more sophisticated in some respects.... The main difficulty
in towns is the cost of any form of mechanical or chemical contraceptives, especially in the poorer groups where the need is greatest.
The same groups also suffer from ignorance, illiteracy and notably
'innumeracy' when attempting to apply the rhythm method—a
fickle method at best" (Spate and Learmonth, 1967:146-147). Still,
the general economic success of the five-year plans themselves
might gradually generate lower birth rates.

The more philosophical aspects of family planning are expressed
by the three principles that extended this program in October 1963:

"(1) each individual should know and feel that the immediate society or community to which he belongs has agreed as a group that having a small family size is the normal, desirable behavior for its members; (2) each individual should have knowledge that a small family is valuable to him personally and should have knowledge of contraceptive methods; and (3) each individual should have contraceptive methods readily accessible" (Raina, 1966: 115-116).

Implementation involving personnel includes, among other things, schools for auxiliary nurse midwives. In the late 1960s, there were over 200 such schools in India, which trained 10,000 nurses of this type. However, 55,000 nurse midwives are needed (Bhatia, 1969:78).

As for the birth control techniques employed, these range from the conservatives' *brahmacharya* (monklike abstinence) to the Y.M.C.A. method (cold baths) and the pill.

One of the reasons why the rhythm method has been common is the fact that, when India requested the assistance of the World Health Organization, the influential Roman Catholic member-nations responded with a great emphasis on this technique. This inadequate approach was rendered less effective by a peculiar practical implementation, namely, a necklace of twenty-eight beads worn by women. Unfortunately, these women were unable to distinguish the red color of the danger beads at night and often moved them in the wrong direction. Even when the experts intro-duced safety catches and different shapes, the women forgot to move the beads or, when sexually excited, moved more than one a day! Besides, in order to preclude criticism by their neighbors, many women hesitated to wear these necklaces (Chandrasekhar, 1965:110, 117). In the villages, ignorance, illiteracy, conservatism, and poverty often led to magic beliefs concerning this method. For instance, "beads representing the menstrual cycle differentiating the most likely period for conception . . . were in fact placed around the neck of a goat, in a village near the experimental clinic in Ramanagaram in Mysore, in order to *induce* a caprine preg-nancy!" (Spate and Learmonth, 1967:147).

Similarly, in the late 1960s when government demonstrators stretched condoms over bamboo sticks, many peasants lost faith in such "magic" when their wives conceived, although they, too, stretched prophylactics on bamboo sticks while having coitus! Still,

the press advertised *nirodh* (protection) condoms and the government subsidized them—the price has been two cents for three
pieces. Thus, in 1968-69, almost 51,000,000 prophylactics were
distributed (Mandelbaum, 1974:6,82).

The number of IUD insertions for 1970-71 was 470,000, or
4,100,000 when previous ones are included. The Lippes loop, which
the government adopted recently, is particularly practical and
promising. Indeed, a test, involving 3,500 Indian women revealed
that 5 per cent of the loops were removed because of discomfort,
and 5 per cent were expelled naturally. Of the remaining 90 per
cent, 99 per cent were effective (Mandelbaum, 1974:82; Lader,
1970:138).

Vasectomy, however, has been approved by the government too
reluctantly and too late (Lader, 1970:137-138). According to Spate
and Learmonth (1967:147), "success with contraception and the
rhythm method has been so limited that the government department concerned has turned, as a desperate remedy, to sterilization,
especially of men once they have say three children including at
least one son; there is even some tendency to regard the planned
increase of medical practitioners as an additional force,of potential
vasectomists, a sterile objective! From the beginning of the campaign to encourage vasectomy in 1956 to April 1962 the total
number of operations performed was only some 98,000 mostly in
Madras and Maharashtra. This form of campaign seems doomed to
failure, probably implying undesirable social, psychological and
international consequences." In the early 1960s, the Madras program "provided 40 rupees for travel and loss of working time as
well as a liberal finder's fee to the already vasectomized. While
that program was in effect it accounted for a large proportion of
the vasectomies in all India and the number was cut by a large
proportion when the finder's fee was discontinued, only to recover
when the fee was reinstated" (Berelson, 1969:356). Still, by 1969,
India had more than 50 per cent of all sterilization operations in
the world (Mandelbaum, 1974:8-10).

Other birth control methods, such as pills, diaphragms, pessaries,
foam tablets, and jellies, require a higher income, modern plum-
bing, bathrooms, adequate lighting, privacy, and diligent application,
which are not prevalent in India (Mandelbaum, 1974:82; Lader,
1970:137-138).

These difficulties explain why, of all Indian couples in the repro-

ductive years, only 13,440,000, or 13.3 per cent, are protected in
some way. Unfortunately, many of these couples include those
using IUDs that have been extracted, and sterilized older persons
who have already had all the children they desired. Accordingly,
the reduction in the birth rate has not been spectacular (Mandelbaum, 1974:8-10).

Abortion. It has been stated that neither "Buddhist nor Hindu
theology contains any scriptural prohibitions against early abortion,
treating it as a social rather than religious issue. In fact, the Indian
government in 1965 began to investigate the legalization of all
abortion, modeled on the Japanese system" (where "no religious or
ethical objections to abortion have ever been raised") "as part of
its policy on population control" (Lader, 1970:94; *Cf.* Kapadia,
1966:100). Nevertheless, Indian classics, such as the *Rig-Veda,
Ramayana, Mahabharata,* and the *Laws of Manu,* do mention abortion and even condemn it as a serious sin, although they recognize
exceptional cases, since there was no agreement concerning the
exact beginning of life. For instance, at least two passages in the
Laws of Manu refer very critically to women "who have caused an
abortion" or "destroyed the embryo" (V, 90; XI, 88).

The first modern law dealing with abortion in India was the
Indian Penal Code of 1860 which, under classical and British influences, defined induced abortion as a crime, the penalties for the
guilty mother and the abortionist being quite severe, unless the
operation was therapeutic (Sections 312-314). Thus, many women
sought illegal abortions that had tragic physical and psychological
consequences, as a result of which public opinion gradually became
more liberal. For this reason, in September 1964, the Ministry of
Health and Family Planning appointed a committee to study
abortion. In December 1966, the committee issued its famous
report, advocating liberalization of the abortion law (Ministry of
Health and Family Planning, 1966). On 7 October 1967, Minister
Chandrasekhar recommended acceptance of this report, and in
1969, the Medical Termination of Pregnancy Bill was introduced
(Chandrasekhar, 1970:246-249). The resulting Medical Termination
of Pregnancy Act of 1971 "allows induced abortion by a registered
medical practitioner, where the length of the pregnancy does not
exceed 12 weeks; or by two registered medical practitioners, acting
together, where the length of the pregnancy exceeds 12 weeks but
does not exceed 20. Pregnancies can be terminated only if the

medical practitioners are of the opinion that 1) there is a risk to the life or physical or mental health of the mother, or 2) there is a risk that the child would be born with physical or mental abnormalities. The law further provides that pregnancies caused by rape or due to the failure of family planning devices are cases where continued pregnancy is considered to have negative consequences for the mental health of the mother. The present abortion law in India is quite liberal and, in many respects, similar to the law in Denmark or Sweden" (Mohan, 1975).

Some studies indicate that in India's provinces, three methods of induced abortion have usually been employed: 1) Introducing a stick with an irritant into the cervix by a barber midwife, this being the most common technique. 2) Medicines obtained from native or homeopathic doctors. 3) Papaya, jaggery, and other self-administered oral medicines (Mandelbaum, 1974:73).

Unfortunately, there are extremely few studies of induced abortion in India (Bhowmik, 1975). Moreover, "vital statistics on spontaneous and induced abortions in India are not available" (Mohan, 1975). A limited 1966 report indicates that "out of every 100 pregnancies, 73 result in live births, 10 in natural abortions (miscarriages), 2 presumably in stillbirths, and 15 are terminated by induced abortions." This would give 3,900,000 induced abortions annually, and at the present time about 4,200,000 (Mandelbaum, 1974:70-71). Other estimates report 5,000,000 cases a year, and that "more than 90 per cent of the women who have induced abortions are married because of the near universality of the marital state in India and the relatively young age at which most Indian girls get married" (Chandrasekhar, 1970:245).

THE PROBLEM

Although social science departments in Indian colleges and universities have emphasized armchair theorizing at the expense of empirical research (Kuppuswamy, 1972), there are countless empirical studies dealing with the Indian family, most of which have been conducted by Indian scholars. These investigations cover the family institution in general (Basham, 1963; Ross, 1967; Shah, 1974; Srinivas, 1942), as well as specific subjects, such as family types (Desai, 1936; Ehrenfelo, 1953; Nimkoff and Gore, 1959;

Orenstein, 1961; Owens, 1971; Singh, 1968), family changes (Rungachery, 1960), exogamy (Karandikar, 1929), kinship (Mayer,
1960), marriage age (Yadau, 1971), housing (Rao, 1974), the
family cycle (Collver, 1963), women (Kapur, 1970; Floris, 1962;
Gupta, 1970), fertility and family planning (Agarwala, 1967;
Dandekar, 1967; Husain, 1970; Prasad and Ghosh, 1956; Rajan,
1967; Vig, 1970), and so on.

Research dealing with young Indians' attitudes toward the family
and other social institutions is also fairly common (Desai, 1967;
Mukerji, 1945; Sinha and Upadhyay, 1960). It seems, however, that
there are no studies of abortion attitudes, although overpopulation
and democratization make such research both timely and useful. It
is for this reason that the author has conducted what appears to be
the first investigation of attitudes toward abortion among
university students in India.

As this is part of a major international study dealing with abortion and oral contraception (Bardis, 1971; 1972a; 1972b; 1973a;
1973b; 1975), it has been theorized, sometimes inductively, that
education and even religiosity constitute influential forces. More
specifically, university education, which generates a high degree of
familiarity with a variety of social systems, epistemological concepts, ontological objects, and axiological principles, tends to result
in intellectual scepticism and cultural relativism, thus operating as
a liberalizing and, attitudinally, even fairly equalizing variable.
Also, conservative religious systems, due to the traditional indoctrination and socialization that they emphasize, usually preclude
the adoption of liberal ideologies by their adherents.

Accordingly, the following hypotheses have been formulated: 1)
University students tend to approve of abortion; 2) such approval
is fairly uniform among university students; 3) religiosity tends
to neutralize the influence of education and thus generate fairly
conservative abortion attitudes; and 4) American Catholic students
are more conservative than Indian students, who are almost as
liberal as American Protestants with reference to abortion attitudes.

METHODOLOGY

To test these hypotheses, the author has collected additional data
among university students in India.

The sample. The 150 students interviewed (with the assistance of Professor K.L. Bhowmik of Calcutta) came from two Calcutta colleges and constituted a stratified random sample, twenty-five males and twenty-five females thus representing each of the first, second, and third college years. The characteristics of the sample were as follows:

1) Sex: 75 males and 75 females
2) Age: an average of 19.69 years
3) Marital status: 126 single, 14 engaged, and 10 married
4) Number of brothers: an average of 2.42
5) Number of sisters: an average of 1.91
6) Order of birth: an average of 2.33
7) Religion: 132 Hindus, 11 Muslims, 6 Christians, and 1 Sikh
8) Religious services attended per month: an average of 1.49
9) Population of home town: 123 at least 5,000 and 27 less than 5,000
10) Education: 50 from each of the first, second, and third college years
11) Major field of study: 66 in science, 64 in the humanities, and 20 in commerce
12) Father's education: an average of 12.49 years
13) Mother's education: an average of 7.57 years
14) Father's main occupation: 7 farming, 9 manufacturing and industry, 37 trade and commerce, 18 teaching, and 79 miscellaneous services
15) Mother's outside employment: 131 not working and 19 working
16) Employed mother's main occupation: 9 teaching and 10 miscellaneous services

The Abortion scale. In order to operationalize and quantify abortion attitudes, the author employed his Abortion Scale (Bardis, 1972b; copies are available upon request from the author). The theoretical range of scores on this twenty-five-item Likert-type instrument is zero (least approval of abortion) to hundred (greatest approval), the five-point scale for each item being:

0=Strongly disagree
1=Disagree

2=Undecided
3=Agree
4=Strongly agree

A split-half reliability test of the scale, based on 30 Indian cases, gave a Spearman-Brown reliability coefficient of 0.89 (Garrett, 1967:339-340, 342-345), which has highly significant (df=28, P<0.001).

Personal data. An additional instrument secured information regarding miscellaneous independent variables (sex, age, education, religion, and the like).

Statistical analysis. The data thus collected were computerized and analyzed by means of various statistical tests.

FINDINGS

The most important statistical findings of the present study were as follows:

Item analysis. The twenty-five scale items were represented by these arithmetic means (theoretical range=0-4):

1) Abortion is all right during the first three months of pregnancy.	2.31
2) Abortion is not murder.	2.28
3) Abortion should be given to single women.	2.34
4) Abortion is not sinful.	2.24
5) Abortion laws should be liberal.	2.40
6) If the family cannot support another child, abortion is all right.	2.50
7) Abortion is not immoral.	2.17
8) Man has the right to destroy life in the womb.	1.89
9) Abortion should be legalized.	2.69
10) If the child is not wanted, abortion is all right.	2.71
11) Abortion is a human right.	1.91
12) Easy abortion will not lower the value of human life.	2.21
13) In cases of rape, abortion should be allowed.	3.40
14) Abortion is right, when the fetus is too young to live outside the womb.	2.51

15) Abortion should be used to reduce illegitimacy.	2.50
16) Abortion should be used as a birth control method.	2.18
17) The embryo is not really a human being.	2.02
18) Abortion is acceptable when the father abandons the mother.	2.56
19) Illegitimacy justifies abortion.	2.55
20) Where the child is likely to be born physically defective, abortion should be allowed.	2.89
21) Just because a child is conceived, it does not mean that it has the right to live.	2.05
22) Abortion is better than marriage forced by pregnancy.	2.79
23) Having unwanted children is worse than abortion.	2.75
24) In cases of incest, abortion should be allowed.	3.39
25) Easy abortion will not increase promiscuity.	2.34

It is significant that, of these twenty-five means, twenty-one were on the side of relative approval of abortion, while two (eight and eleven) represented relative disapproval of the right to destroy life, and the remaining two (thirteen and twenty-four) indicated considerable approval of abortion in cases of rape and incest.

Mean values. The arithmetic mean of total abortion scores (theoretical range: 0-100) for the entire Indian group was 61.58, that for the 132 Hindus alone being 63.12. When the Hindu value (63.12) was compared with the means of certain other groups (Bardis, 1972a; 1972b; 1975), the tests (McCall, 1970:177-190) gave the following results:

1) American Catholic college males: N=100, mean=42.20, t=3.86, df=230, P<0.001.
2) American Catholic college females: N=100, mean=28.52, t=4.27, df=230, P<0.001.
3) A mixed sample of American Catholics: N=45, mean= 37.22, t=4.21, df=175, P<0.001.
4) A mixed sample of American Protestants: N=45, mean= 69.03, t=1.89, df=175, 0.10>P>0.05.

The abortion means of the various subsamples and the t values for comparisons of pairs of means for the Indian group alone were as follows:

1) Males, 66.11; females, 57.05: t=2.41, df=148, 0.02>P>0.01.

2) Single, 62.04; married, 64.30: t=0.29, df=134, P>0.70.

3) Hindus, 63.12; Muslims, 26.91: t=3.98, df=141, P<0.001.

4) Population of home town: at least 5,000, a mean of 60.95; less than 5,000, a mean of 64.44: t=0.70, df=148, P>0.40.

5) Commerce majors, 71.60; humanities majors, 53.58: t=2.96, df=82, P<0.005.

6) Commerce majors, 71.60; science majors, 66.30: t=2.29, df= 84, P=0.025.

7) Humanities majors, 53.58; science majors, 66.30: t=2.68, df=128, 0.01>P>0.005.

8) Father's occupation: trade and commerce, 68.00; teaching, 48.00: t=3.19, df=53, 0.005>P>0.001.

9) Children of working mothers, 61.21; children of nonworking mothers, 61.63: t=0.21, df=148, P>0.80.

Correlations. When the total abortion scores were correlated with selected independent variables, the resulting Pearsonr's (Marascuilo, 1971:416-442) were as follows:

1) Abortion versus age: 0.05.

2) Abortion versus number of brothers: .09.

3) Abortion versus number of sisters: 0.00.

4) Abortion versus birth order: 0.02.

5) Abortion versus religious services attended: —0.38 (df=148, P<0.001).

6) Abortion versus class rank: —0.12.

7) Abortion versus father's education:—0.21 (df=148, 0.05>P >0.02).

8) Abortion versus mother's education: —0.03.

9) Abortion versus attitudes toward violence in general:—0.04. This interesting findings suggests some sort of independence between generalized violence attitudes and the violence or destruction involved in abortion. The subjects' violence scores were obtained during the same survey by means of the author's Violence Scale (Bardis, 1973b; copies of this scale are available upon request from the author).

DISCUSSION

Hypotheses. To a great extent, the above statistical data corroborate all four hypotheses, namely, that university students tend to approve of abortion; that such approval is fairly uniform among them; that religiosity tends to neutralize the influence of education and thus generate fairly conservative abortion attitudes; and that American Catholic students are more conservative than Indian students, who are almost as liberal as American Protestants with reference to abortion attitudes.

Indeed, the Indian abortion average reflected definite, although not overwhelming, approval of abortion. Moreover, such approval was somewhat homogeneous, since many variables did not seem to affect abortion attitudes significantly—these were age, marital status, birth order, number of brothers, number of sisters, mother's education, mother's employment, and population of home town. Of course, additional samples might throw further light on this issue. Then, religiosity, expressed in terms of institutional affiliation and number of religious services attended, remains an influential force, Catholics being more conservative than Hindus and Protestants, and Hindus almost as liberal as Protestants, while there is an inverse relationship between abortion liberalism and frequency of religious services attended.

More specific findings may be interpreted as follows:

Urbanization. The nonsignificant difference between abortion scores representing urban and smaller population centers recalls the conflicting findings of various investigators. For instance, the development theory, which is based on the demographic transition theory, and which states that urbanization and industrialization in the Third World will generate lower fertility rates, has not always been supported empirically, thus leading to the conclusion that the U.S. Agency for International Development has not been entirely successful (American Association for the Advancement of Science, 1974). Similarly, it has been asserted that, although urban populations are more likely to adopt various birth control methods, they are not usually and really characterized by lower fertility rates (Robinson, 1960-61). The opposite has also been averred concerning both fertility and abortion (Mandelbaum, 1974: 46-51, 73). Moreover, it is frequently "assumed that urban families tend to be smaller than rural ones, and that this may afford at least to neo-

Malthusian thinkers an additional reason for favoring rapid urbanization" (Spate and Learnmonth, 1967: 137). Then, according
to the multilinear convergence hypothesis, in the West and the
Third World, although "urbanization begins in very different cultural contexts, in each instance the trend soon begins to reproduce
phases and patterns that have occurred in other times and places"
(Hawley, 1971:313)

Sex. The significantly lower abortion scores of Indian females
seem to suggest that, as among Roman Catholics, in traditionally
oriented cultures, females tend to be more conservative due to their
lower education, their acceptance of higher social status for the
males, and the like. To some extent, such conservatism often persists even among educated females until more drastic social changes
occur.

Education. The somewhat liberalizing influence of education in
regard to abortion has also been mentioned by other authors, who
have considered both attitudes and actual behavior among Indian
women (Mandelbaum, 1974: 73). The same effect is found in the
area of fertility rates, which tend to be lower among educated persons, as well as among those with higher incomes—of course, education and income are usually positively related (Mandelbaum,
1974: 42-44, 51-59). It is true that, in the present study, the correlation between class rank and abortion scores was too low. Nevertheless, one may speculate that the small number of class ranks,
namely, three, resulted in some degree of homogeneity that, in view
of the slow cumulative effects of education, precludes higher correlation coefficients. It is revealing that, when, in another part of the
present international survey, many more educational levels were
included, the liberalizing influence of education was statistically
highly significant (Bardis, 1972a).

The relationship between abortion scores and major field of study
was interesting. The most liberal subjects were the commerce
majors, followed by those in the sciences, while students of the
humanities were the most conservative. All differences were statistically significant. Although, as usual, one would have expected the
humanities majors to be much more liberal, the opposite was true,
and this may probably be explained in terms of their education.
which is more philosophical, traditional, and life-negation oriented
than in the West (Ministry of Education, 1957; Jones, 1953; Gupta,
1968). Commerce students, on the other hand, appear to be more

pragmatic and life-affirmation oriented, while science majors, with their emphasis on experimentation and empiricism, are found between the two extremes. It does not seem coincidental that the subjects with fathers in commerce and trade were also significantly more liberal than the children of teachers.

Religion. As was hypothesized, despite increasing secularization, religiosity was found to be exceedingly influential. First of all, American Catholics were most conservative as regards abortion attitudes, American Protestants being the most liberal, while the Indian subjects were below and close to the Protestants. Moreover, Hindus were much more liberal than Muslims, and the correlation between the variables of abortion and religious services attended was high and negative. Other authors have found that, for strong religious reasons, Indians value procreation of children, especially sons, and that religiosity, although less than education and income, affects fertility rates, which tend to be higher among Muslims than among Hindus. Moreover, Hindus stress religious celibacy and abstinence, while Muslims are less likely to employ contraceptive devices. Of course, there are some exceptions (Basham, 1963: 161; O'Malley, 1941; Mandelbaum, 1974: 44-46).

But what are the basic and relevant doctrines of the two faiths?

Hinduism, first of all, is considered *sanatana* (eternal). The soul is believed to transmigrate, but good *karma* (action) and *jnana* (knowledge) can lead to *moksha*, that is, merging of the soul into the *paramatma* (supreme soul) and, thus, to freedom from rebirth and the sorrows that the human body is heir to. Its outward symbols are the caste system and the Vedic hymns, with modern additions. Sacrifices to the divine beings are recommended, but devotion and knowlege are regarded as more important. Worship is mainly individualistic and religious dissent is tolerated—the bloody feuds of Roman Catholics, Protestants, and Muslims are alien to Hinduism. The main source of Hindu philosophy is the *Upanishads*, although Hindus esteem many of the ideas found in the epic masterpieces, the *Ramayana* and the *Mahabharata*. Its sects are many, the chief ones being the worshippers of Siva, or Saivas; the worshippers of Sakti, or Saktas; and the worshippers of Vishnu, or Vaishnavas (Bhattacharya, 1967: 421-423).

With reference to Islam, suffice it to say that, in "Mohammedan lands, the Islamic belief is that life begins in the fetus only after 150 days" (Lader, 1970: 94). The *Koran* itself does not mention *isqat* (abortion), but, as is stated in the *Fatawa-i-Alamgiri*, "it is forbidden after the child is formed in the womb. Muhammad is related to have ordered prayers to be said over an abortion, when supplication should be made for the father and mother, for forgiveness and mercy" (Hughes, 1965: 4; Ansari, 1955).

Of course, such beliefs must be compared with the attitudes and practices of additional Indian students, since the sample of the present study included only—eleven Muslims. Still, it is significant that religiosity remains influential in the modern world, which presents a formidable challenge to religious leaders, who should contribute to the solution of major social problems by adopting gradual changes that do not compromise any of their more valuable doctrines.

Paternal education and occupation. It is not clear why father's education and student's abortion score were correlated highly and negatively. It may be that, as in the case of humanities majors, paternal education a few decades ago was also traditionally oriented, and even more so then, education thus still being influential, but in rather conservative fashion, at least in some respects.

As regards paternal occupation, fathers in trade and commerce had children with more liberal abortion attitudes than teachers did —the findings concerning the subjects' own major fields of study were similar.

Perhaps these two statistics mean that, in India's somewhat male-oriented culture, family life styles and attitudes are primarily determined by the father's, not the mother's, education and occupation. This also indicates that, to some extent, type of education and economic development may be among the forces that could mitigate the overpopulation problem.

Family planning versus economic development. This problem, which involves, not only India, but the entire planet, was dealt with by the August 1974 United Nations World Population Conference in Bucharest, the first global conference of representatives of governments to concern itself with population control. Unfortunately, the 1,100 delegates from 141 countries reached little agreement, since these leaders "seemed motivated more by national pride and ideology than concern for the hunger that already blights many poor nations" (*Time*, 1974). The "plan of action," which "called for a reduction of birth rates that would be proportionate to a country's population," and which "proposed that governments should provide the education, information and means for family planning, if the families so desire," was attacked severely (*Time*, 1974). Algeria's Ali Oubouzar, chairman of the working group that revised the plan, objected that the underdeveloped countries prefer economic and social development to family planning. "The onslaught was led by a bizarre alliance of Communist and Latin American countries. According to these delegations, overpopulation is a myth invented by the rich to exploit and subjugate the poor" (*Time*, 1974). Soviet Deputy Minister of Health Lev Volodarsky asserted that overpopulation has nothing to do with the Third World's problems, and Chinese Deputy Minister of Health Huang Shu-tse expressed a similar opinion. In general, the Marxist position was that "capitalism rather than population is the root of the developing nations' problems" (Walsh, 1974: 1144). Even India's delegates, although they occasionally emphasized a healthy combination of population control and economic development, failed to stress family planning (*Time*, 1974; Walsh, 1974 : 1144). Finally, the "Conference recognized that constructive changes in the consumption patterns of affluent countries are vitally necessary to cope with the limited resources of the planet; that mere access to contraceptives and safe abortion will not reduce growth" (Mead, 1974: 1113).

It seems, then, that, since in the underdeveloped countries of Asia and Africa, which have more than 50 per cent of the world's people, the population is increasing by 2.3 per cent annually, that is, much faster than the means of subsistence; and since drought in India and Africa has been intensifying this crisis, the salutary effects of foreign aid, industrialization, and modern agriculture are being constantly neutralized by high birth rates. It is no wonder that Kim Jae Hee, an executive of South Korea's Planned Parenthood Federation, has desperately declared a "No Pregnancy Year," a program using rallies, banners, window stickers, campaigns by movie stars, and so on. But, as Director Roger Revelle, of Harvard University's Center for Population Studies, has observed: "Any contraceptive program probably needs to be backed up by a system of legal, safe, and inexpensive abortion, such as exists in Japan, the Soviet Union, and the Scandinavian countries" (Lader, 1970: 139).

In brief socio-economic justice is desirable, but not sufficient. Family planning is helpful, but not enough. A combination of both is urgently needed. Couples should at long last realize that they must emphasize both their own welfare and that of others. And states should at long last understand that they must stress both domestic freedom and international responsibility.

CONCLUSION

A study of abortion attitudes among university students in India has revealed that the subjects rather favored abortion and did so somewhat uniformly. Education and religiosity were particularly influential. It was further concluded that, family planning, including abortion, must be combined with economic development, if it is to be effective. ·

Additional surveys (comparing with less educated Indians, testing for possible selectivity in the student groups even before college, and so on) are needed in order to throw further light on this subject, especially now that overpopulation is a serious problem, and modern democratic ideals have made the study of attitudes both timely and useful.

REFERENCES

Agarwala, S.
　1967 "Family Planning Program in India." *Asian Survey*, 7 (December). Pp. 851-859.
American Association for the Advancement of Science.
　1974 *Culture and Population Change*, Washington.
Ansari, G.
　1955 "Muslim Marriage in India." Wiener Volkerkundliche Mittelungen, 3. Pp. 191-206.
Bardis, Panos D.
　1971 "Modernization and Birth Control: An International Survey of Attitudes Toward Oral Contraception." *International Journal of Sociology of the Family*, 1 (March). Pp. 21-35.
　1972a "Abortion and Public Opinion." *Journal of Marriage and the Family*, 34 (February). P. 111.
　1972b "A Technique for the Measurement of Attitudes Toward Abortion." *International Journal of Sociology of the Family*, 2 (March). Pp. 1-7.

1973a "Attitudes Toward Oral Contraception Among Italian University Students." *Social Science*, 48 (Summer). Pp. 167-176.

1973b "Violence: Theory and Quantification." *Journal of Political and Military Sociology*, 1(Spring). Pp. 121-146.

1975 "Abortion Attitudes Among Catholic College Students." *Adolescence* (in press).

Basham, A.
1963 *The Wonder That Was India*. Revised edition. New York: Hawthorn.

Berelson, Bernard
1969 "National Family Planning Programs: Where We Stand," in S. Behrman *et al*. (eds.), *Fertility and Family Planning*. Ann Arbor, Michigan: University of Michigan Press. Pp. 341-387.

Bhatia, D.
1969 "India: A Gigantic Task," in B. Berelson (ed.), *Family-Planning Programs*. New York: Basic Books. Pp. 67-80.

Bhattacharya, S.
1967 *A Dictionary of Indian History*. New York: Braziller.

Bhowmik, K.
1975 "Abortion in India." *Social Science* (in press).

Chandrasekhar, S.
1965 "A Billion Indians by 2000 A.D.?" The *New York Times Magazine*, (4 April). Pp. 110, 117.

1970 "Abortion in India" in R. Hall (ed.), *Abortion in a Changing World*, Volume 1. New York: Columbia University Press Pp. 245-250.

Collver, Andrew.
1963 "The Family Cycle in India and the United States." *American Sociological Review*, 28 (February). Pp. 86-96.

Dandekar, K.
1967 *Communication in Family Planning*. London: Asia Publishing House.

Deasi, B.
1967 *The Emerging Youth*. Bombay: Popular Prakashan.

Desai, N.
1936 *Report on the Hindu Joint Family*. Baroda: Baroda State Press.

Ehrenfelo, U.
1953 "Matrilineal Family Background in South India." *Journal of Educational Sociology*, 26 (April). Pp. 356-361.

Floris, G.
1962 "India's Women on the March." *Contemporary Review*, 201 (January). Pp. 21-23.

Garrett, Henry
1967 *Statistics in Psychology and Education*. Sixth edition, London: Longman, Green.

Gupta, A.
1968 "A Study on the Promotion of Knowledge of Contraception by

Education Programme in Family Planning, 1965." *Indian Journal of Social Work*, 28 (January). Pp. 427-452.

Gupta, S.
1970   *A Study of Women of Bengal.* Calcutta: Indian Publications.

Hawley, Amos
1971   *Urban Society.* New York: Ronald.

Hughes, Thomas
1965   *Dictionary of Islam.* Clifton, New Jersey: Reference Books Publishers.

Husain, I.
1970   *An Urban Fertility Field.* Lucknow, India: Lucknow University.

Jones, Charles.
1953   "Notes on Indian Education." *Journal of Educational Sociology*, 27 (September). Pp. 16-23.

Kapadia, K.
1966   *Marriage and Family in India.* Third edition. London: Oxford University Press.

Kapur, Promilla
1970   *Marriage and the Working Woman in India.* Delhi: Vikas Publishing House.

Karandikar, S.
1929   *Hindu Exogamy.* Bombay: Taraporewala.

Kuppuswamy, B.
1972   *Social Change in India.* Delhi: Vikas Publishing House.

Lader, Lawrence
1970   *Abortion,* Boston: Beacon Press.

Mandelbaum, David
1974   *Human Fertility in India.* Los Angeles: University of California Press.

Marascuilo, Leonard
1971   *Statistical Methods for Behavioral Science Research,* New York: McGraw-Hill.

Mayer, Adrian
1960   *Caste and Kinship in Central India.* London: Routledge and Kegan Paul.

McCall, Robert
1970   *Fundamental Statistics for Psychology.* New York: Harcourt, Brace, and World.

Mead, Margaret
1974   "World Population: World Responsibility," *Science,* 27(September). P. 113.

Ministry of Education
1957   *A Review of Education in India.* Delhi: Albion Press.

Ministry of Health and Family Planning
1966   Report of the Committee to Study the Question of Legalization of Abortion. New Delhi.

Mohan, Raj
  1975 "Abortion in India." *Social Science* (in press),
Mukerji, M.
  1945 *Indian Adolescence.* Lucknow, India: Teachers' Cooperative Education Journals.
Nimkoff, M., and M. Gore
  1959 "Social Bases of the Hindu Joint Family." *Sociology and Social Research,* 44 (September). Pp. 27-36.
Norman, D. (Editor)
  1965 *Nehru.* New York: Day, Volume 2.
O' Malley, L.
  1941 "Family and Religion" in L. O' Malley (ed.), *Modern India and the West.* London: Oxford University Press.
Orenstein, Henry
  1961 "The Recent History of the Extended Family in India." *Social Problems,* 8 (Spring). Pp. 341-350.
Owens, R.
  1971 "Industrialization and the Indian Joint Family." *Ethnology,* 10 (April). Pp. 223-250.
Prasad L., and L. Ghosh
  1965 "Field Experience in Family Planning." *Journal of Family Welfare,* 2 (March). Pp. 98-100.
Raina, B.
  1966 "India" in B. Berelson *et al.* (eds.), *Family Planning and Population Programs.* Chicago: University of Chicago Press. Pp.111-121.
Rajan, K.
  1967 "La Planification Familiale en Inde." *Finances et Developement,* 4 (December). Pp. 289-299.
Rao, D.
  1974 "Housing of Squatters in Delhi: Search for a Solution." *Ekistics,* 38 (July). Pp. 57-62.
Robinson, W.
  1960- "Urban-Rural Differences in Indian Fertility." *Population Studies,*
  1961   14. Pp. 218-234.
Ross, Aileen
  1967 *The Hindu Family in Its Urban Setting.* Toronto: University of Toronto Press.
Rungachery, S.
  1960 "The Family in Transition." *March of India,* 12 (August). Pp. 63-65.
Shah, A.
  1974 *The Household Dimension of the Family in India.* Los Angeles: University of California Press.

Simmons, G.
  1971 *The Indian Investment in Family Planning.* New York: Population
        Council.
Singh, J.
  1968 "Sikh Marriage in Transition." *Social Action,* 18 (May-June).
        Pp. 224-230.
Sinha, A. and O. Upadhyay
  1960 "Stereotypes of Male and Female University Students in India
        Toward Different Ethnic Groups." *Journal of Social Psychology,*
        51 (February). Pp. 93-102.
Spate, O., and A. Learmonth
  1967 *India and Pakistan,* Third Edition. Bungay, Suffolk: Chaucer
        Press.
Srinivas, M.
  1942 *Marriage and Family in Mysore.* Bombay: New Book Company.
Time
  1974 *"Population."* (9 September). Pp. 37.
United Nations
  1974 *Statistical Yearbook.* 1973, New York.
United States Bureau of the Census
  1973 *Statistical Abstract of the United States.* Washington: Government
        Printing Office.
Vig, O.
  1970 "Demographic Effectiveness of Sterilization Programme in India."
        Artha Vijnana, 12 (September). Pp. 398-406.
Walsh, John.
  1974 "UN Conferences." *Science.* (27 September). Pp. 1143-1144,
        1192-1193.
Yadau, S.
  1971 "Trends in Marriage Age of Girls in India." *Artha Vijnana,*
        13 (March). Pp. 119-138.

CHAPTER V

Modernization and Social Change—the Family in Pakistan[1]

J. HENRY KORSON

INTRODUCTION

Prior to the second world war, not much attention was paid by social scientists to the concept of modernization, although considerable thought was given to some of the problems of colonial societies. But in the post-war period, considerable attention has been paid to these societies, which have variously been referred to since World War II as "underdeveloped," "developing," or "modernizing." Implicit in this is the assumption that Western Europe and North America represent the "modern" nations of the world, which the ex-colonial societies should use as models and, therefore, strive to achieve a more satisfactory level of living for their people.

Of the major social institutions to which the social scientists have applied themselves in their studies of the developing societies, it is not surprising that the greatest interest has been shown in the economic

[1]A part of this chapter was presented at the National Seminar on Pakistan at Columbia University in November 1971, and another part at the Twelfth International Seminar of the Committee on Family Research, International Sociological Association, sponsored by the Soviet Academy of Sciences in Moscow, April 1972. The writer is indebted to the National Seminar on Pakistan, Columbia University, and to the University of Massachusetts Research Council for the financial support of this project. The data presented in this chapter cover up to the period of early 1970s.

and political institutions. Some interest has also been indicated in educational development and, as might be expected, far less interest has been manifested by social scientists in the social institutions of religion and the family.

Although the study of the new young nations has attracted scholars from the various social science disciplines, it is interesting to note the different emphasis in terminology. The terms "development" and "developing societies" appear to have been used most frequently by economists, or at least in the context of developing *economies*, largely, I dare say, because of their inclination to think in terms of economic development. Political scientists, while they may also use the term "developing" in referring to new nations, are and have been more concerned with the processes of governance and political power. And since political power must be legitimized in one form or another, *constitution building and nation building* became their major areas of interest. Other areas of interest, however, were not excluded from the purview of the political scientists, and many insightful studies concerned with political leadership, political parties, and administrative science, as well as some peripheral areas, have also been the center of scholarly interest. (Historians, of course, have also shown scholarly interest in many of the young nations, but their efforts have frequently been limited by the availability of source materials.)

The terms "modernization" and "modernity," however, carry with them the implication of change for the total culture, that is, that positive efforts have been, or are being, made by the government or other leaders to move the society away from the traditional practices of older generations in an effort to achieve previously established goals. The latter term, then, has taken on the connotation of rational, planned change, with definite objectives and goals in mind, and usually *away* from the traditional and previously accepted pattern of action. And these plans are usually not approached with a laissez-faire philosophy about the solution of a particular set of problems, but with a time limit, such as a four-year or five-year plan or series of plans within which the goals are to be met.

But if we were to leave off the discussion at this point, we would find ourselves trapped in a bit of intellectual circularity, because the discussion has not yet moved away from the basic social institutions of economics and government. But to put it simply, while the new nations are, and have been, primarily concerned with economic and political matters and, secondarily, with the systems of education, the two other major social institutions, where planning in these young nations has, in large measure, been ignored, are religion and the family. Where the established religion has been felt by government leaders to be unsympathetic or even a threat to their political goals, the Church's powers and influence were circumscribed. But where religious ideology was in consonance or sympathetic with the political goals of the nation's leaders, the religious institution was co-opted in support of these goals. It will return later to an extended discussion of the role of the family in the whole process of modernization.

The great desire of these new nations not only to assert their political independence, but economic independence, has seen their head-long rush into the 20th century from the disabilities and limitations of the 19th and earlier centuries. With the assistance of large amounts of economic aid since World War II, not only from the former colonial powers, but also from many non-colonial powers, these new nations have experienced the problems of industrial and commercial development with the demographic transition telescoped into one generation—what older nations witnessed over a period of a century and more. In the field of education, for example, their commendable concern with the achievement of universal literacy has seen these nations attempt to achieve in one generation what older nations took a century and more to accomplish.

Political independence appears to be the primary goal to newly established nations, usually with a stated political ideology. When Great Britain gave up sovereignty of the Indian subcontinent in 1947, Muslim political leaders who had been agitating for a separate state based on Islamic ideology gained their objective, and a new nation, Pakistan, was founded (Wilcox, 1963). A massive exchange of populations occured immediately after independence, followed by continued immigration of Muslims into West Pakistan (and what was formerly East Pakistan, now Bangladesh), so that today Pakistan is approximately 97 per cent Muslim. Pakistan, then, presents the social scientist with an almost completely homogeneous population in terms of religious and social values, although there are cultural variations among regions and social classes, and these values dominate the social structure of the family in Pakistan.

Although the institution of religion is not of direct concern in this paper, it must be stated that Max Weber probably made as percep-

tive an observation as any social scientist concerning the role of
religion in the modernization of Asian nations. In assessing Weber's
analysis, Singer (1966:55) states that Weber viewed "Asian religion
[as] a major obstacle to modernization because of its bulwark of
traditionalism and a repository of beliefs and values incompatible
with modern science, technology, and the ideology of progress." On
the other hand, few religious leaders have hesitated to adopt any
technology that might be useful to further their religious ideology.
I do not know whether the *muezzins* in Karachi climb the many
steps to the top of the minarets to use the public address system to
call the faithful to prayer five times daily, or merely perform this
duty from the ground floor level with the use of a microphone. It
would appear, then, that traditional Asian religions are perhaps
not opposed to modernization, *per se* provided it does not threaten
their vested interests.

Although there is considerable variation in the degree of religiosity among Muslims in Pakistan, the Islamic roots that underlie the
social fabric of the people are deeply imbedded and are not likely
to change radically in the near future. Some changes that have
occurred in the last generation that affect the family, however,
will be discussed in detail below, and these changes are indicative of
what is likely to happen in the future.

Since this paper is concerned with the concept of modernization,
and since the concept itself must be thought of in relative terms, it
might be well to think in terms of scaling all Muslim societies along
a continuum from the most conservative to the most liberal. Turkey,
which had its social revolution almost a half century ago, would
probably be placed at the liberal end of the continuum, while Saudi
Arabia and the Trucial states would be scaled at the other end, with
Pakistan placed near the conservative end.

THE SOCIAL STRUCTURE OF THE FAMILY

Perhaps a brief sketch of the social structure of the family in
Pakistan is in order at this point. The family can be considered a
traditional one, and by traditional is meant that the value system
which supports the social structure of the family has remained
largely unchanged for a number of generations: patriarchal, patrilineal and patrilocal—in large measure. The terms extended family

and joint family are well known in the literature and are frequently used interchangeably, and just as frequently confused. Litwack (1960:9) has defined the extended family "in terms of geographic propinquity, occupational dependence and nepotism, a sense that extended family relations are most important, and a hierarchical authority structure based on a semi-biological criterion, that is, the eldest male." The extended family is here defined as one of three or more generations living in one household, or within one compound, with the grandfather actively serving as the family head, and with married sons and their families, as well as unmarried sons and daughters. This form appears to be the epitome of the patriarchal, patrilocal, and patrilineal family, with the family head as the power center and the major decision-maker. The joint family, on the other hand, is usually limited to two generations, and consists of two or more brothers, married or unmarried, with their spouses and children and unmarried sisters living in one household, or within a compound. The oldest son usually assumes the headship upon the death or disability of the father. Married sons, of course, are not required to live with the family head, but, once again, this appears to be the ideal to be achieved.

Although the extended family is viewed as the ideal form in Pakistani society, in 1958 only 17.3 per cent of all families in Karachi were of the extended type, and another 15.1 per cent of the joint type, for a total of 32.4 per cent of all family types in the city (Hashmi, 1964:32). Nevertheless, it would appear that the *influence* of the extended family type is far stronger than the figures above would indicate, largely because these data were the result of a *household* survey. Although the great majority of families were of the nuclear type, many extended and joint families live in very close proximity to one another, so that constant visiting of family members is very evident with the result that the influence of the extended family is everpresent as a source of social control, and as a socializing force for the young (Ghani, 1963:324; Goode, 1963:123-129).

The Biraderi

Even though the extended family is viewed as the ideal in Pakistan, it can be seen from the brief statement above that only a minority of Muslim families do indeed fit that description, or even that of the joint family. Perhaps what is even more important in an examination of the social structure of the family is the *biraderi*, or larger kin group. *Biraderi*, a term derived from the Persian *birader*, brother, means brotherhood. Although there is not complete agreement among sociologists and anthropologists concerning its definition, consanguineal ties appear to be stronger than affinal ties. "The size of the *biraderi* is as large as the distance at which one can recognize one's relatives" (Wakil, 1970:700). Eglar (1960:75-76) limits membership to the male line of descent, and, as a patrilineage, "all men who can trace their relationship to a common ancestor, no matter how remote, belong to the same *biraderi*. Daughters belong to the *biraderi* of their fathers, but after marriage are included in the *biraderi* of their husbands also." The widest possible group of people who are recognized as being related to one another is called the *saak* (Eglar, 1960:81). Others have claimed that a *biraderi* is a group made up of kin whether related by blood or marriage, regardless of how far removed. At one time the *biraderi* was as much fixed by close geographical proximity as by occupational ties, but with increased migration of males (especially), these ties appear to be weakening.

Even in the urban setting, if siblings or other close kinfolk are within relatively easy reach, kin ties are continually reinforced by almost daily visits. There appears to be little difference in the behavior or attitude toward this form of leisure time activity among the different social classes. One university professor, in discussing the importance of kinship ties, reported that he and his four brothers, all married, and all living in the same city, took turns visiting one anothers' home one evening per week on a regular basis. These visits included wives and children. "This left two evenings per week to visit my wife's relatives."

Members of a *biraderi* will gather to help celebrate major family events, such as births and marriages, and to assist in the mourning of the dead at a funeral. Otherwise, the strength and effectiveness of these kin ties depend largely on the amount and degree of use to which they are put. From Eglar (1960), we learnt that *biraderi* is a highly complex, yet very functional, system of favors and obligations which include an intricate system of gift-giving.

Individualism is a concept not in tune with the Muslim ethos, because individual ambition and success are translated to mean improving the position of the whole family, whether in financial, social, or prestige terms. Older children are expected to assist their younger siblings to achieve their goals in education, in the search for occupational placement, or even in the selection of marriage partners. The Muslim who succeeds in business or in some other field of endeavor might find himself under obligation to employ or even support to the limit of his abilities more and more relatives.

Intergenerational continuity provides the kind of support for the individual in need that is usually absent in the Western nuclear family, and the abrasive, if not shattering, experience of independently finding one's own way—which in the West is condoned as a welcome part of the maturation process—is often absent in the Muslim family. The extended family and, even more so, the *biraderi* in Pakistani society play the supportive role of the "great umbrella" with protection for all who qualify by kinship. "Muslims place great emphasis on kinship. Traditional reciprocities between grandparents and grandchildren, uncles and aunts, and nieces, nephews, and cousins, as well as those between members of nuclear family units, create close family ties" (Blitsten, 1963:200).

So highly institutionalized is the dependence of the individual on his family and, beyond those limits, his *biraderi*, or kin ties, for his short-term and long-term needs, that the usual first step in gaining an objective is to enlist the support of a relative, who might have a friend, or a friend of a friend, who might be under obligation to lend assistance to gain the objective. So well socialized is the individual in this system of functional exchange that this kind of normative behavior comes almost as second nature.

Seeking assistance to cut through bureaucratic red tape is well known and practiced in all societies to one degree or another, but it is usually attempted as a last resort. To the outside observer, the apparent difference in Pakistan is that the individual *begins* his undertaking by seeking assistance from relatives, and through them friends, and friends of friends, and assumes that he will receive this sought-for assistance without question. The individual whose assistance is being sought may, indeed, be under obligation to the one seeking help, or, perhaps a member of the supplicant's family. Or the request can be looked upon by the recipient of such a request as an opportunity to establish "credit ' to be used at some future time. Not all requests for assistance can be met, of course, but it is incumbent upon the individual whose assistance is being sought to make an effort to help. A flat denial would immediately mark him as one "beyond the pale"—as one who had failed to live up to a fundamental tenet of Muslim family structure.

The *biraderi*, then, functions not only as a mechanism for group survival, but even group enhancement. It appears that there is even a degree of intergroup rivalry, which would inevitably occur when two or more individuals or their *biraderis* might seek the same goals. The criteria are the same in both urban and rural areas, but since the great migration movement following partition, and the continued internal rural-urban migration in the last two decades, it would seem reasonable that the influence of the *biraderi* is weakening. The urbanites, however, attempt to re-establish their kin ties at the earliest opportunities, if, indeed, they are ever truly broken. One would expect the *biraderi* to function best in a rural and feudalistic society, because the urban migration of males would tend to weaken it. Industrialization creates the need for geographic mobility of the industrial worker, which is in sharp contrast to the traditional needs of the agricultural worker usually rooted to the land, either as an owner or farm laborer. This does not mean that the kin network is lost in the urban environment, but it is apt to be weakened. In the work situation the *biraderi* is likely to contribute to bureaucratic inefficiency and is in contradiction to any system based on meritocracy, the theoretical goal of a democratic system. A Pakistani would be quick to point out, however, the advantages of favoring a relative over a nonrelative when a new employee or partner is to be added: loyalty, trustworthiness, and dependability, since the "best talent available" may not be a prerequisite. Furthermore, in a society where the great majority of the population know economic insecurity firsthand, over the long run sharing limited resources has its advantages. For these reasons (as well as limited employment opportunities), many businesses and government agencies will appear to have a surfeit of clerks and other employees who are obviously underemployed. Generally speaking, then, it would appear that to the degree that an organization seeks to fill its ranks from within kin groups, to that degree is the organization limited in its search for the best talent.

There appears to be a rank order of *biraderis*. Indeed, some have greater prestige and influence than others, since they do take on some aspects of a caste system. The higher ranking *biraderis* have greater prestige and influence in government and business circles, so that the vast majority of the population feels it is denied any opportunity to take advantage of the system. Since the kin ties of members of the lower class carry little influence, this segment of the population feels deprived. It is not that they disapprove of the system as such, it is just that they want "a piece of the action," and are the first ones to attempt to appropriate or participate in the system should the opportunity present itself.

In the last analysis, modernization indicates an increase in urbanization and, with it, inevitably, the increased possibility of anonymity and the drift toward individualism and away from the dependence on the strength of kin ties. When General Yahya Khan displaced Mohammed Ayub Khan from the presidency in 1969, one of the charges leveled at the latter was the high degree of "corruption and nepotism" in the central government. Nepotism is a logical consequence of a society so heavily infused with the ideology of the importance of kin ties, and it is taken for granted in a social system organized around the *biraderi.* "Nepotism in the technical sense...is only one form of spread of family considerations to non-family contexts" (Levy, 1966:386).

URBANIZATION

Although the urbanization of populations is current in all nations, urbanization has even more telling effects in Pakistan, most especially on the sex ratio and the social structure of the family. Whereas most nations have a sex ratio showing a higher number of women in their population, the 1961 census showed Pakistan to have a ratio of 111 males to 100 females. Continued internal migration to the cities has accentuated this problem, because the same census indicated a sex ratio of 131 males for each 100 females in the city of Karachi. This continued migration inevitably affects the structure of the family in a number of ways. Rather than serving as a haven or attraction of women into the labor force, as is found in most nations, just the opposite holds true in Pakistan. Unmarried men who leave their villages to seek work in cities are almost certain to delay the time of their marriage, while married men leave their families behind, with the expectation of making annual home visits. This loosening of family ties will inevitably affect the social structure of the family.

In the West, a major life goal appears to be individual happiness however, that is defined or achieved, and parents commit themselves to helping children achieve that goal. One might say that Westerners are "inner directed" in their search for individual achievement and happiness, while the socialization process in Pakistan with its great stress on loyalty to kin helps to ensure that the individual is "other directed" and his participation in the social interaction of the group both as a recipient and giver of assistance and support is continued. Evidence in support of this position is offered below in the section devoted to mate selection.

PURDAH

No discussion of the family in Pakistan would be complete without an examination of the highly institutionalized system of sexual segregation known as *purdah*. As Papanek (1964:160) has put it, "the status of women in a *purdah* society is a characteristic of major importance of the entire social system, and must be confronted at every turn." All Muslim societies practice, or have practiced in the past, forms of *purdah*, and it is also found in some segments of Indian society (Jacobson, 1970).

One of the major problems in any discussion of *purdah* is the lack of empirical data. It is not difficult to understand the lack of "hard data" in this area of investigation because the vast majority of the scholars working on this subject are men, and this automatically eliminates them as possible field researchers. Papanek (1964:160) explores this problem in some depth. Although quantitative data are lacking, important material can be gathered by observation and discussion and probed for significance.

In a very limited sense, *purdah* includes a spatial aspect which might mean restriction to women's quarters, traveling in a *purdah* railway car, or the *purdah* section of a public bus in Karachi, or sitting in a segregated section of a public building. The literal interpretation of the term *purdah* (curtain) is the seclusion of women. In Pakistan the term refers largely to the minority of women who wear the *burqa*, or veil, in public. But it might also be thought of as a whole syndrome of the segregation of women from men who are not their relatives, and the maintenance of modesty in dress and manner. Regardless of costume or style, women are fully covered from neck to ankle, and women are expected to have as little contact as possible with men who are not relatives. In a wider sense, it includes what Papanek (1971:517) refers to as "symbolic shelter," the kind of social-psychological support the woman receives from her kinfolk in this very complex area of human interaction.

Islamic philosophy has always assumed that women must be protected from the sexual advances and aggression of males so that the protection of women (and their proper behavior as "sheltered persons") has always been paramount. It is also a prime ingredient of the family's *izzat* or honor. The term probably comes from the Arabic *ird*, literally, "to show one's face." In other words, the women in a family, through proper behavior bring honor to the men of the family so that their honor and prestige (and, secondarily, that of the women) are maintained, if not enhanced. For this reason (according to tradition), if a daughter in a family has made a misstep, it is she who is punished by the men in her family, rather than the male transgressor.

In a wider sense, the practice of *purdah* in the urban areas has been associated not only with the honor and prestige of the family, but it would also appear to depend on the socio-economic status of the family, that is, "those who can afford to provide it" (Bertocci, 1971:43). Some observers even claim that *purdah* is less likely to be found among peasant women than among urban dwellers, because its practice (especially the wearing of the *burqa*, or veil) would interfere with their work in agricultural chores. The family's degree of religiosity is also a contributing factor in the behavior of women.

Perhaps the most important factor that contributes to social cleavage in Pakistani society is sex. In a strongly male-oriented society, sex is the primary category for defining the role of the individual. "Emphasis is placed on the mutually exclusive but complementary roles of men and women both in the family and in society at large. Distinctions are made from the moment of birth and increase in number and emphasis as the child grows into adulthood" (Wilbur, 1964:25). A girl is not always viewed as an asset, although she is treated kindly. Since she grows up in a patrilocal society, the family fully expects her to leave the household upon marriage and take up residence with her husband's family. This kind of perceived economic loss does not call for a large investment in training, aside from the domestic duties a girl is expected to learn. Her behavior, however, before marriage is of concern to her family. Before marriage, any improper behavior would weaken her chances of making a good marriage, and would certainly serve to threaten the family's honor and prestige.

In the socialization process, a girl is taught or encouraged to be modest, docile, obedient to her elders, unassertive, and to defer to male members of her family. One of the major goals in the socialization process is to inculcate the psychological feeling of dependence on the male, and *not* to be self-reliant. Obviously, not all families are successful in achieving this norm, nor for that matter do all families subscribe to it. Patterns of behavior vary widely from region to region, and among the social classes. Urban middle and upper class women usually do not go to the food markets. This activity is usually assumed by male members of the family, or, more frequently, by servants. But it is acceptable for women to shop for other household necessities in the bazaars, and even in this situation they will not go alone on such missions but frequently with other female relatives or friends.

How strictly *purdah* is observed can vary widely from family to family within the same social class, and frequently its observance depends on the degree of religiosity of the exended as well as the nuclear family. It is far more difficult for a young lady to attempt to break or even bend some of the norms when aunts, uncles, and even grandparents are present in the household (or nearby) to lend psychological support to the girl's parents in the maintenance of the traditional norms. Since decision-making rests with the adults in a family, and especially with the family head, they are more likely to support each other rather than members of the younger generation in the observance of traditional norms.

That there has been a considerable amount of social change in the traditional observance of *purdah* can be readily noted in such cities as Karachi and Lahore. For those girls who attend school, except for the earliest years, classes are segregated through the college level. Only at the graduate level, in the university, is coeducation found. And even this devolopment has not met with complete consensus because one of the major issues in the student difficulties in December 1964 and January 1965, at the University of Karachi, was the demand by some men students that the government of Pakistan build a separate university for women students. The men students claimed that it was against the finest Islamic tradition to have men and women attend the same university. (As a faculty member at that time, I can report that hardly a week passed that a memorandum was not distributed to all teachers, to be read to each class that coeducational use of seminar rooms behind closed doors or similar "coeducational behavior" was a violation of university rules, and reminding students that proper behavior on their part was expected at all times. Today, however, many girls and boys can be seen chatting together in groups—something that would have been frowned upon a few years ago.

Although only a minority of the women students wear a *burqa*, and then only during their travel to and from the university, it is difficult to comprehend the vast gulf that must exist between these university women students and their mothers. One study (Korson, 1970:87) will serve to demonstrate the great difference in educational achievement between the two generations. This study shows that the mothers of the girls who received their Master's degrees from the University of the Punjab in 1966 had an average achievement of elementary school education, and that 45 per cent of their mothers had no formal schooling. The sample taken of the same class (1966) at the University of Karachi showed an even lower educational achievement for the mothers, with 63.4 per cent indicating no formal schooling. Only 2.8 per cent of the Karachi mothers had achieved a Bachelor's degree or higher, and only one per cent of the Lahore mothers could make the same claim. Karachi fathers had achieved higher educational levels than their Lahore counterparts: 62 per cent held Bachelor's degrees or higher, against 40 per cent for the Lahore fathers.

The system of *purdah* almost dictates that some vocations will either be monopolized by women or be well represented by women, and this is especially true in a "contact" occupation, such as medicine. For example, there are separate medical colleges for women in Pakistan, and women patients normally seek out women doctors for medical care. The *dai*, or midwife, has traditionally played a very important role in Muslim societies. Nursing, on the other hand, has never attracted Muslim women in Pakistan in any numbers for several reasons. A relatively small number of Muslims use in-patient hospital facilities as such, because bed care has always been considered a family responsibility, rather than the expectation that complete strangers in an impersonal institution such as a hospital would play the nursing role. The status of a nurse has been depicted as hardly more than as cut above that of a servant, hence middle class girls who would form the most likely cohort of candidates for nursing training because of their level of educational achievement are quite likely to spurn this occupational opportunity. The growth of modern nursing as a profession for women in Pakistan has been exceedingly slow. Although various aspects of *purdah* dictate a discriminatory process against women, some advantages do accrue. For example, thirteen seats in the national assembly are set aside for women. Although women have the franchise and are free to run for public office, no women were elected to the national assembly in the December 1970 elections. If any of the candidates who had run at that time had been successful, they would have served in addition to the thirteen allotted by the constitution. The latter were not elected in the general election, but, rather, by the regularly elected members. The reservation of at least thirteen seats assures some representation for the women.

THE ROLE OF EDUCATION

This discussion of the role of education and its contribution to the changing status of women in Pakistan will be limited to higher education and, more specifically, to graduate education. In spite of the fact that the illiteracy rate in Pakistan is high (about 80 per cent) the rate does vary among regions, rural-urban areas, socio-economic classes, and between the sexes. As might be expected, the rates are higher for women than men, but what is surprising is that in the late 1960s slightly more than 50 per cent of the graduate students at the University of Karachi were women, and during this same period women made up about 30 per cent of the graduate students at the University of the Punjab in Lahore. To my knowledge women were not discriminated against in admission at Karachi, nor was there discrimination in the choice of fields of study. I cannot speak to the situation at Lahore, but I have no reason to believe that the women students were restricted in their choice of fields.

In recent years the total number of graduate students in all the universities in the country was estimated to be about 25,000, an exceedingly small number for a nation of 125,000,000 or more people, including Bangladesh, formerly East Pakistan. If women are represented in the same proportion at the universities, a rough estimate would yield the figure of about 10,000 women participating in a variety of programs which will fit them for a variety of other careers in the labor force. Although women are admitted to the law colleges, they constitute a small number, perhaps 5 per cent, of the student body.

This raises the question of female participation in the labor force. The pool of highly trained personnel is probably of greater importance in a modernizing nation than in one of the more highly developed nations, and since the key to training is the educational system of a nation, it is surprising to note that Pakistan's expenditure for its entire educational system in 1961 was 1.3 per cent of its gross national product. By 1965 the planned percentage was 2, but did not exceed 1.5 per cent. At that time (1965), it placed Pakistan in the lowest group of nations in terms of educational expenditures. The long-range plan called for a steady increase so that by 1985 the percentage would reach 4 per cent of the gross national product. In the same year, the Soviet Union spent about 7 per cent on its education system (Huq, 1965:239).

Although increased sums have been appropriated by both the central and provincial governments, the continued population increase, in the order of 2.5 to 3 per cent annually, has tended to dissipate any projected gains in this area of development. At the university level, budgets have been only slightly expanded to care for increased pressure for admission, and capital outlay for new buildings has been relatively small. In spite of severe budget limitations and continued pressure for admission, there has been no apparent change in the policy toward the admission of women. At the lower levels (even though schooling is supposedly open to all), in 1961-62, girls made up only 25 per cent of the student body in the primary grades and about 14 per cent in the middle and secondary schools (Huq, 1965:218). (The 1971 decennial census, which was planned for January 1971, was postponed and carried out in September 1972.) As of this writing, results were not available.

WOMEN IN THE LABOR FORCE

At the time of partition, the subcontinent, which had known
colonial status for over 200 years, and feudalism before that, much
of which continued into the colonial period, the status of women
had seen relatively limited change. Little schooling had been
available for the masses in Muslim society, and even less for its
women. In the last two generations, some women of the middle
and upper classes did make their way through the social barriers
to reach levels of higher education, and a number achieved
professional status, especially in the fields of medicine and
teaching.

All Muslim societies are noted for the low rate of participation
of women in their labor forces, and Pakistan is among the lowest.
From the 1961 census we learn that only 9.6 per cent of the
women twelve years of age and over were classified as economically
active (Bean, 1968:401). This is typical of those nations among the
least economically developed where the female population is
made up of largely unpaid family labor. This contributes to a
very high dependency ratio, so that each employed male member
of the labor force has a much higher number of family members to
care for, without much assistance from other members, particularly
the women, of his family.

Hashmi, Khan, and Krotki (1964: 26) have conducted one of the
few studies of the labor force of Karachi. They were able to
demonstrate that women made up only 2.6 per cent of the labor
force. Of this group the great majority, 67.3 per cent, were
employed as servants, semiskilled and unskilled workers; 9.9 per
cent as skilled workers; 3.6 per cent in clerical and sales; 2.7 per
cent administration and management; and 16.5 per cent in the professional and technical fields. Since Karachi, as the major
industrial and commercial city of the nation, provided so little
paid employment for women workers, it appears very likely that
other cities and towns were able to provide even less. It is not
difficult to understand the high dependency ratio which prevails in
the nation, and which continues to retard its economic growth.
Since 0.5 per cent of the total labor force in Karachi is made up of
women in administrative, management, or professional fields, it is
interesting to examine the careers of recent women graduates of
the Universities of Karachi and the Punjab.

In the study referred to above (Korson, 1970), in which samples were taken of the class of 1966 (Master's degree), from the Universities of Karachi and the Punjab, it was found that women graduate students, two years later in 1968, were not fully engaged in the labor force. It is evident that the Karachi graduates are far more active in the labor force, with a total of 64.1 per cent of the sample employed at the time of the study. Of the total sample, 38 per cent were employed as teachers at various levels; 14.1 per cent held positions as research assistants; 0.7 per cent were employed in social work; and 11.3 per cent held positions in government agencies or in business organizations. This compares with 21 per cent of the Lahore women employed in teaching positions; 6 per cent in research; 3 per cent in social work; and 3 per cent in administrative or business positions.

Also included in the labor force were those who had been employed, but were unemployed at the time of the study and were seeking work. These made up 4.9 per cent of the Karachi sample and 1.0 per cent of the Lahore sample. Those who had never been employed, but were seeking employment at the time of the study made up 10.6 per cent of the Karachi sample and 31 per cent of the Lahore sample, almost three times that of their Karachi peers. Women graduates not in the labor force were made up of those who were continuing their education for advanced degrees: Karachi, 5.6 per cent, and Lahore, 10 per cent; those formerly employed, but now married and not seeking employment: Karachi, 2.1 per cent, and none in Lahore; those married, never employed, and not seeking employment: Karachi, 5.6 per cent, Lahore, none; and those who were unmarried, were never employed, and not seeking employment: Karachi, 7 per cent, and Lahore, 25 per cent.

Karachi, as the leading industrial and commercial center of the nation, has experienced far greater growth than Lahore, which probably accounts for greater employment opportunities for university graduates. The marked difference in labor force participation between the two samples can also be interpreted as reflecting the social "conservatism" of the Lahore women with the more "progressive" approach of the Karachi women. Lack of employment opportunities may, indeed, explain the very considerable differential between the employed women in Karachi and Lahore (64.1 per cent and 33 per cent, respectively), as well as those who are unemployed, but seeking employment (15.5 per cent and 32 per cent, respectively). But when those not in the labor force, who are unmarried, were never employed, and were not seeking employment, were found to be more than three times as great in Lahore as in Karachi (25 per cent compared with 7 per cent for Karachi), then the thought suggests itself that the families of the Lahore women are far more "conservative" and closer to the constraints of *purdah* than are the Karachi families and their women. It is also suggested that more Lahore families either do not encourage their daughters to seek employment or even actively discourage them from doing so (Korson, 1970:91-92). Aside from this small number of university graduates, it can be safely generalized that so long as Muslim traditions and values persist unchanged, it is difficult to imagine rapid change in labor force participation of women in Pakistan.

Basic to any long-range career goals the individual student might have would be the socialization experience, and the form this socialization takes would certainly have a strong influence on the decision-making process. Not only are adolescents fully aware of the societal norms which tend to limit their decisions, but they are also sufficiently perceptive of their family's attitudes in regard to the role that daughters are expected to play. As in all societies, the norms at any given time might be thought of as the mode, and response to the norms can be scaled in relation to the ideal that is verbalized.

Within the context of middle and upper class Pakistani society, employment outside the homes for adult women presupposes higher education or training in a specialized field. The enormous differential in educational achievement between the mothers and their daughters has been noted above and is readily apparent, and it is evident that few of the mothers have achieved sufficient education to hold the positions in the labor market their daughters do today.

In a nation only generation old, whose people made great sacrifices to achieve political and social independence based on a religious ideology, it is natural to expect that the social values would be supported and reinforced by that ideology. In traditional societies it is to be expected that the religious institution would support the traditional family values. It is not surprising, then, that the sexual segregation on which *purdah* is based would impinge on the freedom of these women to enter the labor force.

In the same study (Korson, 1970), with reference to a question concerning the attitudes of their parents toward seeking and taking employment, it was found that 11.3 per cent of the Karachi parents and 25.0 per cent of the Lahore parents either "do not want ' or "will not permit their daughter to work." Two major reasons are offered for this position: 1) some middle class families felt quite defensive about a daughter working outside the home for money. They were fearful that friends and relatives would believe the family needed the financial assistance of the daughter, and that in the long run this would damage her marriage prospects; and 2) although they were willing to have the daughter achieve higher education while she waited for the propitious time for marriage, the family was either bound by the constraints of *purdah*, or otherwise considered it improper for a female member of the family to enter the labor market. This attitude was supported by the second option the students chose, namely, that their families would only permit them to work under *purdah* conditions, such as at girls' schools or colleges. This response was chosen by 52 per cent, or more than one-half, of the Karachi students, and two-thirds, or 67 per cent, of the Lahore students. These attitudes would appear to reflect the "heavy influence of the *purdah* mentality," as some have put it. A few parents, 1.4 per cent of the Karachi sample and 2 per cent of the Lahore sample, had other objections, which were not specified.

At the "liberal" end of the scale were those parents who "do not object to any kind of work" the daughters might decide to undertake. Here it was seen that 35.2 per cent of the Karachi students but only 6 per cent of the Lahore students responded positively to this option. An examination of all the options would indicate that far more Karachi students came of liberally inclined families, and that the freedom of action in the matter of career choice was far greater than that of their Lahore peers. This evidence offers further support that the middle and upper class families in Karachi generally take a more liberal stance in regard to the behavior of their women than do their peers in Lahore (Korson, 1970:95).

Reasons offered for the variety of the families' attitudes toward the pursuit of the higher degrees for their daughters ranged from "it's a good thing for the girl to do while she waits for a marriage to be arranged by her family" to a more mundane and realistic, if not materialistic, approach, such as "will strengthen our bargaining position in arranging a marriage," "a second income is always desirable," or "it is a good thing for a girl to be able to support herself in case of failure of the marriage or widowhood." From the women who were employed came the clear signal that the egalitarianism between the sexes which is taken for granted in the West was making itself felt (Korson, 1970: 98).

Certainly the majority of women graduate students who have completed their Master's degree work at the two major universities in Pakistan can be assumed to perceive their role as young adults in a traditional Muslim society quite differently from that of their mothers. Although there are no data on the employment history of the students' mothers as young adults, the fact that their educational achievement is so low precludes a very high level of participation in the labor force. This intergenerational difference points to the mothers' generation as one of almost complete economic dependence on their families, while many of these young women are either in the labor force, or could participate in the labor force if necessary. In any case, it can be assumed that very important segments of the middle and upper class young women in Pakistan who have completed their graduate work have manifested attitudinal changes in their roles that are in sharp contrast to those of their mothers a generation ago. Certainly the économic independence of the employed graduates is something their mothers never had a chance to experience, and this will undoubtedly have its effect on their relationships with their future husbands and other members of their families. In the area of decision-making it can be safely predicted that "economic independence breeds social independence" (Korson, 1968:61).

Perhaps a modification of Lerner's typology (1958) is in order at this point. Since the mothers of the respondents in this study show a very low level of educational achievement and participate in the labor force hardly at all, they might, indeed, be termed "traditional." Those students who completed their graduate training, but whose families do not want or permit them to work, might be termed "transitionals," because they have broken out of the tradition of *purdah* to the extent that they have sought higher education and training and have maximized or at least taken advantage of the opportunity to satisfy their intellectual curiosity. (It is also claimed that a highly educated girl can hope to make a better marriage, and, therefore, it is felt to be a "good investment.") Those students who have sought and found employment in the labor market have also established a degree of economic independence which their unemployed peers lack. These girls might indeed be classed as "moderns"—willing, with the moral support of their families, to challenge the traditional norms of their society.

In a developing nation where the social norms limit the participation of women in its labor force, the question arises whether it is economically sound for the government to subsidize the higher education of women when the norms largely deny them the opportunity to put their knowledge and abilities to use in helping advance the economic and social development of their nation. Much has been said in recent years about the "brain drain," the migration of highly trained personnel from the less developed nations to the more prosperous nations of the world. This has represented a serious loss of any important human resource to the poorer nations. Since all the universities in Pakistan are government supported, little has been said about the economic loss to the nation of those who do not enter the labor force, largely because of social constraints. Here, indeed, is an excellent example of cultural lag, but at a considerable price to the nation.

Even though all the universities are government supported, no effort has been made to limit the admission of women to those who will promise to enter the labor force after completion of their degree work. In 1969 the government of Pakistan proposed a National Literacy Corps, similar to the one in Iran, in which college and university graduates would be asked to serve in both rural and urban areas as a form of national service, but the plan was never implemented. On 15 March 1972, President Bhutto announced a new Education Reform Policy which included a National Service Corps in "which all youths between the ages of 17 and 23 will be encouraged to serve for a total period of one year after passing the intermediate examination" (twelfth grade) (*Morning News*, 1972·6). Although details of the plan have not yet been announced, it is assumed that this group would constitute the base for the formation of an adult literacy corps, and that suitable incentives would be offered to induce and encourage young people to participate in it. "From a development point of view, the purpose of education must be to rationalize attitudes as well as to impart knowledge and skills" (Myrdal, 1968:1621).

Unquestionably, those respondents who have entered the labor force have not only made a sharp break with the norms of the previous generation, but the syndrome of the attitudes inherent in their new status will inevitably affect the social processes of their interpersonal relations with their parents' generation and with the males of their own generation. Islamic ideology calls for all Muslims to marry, and the norm in Pakistan calls for all marriages to be arranged by the families of the principals. Two years after these women had received their degrees, only 12.4 per cent had married (Korson, 1970:85). Young women who have achieved higher education and a degree of economic independence that usually results from their participation in the labor force are hardly likely to emulate the behavior patterns of their mothers in decision-making. The latter have had relatively little formal education and almost no opportunity to achieve a degree of economic (and social) independence that their employed daughters have. It is suggested that the greater their degree of participation in the labor force as wage earners, the greater the degree of economic and social independence the women graduates will achieve. The drift towards egalitarianism between the sexes, so widespread in the West, will be slow, but it is difficult to see how the process, now well under way, will be reversed.

AGENTS FOR CHANGE

Government

The founding of a new nation gave the early government leaders of Pakistan an unexcelled opportunity to institute a number of desirable changes in the social life of its people. But when one uses the term "desirable," one is immediately confronted with the possible accusation of introducing personal bias as reflected by one's value system.

In the early years of the nation (and since), many conservative religious and political leaders espoused a return to the "true" Islamic values by the institution of religious norms reinforced by a legal code. These leaders felt that some of the cultural intrusions from the West during the period of colonial rule should be excised, and the nation put on the road to a "true" Islamic state. Other leaders felt that desirable changes should be made that would enhance the welfare of the great majority of people; and that laws should be passed to correct many of the ills of the society and, most especially, to improve the welfare and status of women and children, a position much more in tune with the social welfare legislation of Western nations.

That the latter group won out is attested by the establishment of the National Commission for the Eradication of Social Evils in 1958, which conducted surveys for several years and studied some of the more serious social problems that confronted the young nation. There were a series of delays with which the commission had to contend, and the final report was not ready for acceptance by its members until May 1963. The commission collected a great deal of material relating to social problems and made a number of recommendations in its report (1965). Although many pronouncements were made in the press, to the writer's knowledge no particular piece of legislation resulted from the work of the commission.

Even before the commission had completed its work, however, *The Muslim Family Laws Ordinance*, with *Child Marriage Restraint Act*, and *Dissolution of Muslim Marriage Act*, was enacted in 1961, and became effective in August of that year. In essence, this act elucidated and codified some of the principles of Muslim family law. It did not introduce many innovations, but helped bring a degree of uniformity and statutory force to the variations of family law that had been practiced over the years. Its intent was to help "ameliorate the conditions in which women have to live in this country, and would give them protection against the tyranny of the male" (Mahmood, 1964:111).

Among the most important changes were the following:

1) It raised the minimum age at marriage from fifteen to sixteen for women and from seventeen to eighteen for men. Proof of age was required.

2) All marriages were to include a marriage contract (*nikahnama*), an outline of which was provided for those who wished it. The contract was registered with the Local Union Council where the bride resided.

3) Polygyny, although still permitted, was more strictly regulated.

4) Divorce was more strictly regulated, and women were given for the first time the right to sue for divorce.

5) The rights of inheritence under Muslim law were made uniform.

6) Legal redress for the maintenance of the wife was provided.

The All Pakistan Women's Association

This organization was started soon after partition by Begum Liaqat Ali Khan, and was first known as the Pakistan Women's Voluntary Service. Its personnel is made up largely of volunteers and is drawn almost exclusively from the middle and upper classes —wives of civil servants, military officers, businessmen, and professionals. It is the counterpart of so many similar women's organizations found in Western nations. It claims not to be a political organization, but is said to have considerable indirect political influence, if for no other reason that many of the women are close to the sources of power in many government agencies. Furthermore, the Begum was a close personal friend of President Ayub Khan, and during his ten year tenure in office she did not hesitate to bring APWA's demands to his attention, and he, in turn, did not hesitate to meet those demands whenever possible (Chipp, 1971: 20). Moreover, the women's activities keep them in the public eye, and they receive a good press. Their membership is estimated to be about 20,000.

According to All Pakistan Women's Association's (APWA) constitution, the basic goals it aims to achieve are:

(a) The informed and intelligent participation of the women of Pakistan in the growth and development of their country; (b) the advancement and welfare of the women of Pakistan through the improvement of their legal, political, social and economic status and rights; (c) the promotion of social, educational and cultural programs and policies in all areas of the country, by affording opportunities of knowledge and learning for women and children of Pakistan; (d) the health and well-being of the people of Pakistan in the home and in the community, including the eradication of disease and prevention of physical and bodily suffering; and (e) the promotion of international good will and the brotherhood of mankind" (**Chipp, 1971:18**).

Their activities are, indeed, in the area of social reform and, as might be expected, they are sometimes referred to as "do-gooders," a term well known in the West. But a supporter of their efforts would counter with the observation that there is great need for such organizations, and their efforts are well recognized.

APWA has been active in pressing for social reform legislation, and a most notable success was the passage of the Muslim Family Laws Act of 1961. For example, APWA never attacked the institution of polygyny directly, only its abuses, pointing out that "civilized" societies considered the practice of plural wives demeaning to the female sex, and pressed for greater protection and consideration of the first wife's rights in any contemplated additional marriage. According to the 1961 census, only 0.8 per cent of the married men in Karachi have more than one wife, and no case of four wives was reported. Other social reform measures have been supported by APWA, some passed, others not; but no one with serious political ambitions would discount their support. APWA receives grants-in-aid from the both the central and provincial governments, as well as from international bodies, such as UNICEF, C.A.R.E., and the Red Cross.

It is clear, however, that the All Pakistan Women's Association has been in the forefront in seeking and achieving legislative changes in an effort to enhance the status of women in the nation. For example, APWA was solely responsible for the inclusion of three articles in the *Interim Constitution* (pp. 7, 9) which was adopted by the national assembly in May 1972. These articles read:

22-(1) All citizens are equal before law and are entitled to equal protection of law.

(2) There shall be no discrimination on the basis of sex alone.

(3) Nothing in this Article shall prevent the State from enacting any special provision for protection of women.

24-(1) No citizen otherwise qualified for appointment in the service of Pakistan shall be discriminated against in respect of any such appointment on the ground only of race, religion, caste, sex, residence or place of birth.

32- Special steps shall be taken to ensure full participation of women in all spheres of national life.

Leaders of APWA are especially pleased with their achievement in having these articles included in the constitution, which came as a direct result of an intensive lobbying effort in Islamabad by the officers of the organization. It is obvious that President Bhutto is sincere in his efforts to bring qualified women into the forefront of national life. For example, in October 1972, he appointed a woman to be the vice-chancellor of Islamabad University, clearly a "first" for this nation.

In the area of social welfare, APWA has sponsored native crafts and cottage industries and provides retail outlets for these products in the major cities. A listing of their activities and sub-organizations would be a long one, but they have concentrated heavily in the area of education for girls, not only literacy classes for the young, but programs for adult women to achieve "functional literarcy." APWA has been very supportive of family planning and sponsors medical clinics, but they are careful to work within the framework of a conservative Islamic social system. They have not, for example, seriously challenged the institution of *purdah*, although their leaders recognize that it presents a serious barrier to rapid improvement of the status of women in Pakistan.

Family Formation

In the area of family formation, it can be hypothesized that whenever kin groups can maintain control over the marriage choices of their members, traditional societies and communities can better maintain and defend their value system against change. As control over marriage choices weakens, the traditional value systems of kin groups weaken, and the latter begins to accept (or perhaps submit to) change.

Perhaps in few other societies is entrance into marriage so carefully controlled as it is in a traditional Muslim society. The norm is for all Muslims to marry, and in Pakistan a marriage is normally arranged by the families of the principals, frequently without a prior meeting of the two principals. The major reasons for entering a marriage are not necessarily companionship, romantic love, and the achievement of "instant" individual happiness, but, rather, "fertility, permanence, and the alliance of two family groups" (Shah, 1960:156). It is incumbent upon all parents to arrange a marriage for each child, and since life expectancy in the subcontinent is not high, it has not been unusual for parents to arrange an early betrothal, frequently before the age of puberty. The marriage, of course, will not be consummated until after puberty, but the parents will have fulfilled their obligation.

Since sexual segregation of women from men who are not their relatives after the age of puberty is the norm, there are literally few opportunities for potential marriage partners to meet, and the exploratory relationship known as dating, which is so common in the West, is largely unknown. Since a very small percentage of adult women participate in the labor force, few females are able to meet men to whom they are not related. Even working women are not employed in situations where they will be in contact with males. As a single cohort of females who do have some freedom to mingle with males on a daily basis, university coeds appear to make up an important group, small as they are in relation to the total population. Even if a young couple should become sufficiently interested in pursuing the possibility of a closer relationship, they would need the support of relatives and friends to intercede with their parents. Since the vast majority of students come from middle and upper class families, the problem of social distance between the two families will probably not be too great.

From a study based on two samples of students taken at the Universities of Karachi and Lahore (Korson, 1969:156), it was found that more than half (52.6 per cent) approved of the current system of arranged marriages, but would like a little more freedom to make a final choice or would like to be consulted by their parents so that they could make their feelings known. Another 18.8 per cent felt the present system (of not consulting the principals) should continue unchanged, while 20.9 per cent stated that the parents should be consulted, but the final choice should be left to the principals. A small percentage (5.6) opted for final veto power, with 2.6 per cent not answering. Male students showed a somewhat greater desire for making choices independent of their families than did the women. In fact, the law requires that the principals agree to a marriage before the contract is signed. It is the rare individual who would oppose the selection of a mate by his family, since this would constitute a threat to the established authority of the family head and set an undesirable precedent. Among other things, the young rebel would then be confronted with the prospect of losing the benefits of membership in his *biraderi*.

Although the students have been socialized in a traditional society and are fully aware of the norms in the choice of marriage partners, when asked to what extent their family would arrange their marriage, 41.7 per cent agreed that their parents would arrange it, but, that they would have some voice in agreeing to the choice. A significant percentage (17.8) felt that they would take the initiative in suggesting who the mate would be. Twenty-three per cent stated they would "consider the whole matter, but in the end make his (or her) choice." Thirteen per cent claimed their parents would arrange their marriage without consulting the principals, and 4.3 per cent offered no answer.

With the limitation of sexual segregation among adolescents and adults enforced by the practice of *purdah*, it is only natural that the young men and women are likely to develop close attachments to those relatives they are permitted to see over a period of time, namely, cousins. Endogamous marriage has been a common practice in Muslim societies for centuries, and even though there have been significant changes in Pakistani society, cousin marriage continues to be practiced, although to a reduced extent. In the same two samples of students, it was found that 24.8 per cent of their parents were first or second cousins before marriage, and 16.4 per cent more distantly related, while of the students' siblings who had married, 12.2 per cent had married first or second cousins, and another 11.0 per cent had married more distant relatives. In other words, the rate of cousin marriage had dropped roughly 50 per cent in one generation. Perhaps the most important reason for the decline was the disruption caused by the migration of great numbers of Muslims from India, following partition. This had the net effect of lossening or breaking family and community ties that had endured for many generations (Korson, 1971). The same samples revealed that when the time came for the students to marry, 9 per cent felt that their parents would select a spouse who was completely unknown to them, and 12.7 per cent stated that their parents would select a relative for a spouse. It is even possible that such a choice had already been made. The more traditionally inclined among the students (19.7 per cent) were uncertain what would happen, but would leave it to their parents to make the decision.

From the above discussion it would appear that a sense of freedom and independence in decision-making among students is becoming evident, even though there may not be many direct confrontations at the family level. A couple that might decide to throw all caution to the winds and marry against the wishes of the two families might well find themselves very lonely people, cut off from the psychological support they have had all their lives and had come to expect.

When a male student plans to go abroad for further study, his family might well arrange a marriage for him as a form of insurance that he will not stray too far from the cultural fold. More than one Pakistani student has returned home on short notice for an arranged marriage when word reached his family that he was growing very interested in a foreign girl. Proxy marriages for students who have gone abroad to study are also arranged, although that presents an added difficulty in the legal admission of the wife to the United States or other foreign country.

An important part of every marriage contract in Pakistan is the sum of *mehr*, or dower, pledged by the bridegroom to the bride. It is not only a tradition, but is required by law, and can be enforced by law. *Mehr* is a bridal gift, and remains with the bride and cannot be revoked by the husband. The wife, however, is free to renounce (but not under duress) any further claim to the *mehr* after marriage, should she find herself in a difficult marital situation, and use the renunciation of the *mehr* as an incentive to gain her freedom from her husband. *Mehr* can be paid under a variety of arrangements agreed to by the two families when the *nikahnama*, or marriage contract, is signed at the time of marriage: on a deferred basis, on demand, or a combination of all three. The sum agreed to is entered in the contract, which is then registered with the union council where the bride resides and becomes a legal document. The threat by the wife to enforce her demand has caused more than one husband to reconsider his behavior seriously. The "on demand" arrangement has the added function of social control when other efforts have failed. *Jahez*, or dowry, is made up of gifts to the bride from relatives and friends, and varies with the economic status of the family (Korson, 1968).

Mehr is a highly institutionalized part of Muslim marriages, and it is thought of as a form of insurance for the bride in case of separation or divorce. In a society with a very high dependency ratio, *mehr* serves a very useful function. Relatively few women are capable of supporting themselves, and a separation of divorce usually means a return to the household of a woman's parents, brother, or other male relative. The sums usually vary with the socio-economic status of the families, as a study based on 1961-64 data showed. The median amounts pledged by members of the upper, middle, and lower classes in Karachi was Rs 8,000, Rs 5,430, and Rs 1,200. Although no specific amount is required by law, a minimum amount of Rs 32, which is known as *Rasooli Mehr*, or "the Prophet's *Mehr*," was registered by approximately 8 per cent of all the registrants of all the socio-economic classes. *Rasooli Mehr* is considered a symbolic gesture to the whole practice, and an indication by the families that they have great faith in the future of the marriage arrangement. For some middle and upper class families, the subscription of large sums "smacks of the marketplace." There is no question that the great majority of families do take the matter of *mehr* seriously, because it forms an integral and important part in the negotiations that lead to a marriage arrangement (Korson, 1967).

All parents are ambitious for their children, and it is natural that they will seek the best possible match for each child. But each child is also keenly aware of the economic status of the family, and is likely to understand the outer limits of possible financial agreements in entering upon a marriage arrangement. Since students are still at the level of economic dependence on their parents, they are also sensitive to continuing or extending that burden beyond their formal education.

The response of students not only to the tradition of *mehr* but also to the current practices of *mehr* and *jahez* of the middle and upper classes is of interest, and must please their parents if the latter were informed of their children's attitudes. In the same samples referred to above, when the students were asked about the significance of dower and dowry in the event of their marriage sometime in the future only 17.3 per cent felt that these elements were "important" or "very important." Another 12.3 per cent believed that these were "somewhat important," but two-thirds, or 67.3 per cent, stated that these were "not very important" or "very unimportant." Another 3.1 per cent did not answer. When the students were asked to evaluate the whole system of dower and dowry, 40.2 per cent felt that it should be abandoned because "it is too great a burden on the families," another 21.6 per cent said that the whole system should be discontinued because the young couple should seek economic independence and not feel under obligation to their parents. At the more conservative end of the scale, 20.5 per cent felt that the system is satisfactory and should be continued on its present basis, 9.7 per cent believed that the dower should be increased to protect women against separation and divorce, while 8.0 per cent offered other responses or did not answer (Korson, 1968:700).

While the commitment of *mehr* is a legal one, and might well affect the future welfare of the wife for years to come, *jahez* is not a legal commitment. Nonetheless, since most arranged marriages are homogamous in socio-economic terms, the gifts the bride receives are usually commensurate with the status of her family. Since the matter of family prestige is invoked (as it is in the case of *mehr*), families will frequently overextend their resources and go into debt in order to "put on a good show." A socially ambitious father may demand (and achieve) a *mehr* of Rs 100,000 for the eldest of several attractive daughters, and from that time his remaining daughters, would have to carry with them the invisible price tag of Rs 100,000. The young are fully aware of the negotiations, but are usually helpless to do much about them. The parents feel that the long-range objective is, indeed, for the welfare of the daughter.

When students at the Universities of the Punjab and Karachi were asked, "What do you believe the appropriate amount of *mehr* should be," 48.8 per cent of the total sample responded in favor of *Rasooli Mehr* (the minimum amount), with the men out-voting the women by a three to two margin. Another 28 per cent of the total sample felt that the sum should be "according to the means of his [the bridegroom's] family," with the women out-voting the men by a two to one margin. The rest of the sample opted for varying amounts that should be pledged, with no significant figure chosen as the ideal. In other words, 76.8 per cent of the students did not place great store in the amount of *mehr* to be committed (Korson, 1968:702). This should come as welcome news to their parents.

One of the most important variables considered by demographers and family sociologists who concern themselves with social change in the institution of the family is age at first marriage. This variable brings into focus a whole host of consequences, not all of which can be dealt with at length in this paper. The fact that the Muslim Family Law of 1961 did, indeed, raise the minimum age in a nation on the subcontinent which in the past has been noted for early marriage is one of the most significant social changes that have occurred in Pakistan since independence. Each nation has its own pride, and for a nation to take legal measures which would place it on par with Western nations in protecting the welfare of its young is a worthy accomplishment.

Even before the 1961 law was enacted, the average age at first marriage in Karachi had been rising: in 1931, 1951, and 1961 it was 21.6, 24.8, and 25.5 years for males, and 15.5, 16.9, and 18.2 for females. The new law undoubtedly had some effect on the last figures, since it went into effect in August of that year. A hypothesis proposed in a recent study completed in Karachi (Korson, 1965) was that the lower the income group, the lower the age at first marriage. This hypothesis was validated when it was demonstrated in that city that the median age at first marriage for women from low, middle, and high income families was 17.3, 18.4, and 19.9 years. The median age at first marriage for men from low, middle, and high income families was found to be 25.3, 25.4, and 26.8 years (Korson, 1965:590, 593). It has also been well established that the higher the level of education achieved, the higher will be the age at first marriage. In 1968 it was found that two years after the women at the Universities of Karachi and Lahore had completed their graduate work (and at that time had an average age of twenty-four years), only 12 per cent had married. One of the net effects of higher education, then, has been to delay marriage for both males and females. (The age differential of approximately seven years between the sexes has long been the norm on the subcontinent.)

FAMILY PLANNING

Although family planning is, indeed, one of the consequences of modernization, the limitation or nonlimitation of family size has been of concern to all socities. Although there has been some opposition from conservative religious leaders, the government has always looked favorably on such programs, and has welcomed aid from a variety of foreign sources. President Ayub Khan specifically encouraged such programs, and there has never been anything but encouragement from government leaders.

While the death rate, with the aid of public health programs, has declined over the years, the birth rate had declined hardly at all until some of the programs came into operation. Before these programs were introduced, the annual rate of increase was about 3 per cent. Today it is estimated to be about 2.5 per cent, and it is hoped that it can be reduced to 2 per cent in the 1980s. The programs have had a moderate rate of success in Pakistan, but the work is continuing. Although Pakistan's economic development since the nation's inception has demonstrated relatively high levels of annual growth, as in most underdeveloped nations, many, if not all, of such gains have been negated by continued high fertility rates.

DIVORCE

No extensive study of divorce has ever been conducted in Pakistan, but from census data as well as a limited (and still incomplete) study by the writer, it is clear that Pakistan has one of the lowest divorce rates in the world. For example, in a sample survey conducted in 1959 in Karachi, Hashmi (1965:71) found that only 0.1 per cent of the population was classified as divorced. In a society where both by religious tradition and civil law it has been relatively easy for a husband to obtain a divorce (but less so for a wife), it is surprising to Westerners that the rate is so low. The opportunity for polygynous marriages (up to four wives at the same time) in a traditional Muslim society may be offered as a reason for alternate arrangements, but this explanation is faulty because only 0.8 per cent of all married men in Karachi have more than one wife, only one has three, and none has four (Hashmi, 1965:65). Recently enacted laws have made it more difficult for husbands to obtain a divorce and easier for a wife to obtain one. Whether this slight movement in the direction of egalitarianism is indicative of things to come remains to be seen. As one compares the more "modern" nations of the world, it would appear that the greater the degree of egalitarianism between the sexes in a society, the higher the divorce rate.

CONCLUSIONS AND OBSERVATIONS

Modernization is more than industrialization, it is a conscious effort to introduce changes in all the institutions of a society. And modernization of a traditional society presupposes the rational uses of *all* resources, including human ones. This would indicate that the longer *purdah* continues to dominate and guide the thinking of the majority of the population, the slower will be the full utilization of women (and especially trained women) in the labor force.

Although all societies have a well-recognized division of labor between the sexes, it might be generalized that the more traditional a society, the more rigidly defined will be the division of labor, and, conversely, the more "modern" a society, the greater the degree of egalitarianism between the sexes, and the less rigid will be the division of labor. Marx is said to have stated categorically that "the progress of a nation can be measured precisely by the status of women in a society." One would have to take into consideration the relative status of its men, hence, equality between the sexes must have been what Marx had in mind. In other words, as the status of women rises to match that of the men in a society, Marx would judge that change to be a progressive one.

As long as the norms of *purdah* are maintained in Pakistan, and as long as major decision-making remains largely the prerogative of the family head, the longer will preference for cousin marriage continue. This will have the net effect of retarding any significant change in the structure of the Muslim family in Pakistan.

The more patriarchal a society, the more rigid are the premarital (and postmarital) sex codes. From the women's point of view, only when her status and position are highly dependent on the male will she have reason for supporting and maintaining such a code. In such a society it can be said that the female's most valuable good in exchange is her sexual activity and, if it is to remain valuable, it must be carefully guarded and preserved. This can be interpreted by some to equate with family honor and prestige. In contrast, when her status and ultimate position do not depend greatly on her father or husband, she need not be so cautious, and she can be less concerned with her "reputation," and her family's "honor." As more women enter the labor force of a society, the more they become economically independent, and, as their economic independence increases, their social independence rises commensurately. In a traditional patriarchal society such as Pakistan, where the earnings of all the family members normally go into the family exchequer, which the family head usually controls, there may be a lag of a generation or two before unmarried girls begin to assert themselves (at least in urban areas). For example, it is almost unthinkable for an employed unmarried woman, even a professional, to live alone or apart from her family as would her counterpart in the West.

Since formal education often accompanies the initiation of modernization and social change, members of the middle and upper classes inevitably have the first opportunities to profit from such an innovation in a society. Universal literacy almost always appears high on the list of the leaders of a developing nation, and the desire for educational and occupational achievement beyond that level soon filters down from the upper and middle classes to the low income groups. Not only these desires, but other aspects of modern life filter down to members of lower class families. With the aid of organized educational systems, a degree of egalitarianism begins to develop among the social classes, as well as between the sexes. Although the "filter down" theory has been used in other contexts, it seems that its use here is quite appropriate.

The more highly developed nations provide a wider occupational choice for the young members who are about to enter the labor force, while the less developed nations offer fewer choices, and for women this means fewer alternatives to marriage. This situation has the net effect of enforcing an occupational rigidity on an inter-generational basis and generally retarding rapid economic growth—and social change. The modernizing nations have the opportunity to choose from a variety of experiences of the more advanced nations, and to borrow or not in the economic and political spheres, as they see fit. But the social institutions of religion and the family are usually considered inviolate, and resistance to significant change becomes readily apparent even when cultural intrusions threaten the *status quo.*

Social change is more apt to come from the younger members of a society, especially those who have been exposed to the rational and scientific training of the natural and social sciences. The humanities, of course, make their own contribution. Students exposed to the intellectual ferment of a university campus, and frequently living away from home and the socializing influence and social control of their families, are apt to feel less bound to support the traditional norms that their parents find meaningful, and therefore might be more receptive to new ideas, influences, and norms of behavior, as well as to new philosophies.

As Gusfield has observed, any consideration of "tradition" and "modernity" as polar opposites in a unilinear theory of social change overlooks the fact that traditional societies have never been "static, normatively consistent, or structurally homogeneous, nor do the relations between the traditional and the modern... necessarily weaken tradition. Both tradition and modernity form bases of ideologies and movements in which the polar opposites are converted in aspirations, but traditional forms may supply support for, as well as against, change" (1967: 351).

Just as there is little basis for the assumption that traditional societies have been static in the past, it is equally invalid to assume that innovators have been, or are always, apt to be in conflict with the "traditionalists." At any given time, individuals are confronted with a wide variety of choices in decision-making, not all of which might bring approbation to the innovator from the traditionalists.

Both tradition and modernity must, at any given time, be considered in a state of flux, subject to the influences and pressures of the innovators, on the one hand, and the resistance to change from those who might feel the need to defend a vested interest or the *status quo*, on the other. "Those members of the younger generation who seek change, for whatever reasons, are not necessarily impelled in that direction because of the lack of vested interest but may, indeed, seek change within the total context of the situation— not in opposition to the system but rather in support of it, although in a modified manner" (Korson, 1968: 706). The question can be fairly asked, if modernization comes to a traditional society, can egalitarianism between the sexes be far behind?

REFERENCES

Bean, Lee L.
1968 "Utilization of Human Resources: The Case of Women in Pakistan." *International Labour Review*, 97 (4 April).

Bertocci, Peter J.
1971 "Social Stratification in Rural East Pakistan." Unpublished paper.

Blitsten, Dorothy
1963 *The World of the Family*. New York.

Chip, Sylvia A.
1971 "Tradition vs. Change: The Status of the Muslim Woman in Pakistan." *Wells College Alumnae News-Express*, IV, 3. Aurora, New York.

Eglar, Zekiye
1960 *A Punjabi Village in Pakistan*. New York.

Ghani, Anna
1963 "Combining Career and Marriage" in Barbara Ward, *Women in the New Asia*. Paris.

Goode, William J.
1963 *World Revolution and Family Patterns*. New York.

Gusfield, Joseph
1967 "Tradition and Modernity: Misplaced Polarities in the Study of Social Change." *American Journal of Sociology*, 72 (4 January). Pp. 351-362.

Hashmi, Sultan S.
1965 *The People of Karachi: Demographic Characteristics*. Monograph 13. Karachi: Pakistan Institute of Development Economics.

Hashmi, Sultan, Masihur R. Khan, and Karol J. Krotki
1964 "The People of Karachi, Data from a Survey." Statistical Paper No. 2. Karachi: Pakistan Institute of Development Economics.

Huq, Muhammad S.
1965 *Education and Development Strategy in South and Southwest Asia*. Honolulu: University of Hawaii.

Jacobson, Dorothy A.
1970 "Hidden Faces: Hindu and Muslim Purdah in a Central Indian Village." Unpublished Doctoral dissertation. Columbia University.

Korson, J. Henry
1965 "Age and Social Status at Marriage: Karachi, 1961-64." *Pakistan Development Review*, 5, 4 (Winter). Pp. 586-600.

1967 "Dower and Social Class in an Urban Muslim Community." *Journal of Marriage and the Family*, 29 (August). Pp. 527-533.

1968 "The Roles of Dower and Dowry as Indicators of Social Change."
      Journal of Marriage and the Family, 30 (November). Pp. 696-707.
1969 "Student Attitudes Toward Mate Selection in a Muslim Society:
      Pakistan." *Journal of Marriage and Family*, 31 (February).
      Pp. 154-165.
1970 "Career Constraints Among Women Graduate Students in a
      Developing Society." *Journal of Comparative Family Studies.*
      Pp. 82-100.
1971 "Endogamous Marriage in a Traditional Muslim Society." *Journal
      of Comparative Family Studies*, 2 (Autumn). Pp. 145-155.

Lerner, Daniel
1958 *The Passing of Traditional Society.* Glencoe, Ill.: The Free Press.

Levy, Marion, Jr.
1966 *Modernization and the Structure of Societies.* Princeton: Princeton
      University Press.

Litwack, Eugene
1960 "Occupational Mobility and Extended Family Cohesion." *American
      Sociology Review*, 25. Pp. 9-21.

Mahmood, Shaukat
1964 *Muslim Family Laws Ordinance, 1961, With Child Marriage
      Restraint Act and Dissolution of Muslim Marriages Act.* Lahore.

Morning News
1972 Karachi. 16 March.

Myrdal, Gunnar
1968 *Asian Drama*, Volume III. New York.

Government of Pakistan
1965 *Report of the Commission for the Eradication of Social Evils*,
      Karachi: Manager of Publications. P. 102.
1972 *The Interim Constitution of the Islamic Republic of Pakistan.*
      Karachi.

Papanek, Hanna
1964 "The Woman Field Worker in a Purdah Society." *Human
      Organization*, 23 (Summer).
1971 "Purdah in Pakistan: Seclusion and Modern Occupations for
      Women." *Journal of Marriage and the Family*, 33 (August).
      Pp. 517-530.

Shah, Khalida
1960 "Attitudes of Pakistani Students Toward Family Life." *Marriage
      and Family Living*, 22 (May). Pp. 156-161.

Singer, Milton
1970 "The Modernization of Religious Beliefs" in Myron Weiner (ed.),
      Modernization, The Dynamics of Growth. New York.

Wakil, Parvez A.

1970 "Explorations into the Kin-Networks of the Punjabi Society: A Preliminary Statement." *Journal of Marriage and the Family*, 32. Pp. 700-707.

Wilbur, onald L.

1964 *Some Aspects of Contemporary Pakistani Society*. New Haven: Yale University Press.

Wilcox, Wayne

1963 *Pakistan: The Consolidation of a Nation*. New York.

CHAPTER VI

Marriage and the Family in Iran

Jacquiline Rudolph—Touba

Introduction

Iran, located at the crossroads between the East and West and bounded by five nations—the USSR, Turkey, Iraq, Pakistan, and Afghanistan—as well as two bodies of water, the Persian Gulf and the Caspian Sea, is generally an arid area due to insufficient rainfall. The main source of water is mountain streams and rivers. For centuries, an intricate system of *qanats* or underground irrigation ditches has carried this precious source of life from the mountain to the valleys which encircle the two great deserts of central and eastern Iran, thus contributing to the population settlement pattern which, in the west, takes the form of a crescent.

Population concentrations are, for the most part, found in these areas lying between the mountains and the deserts or between the mountains and either the sea or national boundaries.

The population of Iran can be divided into three major groups: the urban population (39 per cent of the 1966 settled population, 25, 078, 923), the rural population (61 per cent of the 1966 settled population), and the tribal population. This last group was referred to as unsettled in the 1966 census and was estimated to include 244, 141 persons (Iranian Statistical Center, 1968: Tables 1 and A). However, reference to this group as unsettled is often a misnomer and local anthropologists prefer the term "tribal population." This group is estimated to consist of 4,500,000 persons, of whom about 2,000,000 make a seasonal migration (Afshar-Naderi, 1971:10).

Since the study of the tribal family is a separate field within itself, there will be no attempt to include it in the present chapter. All references made to marriage and the family in Iran are, therefore, restricted to the urban and rural populations. In addition, generalizations pertain to the Muslim family, since in the 1966 census, 99 per cent of the population was reported to be followers of Islam. It should be noted that the form practiced in Iran is Shiism. This sets Iran apart from the rest of the Muslim world, which adheres to Sunni Islam.

The 1960s marked a period of political stabilization, thus allowing for concentrated endeavors to accelerate economic growth and social development. These efforts are reflected in the third and fourth five-year development plans of Iran.

At the same time, value changes resulted in the formulation of new laws which put agricultural lands into the hands of the rural population and forced private investment into areas other than land. Private industry sprang up in the capital and large cities of Iran, thus attracting the agricultural population, as well as urban dwellers from smaller cities to the larger urban areas. Mass education and improved health conditions became important and institutions were created using military conscripts to insure realization of the programs.

Thus, the 1960s marked a transition period which had repercussions on marriage patterns and the family, as will be observed in the following pages. The first section of this chapter will include an introduction of types of mate selection, marriage patterns. and norms related to these activities. In the second part. the family system, its structure and processes, as well as recent changes in the family, will be discussed. The role of family planning in Iran will also be noted. Finally, a look will be taken at the disintegration of the family as a result of divorce and widowhood.

The material presented in this chapter is based on the most recent research findings available in Iran, dating in most cases from the mid-sixties. Some of the discussion is based on the author's own knowledge and interpretations of available data. Future research will no doubt shed new light on Iranian marriage and family patterns, thus making some of the material presented here relevent only to the body of literature available at the present time.

MATE SELECTION

Types of Mate Selection

In Iran, there are a number of ways in which the bride for a prospective bridegroom can be found. More often than not, a spouse is sought within the extended family network. There is a proverb which says that the hands of first cousins are united in marriage in heaven (Behnam, 1968:100). Aside from traditional attitudes, marriage is often a mechanism through which families maintain and expand their power, as well as solve interfamilial conflicts (Behnam, 1968:100). Endogamy is also motivated by a desire to keep property within the family (Khazaneh, 1968:121). In the past, endogamy was further encouraged in many areas of the country because of the obstacles imposed by geographic isolation, as well as the concentration of families in certain areas of the city.

Although first cousin marriage on either the mother's or the father's side of the family is desirable, mate selection from the father's side is preferred. Research has demonstrated that endogamy, especially among first cousins, is still prevalent, even in large cities such as Tehran (Khazaneh, 1968:122). When someone eligible is available within the kinship group, the parents of the prospective couple already know each other, and thus, the arrangements can easily be made. When no one suitable is available, parents are found by means of *khastegari* (an arranged proposal of marriage), which involves different methods. In the past, there were women called *mashateh*, who would go to homes where an eligible young girl was known to be relising. The *mashateh* would look the girl over and report her physical features and information concerning the family to the prospective groom or his parents. The *mashateh* would continue to act as a go-between in the preliminary stages of the discussion.

Although the *mashateh* performed this important role in the society, it was secondary to her primary function of hairdresser. In the past, hairdressers went from house to house performing their service and so were able to seek out attractive and well-to-do brides.

At the present time, recourse is not being taken to the *mashateh*. This institution has been replaced by a system in which the mate is sought with the help of the family or friends. However, the investigating and reporting aspects still take place by a family member or friend. He may even go to the person's (usually the groom's) place of employment to inquire about him and his family. When a girl is located and investigations are completed, the parents of the boy go to discuss the possibilities of marriage with the parents of the girl.

At the most traditional end of the continuum, neither the girl nor the boy in question is consulted, all arrangements being made by the parents. If the family is somewhat less traditional, the boy may accompany his parents to the home of the girl. If the parents of the girl are less traditional, she may be given the opportunity to reject the proposal. If the parents are still less traditional, they may give the couple the opportunity to see each other before the final decision is made.

At the modern end of the continuum, the mate is not sought through *khastegari*. This means that a spouse is sought through the assistance of the parents or friends. This form of mate selection has only recently evolved in Iran and is mainly found in the large cities and among better educated families. It might be said that the basis for this form of mate seletion is "romantic love." However, since a couple rarely decides to marry without parental consent, the socio-economic and religious status of the family is usually considered by both parties and their parents before final decisions are made. If the parents have been educated in a Western society or are very progressive in their thinking, they may accept the selection of their children.

The extent to which this modern type of mate selection occurs is not known for the total country. However, one study of 750 students at the University of Tehran seemed to indicate a preference for self-selection with the final consent of the parents being considered important (Touba, 1966). Another study of 834 female secondary school students in Tehran indicated that 93 per cent wanted to have a voice in the selection of their mate, and of these, 27.3 per cent preferred self-selection, while the remainder felt selection should be made with parental consultation (Ziadlou, 1967).

Norms Related to Mate Selection

If a male is selected through *khastegari*, a number of problems must be solved before the parents of the prospective bride, or the girl herself, decide to accept the marriage offer.

In some parts of the country, *shirbaha* must be paid to the bride's parents. This might be compared to the bride price found in other parts of the world. Although, literally, this means payment for that milk which the girl has taken from her mother, it, in fact, means compensation for the expenses the parents have suffered in raising the girl and preparing her for marriage. It is also considered a counterbalance to the dowry which the girl's parents must provide. *Shirbaha* has never been more than a custom, therefore, it was never formalized into a law. Today it seldom occurs, and when it is found, it is usually in rural areas.

The provision of a dowry is a custom which is still quite prevalent in Iran. It is a specific requirement to be negotiated if the mate is selected through *khastegari*. Although the material goods given by the parents of the girl remain her property, the fact that they are supplied by the parents of the bride reduces the male's immediate economic expenses.

The final point to be negotiated before any decisions about the marriage are concluded is the amount of the *mahriyeh*, which is usually written in the marriage contract.

As opposed to the *shirbaha*, the *mahriyeh* is given to the bride and, therefore, cannot be equated with bride price. Originally, in Shiism (that form of Islam practiced in Iran), the *mahriyeh* could be in the form of transferable goods, furniture, and money (Tavassoli, 1968:3).

Among some very religious families, a Koran and candlestick might be pledged for the *mahriyeh*. Since this has no monetary value, it means that the woman, in fact, has no financial security at all. However, at the present time, it is usually the custom to pledge money rather than other types of goods.

Although it is the legal right of the bride to ask for the amount specified in the marriage contract at any time after marriage, it is usually requested only in the case of divorce, or it may be subtracted from the husband's estate if the male should succumb before his wife. If the *mahriyeh* cannot be paid on demand, the male can be imprisoned. However, he is normally allowed by the judge deciding the case to pay, in monthly installments, the amount being determined by his income. The amount of the *mahriyeh* varies among socio-economic groups and from period to period. For example, one study of the amount of *mahriyeh* pledged in Tehran showed that, while the largest corresponding amount in 1337 (1958-59) was 20,000 rials to 50,000 rials, by 1345 (1966-67) this amount had risen to between 50,000 rials and 200,000 rials (Tavassoli, 1968:8).

Often poorly educated persons with low incomes pledge amounts beyond their ability to pay, while highly educated persons either pledge little or nothing or a great deal, which also may or may not be in the realm of realistic ability to pay. The amount pledged is related to the prestige attached to the *mahriyeh* by the persons involved and is also affected by the desire to compete with other family members or friends. Since it is often a status symbol to have one's daughter receive a large *mahriyeh*, it may be previously agreed upon to have the groom pledge an amount far beyond his means, but officially write in the marriage contract that it has been already paid, either in part or in full.

When the amount pledged is unrealistic, the *mahriyeh* may discourage the husband from dissolving the union. Therefore, it not only serves the function of providing some economic security should a divorce occur, but also a certain amount of economic security during the marriage itself. Today, since women are allowed to initiate divorce, it may further strengthen the position of women in the family.

If the bride is self-selected, the dowry and *mahriyeh* are still frequently negotiated, but more often the couple involved makes the decision concerning the amount to be paid. There are instances where no dowry is given by the girl and a token such as the Koran, mirror, or candlestick is pledged by the male.

However, this situation occurs only among the most modern and better educated families residing in the large cities, and more frequently in Tehran.

MARRIAGE

Types of Marriage

There are a number of different forms of marriage in Iran. First, a distinction must be made between a form of temporary marriage termed *sigheh* and permanent marriage. *Sigheh* is often equated

with concubinal union and implies a situation in which the wife has
inferior status. In this form of marriage, law requires the male to
pledge something of material value or a sum of money which must
be mentioned in the marriage contract. It is impossible to pledge
nothing or a token without monetary value as is possible in the
permanent marriage (Owsia, 1968: 4). This form of marriage is called
temporary because the duration of the union is decided upon by
the couple and written into the contract. It can range from a few
hours to ninety-nine years.

This form of marriage may be chosen for a number of reasons.
In some cases, it is hardly more than an institutionalized form of
prostitution. The children are recognized as legitimate, but no
inheritance may be expected by the wife. In addition, the wife has
no right to expect any support at all, unless it is previously agreed
upon in the marriage contract.

A temporary wife may be taken to bear a child when a permanent wife is unable to have children, or may be a way of testing
male virility in case no child resulted from a permanent marriage.

There are no readily available statistics indicating the rate
of occurrence of temporary marriage in Iran, in the past or
present.

Permanent marriage in Iran takes two major forms, monogamy
and polygyny. According to Islamic law, a male may take up to
four wives, but should be able to provide equally for their economic and psychological well-being. Polygyny is practiced for a
number of reasons: to insure a large number of children, to provide
necessary female manpower for caring for flocks, and to satisfy
other economic and social conditions.

In the past, a man could take an additional wife at any time
without consulting his first wife. However, with the passing of the
Family Protection Law in 1968, a man must first seek the permission of the court to take another wife, as well as obtain his first
wife's consent. The court investigates the husband's ability to treat
each wife equally and makes the final decision.

A study of the effect of this new law on marriage forms in
Tehran indicated that within the first three months after the new
law was passed, only 14 men took a second wife, as compared to
456 cases reported for the same period of the previous year
(Hessam-Vaziri, 1968: 15). More research is necessary to determine
the specific reasons for choosing this marriage form, and to find its

differential distribution, both geographically, as well as socio-economically.

The other type of marriage form which occurs in Iran, is monogamy which is practiced by the majority of couples in Iran today. The changing economic situation, as well as changing legal forms and traditions, is promoting an increased incidence of monogamy.

Within these two marriage forms, sororate or levirate is sometimes practiced. In the former type of marriage, a man may marry his wife's widowed, divorced or unmarried sister. In the latter form, a man may marry his widowed sister-in-law. The frequency of either sororate or levirate is unknown in Iran.

Norms

The wedding ceremony. There are often two ceremonies performed in the case of permanent marriage. The first is called *sigheh aghde*, which is usually performed in the bride's home. It is during this ceremony that the *mahriyeh* is pledged and recorded in the marriage contract by a mullah (a religious man). This mullah recites the marriage pledge and a number of verses from the Koran, while the bride and bridegroom either read from the Koran, if they are literate, or simple listen to the verses, if they are not. It is customary for the groom to give a mirror to the bride before which the couple sits while reading or listening to the verses. Since they are not yet married, they are supposed to look only at each other's image in the mirror. The mirror is meant to symbolize the hope for a bright and successful future for the couple.

After reciting some verses, the groom is asked whether he accepts the bride and *vice versa*. As a matter of custom, the bride often declines to answer until asked the third time. This is usually done to give the bride a chance to think for the last time and be sure of her answer. Once this ceremony is performed, the couple is considered legally married. However, often a bride will not leave her parents' home to live with her husband until a second ceremony called *arusi* has taken place. This is actually the celebration of the consummation of the marriage. At this time, dinner and dancing are enjoyed by the guests and congratulations are paid to the families. The form and elaborateness of the *arusi* depend on social traditions and the socio-economic status of the families involved. In villages, it is only after the celebrations are held separately for members of each sex and the group is ready to wish his bride away to his own home that he comes to see her. Sometimes the celebrations are held jointly with elaborate dancing. One's finest clothes are saved for this occasion.

In the large cities, joint celebrations are often held for both sexes and the couple stays together while congratulations are being made. Among the higher socio-economic classes, famous entertainers are hired to perform and elaborate traditional Iranian dishes are served to the guests.

The length of time between the *sigheh aghde* and the *arusi* varies, depending on the situation. Sometimes a young child is promised to a man and the *sighe aghde* is performed, but she remains with her parents until puberty or until an age at which her parents consider it appropriate for her to join her husband. Sometimes a home for the new couple has not been completely constructed or all the dowry has not been secured, thus temporarily delaying the *arusi*.

In other cases, *sighe aghde* is performed just before the *arusi* and the bride joins her husband the same day.

Intermarriage. Intermarriage between different religious groups is not readily accepted by the majority of the population. When it does occur, it is easier for a Muslim male to obtain permission to marry a non-Muslim female than *vice versa*, since it is assumed that the male will dominate the family and the children will automatically become Muslim. Therefore, it is not necessary for a woman to convert to Islam unless she so desires. However, if a non-Muslim male wishes to marry a Muslim woman, he must first convert to Islam and be married according to Islamic law, if the couple expects their marriage to be officially recognized in Iran. If the couple plans to reside outside of Iran, no problem arises.

Usually, intermarriage across religious lines also involves marriage between different nationalities. With an increasing number of Iranians going abroad to study, the incidence of intermarriage has increased. This type of intermarriage is, of course, more likely to occur among highly educated persons. Somehow, a foreign non-Muslim is more easily accepted by an Iranian than a mate from a religious minority group within his own country. The reason for this has not been studied, but provides an interesting area for future research.

Age at marriage and age differences between spouses. At the present time, the legal age for marriage is eighteen for girls and twenty years for boys. If a girl wishes to marry before the age of eighteen legally she must not only have the permission of her parents, but also must be examined by a court doctor to establish whether she has reached the age of puberty (Ministry of Justice, 1971: 121). If a girl is under fifteen years of age and marriage results in her becoming deformed or ill, her spouse can be imprisoned (Kamangar). It was thirteen a few years ago.

Previous to the passing of the above law, a girl was often married before the age of fifteen years, *sighe aghde* having occurred during childhood. Recent research is uncovering evidence that some parents now prefer their daughters to marry at the age of fifteen years or even later, especially among urban dwellers (Touba, 1971, 1972a). However, the extent to which this attitude prevails nationally can only be established by future research.

Although there is no law regulating age differences between spouses, custom demands significant age gaps. Whereas age gaps often as much as fifteen years are found, it is not uncommon for a man to be as much as twenty years older than his wife. This has created a "self-fulfilling prophecy," for few women are available in a man's own age group, thus forcing him to seek younger women. In 1966, there were more than two men for every female of fifteen years or younger still available for marriage in both the urban and rural areas. As the ages increased up to thirty-five, the proportion of females available for marriage decreased rapidly. For example, in the age group of twenty to twenty-four, there were more than four single males for every single female; six single males for every single female in the twenty-five to twenty-nine range; and more than five males for every single female of thirty to thirty-four years of age (Touba, 1970: 20).

This custom has had significant social repercussions. In the case of divorce, a male can easily take a young wife and begin another family, but a woman having passed the marriageable age usually remains unmarried. This presents a difficult situation for the female divorcee who can seldom look forward to a normal family life.

Similarly, the large age gap has meant an extremely large proportion of widows in the population. In the 1966 Iranian Census, it was reported that nearly a fourth of the females aged fourty-five to fifty-four were already widowed and nearly half of all famales aged fifty-five to sixty-four were widowed. These proportions are higher in the urban areas. This may be due to the equally difficult living conditions for rural females and males, which results in early female mortality in rural areas.

Place of residence. When newlyweds choose to live with their in-laws, there is a tendency toward patrilocal residence, although matrilocal residence also occurs, depending on the village or city in which the couple chooses to reside and the economic status of the bride's family. Often a couple will live with their in-laws immediately following the marriage, until such time as they are able to secure a house of their own, either by renting, purchasing, or building. It is preferable for sons to build homes close to their father's. Often a large garden is divided among a man's children and their houses are built adjoining one another.

This pattern is not universal and with increasing urbanization and migration, children are moving to other villages or cities, thus forming neolocal units. However, after the death of a parent, an elderly mother or father may again join one of the children, even if it means migrating to another region of the country.

FAMILY SYSTEM

Structure

It is difficult to make a direct comparison between the nuclear family as conceived in the West and in Iran. Often the term *khanevadeh* is used to indicate the basic family unit, but this sometimes includes married or unmarried children who live separately and are still considered a part of the basic unit by the parents.

If the members of a family are determined by living arrangements, there is still another problem, for in Iran a house is usually a compound with many rooms arranged around a central courtyard. Often sons, brothers, and sisters, as well as nonrelatives, may live within the compound and are, therefore, considered part of the dwelling unit. If these persons eat together at the same table, or *sofreh*, they are usually considered economically dependent on one another.

On the other hand, sons may eat at a separate *sofreh*, but live adjacent to their parent's home and cooperate in economic activities, so that in fact they are economically dependent on one another.

The extent to which these different forms exist has not been nationally documented, but research carried out in some areas of Iran indicates that each one does exist, even if infrequently. For example, whole villages may consist of a few *taiefeh*, or kinship groups, although living arrangements may take a neolocal form. Therefore, to discuss a change from the extended to the nuclear form of residence pattern, or from the nuclear to the extended one needs a clear definition of what a family is so that cross-cultural comparisons can be made.

At present, the Iranian Census provides the only national statistics on the family. For purposes of the census, the family was defined as those persons living together within a single housing unit. This may refer to an entire structure or an independent section therein. These persons should share expenses, as well as the principal meals. Therefore, all of the members of the household may not be related (Iranian Statistical Centre, 1968:b). Accordingly, 73 per cent of both urban and rural households were found to consist of parents and unmarried children. Vertical extended families living within a housing unit were found to constitute a very small proportion. However, due to the type of housing units, especially in rural areas, this may be an extreme understatement of the degree of matrilocal or patrilocal residence (See Table 1).

In a recent study of the family in a region undergoing planned industrialization (Arak), a slightly different definition of the family was employed (Touba, 1972). Here, the definition of a family included those persons related by blood or marriage living in the same dwelling unit and eating at the same *sofreh*. Although one of these members might be temporarily absent from his place of residence for purposes of work, education, vacation, sickness, visiting, shopping or military service, the other family members assume that he will return and rejoin them. Included were persons not related by blood or marriage, but legally adopted, living under the same roof, eating at the same *sofreh*, and being economically dependent on the family. In a sample of 105 rural families from 10 villages, nearly half consisted of a father, mother, and unmarried children; a fourth were extended families which exhibited both matrilocal and patrilocal types of residence patterns; and a few other types

TABLE 1. *Types of private households in Iran and the outlying urban and rural areas, 1966*

Type of Household	Total country		Urban						Rural	
			Total		Tehran City		Other urban areas			
	No.	%	No.	%	No.	%	No.	%	No.	%
Total	5,029,320	100.0	1,960,701	100.0	565,968	100.0	1,394,733	100.0	3,058,619	100.0
Married couple No children	545,480	10.8	210,395	10.7	61,287	10.8	149,108	10.7	335,085	11.0
Parents and Unmarried children	3,671,878	73.0	1,427,474	72.8	405,275	71.6	1,022,199	73.3	2,244,404	73.4
Parents, married children, No. grand children	62,155	1.2	26,458	1.4	6,816	1.4	19,642	1.2	25,697	0.8
Parents, married children, and grand-children	234,104	4.7	60,520	3.1	14,352	2.6	46,168	3.3	175,584	5.7
Other	515,703	10.3	235,854	12.0	78,238	13.8	157,616	11.3	279,849	9.1

Source. National Census of Population and Housing, November 1966, Total Country-Settled Population, Volume 168, Tehran: Plan Organization, Iranian Statistical Center, March 1968, Table 41; and Tehran Shahrestan. Volume 10. August 1967.

were either polygynous, with the wives living together in one household, or incomplete units due to the death or temporary absence
of a parent.

Among the 112 urban sample families, slightly more than two-
thirds were nuclear, 15 per cent were extended, and the remainder
were similar to the other types previously mentioned. In using the
above definition in taking these samples, the proportion of nuclear
families in relation to other types was much less than that indicated
by the Iranian Census.

Behnam (1968 : 105) has classified families in another way, divid-
ing them into those characterized by either rural or urban family
structure. His method of classification centers on the focus of power
and economic dependence, as well as the type of residence pattern.
Behnam has typed urban families as being:

1) Independent conjugal units with no other relatives.
2) Independent conjugal units with additions consisting of a
dependent aged parent.
3) Independent, conjugal immigrant units with or without a
relative in residence.

These three are said to function with relative independence of the
larger kinship structure.

4) Extended particentric families, in which power is vested in
the father and married sons who are dependent on him.
5) *Taifeh*—the larger network of relatives.

Rural families have been classified as follows:

1) Independent conjugal units usually with few or no relatives
in the villages. These are often nuclear migrant workers.
2) Seemingly independent structures supervised by the extended families, neolocal residences which are economically tied to the
parents.
3) Disintegrated conjugal units in which the head of the household or a spouse is either temporarily or permanently absent;
members of this unit may live alone or return to their parents.
4) Extended particentric families (similar to urban particentric
ones). This type has a special name in some regions. For example,

boneh, an independent communal agricultural unit found in many villages, was often another name for the extended family.

5) *Taifeh*—the larger network of relatives.

It is clear from this presentation that simplified discussions of nuclear or extended families, so often found in Western documents, do not directly apply to the case of Iran. In Iran, even in urban areas, a seemingly isolated nuclear unit may be tied to a *taifeh* through marriage. This relationship is sustained by attendance at weddings and funerals, visiting during the New Year or other religious holidays, and meeting at the time of illness of a family member, as well as by regular meetings in tea houses. Moreover, such a unit serves as a source of assistance to other taifeh members (Behnam, 1970: 127).

The conjugal unit must be studied within the context of the larger kinship networks, with consideration being given to power relations and economic dependency, as well as residence patterns.

A neolocal living arrangement does not necessarily mean that the unit is not strongly tied to a larger kinship group, both socially and economically. As mentioned previously, villages are often composed of a few *taifeh* or kinship groups. These *taifeh* originated as an assemblage of families linked by such factors as geographical proximity, loyalty to a common chief, etc. (Behnam, 1970: 122). Due to physical isolation, these families eventually intermarried and the kinship group was thus enlarged.

A study of the places of origin of workers in Tehran indicated that in 93 per cent of the villages, *taifeh* were in existence (Vielle, 1965). Cities also have been found to have either *taifehs* or concentrations of close relatives living within one block or one neighbourhood of each other (Behnam, 1970 : 122).

Processes

Authority patterns. The predominant authority pattern which prevails in Iranian families is traditionally patriarchal. Although women had certain recognized rights during the pre-Islamic period and acquired other benefits with the coming of Islam, later invasions, especially that of the Mongols, pushed women to a position of powerlessness due to illiteracy, ignorance of social affairs, superstition, and a limited defined role within the family. With no knowledge of social matters, women became dependent on their husbands to make major decisions for the family. In addition, children, especially girls, had no voice in deciding their future.

Today, illiterarcy is being combated in urban areas and attempts are being made in rural areas, but their success have yet to be determined.

Women in certain social groups participate more fully in society and are becoming economically independent. However, since this only applies to a relatively small proportion of the population, traditional patriarchal authority patterns are still likely to persist. Those evidences of changing pattarns which do exist need further research. A woman may subtly come to possess a certain amount of power in family affairs. However, in which affairs and under what conditions have yet to be studied.

An important law still exists which serves to remind even the most wealthy and educated women that they must bend to the authority of their husbands if they wish to travel abroad. This law requires a husband to give his wife written permission each time she wishes to travel abroad, whereas he may leave the country without her consent.

Socialization. Since research in the area of the family is just beginning, only a sketch of the socialization process from isolated research findings can be presented. A study of personality development in an Iranian village found significant differences in patterns of socialization for boys and girls. The study reported that parents cater to the desires and demands of boys in all situations in which males and females are involved. Females were found to be quiet, obedient, subservient, and accepting of their destined role as wives and mothers (Kendall, 1968). This study emphasized female socialization patterns.

Another study of three villages found a similar priority given to male children (Touba, 1971: 54). However, for both sexes, parents expressed the need to control behavior, for boys outside the home and for girls inside the home. Girls have little opportunity to play freely outside after a certain age. In general, parents stressed obedience and submission as ideal child behavior. Most parents wanted passive, obedient, polite children who would not be a bother.

In a similar study among urban families, fathers were found to be more interested in the achievements of their children, while mothers held ideas similar to those exhibited by rural parents.

However, a father's concept of a bad child was also one who disobeyed and opposed social standards (Touba, 1972a).

The demand for submission to authority figures seems to be a cultural pattern in Iran: first, submission to God, as implied by the meaning of the name of the dominant religion, "Islam"; then, to the leader of the nation; next, to those who hold a position higher than oneself, and, finally, to the authoritarian parent. It is questionable whether children can be creative and whether they can innovate social forms, since the parents, the formal educational system, and religious training all attempt to socialize children into the traditional norms of society.

RECENT CHANGES IN THE FAMILY AND PROJECTIONS FOR THE FUTURE

The second world war period marked the beginning of large scale migration to urban centers, particularly those under British occupation. After the war, some families returned to their homes and others remained in their new setting or migrated to Tehran and other large cities. Following the war, when the oil industry was nationalized, a period of instability ensued. However, by the end of the 1950s, oil resources and the establishment of political stability made money available. Thus, the country embarked on a path of economic and social development. The large cities, especially the capital, began attracting people due to their industrial, educational, and other social facilities. Members of rural families began migrating to nearby cities in search of work during periods of unemployment in the fields. The new advantages available in urban areas were drawing many people who often left their extended family unit to seek a new life. However, as mentioned previously, kinship ties often remained strong in spite of distance. Individuals who had moved away still maintained the sphere of influences by frequent visiting.

Value changes connected with the role of women in society resulted in increasing emphasis on women's education, at least in urban areas. Opportunities for female participation in the labor force at the white collar level also increased. These occurrences were brought about partly because new types of jobs were being created in conjunction with economic development. Moreover, there was a corresponding rise in the educational level reached by women and middle class families began accepting the idea that women could use their education, at least in a few fields such as teaching, nursing, and other traditionally females occupations. The increasing possibility of achieving some economic independence was to have drastic effects on the middle class family. Women in rural areas were previously active in the labor force, to be sure, especially in the carpet weaving industry, but this was a home industry and their illiteracy status still made them dependent on their husbands or fathers in handing secular affairs outside the home.

The value changes taking place among the power elite, and the new intelligentsia often educated abroad, culminated in a number of institutional changes during the mid-60s, which had a great impact upon the family, as well as the role of women in society. The full impact of the programs initiated at that time, such as land reform, the nationalization of forests, the electoral law, the establishment of the Literacy Corps, the Health Corps, and the Development Corps (involving the use of military transcripts to teach and provide medical service, as well as engineering or agricultural techniques to rural areas), has not yet been evaluated. However, recent research has shown changes in marriage forms and decision-making patterns and has revealed greater female participation in political affairs (Touba, 1972b). The Family Protection Law established toward the end of the 1960s probably had the most direct effect on the family, for it not only gave women the right to initiate the divorce, but made the first wife's permission compulsory before taking a second wife. This has undoubtedly given women more power within the family.

The role the extended family has played in the industrialization process has yet to be documented. However, some discussion can be undertaken. Rather than simply saying that the family retarded industrialization, it seems more approximate to consider the kind of investment which stifled industrialization per se before land reform. Previously, acquisition of land was viewed as an appropriate manifestation of wealth, but after land reform, capital was being directed into industrial enterprises. In addition, capital was often sent abroad until the period when the newly acquired political stability created enough security to make investment in Iran itself possible, as well as advantageous.

Nevertheless, family ties may still have affected the process indi-
rectly. For example, acquiring an industrial labor force from a local
rural population often meant a mass turnover at harvest time when
workers preferred to return to their villages and help the family. In
addition, rural migrants to cities often worked just long enough to
save some money to begin some local enterprises in their own
villages. Finally, highly, trained personnel were often unwilling to
leave the city where their extended family was residing even if they
had already been operating almost as a nuclear unit most of the
time. When a country wants to industrialize, it must decentralize
its industry and securing a technically trained labor force for some
areas of the county is frequently retarded by family ties.

Certainly, some ecological and demographic processes have already separated families physically. Moreover, continued industrialization and urbanization will undoubtedly result in the next
generation's searching for new opportunities and put them in
touch with new ideas which will be opposed to older traditional
values.

In the large urban centers, contact with Western culture through
returnees who studied abroad, movies, foreign books, newspapers,
imported material goods, new techniques, etc. is affecting relationships between the generations. Youth are breaking away from old
religious traditions and expect more freedom of thought and
movement.

Increased female education, accompanied by economic independence, is resulting in the fact that women are acquiring the power
to think for themselves. They will inevitably demand a greater say
in family affairs, not only in the matter of choosing a spouse, but
also in making decisions concerning the family as a whole. The
new divorce laws could have either of two effects: either an
increase in divorce, since half the population which was previously
without any say in marriage matters can now initiate divorce procedures, or a decrease in divorce, since women are no longer
compelled to accept all their husbands' demands and can pose a
threat through legal procedures.

It is hoped that systematic research will provide additional information on the changing family in Iran so that more concrete
predictions of future variations can be made.

Family Planning

Two major researches occurred in 1966 which brought the need for family planning to the attention of the Iranian government. The first was a fertility study conducted in four regions of Iran by the Institute for Social Studies and Research, University of Tehran (Chasteland, *et al.*, 1966). The second was the Iranian Census of 1966. Since the latter was the second national census, population growth was rapidly apparent and demographers calculated a growth rate near 3 per cent. The fear of population explosion was so great that the government launched a family planning program in 1967 with the aid of the Population Council in the United States, and a family planning Unit was established under the auspices of the Ministry of Health (Sardari, 1969).

As with the introduction of any new program, a certain amount of resistance was encountered by political, economic, and religious leaders. However, after the Shah of Iran pledged his support, and a concerted effort was made to enlist the cooperation of various leaders, the family planning program gained recognition. Family planning programs were set up in many public clinics, first in Tehran and the Central Province and then in the remainder of the country. An educational training program was conducted for medical and paramedical personnel to help clarify points about birth control and to encourage communication of the message to the general population. After military selection was extended to include women, many were sent to work in family planning clinics.

However, although a concentrated attempt has been made since the establishment of the program, most of the energy and funds have been spent in the clinics themselves, rather than for a communication campaign in the society at large. The Esfahan *shahrestan* is one area with an extensive communication campaign, which has included a built-in evaluation of the family planning program and of the communication campaign itself. This program was supported by the Population Council of the United States and sponsored by the Esfahan Ministry of Health (Gillespie, 1972). Later this program was extended to six *ostans*, but its evaluation has yet to be completed.

Communication of the family planning program message is absolutely vital for the acceptance of the program by the population at large because of the traditional attitude of Iranians toward children.

In Iran, the saying, "Who gives teeth, gives the bread," meaning that God gives the children so he will also provide for their necessities and the family should not worry, is indicative of this attitude. Children have traditionally been highly valued for their economic worth, especially in rural areas, since boys labor in the fields and provide a means of support for aging parents. Girls contribute to the income of the family through carpet weaving, at least until marriage. Although urban life is now making a large number of children more of an economic burden, the extended family pattern, which expects children to be a source of emotional and economic support to the elderly and widowed and provides a way of building a family power structure, still contributes to the desire for large families. Some men consider children proof of male virility. In other cases, there is a fear of contraceptives.

Large scale evaluation of the national family planning program has yet to be undertaken. Thus, an overall statement about the gains and the degree of acceptance of the program by the population at large remains the task of future research.

DISINTEGRATION OF THE FAMILY

Divorce

Until the passing of the Family Protection Law of 1968, in almost all cases, it was the man's prerogative to initiate divorce. Although it was sometimes possible to include a promise of equal divorce rights under certain conditions in the marriage contract, in practice such guarantees were not successful in the actual event of divorce. However, after the passing of the above law, women were empowered to initiate divorce. Moreover, all cases of divorce were henceforth to be mediated by the courts. Article II of this law gave either spouse the opportunity to obtain a divorce on any of the following grounds: "Either spouse receives a sentence of imprisonment of five years or more, when either is addicted to dangerous drugs that affect the continuation of family life, if the husband marries another wife without the consent of his first wife, if a spouse abandons the family or if a spouse is convicted of an offense unbecoming to family prestige or social standing of either spouse."

Previous to the passing of the Family Protection Law, divorce rates in Iran seemed quite high. During the twenty-year span from 1942-47 to 1962-67, divorce was more prevalent after the war than in more recent times. However, the divorce rate still remained high for the period as a whole. For example, "the ratio of divorces to marriages was as high as one to four during the 1942-47 period, declined to one to six from 1947 to 1962, and increased to one to five from 1962-1967" (Hessam-Vaziri and Djilani, 1968: 3). (See Table 2).

TABLE 2. *Ratio of divorces per 100 marriages in Iran, 1942-67*

Years	Average divorces per 100 marriages
1942-47*	24.8
1947*-52	24.1
1952-57	18.8
1957-62	17.5
1962-67	19.2

*The Persian year ends 20 March and begins 21 March in the Western Calendar.

Source. Hessam-Vaziri and K. Djilani, "Divorce in Tehran: A Research Report," Tehran: Institute for Social Studies and Research, 10th International Seminar on Family Research, 5-12 March 1968.

Another report on divorce in Tehran during the years 1968 to 1972 indicated a numerical increase in divorce, but a sharp decrease in the ratio of divorces to marriages after 1968 and the passing of the marriage law. It also revealed a stabilization of the ratio at about one divorce to every five marriages (see Table 3).

TABLE 3. *Number of divorces and marriages, and ratio of divorces per 100 marriages in Teheran, 1968-72*

	Number of divorces	Number of marriages	Ratio of divorces per 100 marriages
1968-69*	9,552	39,000	24.5
1969-70	10,500	50,000	21.0
1970-71	10,200	46,800	21.8
1971-72	11,000	50,400	21.8

*The Persian years ends 20 March and begins 21 March in the Western Calendar.

Source. *Kayhan Journal*, No. 8605, Tehran (29 Esfand 1350), 1971.

Observations made during the 1966 census demonstrated considerable regional differences in the total number of divorced persons
in the population, as well as differences between the sexes. Urban
areas demonstrated a larger percentage of divorce than rural areas,
but the differences found between females and males were more
significant, with females having nearly twice as many divorces than
males (see Table 4).

TABLE 4. *Marital status in rural and urban areas
of Iran by sex, 1966*

Marital status	Total country		Urban		Rural	
	No.	%	No.	%	No.	%
Males:						
Total	8,546,238	100.0	3,537,257	100.0	5,008,981	100.0
Married	4,830,316	56.5	1,838,882	52.0	2,991,434	59.7
Widowed	148,164	1.7	43,584	1.2	104,585	2.1
Divorced	40,418	0.5	19,623	0.6	20,795	0.4
Never married	3,492,007	40.9	1,618,030	45.7	1,873,977	37.4
Not reported	35,328	0.4	17,138	0.5	18,190	0.4
Females:						
Total	7,989,606	100.0	3,209,182	100.0	4,780,424	100.0
Married	4,877,170	61.0	1,818,335	56.7	3,058,835	64.0
Widowed	862,172	10.8	363,919	11.3	498,253	10.4
Divorced	75,642	1.0	54,169	1.4	30,473	0.7
Never married	2,132,117	26.7	959,269	29.9	1,172,848	24.5
Not reported	42,505	0.5	22,490	0.7	20,015	0.4

*Source. National Census of Population and Housing, November 1966, Total
Country-Settled Population*, Volume 168, Tehran: Plan Organization, Iranian
Statistical Center, March 1968, Table 4.

This distributional difference between sexes may be related to the
fact that a divorced man can easily marry a woman many years his
junior, while an older woman has little chance to remarry. In
addition, a double standard prevails which makes it acceptable for
a male to divorce, although a divorced woman is often looked
upon as being degraded.

Regional differences in divorce matters may be due to tradition.
Marriage is an institution which is used as a mechanism for
binding families together, especially in rural areas. Thus, divorce
is not necessarily an individual affair. The economic interdepen-

dence of all members of the family on one another may be another deterrent to divorce.

Not only were differences exhibited between urban and rural areas, but, in addition, certain provinces and governorships demonstrated a larger proportion of divorces than others. It is interesting to note that although the central Ostan, containing the capital city of Tehran, is among the five provinces which have the highest divorce rates, as are three provinces in the south and southeast of the country, for example, the Ports and Islands of the Omman Sea, Kerman, Sistan, and Baluchestan. Whether location, economic or social and cultural factors are at play in these areas, it would be an interesting topic for future research (see Table No. 5).

Some causes of divorce in Tehran may be cited on the basis of available research. One study of 340 divorces conducted in Tehran in 1965 showed a number of factors causing divorce (Hessam-Vaziri and Djilani, 1968:12). The dominant causes mentioned in this study were incompatibility and failure to adjust to marital life. In addition, extramarital relations, lack of adjustment in sexual relations, interference of relatives, drug or alcohol addiction, and economic factors contributed to divorce in the capital city.

An earlier study seemed to find unsatisfactory sexual relations, overwork on the part of the husband, interference of relatives, economic factors, and lack of children as major reasons for divorce (Katanchi, 1963). Untill now, only a few research studies delving into the underlying causes of divorce are available and they usually utilize only Tehran samples.

After divorce, a woman usually returns to the home of her parents or other family members. If she is left without any means of support, either financially or emotionally, she often has no alternative. In the larger urban areas, an educated woman may find rewarding employment and go on leading an active life. But even these women will most likely seek the emotional support of their own parents. Since it is extremely difficult for a woman to live alone in an apartment without acquiring an undesirable reputation, she has little choice other than returning to her family.

There are specific regulations concerning the custody of the children. Normally, the mother is allowed to keep a son until the age of two years and a girl until the age of seven. If the mother marries or becomes mentally ill, the children automatically become the responsibility of the father.

TABLE 5. Divorced males and females in the Ostans and Farmandarikols of Iran, 1966

	Females			Males		
	Total	Divorced		Total	Divorced	
		No.	%		No.	%
Ports and Islands of the Onman Seas F.	114,230	2,046	1.8	119,996	1,259	1.0
Central	1,632,795	23,697	1.5	1,799,780	10,041	0.6
Kerman	247,489	3,003	1.2	252,920	1,057	0.4
Sistan and Baluchestan	144,954	1,593	1.1	151,040	663	0.4
Kermanshahan	237,801	2,336	1.0	270,283	1,773	0.7
Khuzestan	493,659	4,503	0.9	530,301	2,167	0.4
Khorasan	815,057	7,493	0.9	849,769	4,533	0.6
Kurdistan	192,482	1,817	0.9	217,334	1,865	0.9
E. Azarbayejan	805,736	6,465	0.8	870,391	3,457	0.4
W. Azarbayejan	330,910	2,486	0.8	368,584	2,081	0.6
F. of Hamadan	279,660	2,369	0.8	296,293	1,300	0.4
F. of Lurestan	207,045	1,578	0.8	225,055	992	0.5
F. of Semnan	70,029	537	0.8	71,450	192	0.3
F. of ports and islands of Persian Gulf	81,824	587	0.7	87,572	328	0.4
Fars	450,781	3,719	0.8	484,761	1,748	0.4
Mazandaran	577,936	3,248	0.6	603,743	2,571	0.4
Gilian	567,199	3,554	0.6	573,943	2,764	0.5
Esfahan	559,101	3,645	0.6	572,903	1,176	0.2
F. Chahrmahal and Bakhtiari	91,335	519	0.6	98,151	236	0.3
F. Kohkiluyeh and Boyar Ahmadi	46,120	268	0.6	50,869	99	0.2
F. of Ilam	43,463	179	0.9	51,100	116	0.2

If the father relinquishes possession of the children, custody can be given to the mother, or if the mother can prove to the court irresponsibility on the part of the father, she may be awarded custody. However, the courts tend to favor giving custody to the father, since, traditionally, he has been the only one economically capable of providing support. As mentioned previously, the *mahriyeh*, although officially payable upon the demand on the wife, is most frequently requested at the time of the divorce. However, this sum is usually not sufficient for a woman to continue supporting herself and a large number of children.

Widowhood

Occurrence. A much more significant and pressing problem than divorce is widowhood among females. In 1966, nearly 23 per cent of all women in the age group forty-five to fifty-four were already widowed and the figure more than doubled for the age group fifty-five to sixty-four (see Table 6).

As mentioned before, traditionally, Iranian males married females much younger than themselves. This resulted in a situation where, in fact, there were few women available to marry within one's own age group. When the age gap between spouses is great, it is clear that the wife is probably destined to widowhood for much of her adult life (Touba, 1970:20).

Widowhood is high among females in all the provinces and governorships of Iran. As the 1966 census demonstrated, at least a tenth of the females in all regions of Iran are widowed. Some areas have a higher incidence of widowhood than others—for instance, the Semnan governorship and the provinces of Esfahan and Fars. In these two provinces, more than 12 per cent of the women were widowed, as compared to the provinces of West Azarbayejan, Gilan, Mazandaran, and Kurdestan, where slightly less than 10 per cent were widowed (see Table 7).

This situation has important social implications, which have not yet been recognized in Iran. Since a large proportion of the female population is illiterate, especially in rural areas where the trend is towards large families, most of those women who are widowed are probably left with little economic support. At present, only government and industrial employees and the military look forward to some social security. However, this only reaches a small proportion

TABLE 6. *Widowed females by age-specific groups for total country, urban and rural areas, 1966*

Age Groups	Total country			Urban		Rural	
	Total female population	No. widowed	% of each age group widowed	Total female population	% of each age group widowed	Total female population	% of each age group widowed
All ages	12,097,258	862,172	7.1	4,697,592	7.1	7,399,666	6.7
Under 25	9,192,072	34,343	3.7	3,545,434	4.1	5,596,642	3.0
33-44	1,237,581	82,926	6.7	478,545	7.6	759,036	4.8
45-54	734,583	168,660	22.9	301,235	26.3	433,348	20.6
55-64	530,101	154,419	48.0	208,769	52.4	321,431	44.5
65 and over	452,917	323,622	71.4	163,708	75.5	289,209	69.1

Source. Jacquiline Rudolph-Touba, *Highlights of Sex-Age Characteristics in Iran, 1956-66: A Sociological Interpretation,* Tehran: Plan Organization, Iranian Statistical Center, 1970, Table 11.

TABLE 7. *Widowed females and males in the Ostans and Farmandarikols of Iran, 1966*

Ostan and Farmandarikol	Female			Male		
	Total	Widowed		Total	Widowed	
		No.	%		No.	%
	1	2	3	4	5	6
F. of Semnan	70,029	8,906	12.7	71,450	1,112	1.5
Esfahan	559,101	69,775	12.5	572,903	7,458	1.3
Fars	450,781	53,896	12.0	484,761	6,814	1.4
F. of Ports and Island of the Omman Sea	114,230	13,139	11.5	119,996	3,173	2.6

	1	2	3	4	5	6
F. of Chahrmanal and Bakhtiari	91,335	10,372	11.4	98,151	1,201	1.2
F. of Hamadan	279,660	31,346	11.2	296,293	4,033	1.4
Sistan and Baluchestan	144,954	16,143	11.1	151,040	3,110	2.1
Kerman	247,489	27,382	11.1	252,920	4,481	1.8
Khuzestan	493,659	54,633	11.1	530,301	8,746	1.?
F. Azarbayejan	805,736	88,673	11.0	870,391	16,615	1.9
Central	1,632,795	178,379	10.9	1,799,780	20,573	1.1
F. of Lurestan	207,045	22,512	10.9	225,055	3,452	1.5
F. of Kohkiluyeh and Boyer Ahmadi	46,120	5,031	10.9	50,869	651	1.3
F. of Ports and Islands of Persian Gulf	81,827	8,828	10.8	87,572	2,112	2.4
F. of Ilam	43,460	4,626	10.7	51,100	942	1.8
Kermanshahan	237,801	24,196	10.2	270,283	6,129	2.3
Khorasar	815,057	81,400	10.0	849,769	20,731	2.4
W. Azarbayejan	330,910	32,672	9.9	368,584	8,892	2.4
Gilan	567,199	56,015	9.9	573,943	10,997	1.9
Mazandaran	577,936	56,235	9.7	603,743	10,966	1.8
Kurdestan	192,482	18,013	9.4	217,334	5,981	2.7

of the group in need. Only future research will be able to clarify
the depth of these problems, and the role played by the extended
family.

Ceremonies. There are specific ceremonies following death, which
both help and hinder the adjustment of the widow. Since, in Islam,
the funeral must take place the day following death, the ceremonies
are reserved for a later date. Relatives of the family usually visit
the home of the deceased to pay their respects. After a few days, a
ceremony is performed in the mosque or at home where again
relatives and other friends come to pay their respects. There are
specific chants recited during the ceremonies which elicit wailing
among the women. This grief seems to be shared by all present.
The family of the deceased is so preoccupied with providing meals
for the family and friends and with participating in the ceremonies
during the week following the death, that there is often little time
for comprehending the events of death.

Not infrequently, relatives will remain with the family of the
deceased for the first week, at the end of which, a return is made
to the grave. Occasionally, relatives will remain with the family of
the deceased for forty days, the last day being marked by another
ceremony and return to the grave. During these forty days, all
secular entertainment is abstained from. Moreover, visiting those
persons who attended the ceremonies during the first week then
becomes a major activity of the widow and the immediate family.
Close female family members continue to wear black for one year
and other female relatives wear black for at least forty days.

These ceremonies and visitation patterns manage to keep the
mind of the widow occupied for some time following the death. In
addition, the extended family usually comes to the emotional
support of the immediate family so that the widow does not feel
completely lost at the beginning of her new life. However, the
wearing of black and numerous ceremonies serve to remind the
family of the tragedy.

Laws of inheritance. If an estate is left, the division among the
beneficiaries is predetermined by law (see *The Complete Manual of
Civil Laws*, 1970:92-104). In order of importance, the beneficiaries
are the children, the spouse, and the parents of the deceased. If
only one child is left, he inherits all except for what is allocated
to the remaining parent. If only boys or only girls are left, the
estate is equally divided, and if there are both boys and girls, two

parts are allocated to the boys and one part to the girls. In case children are left, the woman inherits only one-eighth of the estate and the male inherits one-fourth. The female spouse inherits one-fourth and the male spouse one-half of the estate when there are no children or grandchildren, and the remainder is passed to the second level beneficiaries in order of importance, these being the grandparents, siblings, aunts, and uncles of the deceased.

In addition, a woman's inheritance can only consist of movable possessions, houses, and gardens which have been sold and divided accordingly. Unless the estate is considerable or the woman has acquired numerous possessions before the death of her spouse, she, in fact, becomes financially unable to support herself from the proceeds of the estate. Therefore, if she is a young widow, she must either return to her parental household or that of other family members. She may also be forced into the labor market. If the children are old enough, she will most likely join one of them. The Iranian Census of 1966 reported 539,751 female parents and 65,979 male parents living in private households (Iranian Statistics Center, 1966:7). Even if both parents were present, more than 400,000 female parents were certain to be living in private households without their spouses. Although it cannot be said with complete accuracy, it may be assumed that about half of the widows in Iran choose this alternative. How well they can adjust to their new situation and can continue to contribute to society requires further research.

THE FUTURE OF THE IRANIAN FAMILY

In his book, *World Revolution and Family Patterns*, Goode analyzed modifications of family patterns in several industrializing societies. His basic conclusion was that similar cross-cultural trends are apparently emerging in the wake of modernization, but that these family changes taking place within the societies will vary as a result of the unique features of each culture. Since Goode's original observation, many comparative family studies have observed this same phenomenon. Analysis of the Iranian family patterns reinforces this conclusion. In this remaining section we will speculate about the future areas of change in the Iranian family and how these changes will most likely be affected by Iranian culture.

The obvious attempts of the government to increase the status of women in Iranian society probably presents the broadest implication for the future of the family. The unveiling of women, the increase prominence of women in the labor force and in education, and the trend toward equalization of divorce laws are expanding the power of women in relation to what has traditionally been a patriarchal family system.

The trend in marriage will continue to move from a system of polygyny to one of monogamy. This movement will continue to increase the power of women by concentrating the authority of the female in the home with only one person rather than possibly two or more women. The more direct role of parents in selecting mates will diminish, particularly in urban areas, and even in rural areas, as television and radio become more common there. With increasing educational opportunities for males and females and less parental control, young people will have more opportunity to choose their friends and future mates. The early betrothal of children will cease outside isolated rural areas. The *mehriyeh*, a kind of economic protection for divorced women in a society controlled by men, will disappear as more women flood the labor force. With this financial burden lifted, the marriage rate should increase. The lack of emotional support from extended families in urban areas should encourage more companionship marriage ventures. The temporary marriage will no longer be functional in the future. Currently, it is limited to seasonal farm laborers and pilgrims on religious journeys.

As discussed earlier, divorce laws are moving in the direction of making divorce more difficult for men and easier for women. Here again, one can observe the implications that women are equalizing their position in relation to men.

Shifts in function will most likely alter the future structure of the Iranian family. As discussed earlier, the surge of government growth and its consequent expansion of influence have led to more government lending programs, increased educational facilities, and more industrial jobs. In essence, this increase of government activity should foster a move from extended to the more nuclear independent family pattern. There will be more security from government and expanding industrialization (particularly from the oil industry), which will provide more services to the family. Economic dependence upon the extended family will diminish and an increasing emphasis upon marriage rather than kinship will emerge as a predominant pattern. In relation to this emerging pattern, there should also be an increase in free mate choice, because, as the focus shifts from choosing a new extended family member to selection of a mutually satisfying husband-wife relationship, free choice could be more functional.

The increasing centralization of government power and influence should lead to a more secular orientation. In this traditionally very religious Muslim country, there is much integrating of state and Koranic law. However, as the government continues to increase its provisions of service to the family through its lending programs, social services, educational corps, medical corps, etc. (traditionally religious charity activities), the family should assume an increasingly secular orientation to life. People will discover that the "will of Allah" has become the will of the government program.

The traditional functions of the Iranian family should be shifting as a result of expanding government. Such traditional family functions as education, protection, and reproduction are going to be shifting toward the public spheres. But where economic and socio-cultural functions will be diminishing, other functions will increase in value. For example, recreation and "togetherness" will probably replace economic functions (division of labor) as the integrating factor in marriage.

The Iranian family will also develop with increasing sophistication in such areas as family planning, management of joint income, care of children, and care of the elderly. Family planning will become increasingly important for the family in Iran because of the loss of the economic contribution by the children with the migration from rural areas to urban centers. When children become economic liabilities, an ideology supporting family planning seems more palatable. With the loss of economic support from children, the entrance of women into the labor market will receive increased impetus. The push to develop Iran's industrial capacity and the already expanding gross national product will demand a ready labor force. The need for labor will overcome ideological resistance to women's employment along a broad base of the economy. Management of joint income will be a new family function, but will be handled primarily by the male With increasing numbers of both parents holding jobs, and children who are likely to spend their time playing and in school, parents are likely

to lose some control over their children. If the supporting institutions in the culture were more democratic, this development
would bring greater problems.

The elderly, like children, lose their faith in a rapidly changing
technological society. The information explosion, along with
broader cultural and educational experiences, brings children to
high levels of knowledge far earlier than their parents. Further,
the new knowledge brings old information into question and,
consequently, renders the carriers of the old knowledge, the
elderly, rather useless and a drain on society. There will be increasing governmental programs in Iran to care for the elderly by the
year A.D. 2000.

The forecasts outlined above represent popular generalizations
which are often presented when the future of the family is considered. However, when these generalizations are made in the light
of Goode's proposition that family trends will vary with each
culture, it becomes important to consider some of the unique
features of Iranian society. One aspect of the culture of Iran which
will influence the development of the family is the governmental
structure.

In conclusion, the trends appear to present a picture of a more
visible nuclear family operating with the help of increasing governmental services independent of the traditional extended family.
While this trend appears to follow patterns set by other industrializing nations, the nature of future Iranian family relationships
will evolve in an atmosphere of authoritarian values rather than
in one of more democratic tones.

SUMMARY AND CONCLUSION

Iran, with about 25,000,000 people, strains toward full membership
in the growing family of technocratic nations of Asia. Economic
conditions in the last decade have made enormous strides with the
gross national product up and the per capita income growing Islam
further unites the country and at the same time hinders its growth
as a modernizing nation. Social problems are within the will of
Allah, and, if so, man need not, even must not, interfere with the
divine will.

The family in Iran is characterized generally as extended and
dominated by the male. In the rural areas (60 per cent of the popu-

lation), ancient and traditional marriage patterns prevail. Polygyny is diminishing even in rural areas, due to the heavy cost and the growing sense of women's rights. In the urban areas there is more choice in selection of mates and more likelihood that marriages will be conjugal in nature. Though slow to change, the male privilege of divorce is cracking. The changes have the effect of curtailing the husbands' total control of divorce, but do not yet give the woman equal power to dissolve the marriage. Child-rearing practices are still quite authoritarian and are likely to remain so.

The effects of cultural change have not yet made significant directional movements in the structure of the family and reform has made a start but still has problems. So in the large rural population the extended and patriarchal family continues. Reliance on extended families continues even in the cities. The base for fundamental change in the woman's cultural position has not broadened sufficiently for significant movement in family change. Mass communication and education are beginning to show a standardizing influence, but are not yet prevalent enough to erode traditional values so resistant to change.

The future, however, should see more movement toward a conjugal family unit, less direct influence of parents in mate selection, and more movement toward female equality. Increasing educational and employment opportunities will play a large role in this change. Polygyny will become outdated and divorce laws will give women increased power. Children will be more of an economic liability and, therefore, family planning will come more into vogue. Families will remain authoritarian as long as the nature of other societal institutions continues to be authoritarian.

Many of the traditional functions of the Iranian family, for example, education, reproduction, and protection, will shift to the public responsibility. The fuel for change is present in Iran. The influence that would normally be expected from the rate of change in thus being held back currently by the failure of circumstances to coalesce at certain fixed cultural points with enough friction impact to spark the fuse (e.g., industry's unpreparedness for the labor market swept in by urbanization patterns). That spark is building up and by the year 2000 not even Iran's ancient traditions may be able to stem the tide of change in the institution of the family.

REFERENCES

Afshar Naderi, Nader
  1971 *The Settlement of Nomads and Its Social and Economic Implications.* Tehran: Institute for Social Studies and Research, University of Tehran.

Amani, Mehdi (ed.)
  1968 *Some Demographic Aspects of the Population of Iran.* Tehran: Institute for Social Studies and Research, University of Tehran.

Asafie, A.
  1968 "Evolution de la Famille Iranienne." Tehran: Tenth International Seminar of Family Research, (March). Pp. 5-12.

Behnam, J.
  1968 "Notes Toward a Typology of Transitional Family Forms in Iran" in Mehdi Amani (ed.), *Some Demographic Aspects of the Population of Iran.* Tehran: Institute for Social Studies and Research, University of Tehran. Pp. 99-112.
  1970 "Nuclear Families and Kinship Groups in Iran." *Diogenes*, 76. Pp. 115-131.

Chasteland, J.C. and Mehdi Amani, F. Aminzadeh, H. Khazaneh, A.Moezi and O. Puech
  1968 *Etude Sur la Fecondite et Quelques Caracteristiques D'Iran.* Tehran: Institute for Social Studies and Research, University of Tehran.

Gillespie, Robert
  1972 *Family Planning Communication Projects in Esfahan.* Esfahan: Esfahan Health Department.

Hessam-Vaziri, A. and K. Djilani
  1968 "Divorce in Tehran." A Research Report. Tehran: Tenth International Seminar on Family Research, (March). Pp.5-12.

Iranian Statistical Center
  1968 National Census of Population and Housing. November 1966. Total Country-Settled Population. Ostan and Farmandarikol Publications. Tehran: Plan Organization.

Kamangar, Ahmad (ed.)
  Manual of Basic Laws-The Penal Code Revised. Tehran: Efsat Golshan Press.

Katanchi, O.
  "Reasons for Divorce as Expressed by a Sample of Divorces in Tehran." Tehran: Department of Sociology, University of Tehran, Unpublished paper.

Kayhan Archives
  1967 *Family Welfare Laws.* Tehran: Kayhan.

Kayhan International
  1971 "Statistics on Marriage and Divorce in Tehran." Kayhan International 8605 (29 Esfand).

Kendall, Katherine Wakeman
  1968 "Personality Development in an Iranian Village: An Analysis of Socialization Practises and the Development of the Woman's Role." Ph.D. dissertation, Washington: University of Washington.

Khazaneh, H. T.
  1968 "A Study on Endogamy and Distance Between Place of Birth of Spouses in Three Rural Areas of Iran and Tehran City" in Mehdi Amani (ed.), *Some Demographic Aspects of the Population of Iran*. Tehran: Institute for Social Studies and Research, University of Tehran. Pp. 119-125.

Owsie, P.
  1968 "A Sketch of Family Law in Iran." Tehran, Tenth International Seminar on Family Research, (March). Pp. 5-12.

Ministry of Justice
  "Family Relationship and Affinity and Divorce and Marriage: Article 1034-1256" in *Manual of Civil Laws*. Tehran. Pp. 121-144.

Sardari, A. M.
  1969 "Family Planning in Iran." *The Journal of Medical Education*, 44, Part 2, (November).

Tavassoli, G. A.
  1968 "Le Mahret son evolution on Iran." Tehran, Tenth International Seminar on Family Research, (March). Pp. 5-12.

Touba, Jacquiline Rudolph
  1970 *Highlights of Sex-Age Characteristics in Iran, 1956-1966: A Sociological Interpretation*. Tehran: Iranian Statistical Center. Plan Organization.

  1972a *Problems of Children and Youth in the Iranian Family: A Pilot Study in Shiraz*. Tehran: Institute for Social Studies and Research, University of Tehran.

  1972b "Impact of Societal Institutional Changes on the Iranian Family." Moscow: Twelfth International Seminar on Family Research, (April). Pp. 17-23.

  1972c *Preliminary Results: A Study of the Family in a Region Undergoing Planned Industrialization in Arak*. Tehran: Institute for Social Studies and Research, University of Tehran.

Touba, J. R. and Z. Sarmad-Bahar
  1969 "Study of Preferred Type of Mate Selection Among Tehran University Students." Unpublished paper. Tehran: University of Tehran.

Touba, Jacquiline Rudolph and William Beeman
  1971 *Problems of Children and Youth in the Iranian Family: A Pilot Study in the Villages of the Kashan Desert Region*. Tehran: Institute for Social Studies and Research, University of Tehran.

Vielle, Paul and Morteza Kotobi
  1965 *Origine de Ourvrier de Tehran*. Tehran: Institute for Social Studies and Research, University of Tehran.

Zahedi, A.
   1970 "An Interim National Training Program for Communication and Motivation." Tehran: International Workshop on Communication in Family Planning, (June). P. 6.
Ziadlou, F.
   1946 "Expectation and Behavior of Female Students in the Second Cycle of Secondary Schools in Tehran." Tehran: Institute for Social Studies and Research, University of Tehran.

CHAPTER VII

The Modern Chinese Family—Ideology, Revolution and Residues*

ALINE K. WONG

INTRODUCTION

The so-called family revolution in China is generally taken to begin shortly after the turn of the 20th century, both as a consequence of China's industrialization, of her increasing contact with Western culture, and of the efforts of a group of intellectuals to modernize various aspects of their cultural institutions. The Ch'ing rulers had made some moderate attempts near the end of the 19th century to modernize the economy and change certain customary practices such as footbinding by women, but without much success. During the first decade of the Republican period, in the early 1900s, the traditional family institution came under heavy fire of the intellectuals involved in "new culture" and nationalistic movements. The traditional family system became the symbol for all obstacles to modernization and national unity. At the same time, increasing educational and economic opportunities for the women resulted in a meteoric rise of their general status. The family revolution had begun. Meanwhile, economic conditions in the big cities and suburban areas were changing rapidly as China's textile industry picked up pace during and after the first world war. The working and the middle classes were growing rapidly. Their new economic statuses affected deeply their family organization and, already by the 1930s, a new pattern of family living was discernible. However, this "natural process" was soon arrested by

*The data presented in this chapter cover only up to the period of early 1970s.

the national upheavals in connection with the Japanese invasion and the civil war, which lasted for two full decades. The Nationalist Civil Code (1931), which embodied the institution of a modern marriage and family system, thus never had the opportunity to be effectively implemented in the backward rural areas.

The Chinese Communist Party (CCP), which came to power in 1949, wrought fresh revolutionary changes in all aspects of life. In 1950, the new Marriage Law was passed and made one of the fundamental laws of the People's Republic for the socialist transformation of the society. By means of mass educational campaigns, by political pressure and persuasion, and at times by drastic measures, the family reform was carried out throughout the country in the early years of the CCP regime. Repeated campaigns in the subsequent decade have certainly brought about drastic changes in family living. The family, as it exists in China today, is not only the product of changing economic conditions under the general socialization of the national economy, but also a product of strong ideological motivation to change the centuries-old cultural institutions in China. The Cultural Revolution aimed at even more radical reforms of basic values.

The modern nuclear family in Western societies has often been described as the "natural" or "necessary" consequence of the processes of industrialization and urbanization. This leads some sociologists to predict that the modern nuclear family will be universal—whether under capitalistic or socialistic economic systems—in so far as industrialization and urbanization are becoming universal phenomena. The modern Chinese family, although similar to the Western nuclear family in many respects, is nevertheless not entirely a product of economic forces, but also the outcome of socialist ideology. This is not to deny the influence of changing economic conditions of life, but certainly changes in the Chinese family have been brought about through the interplay between ideology and pragmatism (of the CCP in implementing social reforms in accordance with economic development). We shall further see that certain cultural traits still characterize the Chinese family today, which distinguish it from the Western nuclear family pattern.

This paper attempts to depict the changes in the Chinese family system up to the early 1970s. In Section II, we shall describe briefly the traditional Chinese family. Then we shall examine in Section III the Marriage Law movement of the CCP in the early 1950s, and trace the development of later policies regarding marriage and family. In Section IV, we shall describe the patterns of marriage and family living in China today, in so far as there is available information. Finally, in Section V, we shall compare two models of the Chinese family, one traditional and the other modern, in order to focus on the revolutionary changes that have been effected by the CCP in this basic social organization. However, such a comparison will have to remain to a large extent on the ideal type level for two major reasons. 1) Much of what we know about the traditional Chinese family actually pertains to the Confucian ideal of the extended family and the Confucian model of basic family relationships, found in practice only among a very small class of landlords and gentry. Although we shall have dealt with the problem of discrepancy between ideal and reality in Section II, it is to be noted that the ideal traditional family itself became an ideology that helped to stabilize the Chinese family institution over 2,000 years before the Republic. Similarly, the most potent forces that led to the fall of the traditional family system were also ideological, as embodied in the New Culture Movement of the early Republican period, and later the socialist ideology of the Chinese Communist party. 2) A large part of the available information on the family in China also consists of descriptions of *ideal* family relationships in the socialist state (such educational material is obviously intended for internal consumption and not meant for propaganda in the outside world). Again, although we shall have discussed in Sections III and IV the discrepancies between ideal and reality, we have to reckon that the *ideal* socialist family has been and will remain the chief shaping force of the family institution in China. The persisting customary practices associated with marriage and the family, as admitted by the party, constitute the residues from the Communist family reform experiment. The future of the Chinese family is a function of the progressive eliminat on of these residues.

II. THE TRADITIONAL CHINESE FAMILY

Concept of the Chia

The Chinese word for family, *chia*, is an ambiguous term. It may mean a group, an estate, a unit of economic activities, or it may mean all three of these elements.[1] However, the most commonly accepted concept of the *chia* is a social group consisting of members related to each other by blood, marriage or adoption, sharing a common budget and common property.[2] Members of the *chia* may be temporarily absent and yet considered as members of the family. On the other hand, there may be relatives or even non-kin living together with the family in the same household (*hu*), but they are not considered members of the same family. Thus, the family is not identical with the household, and while the former is the basic unit of social organization in the traditional society, the latter is very often more important from the administrative viewpoint, for census-taking purposes, for taxation, conscription, and local security purposes. Moreover, although the family is the basic unit of social life, it is often overlooked that there has always been quite a large population, especially in the cities and market towns, who do not live in family units, but either remain single or are separated from their families for long periods of time. Such people include poor farm laborers, itinerant workers, shop assistants, apprentices, beggars, and monks.[3]

Form and Size

Sociological and anthropological researches carried out in China in the 1920s and 1930s have clearly shown that the commonly held

---

[1]The ambiguities of the term *chia* are fully explored in Myron L. Cohen's "Developmental Process in the Chinese Domestic Group" in Maurice Freedman, *Family and Kinship in Chinese Society*, Stanford: Stanford University Press, 1970, pp. 21-36.

[2]Daniel Kulp, studying the conditions of life in rural China in the early 1920, was convinced that the economic group was, what was commonly referred to by the Chinese as the family. "It is a group of people who on the basis of blood or marriage connection live together as an economic unit." See Daniel H. Kulp II, *Country Life in South China*, New York: Teachers College, Columbia University, 1925, p. 148. Olga Lang also adopted this definition in her *Chinese Family and Society*, Archon Books, 1968; first published by New Haven, Conn: Yale University Press, 1946, p. 13.

[3]For these people, going to prostitutes constituted the only means of sexual gratification. In spite of the strict moralistic codes of Confucianism, prostitution was quite common among the poor people, and courtesans' houses were popular with the wealthy people, who sought both love and sex outside their loveless matches.

conception of the Chinese family as a large, extended family, consisting of several generations and including one or two dozens of people living in the same household, is only a cultural ideal and is found rarely in practice. Similarly, many of the marriage and family institutions associated with this large family ideal are more of cultural norms, conformed to largely by the Confucian-educated gentry classes, rather than by the majority of the commoners. Even among the former groups, the difficulties of maintaining family harmony and solidarity when so many individuals are involved in large family arrangements, the short life expectancy of the individual, as well as the much frowned upon but still practiced division of household, make the large, multi-generational family still a precious rarity among the rich.

Thus, in practice, there are four different forms of the Chinese family coexisting at the same time, with each dependent mainly on the social-economic background. We have already indicated that the *extended family* in which the *pater familias* lives with his married sons and their families, together with his other unmarried sons and daughters, exists mainly among the wealthy people. The most prevalent form is the second type, the *stem family*, in which one or both parents live with the family of one of the sons (usually the eldest), together with the other unmarried children. A third type is the *joint Fraternal family* in which one of the brothers (usually the eldest again) presides over his married and unmarried brothers, with their wives and his and their children. However, this type of family arrangement can seldom last long; without the authority of the *pater familias*, the authority of the eldest brother can seldom hold the families of the brothers together for a long time. A fourth type is the *nuclear family* found mostly among peasants, tenants, petty merchants and artisans, and among younger sons who have been separated from the parental family upon division of the household, and who therefore temporarily live in nuclear families until they acquire their own stem or extended families.

Olga Lang's survey of villages in North China, non-industrial cities in North China, and the industrial city of Shanghai in the mid-1930s showed that the nuclear family was the predominant type of family organization among the farm laborers, wage earners, and industrial workers. On the other hand, the extended family was present in only slightly over 50 per cent among the landlord class in the rural areas (the landlords being a numerically insignificant class in the total rural population), and was found in only 20 per cent of the upper class families in the non-industrial cities, while it was totally absent from the sample of upper class families in Shanghai. By contrast, the conjugal family was 50 per cent and over among the upper classes of both the non-industrial cities and Shanghai (Lang, 1968: 136-137). Furthermore, there were only 40 families comprising four generations out of 1,717 urban families (2.3 per cent), and 15 out of 528 rural families (2.8 per cent) (Lang, 1968: 137). Comparing town and country, while holding social class constant, her study revealed that there were more conjugal families and fewer joint families in the cities than in the country (Lang, 1968: 138). Fei's study of Kaihsienkung in Kiangsu also showed that the typical family in the village was composed of only one married couple, living with an older relative—in other words, the broken stem family. (Fei, 1939:29).

Similarly, the size of the family has been rather small. Census materials published by the Nationalistic government in the 1940s indicated an average of five persons per family (Yang, 1959:7-8). The village community studies done by various people, including Fei, Gamble, and Lang (Fei, 1939; Fei, Chang, 1945. Gamble, 1954; Lang, 1968), also showed that the average size of the family in the vast rural areas in China was anything but large. The size of the family varied in fact with the economic resources of the family. Thus, J. L. Buck's survey in the 1920s revealed that the size of the family was closely related to the size of the farm (Buck, 1930:63). A recent re-analysis of Buck's data by Irene Taeuber showed some regional differentiation also: nuclear families were more predominant in the southeast and southwest regions and the Lower Yangtze, where total family size was smaller (Taebber 1970:73,81). A Nationalist government report in 1947 found an average which ranged from 4.1 persons in the province of Jehol to 5.9 persons in Anhwei per family. The province of Kirin in Manchuria had an unusual average of 6.9, "which is reminiscent of the large frontier family in early American history" (Yang, 1959:8).

Functions and Kinship Structure

Given the small size of the traditional family, it seemed surprising that this unit of social life could have performed a multiplicity of functions for the individual for so many centuries. On the cultural-religious plane, the most important function of the traditional family is procreation. In fact, the cultural emphasis on the continuity of the family line and the practice of ancestor worship lead directly to the large family ideal. The family is also a unit of social-economic life. It is a unit of economic production and consumption. It is mainly responsible for the socialization and education of the children. It provides both status and occupational placement for the grown-up members; it is the center of their social and cultural life.

That the traditional family unit is able to perform all these functions is not so surprising if we look beyond the family itself to the kinship structure as a whole, which serves both to support the family and absorb it into a wider social network. The kinship ties most relevant to the individual are his clan or *tsu*, composed of members supposedly coming from a common ancestor and bearing the same surname. The major functions of the clan are religious, being concerned with rites which honor the clan ancestors. It also runs schools, upkeeps irrigation works, roads, bridges, and the like, deriving its income from the clan-owned land. Often the clan also takes up the function of local defense and the maintenance of law and order.

Internal Structure and Family Relationships

The ideal Chinese family is patrilineal, patrilocal, and patriarchal. Within this family, the oldest male member from the highest generation rules supreme. He allocates the productive tasks to the individual members within the family, dispenses the family purse, and carefully sees to it that harmony is obtained.

A lot has already been written on the nature of relationships within the Chinese family (Levy, 1949; Fried, 1953). The division of labor between the sexes is little different from that obtained within patriarchal families of Western societies in traditional times. The father's instrumental role and the mother's expressive role are universal among traditional families; the emotional ties between mother and son, between mother and daughter, and the affectional relationship between father and young daughter but later the avoidance on account of the incest taboo, are also familiar themes. However, the traditional Chinese family is characterized by two very distinct and perhaps accentuated principles of internal organization, namely, the generational hierarchy and the sex hierarchy. The former makes for the very strong father-son relationship, which is in fact the most central relationship within the family, while the latter results in the extremely subordinate status of the Chinese women, as is well known to the West.

The cultural emphasis on continuity of the family line and the cult of ancestor worship have produced a prominent father-son identification, so that one always lives under the authority of one's father and under the shadow of one's ancestors.[4] However, this relationship is not entirely free of conflict. In the old days, when the son's means of livelihood were completely dependent on family and relatives, such inter-generationl conflict was seldom allowed to flare up in the open. But under the forces of modernization, the generational conflict is fully unleashed as is so well depicted in the literature of the 1920s and 1930s.

Status of Women

The extended family ideal is supplemented by a doctrine of subjugation of women. The stress on male lineage automatically means the downgrading of women and the relegation of the female role to reproduction and household work. Girls from the day of birth are subjected to a lifelong discrimination as is so well described by the popular code of feminine ethics, the Three Obediences, which prescribe that a woman is to obey her father at home, her husband after marriage, and her eldest son after the death of her husband. Female infanticide is known to be quite a common practice since ancient times, and even lasting right up to the early 20th century.[5]

[4]The theme of the father-son identification is fully explored in Francis L.K. Hsu *Under the Ancestors' Shadow*, London: Routledge & Kegan Paul, 1949.

[5]Ho-Ping-ti, in his *Studies on the Population of China, 1368-1953*, Cambridge, Harvard University Press, 1959, points out that infanticide was common since the historical past. The practice of female infanticide continued well into the 20th century, as reported by Olga Lang, *op. cit.* However, lacking accurate census figures on the sex ratio at birth, it is not easy to assess the extent of this practice in the traditional society. Also, it was clear that the practice was never institutionalized. It came about mainly on account of economic hardship; poor families would prefer to devote their resources to bringing up the male children rather than the female.

The selling of young girls by poor families to become servants in rich families is also quite common. Even within their own families of orientation, girls are segregated in the women's quarters of the house, and at an early age, they are made aware of the fact that they would sooner or later be married out of their families. A girl is taught to be gentle in disposition and pleasing in appearance, to be chary of speech and to be assiduous in the performance of her domestic duties. The low status of women is further maintained by the withholding of educational and economic opportunities. The popular saying goes, "Lack of learning is a woman's virtue." Women seldom do any productive work,[6] and are therefore rendered totally dependent on their families. The practice of footbinding, prevalent especially among the rich, symbolizes the extreme subjugation of women.[7]

After marriage, a woman's prime duty is to produce sons for the family line. She is also to serve her husband's parents and be obedient to her mother-in-law. The relationship between the wife and the mother-in-law is often full of conflict and oppression of the former by the latter. To her huband, the woman owes complete allegiance and loyalty, while her husband enjoys the double sex standard to the full. Her position in the husband's family is only slightly improved after she has given birth to sons, and later after she has become a mother-in-law herself. However, she is still subjected to her own grown-up sons.

The failure to produce sons constitutes the main excuse for the male to take concubines. The institution of concubinage is even older than that of footbinding, but its extent has never been great

---

[6]In the rural areas, women have always participated in farm work, especially during the busy peak seasons. However, even the peasant women have never had agricultural work as their major occupation. Their main roles are still in the homestead.

[7]The practice of footbinding probably started in the 10th century. It was at first practiced among the rich families, but it gradually spread to even the peasant population. One Western observer wrote in 1835 that the majority of women in the large towns and cities, as well as in the most fashionable parts of the country, had their feet bound. He estimated that five to eight out of every ten females had bound feet, depending on locality and their social class background—with a tendency towards applying the bindings more tightly and rigorously as one went up the social scale. See Howard S. Levy, *Chinese Footbinding, The History of a Curious Erotic Custom*, New York, Walton Rawls, 1966, p. 52.

for obvious economic reasons.[8] The position of the concubine is always lower than that of the wife. She is obliged to serve, obey, and respect the wife. Children born by a concubine owe their filial duty to the wife and not to their biological mother.

The low status of the traditional Chinese women is a subject well written on. Nevertheless, it is to be noted that the extreme subordination of women and "ideal womanhood" are only approximated by the gentry and wealthy classes. Among the masses in peasant areas, females are subject to less segregation, and their participation in the economic activities of the household has given them a certain degree of self-assertion and freedom of action.[9] In the same way, child brides, concubinage, footbinding, prostitution, etc., are class-related phenomena in practice.

Love, Marriage and Divorce

Romantic love has no place in the traditional marriage system. In fact, it is considered highly improper behavior and the segregation of the sexes at an early age is one of the devices to ensure that young people do not get involved before they are married. In the matter of marriage, the young people have absolutely no say. The choice of marriage partners is completely in the hands of the elders, and the marriage contract, usually involving an exorbitant bride price, is drawn up by go-betweens who act according to the instructions of the parents of both parties. Boys and girls are matched according to both mystical and mundane criteria: their

[8]Concubines were found in less than 1 per cent of the families in Ting Hsien. Sidney Gamble, *Ting Hsien. A North China Rural Community*, New York: Institute of Pacific relations, 1954, p. 38. In Lang's study of 1,700 college and high-school students during 1936-37, it was found that only 11.48 per cent of the students admitted the existence of a concubine in the family, and in another 5.8 per cent of the cases, concubines were suspected though not admitted. Lang, *op. cit.*, pp. 220-221.

[9]In an oft-quoted passage, Mao Tse-tung described the "freer" position of the peasant women: "As to the authority of the husband, this has always been weaker among the poor peasants because...their womenfolk have to do more manual labor than the women of the richer classes and therefore have more say and greater power of decision in family matters." Mao Tse-tung, "Report on an Investigation of the Peasant Movement in Hunan," March 1927, in *Selected Works of Mao Tse-tung*, I, Peking: Foreign Languages Press, 1967, p. 45.

horoscopes as well as their socio-economic backgrounds are cross-examined.

The *Book of Rites*, which contains the Confucian rules of conduct, indicates that men should get married at the age of thirty and women at twenty or twenty-three, but these are interpreted to be maximum ages of marriage. Boys and girls are betrothed quite young, in some places, as early as the age of eight or ten. However, young people are not married until their late teens. There is some slight variation between the different social strata, with the rich tending to marry their children at a somewhat earlier age,[10] while some very poor peasants remain single throughout their life because they cannot afford to pay a bride price. In some areas, particularly in the south and southeastern provinces, the practice of taking in foster child brides (who very often are a few years older than their intended husbands) into the family is quite common among poor people, in order that the labor power of the daughters-in-law can be utilized as early as possible.[11]

Although divorce is enacted, marriages are considered life bonds and divorced persons (especially females) are looked upon with great disgrace. Under the Ch'ing code, there are seven grounds on which a married women can be unilaterally divorced by her husband. These are: failure to serve the husband's parents and disobedience to them, failure to give birth to a son, dissoluteness of manners, jealousy, loquacity (talkativeness and quarrelsome conduct), malignant disease, and larceny. On the other hand, there are only three grounds on which a husband has no right to divorce his wife: if she has participated in the three-year mourning of either of her husband's parents; if her husband's

[10]Data from Ting Hsien, for example, showed that while one-third of the males in the couples in families with less that fifty *mu* of land were married before they were fifteen years old, the proportion was 80.5 per cent in families with hundred *mu* or more. In the latter group 40 per cent of the males were married when they were fourteen years of age. The effect of economic status for the age of marriage of girls was less striking but still noticeable. Sidney Gamble, *Ting Hsien, op. cit.,* pp. 43-44.

[11]The practice of taking in foster child brides (*t'ung yang hsi*) was rather common among poorer families in the south and southeastern parts of China. In Phenix Village in Kwangtung, for example, the age of marriage for girls was eighteen years, and for boys one year to one-and-a-half years younger. The boys and girls were married approximately ten years after betrothal. See Kulp, *op. cit.,* p. 175.

family was poor before the marriage but has become rich after; or if, after divorce, she has no home to return to.[12] The law also provides for divorce by mutual consent, but in practice a woman would never willingly agree to such an action, since she will be subjected to great social sanction and will have to lead an extremely ostracized life thereafter. On the man's part, if he is not satisfied with his wife, he has the recourse to concubinage. The divorce rate in China has therefore been very low.[13]

While remarriage of widowers and widows does occur, especially among the poor,[14] the doctrine of chaste widowhood has long been given official consecration since the Ming Dynasty, which started the practice of honouring chaste widows who would not remarry.

Stability of the Traditional Family System

The traditional family remained stable and relatively unchanged as an institution for nearly 2,000 years. It earned the name of being one of the world's most ancient and stable cultural artifacts. That it was able to remain so was due to a set of social-cultural, economic, and political factors. Economically speaking, traditional China was largely an agricultural country with the family farm as the most basic unit of cultivation. This provided for the economic self-sufficiency of the peasant household, but at the subsistence level, and made a large family valuable in itself because of the available labor. Politically speaking, China had very rarely been able to establish effective political control from the central administration, so that local communities had always enjoyed a large measure of auto-

---

[12]For a comprehensive analysis of the Ch'ing Code, particularly with reference to the provisions for divorce, refer to Vermier Y. Chiu, *Marriage Laws and Customs of China*, Hong Kong: The Chinese University Press, 1966, pp. 61-68.

[13]Kulp found no single case of divorce in Phenix Village, nor could one case be remembered by his informants. Kulp, *op. cit.*, p. 184. Similarly, Gamble recorded only two divorces among the 515 families in Ting Hsien. Gamble, *Ting Hsein, op. cit.*, p. 38.

[14]For example, Gamble found that 14 per cent of the women who had lost their first husbands had remarried. Gamble, *Ting Hsein, op. cit.*, p. 38.

nomy.[15] Thus, the village community consisting of clan(s) came to have much political control over its constituent families and the individuals. Of far greater significance than either of these factors were the cultural-religious tenets of Confucianism. Of the five cardinal social relationships designated by Confucius, three were basic family relationships.[16] And among these three, the father-son relationship was the most important and was well guarded by an elaborate set of behavioral norms collectively known as the *hsiao-tao* (doctrine of filial piety). Even though the finer details of Confucian doctrines were embraced only by the educated classes, the main teachings have been popularized among the common people, being incorporated into a body of folklore and folk religion. Thus, the Han culture was essentially Confucian, so that even though the large, extended family was seldom realized in practice, it had remained the cultural ideal of both gentry and commoners for generation upon generation.

The Family Revolution

The solidarity and stability of the family institution began to be challenged by modernizing forces, which we have already referred to in the Introduction, around the turn of the 20th century. During the Republican period, a modern family was emerging in the urban centers. Given a modern education, economic independence, and a new social and national consciousness, young men and women began to cherish new ideas about their roles in society, questions of love, and marriage. The most significant social phenomenon that happened during this period was the feminist movement. Under the initiative actions of foreign missionaries, natural foot societies sprang up all over the country. Coupled with the effects of Nationalist legislation against footbinding, the practice finally came to an end in the early 1920s. The Republican constitution gave women the rights to be educated, to marry by free choice, and to

[15]By the end of the 19th century, the bureaucracy of the Chling government had become almost completely ineffective, so that the local villages enjoyed a large degree of autonomy. See Hsiao Kung-chuan, *Rural China, Imperial Control in the Nineteenth Century*, Seattle: University of Washington Press, 1960.

[16]The five cardinal relationships are: ruler-ruled, father-son, brother-brother, husband-wife and friend-friend.

participate in the national political life. Co-education in universities and schools came to be established since 1919. Women's rights organizations and women's unions began to appear under various labels. Various publications on the subject of modern womanhood quickly appeared and were eagerly read by the newly literate women. Furthermore, the female students' active participation in the nationalistic movements of the 1920s and 1930s greatly raised their own political status. There was an accelerated pace in the development of both educational and economic opportunities for women, and their appearance on the social scene (as contrasted with their former seclusion) was rapidly becoming an accepted fact.[17]

It can be said that during the Republican period, the principle of sex equality was generally accepted by the urban intelligentsia, the upper, and the middle classes. Modern marriages contracted under the new Civil Code (1931) increasingly took the place of arranged marriages, and divorces were becoming quite common in the big cities (Lamson 1935:532-536). However, in the backward rural areas, traditional practices still held strong; and ideas and outlooks remained essentially untouched by the revolutionary changes in the urban sector, until the CCP carried out vast marriage reform compaigns in the countryside two decades later.[18]

III. The CCP Family Reform Policies

The Marriage Law of 1950 and Its Implementation

A few months after the CCP came into power, the Marriage Law was promulgated in May 1950 as one of the first social reforms made by the Communist government. It can be viewed as the product of an intellectual and emotional drive to build a new social order based on a new form of family and social relationships

[17]See Lin Yutang's *My Country and My People*, New York: The John Day Company, 1935 for an interesting description of the fashions and fads that appeared in the mid-1930s, in connection with the "sexual liberation" of the Chinese women, p. 170.

[18]The forces of change in connection with the so-called Family Revolution in modern China were analysed in Lang, *op. cit.*, as concentrated in the urban sector only, while the majority of the population in the backward rural areas remained untouched, p. 193.

between men and women. The law itself is the culmination of a series of earlier legislation introduced by the CCP in the Soviet areas in the 1930s to bring about the socialist ideal of sex equality.[19] The Marriage Law purports to replace the "arbitrary and compulsory feudal marriage system" by a "new democratic system based on the free choice of the partners, monogamy, equal rights for both sexes, and the protection of the lawful interests of women and children." Polygyny, concubinage, child marriage, interference with remarriage of widows, and the exaction of bride price are prohibited. Husband and wife are bound by law to live together as companions, to love, respect, and take care of each other. They are to enjoy equal rights with regard to the home, their work, and their social life. The freedom of divorce is guaranteed. The Marriage Law requires the registration of all marriages as well as the investigation of all applications for a marriage certificate. This ensures that the provisions of the law are adhered to, so that traditional practices can be effectively checked. The Marriage Law was later supplemented by the "Regulations Governing Marriage Registration," passed in June 1953, which entrusted the matter of registration to grassroots organizations such as the street committees in the urban areas, and the *hsiang* (administrative village) or *chen* (town) people's councils in the rural areas.

The social and political implications of the Marriage Law are apparent. The CCP makes it quite clear from the start that it intends to break down the traditional family system, and to build up a new socialist order based on a new family system. The freedom of marriage granted to both men and women would affect the solidarity and the structure of the traditional family profoundly. Instead of centering around the parent-child relationship, the modern family centers around the two marriage partners, thus giving rise to a conjugal two-generational unit. Within this unit, the husband-wife relationship is no longer subjected to alienation by parental interference, and the quarrelsome relationship between the mother-in-law and daughter-in-law can be avoided. Family continuity is no longer stressed; the size of the family would thus be affected in favor of small families. And instead of owing their

[19]For a detailed account and analysis of the earlier marriage legislation of the CCP in the Kiangsi Soviet and the Border Areas in the early 1930s and 1940s, see M.J. Meijer, *Marriage law and Policy in the Chinese People's Republic*, Hong Kong: Hong Kong University Press, 1971, Chapter 2 and 3.

primary allegiance to kith and kin, the family members can now be made more pliable to the demands of the country. The new marriage system also has its economic implications. The integration of the traditional family is largely supported by the economic interdependence of the family members. With the marriage reform, the status of women is raised and their role in national life would be increasingly important. Freeing women from the ties of the family means the release of a tremendous labor potential which can be utilized for national economic construction. Their free participation in public life in turn hastens the decline of the traditional family.

When the Marriage Law was promulgated, the CCP claimed that for the first time in China's history the women were given equal rights with men. This claim, however, cannot be substantiated in the light of history. As we have already described, the family revolution had started long before the CCP came to power; and before the CCP made nationwide legislation regarding the family, there was already the Nationalist Civil Code. The effects of the previous family reforms, nevertheless, were limited to the educated and upper and middle classes. Thus, the CCP's marriage reform campaigns were designed to quicken the pace of social change in the rural areas. Some of the drastic measures employed during this initial period of the Marriage Law movement can be seen as deliberate (and perhaps necessary) steps to "break the ground," to shake the roots of the traditional social order. A government directive in September 1961 ordered that "the people must be brought together at public accusation meetings to expose those who have failed to live up to the standards of the new law. There must be huge mass trials; the marriage reform is to go hand in hand with the Land Reform and the same techniques are to be used for both" (jih-pao, 1951). Encouraged by the government, some overenthusiastic cadres went into extremes and there were reports of arranged marriages being forcibly dissolved, child brides returned home, concubines and widows being remarried, and cruel punishments inflicted on husbands (Jen-min jih-pao, 1953; Nan Fung, jih-pao, 1952)."

Almost immediately, there was a great social upheaval, as reflected in the large number of marital disputes,[20] the number of

[20]The *Jen-min jih-pao* reported on 29 September 1951, that immediately after the promulgation of the Marriage Law, people took their family quarrels to court. Thus, in the first five months of 1951, the people's courts in the

suicides attributable to matrimonial difficulties,[21] and the large number of divorces.[22] The alarming state of affairs warranted a government investigation in September 1951 into the working of the Marriage Law. Consequently, the extreme measures were checked and the vigorous implementation of the Marriage Law halted until 1953. In March that year, a Marriage Law Month was staged, during which an intensive indoctrination campaign, aimed at both cadres and masses, was mounted to educate the people in "model" family relationships under the new socialist regime. This campaign was carried out in 70 per cent of the countryside. It also marked a change in the CCP's family reform policy towards moderation in the tactics of implementation and a new stress on family harmony.

Beginning therefore in 1953, and becoming more and more apparent since 1955, the marriage reform was relaxed so that all efforts could be concentrated on the first five-year Plan (1953-57) and later the collectivization of the economy. The success of the Marriage Law movement from 1950 and up till the eve of the communes (1958) was difficult to evaluate. In spite of the large amounts of published materials during the first few years of the reform movement, such information was scrappy and was obviously intended for

---

central-south region handled 32,881 matrimonial cases, which constituted more than 60 per cent of all civil suits of the entire region. Newspapers outside of China also reported the sudden upsurge of marital disputes taken to court. For example, in the rural areas of the southern regions, matrimonial cases accounted for 90 per cent of the civil cases passing though the people's courts between January and August 1952, as reported in the *Wah-kiu yat-po*, Hong Kong, on 8 September 1952.

[21]In 1950, the number of women who committed suicide or died for marital reasons was over 10,000 in the central-south region; 1,245 in Shantung; and 119 in North Kiangsu. *Hsin Chung-kuo yueh-k'an (New China Monthly)*, No. 24, October 1951, p. 1244.

[22]The *Jen-min jih-pao* indicated that during 1950-51, the proportion of divorces to matrimonial cases ranged from 46 per cent to 84 per cent for four metropolitan cities, and from 54 per cent to 90 per cent for seventy-one counties in north China (*Jen-min jih-pao*, 29 September 1951). For the country as a whole, divorce cases received by local courts reached 186, 167 in 1950, and rose further to 409, 500 in 1951. In the first half of 1952, there were 398,243 divorces, *ibid.*, 20 March 1953. The major grounds for divorces granted during these early years were: arranged marriage, child brides, marriage by "purchase" cruelty, bigamy, adultery, aud desertion.

internal propaganda-educational purposes. The statistics available cannot form any valid basis for interregional comparisons, and national figures were not made known.[23] But it was clear that the Marriage Law met with a great deal of conservative opposition from the rural population, even from the ranks of the cadres who had to be redoctrinated in the letter and the spirit of the Law periodically. The CCP learned the lesson quickly. It soon came to realize that social reforms, especially those affecting deep-rooted institutions like the family, had to take a long time to take effect. The party had to be reconciled with the fact that, once the indoctrination campaigns were slackened, customary practices re-emerged almost immediately in the second half of the 1950s. Thus, it was reported in the official press that the demand of bride price, arranged marriages, and early marriage had revived in many rural districts. (Chung-Kuo ching-nien pao, 1956; Jen-min jih-pao, 1954; Kung-jen jih-pao, 1956; Chung-Kuo ching-nien, 1958).

The Communes and the Emancipation of Women

With the launching of the communes in 1958, the family came under fresh attack. The people's communes were said to herald in a new form of social organization in which complete equality of the sexes and total emancipation of women could be achieved. Large numbers of nurseries, kindergartens, communal dining halls, laundry service units, etc., were established to free women from household work, thus enabling them to join in the production campaigns known as the Great Leap Forward.[24]

The coming of the people's communes was a surprise to the outside world, mainly because the time span between the beginning of China's collectivization program (1956) and the emergence of the rural communes was so short. From the sociological standpoint, the

[23]Moreover, some free marriages were said to have the "agreement of the parents on both sides." In such cases, it is extremely difficult to judge the relative weight of free choice and parental pressure.

[24]In a rural commune in Pihsien, Szechwan, 432 dining rooms were set up in 1958 to serve the 16,900 households—75,700 men, women and children were thus fed by these communal facilities. In addition, 17,000 women were "freed" to participate in economic production. This at once solved the labor shortage problem. Chuan Nung-tiao, "How Commune Dining Rooms Serve the Peasants," *Peking Review*, No. 2, 12 January 1960, pp. 16-17.

communes represented a continuous effort of the CCP to push through its socialist ideals by one broad sweeping action. The most prominent slogan during the commune movement was the complete emancipation of women. The advantages of the communes were said to be the establishment of a "new" type of marriage and family relationships based on the true liberation of women and absolute equality between the sexes. With equal economic opportunities, with equal pay, husbands and wives could now be real companions according to the spirit of the Marriage Law (Teh-chuan, 1959; Teh-chuan, 1960).

Up to the coming of the communes, the majority of women had not yet been fully involved in production activities, although they had been successfully organized in peasants' associations, local women's federations,[25] and trade unions. While the female industrial labor force continued to grow throughout these years,[26] the greatest proportion of the peasant women was still tied to household work, and agricultural production still remained women's subsidiary occupation. They were encouraged to abide by the *wu-hao* (five virtues)—to be good at harmonizing family and neighbor relationships, good at managing the household, good at educating the children, good at encouraging the family members to work and study, and good at their own ideological studies. Thus, their roles were still essentially those of housewives. The communes, by providing communal services on a large scale, posed a radically different situation. Official figures showed that in 1959, the number of women who worked in the rural communes generally stood at 90 per cent of the total female labor force. Whereas in 1957, the men worked an average of 249 days in the rural areas and women worked 166 days, in 1959, the figures were 300 days for men and 250 days for women (Peking Review, 1960:6-9). In the cities, it was reported that by

[25]The All-China Democratic Women's Federation was formed in April 1949. It functioned through a system of women's representative congresses which permeated every province, every county, subdistrict, city, town, and village. In 1950, there were 30,000,000 members of the federation; by 1953, its membership had grown to 76,000,000. See Chao Kuo-chun, *The Mass Organizations in Communist China,* Cambridge, Center for International Studies, M.I.T. Press, 1953.

[26]The female industrial labor force grew from 2,000,000 in 1952 to around 8,000,000 in 1959. *Ten Great Years,* Peking: State Statistical Bureau, 1960, p. 182.

mid-1960, 27,000,000 women had become members of urban communes and their labor was fully utilized in "street factories"
(Lethbridge, 1961:22-23).

It is interesting to note that at this point, domestic work came to
be condemned. Before the communes, domestic work was glorified
somewhat as a necessary activity in order that the men might devote
their full time to their jobs and their ideological studies (Jen-min
jih-pao, 1956). However, when the people's communes were formed
in 1958, the labor shortage artificially created on account of the
production campaigns demanded the immediate and extensive
mobilization of women. This was made possible by the large-scale
socialization of domestic services and child care. Engels and Lenin
were copiously quoted with regard to the "petty, dirty, heavy and
dull" nature of domestic work, and its "deadening, stultifying"
effects on the female personality. Thus, it was claimed that only
with the socialization of domestic work and collectivization of child
care could the full emancipation of women be finally achieved.

Viewed from every angle, the organization of the communes was
bound to have very deep effects on the family. With large numbers
of women attaining economic independence, there would also be a
general rise in their social status. This meant that they would have
more and more say over their mate selection, and whatever still
remained of traditional practices such as arranged marriages and
child brides would decline much sooner than if the women were not
fully mobilized by the communes. On the other hand, the communes
also produced immediate effects on the pattern of family living.
This is particularly true of the early communes which were keen on
the principles of collective working as well as living arrangements.
With the socialization of domestic work, it would mean that the
family could no longer stay as a consumption unit. With the children
placed under institutional care, the family would no longer be responsible for the socialization of the children. And with old people
cared for in old-age homes, the family would also lose its function
of economic security and maintenance. The family would in effect
be reduced to a two-generational family—or, where the children
were away most of the time, to a conjugal family only. The ideological fervor that accompanied the commune movement, and the
vast amount of propaganda on communal living, therefore, caused
many Western observers to conclude that the family was altogether
abolished in China.

The commune movement, however, was short-lived. After the failure of the production campaigns, the rural commune were reorganized by the end of 1959 and the earlier radical tendencies in communal living were checked. The development of the urban communes was similarly halted since 1960. The family once again resumed many of its former functions and the women had to take back their domestic duties. As the national economic crisis deepened in the first two or three years of the 1960s, all talk of marriage and family reform was quietly dropped. There is quite a bit of evidence that, up to the present day, the family is still functioning as a unit of living, so that the fears of the Western observers at the beginning of the commune movement proved to be alarmist.

The Cultural Revolution and the Crumbling of the Age Hierarchy

The commune movement marked a distinct phase in the CCP's family reform policies. During this phase, criticism was concentrated on the sex hierarchy within the family and discrimination of women in society. The Cultural Revolution, which started in 1966, marked a fresh attack on the family from a different angle. Especially during the first part of the campaign, which focused more on social, ideological, and cultural reforms, the traditional age hierarchy within the family came under heavy fire. Young people were urged to expose their parents and elders for their ideological shortcomings, (Wen-hui pao, 1968), and they were asked to devote all their energy to ideological studies and serving the country. The family was depicted as harboring selfish ideas and self-interest. Hence, young people were exhorted to revolutionize it from within. They were to organize ideological study groups and "struggle-criticism" meetings inside the family, during after-work hours, during meal times, etc. (Jen-min jih-pao, 1967; 1968). By encouraging young people to make long pilgrimages to revolutionary shrines in faraway places, with or without the consent of their parents, the Party was preparing the young generation to be "revolutionary successors."

With the revolt of the youth and with "politics taking command," family relationships were described in the official literature on the Cultural Revolution as "comradeship relationships based on revolutionary ideology." Every individual was not only a member of the "big socialist family," that is, the nation, but also a revolutionary comrade to his parents, brothers, and sisters. Inside each family

Mao Tse-tung should be made the household head, and the *Thoughts of Chairman Mao* should be made the new family law (Jen-min jih-pao, 1968; Wen-hui pao, 1968).

The turmoil of the Cultural Revolution lasted between two to three years, and it was not until the early 1970s that the dust began to settle, and glimpses of the aftermath were possible. However, since the Cultural Revolution, the two major sources of information on the family (the *Chinese Youth* and the *Chinese Women*) have been suspended. What little we know of the social effects of the Cultural Revolution comes from travelers' accounts and journalistic reports. They seem to indicate that trends in marriage and family living, which have already started before the recent political upheaval, have continued. It is clear that a modern family has been steadily emerging in China for the past two decades of Communist rule.

IV. THE FAMILY IN CHINA TODAY

Love, Dating, and Marriage

Up to the eve of the Cultural Revolution, some traditional customs, such as marriage matches and the payment of bride price, were reported to be existing still in the rural districts. However, whenever cases like these happen, young men and women are able to bring their grievances to the attention of the various women's organizations, street committees, the Party cells, and the commune organization at various levels. Thus, freedom of marriage is in effect guaranteed. Concubinage has disappeared. On the other hand, due to the strong reaction against the ease with which divorce was granted at the beginning of the Marriage Law movement, divorce is now treated with much greater care. Young couples are advised to look at their marriage with serious purpose and intent.

Romantic love is not banned as under the traditional family system. Neither is it encouraged, for the obvious reason that it would result in dyadic withdrawal, and the energy of the young men and women would be sapped. Dating is not forbidden. In fact, journalistic accounts have reported young couples (students and workers) engaged "not just in holding hands while taking evening walks, but necking on park benches and in dark corners."

(Taylor, 1966:94-95, 104). Premarital sex is evident from reported cases of abortion performed for unmarried mothers.[27] However, such kinds of behavior are severely punished if known to officials. Incidents of forced separation have occurred when couples are suspected to have indulged in premarital intimacies (Lucas, 1965: 185-187). The general prevailing atmosphere is one of self-denial, self-restraint, and absention. Neither love nor sex is allowed to occupy much of one's thinking, as they would interfere with work and studies. It is ironical in a sense that, after the sudden removal of the traditional barrier between the sexes, and the breaking down of the reserve so long cultivated between men and women, they should now be subjected to the strict surveillance of the Party cadres and their peers.

In spite of official pressure and social criticism, young people apparently have not been totally won over by the party policy. Shortly before the Cultural Revolution, there was a great deal of concern over young people's preoccupation with love and marriage, apart from a host of problems universally associated with youth and adolescence, such as sex and occupational choice. Between the months of February and September 1964, the widely-read journal, *Chung-kuo Fu-nü* (*Chinese Women*) published a series of "letters to the editor," sent in by its female readers upon the editor's invitation to voice their opinions on love and marriage. It was said that as many as 2,000 letters were received, a number of which were printed out. From these revealing autobiographic accounts, it was evident that in Communist China, even after twenty years of socialist indoctrination, young women still cherish "bourgeois" ideas on marriage and family. The most commonly expressed desires are: a good marriage, secure income, and happy family life. This is a far cry from the official statement that "in choosing their marriage partners today, young people are more and more inclined to demand in the first place conscientiousness in work and in ideological study, as well as a progressive outlook. This is a step forward to real freedom in marriage and husband-wife relationships characterized by mutual respect and mutual love." (Peking Review, 1964:19). That the "bour-

[27]The *China News Analysis* (Hong Kong) reported that many unmarried girls have applied for abortion. Information on this was obtained from refugees who came out from China. No. 842, 21 May 1971.

geois" concerns of young people with love and marriage are not easy for the Party to accept, much less to admit, can be seen from what happened to the journal during the Cultural Revolution—the editor was fired, and the journal was suspended indefinitely.[28]

It is worth nothing that in all these published letters, the authors indicated that they were married according to their own choice—hence, pointing definitely to a new trend of free marriage according to love, whether in the true spirit of "proletarian love" or not.

Although there is a considerable amount of interclass marriage, resulting from the freedom of choice, there is still strong social pressure against women entering into hypogamous unions. In particular, the marriage of a city girl to a peasant is generally frowned upon. (Chung-Kuo Fu-nü, 1964; Chung-Kuo Ching-nien, 1965).

Age of Marriage, Birth Control, and Family Size

In general, there has been a trends towards late marriages in accordance with the government's new population policy after the Great Leap Forward. The Marriage Law of 1950 set the age of marriage at twenty for men and eighteen for women. However, since the birth control campaign started in 1956-57, and was reactivated in 1962, men and women have been constantly subjected to educational propaganda on the advantages of late marriage—for example, physical and emotional maturity, the care and education of the next generation, and more time and energy for work and study. The age of marriage recommended for women is twenty-three to twenty-seven, for men, twenty-five to twenty-nine. (Chung-Kuo ching-nien pao, 1962.)

Married couples are encouraged to practise birth control in the interest, again, of physical health and the economic participation of women. Recent visitors to China reported that contraceptives are available at low prices and abortion is free and permitted on medical advice. Sterilization is getting more widely accepted, even among men. In late 1967, Han Suyin wrote, "two or three children

---

[28]A complete translation of all the letters published in those issues of the *Chung-kuo fu-nü* can be found in the Supplement to the 1 July 1964, issue of the *Current Scene*, Vol. II, No. 36.

were now considered the ideal family. Among rural people, six children were thought enough." (Freeborne, 1963:9). A more recent visitor to China reported in April-May 1971 that the birth control campaign has produced great effects even in the countryside. Two are considered the right number, and the largest family on one farm in a commune near Shanghai has only four children (Durdin, 1971:11).

Family Relationships, Structure, and Functions

Within the modern family, a companionship type of husband and wife relationship has emerged, especially among the professional and technical workers, the educated people, party workers, and civil servants. This companionship relationship has come about through the general rise in women's social, economic, and political statuses. Sex equality is gradually being accepted, not just by the urban population, but also by the rural people. In place of the traditional image of the fragile, home-bound woman, the new socialist woman is always depicted in popular literature as a strong-willed, robust worker in the fields or in the factories, who can do whatever the men do and even do better at jobs traditionally considered as "men's work." (China Reconstructs, 1971:36-37) In place of traditional virtues such as obedience and chastity, the new woman is supposed to win respect from her husband by her industriousness, frugality, and correct ideological thinking. She is her husband's helpmate. The good wife is one who manages the household so that the husband can devote his whole heart to socialist construction, and the children can be brought up as revolutionary successors of the country.

The new emphasis on the husband-wife relationship is in direct contrast to the traditional emphasis on the father-son relationship. Family continuity is no longer stressed. Whereas the married woman could formerly be divorced on the ground of failure to give birth to sons, the reasons for obtaining divorce now include personality incompatibilities and discrepancies in ideological standpoints. Thus, the family institution itself is devoid of any mythical-religious context; and ancestor worship is no longer practiced by young people, although it is not banned among older folks.[29]

[29]This is evident from the large numbers of people from Hong Kong going back to "sweep their ancestors' graves" in China, each year during the Ching Ming and the Chung Yeung festivals.

Wedding ceremonies are now completely secularized. The Communist views on revolutionry love and marriage also lead to the advocacy of economy and simplicity in wedding celebrations, which commonly take place in factories, schools, and offices, rather than at homes. Although large dinner parties are reported to be held still in some places and by some families well into the late 1960s (such families, however, are subject to strong criticism), the general trend is toward giving small parties where only cakes and sweets may be served (Taylor, 1967:97).

With the gradual realization of sex equality, and the recent strong emphasis on youth comes a more equalitarian form of family structure. The traditional sex and age hierarchies can no longer stand so long as wives can criticize husbands, and sons are encouraged to expose parents for "counter-revolutionary" ideas. Thus, family decisions tend to be made jointly by the spouses, and children's opinions can no longer be ignored. There is plenty of evidence to show that the traditional division of labor between the sexes is breaking down. While women are engaged in work outside the home, the men have to take up more household responsibilities. Among the professional people in particular, whose duties demand that they be away from home for the great part of the day, and even for a continuous period, it is commonly accepted that husbands and wives should take turns to do the housework and take care of the children (Taylor, 1967-92).

A lot of "exemplary stories" about family life deal with how mothers-in-law and daughters-in-law can now live together in peace under the guidance of the *Works of Chairman Mao*. Others tell of how grandparents are a great help in the household, and how grandchildren have patiently helped their grandparents to correct their conservative ways of thinking. The advantages of having the old folks around the house are very real, especially when the housewife goes out to work.[30] These stories reveal an important

[30]In fact, one letter in the 1 April 1966, issue of the *Chung-kuo-fu-nu*, sent in by a working mother, complained about her mother-in-law living in the same household who did not give the writer sufficient help in the household work, so that her work and studies were impaired. Fortunately, as the story always goes, after indoctrination with Mao's thought, the mother-in-law changed her attitude and became very helpful from then on. *Chung-kuo-fu-nu*, No. 4, 1 April 1966, p. 28.

fact about family organization in China today, that is, the survival of the three-generational family or the stem family. Although there is no way to estimate the proportion of families belonging to the stem family type, it is quite apparent that this form of family is commonly found among both peasant and urban households. Apart from the obvious advantage of having more available labor to help in household tasks, the deep cultural tenet—that one is obliged to support one's parents when they grow old—is an important factor holding the three-generational family together up till today. Thus, it is more often those old people who have no near relatives to take care of them who live in old people's homes. Even in such institutions, care is taken to show that the old people are not only given material support but also treated with respect. In fact, the old-age homes are called homes of respect for the old—another indication of the deep-rooted cultural value of veneration of the old. In spite of the exaltation of youth as "revolutionary successors," old people are by no means to be neglected in the "big socialist family"

While the new husband-wife relationship is more intimate than even before, and the mother-in-law and daughter-in-law relationship much less difficult, the parent-child relationship is often strained, because in many ways young people are taught to be less dependent on family and parents than ever before (Lethbridge, 1965:51). Also, "adults are more cautious with children...not (except in very rare cases) because they are afraid that children will be called upon to betray them. It is because children often lack precautions in talking to others...and they might unwittingly blurt out revealing information" (Vogel, 1965: 52).

Apart from the production of some subsidiary food for private consumption or for sale on the open market, the family is no longer a unit of economic production. But it is still a unit of consumption, although for a period at the beginning of the commune movement, this function was taken away by the free supply system of the communes. More significantly, recent visitors have come out from China with reports that the family unit is still a unit of living, with the family members pooling their wage earnings together in a common budget. And the household is still a basic unit for administrative and accounting purposes, as well as a

unit for the organization of production activiti es.[31] As Audrey
Donnithorne, (1967:91), the widely known authority on the
economy of Communist of China, remarks:

> The resurgence of the rural family as the basic unit of con-
> sumption, and of a considerable part of production, has been the
> most striking feature in China's countryside. Its efficiency as an
> economic unit is due to the immediacy of the incentives to hard
> work and thrift and to the convenient way in which its multi-
> farious aspects dovetail into each other.

With the retreat in the commune movement, many of the service
units formerly established to facilitate collective production have
been withdrawn. The temporary setups, such as day nurseries
and seasonal nurseries, have been withdrawn at the earliest. Therefore, the family still remains the major center for the early socialization of the children. After the reorganization of the communes,
the government stressed again the family's share of responsibility
for the socialist education of the younger generation. During the
Cultural Revolution, parents were described as not only having
blood ties with the children, but also "revolutionary ties." Thus,
being comrades in the revolution, parents and children have the
mutual responsibility of educating each other in revolutionary
thoughts.

Within the modern family, the quality of family living must have
been greatly affected by the fact that the home is no longer "a
man's castle." Although the joys of domestic life are still real and
the family is the place for the individual's emotional and sexual
gratification, personal life can scarcely stay private; what goes
on inside the family is not free from the close observation of
neighbors and party men.

V. THE FAMILY—PAST, PRESENT AND FUTURE

The Chinese family has gone a long way from the traditional

---

[31]Myra Roper, visiting China in 1963, reported that the village today still
counts its inhabitants by households rather than individuals, that the family
is still the important unit, and the "average family wage" is still talked
about. Myra Roper. *China—The Surprising Country*, London: Heinemann,
1966, pp. 41-47.

patriarchal form. The pattern of family living now is so radically different from that in the past, that the changes which have occurred in these two decades can be described as truly revolutionary. The implementation of the 1950 Marriage Law was characterized by its erratic nature. The picture one gets is a series of waves of enthusiasm followed by periods of relaxation, each ebb and flow developing according to the national economic and political policies of the time. However, two decades of ideological training have produced profound effects for the family system. The following schematic comparison between the traditional family model and the modern one will throw more light on the drastic changes which have been wrought by the CCP government.

The Traditional Chinese Family	The Modern Chinese Family
Concept of the Chia	
Members related by blood and marriage; common budget; common property	The "big socialist family"—the nation—composed of members with "revolutionary ties"
Family interest comes before individual or nation	Interest of the party and the nation before family or individual
Ideal Form	
The large, extended family	The small, nuclear family
Family Formation	
Arranged marriage	Freedom of marital choice
Child betrothal and early marriage	Late marriage
Romantic love disfavored	"Love of the proletariate" based on common revolutionary pursuits
Matching of horoscopes and socio-economic backgrounds	Compatibility of personalities and ideological stands as choice criteria
Internal Structure	
Patriarchal	Democratic and equalitarian
Patrilineal	Bilateral
Patrilocal	Neolocal
Generational hierarchy	Exaltation of youth
Subjugation of women	Sex equality
Authority of the clan	Clan has no claim over family or individual
Functions	
Emphasis on continuity of family line; procreation most important function	Family continuity unimportant Birth control advocated
Ancestor worship	Family completely secularized
Unit of production; economic cooperation	Little economic cooperation

Unit of consumption; all earnings and property shared	Unit of living; individual earnings but some pooling of resources
Status ascription	Stress on individual achievement
Socialization and education of children	Socialization and early education shared with state
Center of social and cultural life	Individual's social and cultural life mainly outside family
Sexual and emotional gratification	Sexual and emotional gratification
Associated Institutions	
Child brides and foster child brides	Prohibited by law
Concubinage	Monogamy
Prostitution	Prohibited
Remarriage of divorced and widowed disfavored	Freedom of divorce and remarriage
Family Relationships	
Father-son as central relationship	Husband-wife as central relationship
Husband-wife as institutional relationship	Husband-wife as companionship
Parent-child relationship charecterized by authority and obedience	Parent-child relationship as comradeship
Difficult mother-in-law and daughter-in-law relationship	Harmonious mother-in-law and daughter-in-law relationship
Family relationships as "private" domain	"Love and marriage are not personal matters"

As we pointed out in our introductory section, both these models are in the nature of ideal types. The large, extended family was found mainly among the wealthy gentry classes in the traditional society, while the modern, nuclear family was more common among the urban, educated, professional or technical and industrial workers. On the other hand, there is no doubt that in either period of China's history, the ideal family model serves as an ideological force. Thus, the Confucian ideal of the extended family was aspired to by both gentry and common folk, and it actually helped to preserve the norms and values of the traditional social order. Similarly, the ideal socialist family is increasingly cherished by the young generation, so that traditional customs and practices will be discarded in due course. The freedom of marriage and divorce has been put to practice, and sex equality has been largely established. Although capitalistic ideas about love and marriage were said to be existing still among some of the young people in the mid-1960s, such "residual" bourgeois ideas are constantly being checked by re-indoctrination campaigns such as the recent Cultural Revolution. It can safely be predicted that the modern form of family will be found increasingly among more and more of the population, and will come to predominate even the countryside.

There is no evidence whatever that the CCP aims to abolish the family altogether. Even during the high tide of the commune movement, it was claimed that a "new" family was to be brought about with the complete emancipation of women. As we have described in the last section, the family is still active as a social unit; it is still performing various functions for the individual and society. The question whether certain functions of the family are "irreducible," or whether the family institution itself is indispensable, is at best an academic question.

REFERENCES

Buck, John L.
1930 *Chinese Farm Economy*. Chicago: University of Chicago Press.
Donnithorne, Audrey G.
1967 *China's Economic System*. London: Allen & Unwin.
Durdin, T., J. Reston & S. Topping
1971 *The New York Times Report From China*. New York: Quardrangle Books.
Fei, Hsiao-t'ung
1939 *Peasant Life in China* London: Routledge.
Fei, Hsiao-t'ung & Chih-i Chang
1945 *Earthbound China*. Chicago: University of Chicago Press.
Fried, Morton H.
1953 *Fabric of Chinese Society*. New York: Praeger.
Gamble, Sidney
1954 *Ting Hsien : A North China Rural Community*. New York: Institute of Pacific Relations.
Han, Suyin
1967 *China in the Year 2001*. New York: Basic Books.
Lamson, Herbert D.
1935 *Social Pathology in China*. Shanghai, China: Commercial Press.
Lang, Olga
1968 *Chinese Family and Society*. Hamden, Conn.: Archon Books.
Lethbridge, Henry J.
1961 *China's Urban Communes*. Hong Kong: Dragonfly Books.
Levy, Marion
1949 *The Family Revolution in Modern China*. Cambridge; Harvard University Press.

Lucas, Christopher
  1965 *Women of China.* Hong Kong: Dragonfly Books.

Taeuber, Irene
  1970 "The Families of Chinese Farmers" in Maurice Freedman, *Family and Kinship in Chinese Society.* Stanford: Stanford University Press.

Taylor, Charles
  1966 *Reporter in Red China.* New York: Random House.

Vogel, Ezra
  1965 "From Friendship to Comradeship: The change in Personal Relations in Communist China." The China Quarterly, 21 (January-March). P. 52.

Yang, C.K.
  1959 *The Chinese Family in the Communist Revolution.* Cambridge: Harvard University Press.

Yang, C.K.
  1959 *A Chinese Village in Early Communist Transition.* Cambridge: Harvard University Press.

CHAPTER VIII

The Korean Family

DAE H. CHANG

INTRODUCTION

The purpose of this chapter is to introduce and examine briefly the Korean marriage and family systems, past, present, and future. There are, indeed, numerous studies that have been made by social scientists—historians, archaeologists, anthropologists, political scientists, economists, sociologists—on Chinese and Japanese social institutions, including the family in the Far East; however, only a few comprehensive studies on Korea and almost none on the subject of marriage and family have been made until recently.

Why is it that, in spite of the fact that Korea has been a center of international struggle and conflict for centuries due to her geographic, economic, and strategic importance, very little attention has been paid to Korean studies? Why, despite the fact that Korea offers a colorful history, in terms of her cultural heritage—written and spoken Korean language, literature, dance, music, art, customs, early science and technology, government, social stratification, family life—only a few Western scholars are attracted to Korean studies. Even though Korean marriage and family practices portray and approximate the early Chinese system, there is abundant evidence to support the thesis that the institution of marriage and the family in Korea is distinctively the product of Korean history, geography, and culture.

Korea today is still considered to be one of the lesser developed nations in terms of industrialization. The nations of the West, particularly the United States, have attempted to support Korean development; Western medicine has laid a foundation in Korea and Western educators have made significant contributions to Korean higher learning institutions. All these, together with various contacts with other cultures, have brought about social change in the country. Today, Korea is changing at an ever accelerating pace in many respects. The traditional family institution is now undergoing marked transformation. The greatest changes are due, however, primarily to the conscious realization on the part of Koreans of the need for technological, scientific, and material well-being and for readjustment of the social environment.

We are living in a period of accelerated socio-cultural change and transformation; some changes are planned, others have occurred violently and thus have produced chaotic social dislocation and disorganization. The 20th century is marked by many revolutions and virtually every institution within a society has been profoundly affected. Until 1900, the Korean family was consanguineous and followed the patriarchal principle. The traditional family was therefore large, multifunctional, hierarchically oriented, and a long-lasting unit of the clan group. Korea had a semi-communal family-clan system in which the eldest male had the vested responsibility of overseeing its members' welfare, including marriage issues. Almost all family-clan activities were collective, whether activities were economic, educational, religious or involved discipline of its members.

Since 1900, particularly 1945, the effects of Westernization, together with the industrialization, urbanization, and politicization of the population, have altered radically the structure and functions of the Korean family. The concept of marriage in which people used to marry for the "perpetuation of the family tree" has been replaced by the new concepts of "love," "companionship," and "individual happiness." Traditionally undisputed husband-father's rights and obligations have been questioned by the new generation. Male superiority over the female has been debated and the backbone of the social order, the law, is gradually shifting to equalitarian principles. The modern family, particularly in urban areas, is no longer an economic unit, nor a religious or educational unit. Intermarriage practices among different social classes are widespread among the young. Care of the aged was not a problem of Korean society for centuries because children automatically assumed this responsibility, and if not, the next of kin would provide for material as well as psychological needs. Today the question of such care is no longer a family matter; it is a political as well as a social issue. This past quarter of a century, as the family has become more mobile due to Korea's economy and the Korean War, it has also become smaller and more nuclear. People marry at a much later age; as a matter of fact, child-marriage (less than fourteen) has been outlawed. The single or unmarrying population is on the rise in Korea today.

These changes have not all occurred smoothly, nor as yet are fully approved by all strata in Korea. As a matter of fact, Korea is still in the midst of rapid socio-cultural change where numerous unsettled, unsolved, and unanticipated problems remain. Farmers have left behind century old clan-village living styles and are seeking a new life in urban centers. They face new problems of adaptation in an environment which is foreign to them. The nation's newspapers, radio, and TV are filled with reports of "collective suicide" by entire families as a means to resolve starvation, shame, and other problems. Children of rural background apparently perform poorly in urban schools and drop out rates are high. Juvenile delinquency and crime rates are high among drop outs and migrants. Drug and alcohol usage is increasing; prostitution by unemployed women is flourishing.

Young Koreans, both male and female, claim their newly acquired right to choose their own mate without parental sanction or intereference. They seek romance, love, affection, and companionship without regard to family name or clan status, which were of crucial importance in traditional Korea. Sexual or physical attraction is a predominant marital issue today. These changes have also influenced divorce. It is natural that, when marriage takes place because of love, divorce would also be natural or even logical when love disappears. Today's success in marriage is not determined by how long spouses live together, nor by economic status, nor by how many children they have. The index of success is, to a large extent, the emotional satisfaction, or "happiness," that a couple can achieve.

Accordingly, the modern Korean family structure has been altered drastically to meet new challenges. The functional aspects —division of labor—have also changed. Monogamy, rather than polygamy, predominates. Couples usually want to have a small family with an average of two to three children. Wives commonly work outside the home prior to the birth of their first child. Child-rearing methods—socialization processes—have changed from negative punishment to more positive reasoning. More and more modern married couples establish their own nuclear household rather than live with their parents. In spite of the many changes that have taken place, in rural communities, the village-centered clan group with a large extended family is still the predominant type. Even people living in a large city still regard their clan village the "primary family" to which they hope to return after retirement. Still, patriarchy, patrilocality and patrilineal descent are prevalent.

The modern Korean family, in its broadest historical context, was initiated by the Japanese when Japan's Overseas Government imposed its civil laws upon the Korean people beginning in 1910 and ending in 1945. For the first time in Korean history, Korea recognized the family as a unit of society; prior to 1910, Korea only recognized the clan as a unit of society.

From 1945, the Western culture began taking its roots in Korea. For the first time in their 5,000 years of history, Korean people saw a radically different from of family—small, nuclear, democratic, conjugal—which existed in the West, where the individual, not the family or family head, was the center of focus. Accordingly, the contemporary Korean society stresses the importance of the individual in determining marital and family matters.

Recently, considerable attention has been given to changing the structure of the traditional Korean family for the purposes of : 1) modernization; 2) democratization of its members; 3) industrialization and urbanization; 4) control of population growth; 5) prevention of crime and delinquency; 6) an effective utilization of human resources; 7) economic and consumer behavior control; 8) understanding social change; 9) combating illiteracy etc. Social scientists, as well as applied scientists, in Korea have recently voiced that the country's future development and stability cannot be expected before sound measures are taken to transform the traditional, autocratic, consanguineous, extended family into a more functional, effective, and flexible family system capable of providing for dynamic modern social needs.

There are perhaps only a few societies in the world that are more consciously aware of their family than Koreans. The Korean family, as we shall see later, has played many vital roles in shaping society for over 5,000 years. Indeed, the family and later the clan have provided its members with an identity. The clan gave status to each member so that his position would be identified and clarified, thus establishing a channel of command. The family regulated the sex drive and reproduction. Through elaborate rules which specified a child's relations to others, the birth order, sex, and generation pyramid usually predetermined his activities throughout his life.

Traditionally, the study of the family has been divided into the following sections: 1) courtship patterns, or modes of marriage partner selection; 2) division of labor among and between family members; 3) regulations, provisions, and customs concerning marriage and the family, that is, legal age for marriage, laws of inheritance, and property succession; 4) patterns of child-rearing and care; 5) kinship systems; 6) treatment of the aged, sick, and disabled; and 7) dissolution of marriage or patterns of separation.

In the following sections, we will briefly examine the history and geography of Korea; concepts of marriage and the family; historical development of the Korean family up to the Yi dynasty (A.D. 1392); the family during the Yi dynasty; the family during the Japanese occupation of Korea (1910-45); the modern family since 1945; and future directions of the Korean family.

GEOGRAPHY AND HISTORY

Korea is a mountainous peninsula with the combined population of North and South Korea exceeding 43,000,000, of which 31,000,000 reside in South Korea. The size of Korea is equal to that of the state of Minnesota, the British Isles, Rumania, or New Zealand—South Korea corresponds in size to Indiana, Jordan, Hungary, Poland, or Guatemala, while North Korea is about the same size as New York State. The combined area of Korea is 220,840 square kilometers; the section north of the demilitarized zone (DMZ), known as North Korea, is 125,608 square kilometers, while South Korea is 95,232 square kilometers.

South Korea is internationally known as the Republic of Korea. The modern term for Korea is "Taehan Minguk," and the country is frequently called "Hanguk" for the sake of brevity. Traditionally, however, Korea has been known as "Chosun," which literally means "The Land of the Morning Calm." South Korea's capital is Seoul, while Pyungyang is North Korea's capital. Korea has a 6,000-mile (9,600 kilometers) long coastline with about 3,000 contiguous islands (Oh, 1958:35). Korea has four distinct seasons. The major portion of the country is mountainous and only 20 per cent is flat land suitable for agriculture. The physical basis of Korea thus limits the potentialities for economic development. Historically, Korea has had strong neighbors; in the north, Manchuria and China, and in the south, Japan. Korea's history has been strongly affected by her geography. In spite of her strong neighbors, she was able to survive as a society and maintain her own culture with her own language, arts, and way of life (McCune, 1950; Ginsburg, 1961:130-154).

Korea is a very ancient land and her history dates back more. than 4,000 years. It is generally agreed by anthropologists that Koreans are descendants of the Mongolian race, and more specifically belong to the Tungusic branch on the Altaic side of the Turanian, another name for the Ural-Altaic. The Tungus were a people who thrived in the northern areas of Manchuria and adjacent Siberian and other regions (Kim, 1970:20). Like many other societies of the world, Korea has her own mythology, including a creation myth, according to which Dankun, a major deity, welded together the various primitive tribes and ruled and taught them the arts of civilization. Even though historians disagree, Korean tradition puts the founding of this civilization in 2333 B C. About 1200 B C., the Shang dynasty was ending in China and the last of the Shang emperors, Chou Hsiu, and a number of his followers migrated and established a Chinese colony. This was the era of Ki-ja (Reischauer, 1960:403). For centuries, numerous tribes from Manchuria and China drifted into Korea. By 57 B.C., various tribal groups were united and established the kingdom known as Silla, just to the south of the Han River. Several decades later, another new kingdom, Koguryo, developed and occupied the vast territory of present Manchuria. In 18 B.C., a third kingdom appeared, that of Paikche. Thus, by 18 B.C., there were three separate kingdoms and this period is known as the era of the Three Kingdoms (Oh, 1958:7).

Paikche was the most active kingdom in terms of cultural contact with China and Japan. Its culture was widely felt in Japan where in A.D. 285, Paikche sent many craftsmen, artisans, tailors, brewers, tile makers and ceramists Silla made many contributions, notably in art, religion, and science. Following the creation of the three kingdoms, sectoinalism and rivalry developed among them. Gradually, struggles intensified and finally Silla crushed Paikche in A.D. 600, and Koguryo in A.D. 668 and thus began a new kingdom known as Koryo, from which the name Korea was eventually derived.

The Koryo dynasty was founded in 918 and lasted until A.D. 1392. During this dynasty, much was achieved but tragedies also occurred. Koryo inaugurated the civil service examination for the first time in Korean history; established schools for the education of the young; instituted taxation laws to stabilize the national revenue; reorganized military as well as political institutions; mobilized labor workers for state projects; and encouraged the development and creation of many different kinds of art including music, metal works, and porcelain, to name a few.

The Koryo period also witnessed strife and struggle. From the beginning of the dynasty, conflict between Buddhism and Confucianism developed. Confucianism flourished but was suppressed and Buddhism became dominant as all decisions on state matters were influenced by Buddhist monks and priests. Throughout its dynastic history, Koryo remained constantly under heavy military pressure, notably from the north. Particularly the latter part of the Koryo period saw the rise of the Mongols, led by the powerful Genghis Khan. The Mongols invaded Koryo in 1231 and their monarch fled to Kangwha, an island off Seoul, where he stayed for thirty years. The Mongols did not occupy all of Korea. By the time they abandoned the idea of conquering Kangwha island, Koryo's monarch and his officials had become so corrupted that it was impossible for the government to manage complex internal and foreign affairs. Finally, one of the entrusted military generals, Sungge Yi, revolted against the king and his government. He and his staff executed corrupt monks and officials and established a new ruling house in Korea, the Yi dynasty.

The Yi dynasty was established in 1392 and the capital was relocated from Kaesong to Seoul. This dynasty enjoyed about 500 years of unique history in terms of socio-cultural and economic-political development. Many of the literary works were written during this period. The Korean written language, "hangul," was inaugurated under Saejong the Great in 1416. Successive emperors appointed scholars to compile national history; banned Buddhism and revived the Chinese Confucian classics; facilitated the invention of the first movable metal type in Korea; and promoted astronomy, medical technology, geography, and marine science. A new mass educational system was initiated for the first time, which included education for women.

Like previous dynasties, the Yi dynasty had internal factionalism. During and after the 16th century, regional differences became so intense that governmental bureaucracies were divided into "uncommandable cliques." While internal factional struggles were going on and conflict between China and Japan intensified, Korea closed her diplomatic door to foreign countries except for China on a limited scale. The Sino-Japanese War of 1894, with the endorsement of British and American governments and Japan's victory, suddenly gave Japan uncontested power in the Far East. In the peace treaty with China, Japan obtained agreement from China that Japanese troops would be stationed in Korea in lieu of Chinese, which later enabled her to pursue her policy aimed at colonizing Korea for her expansion into Manchuria and further into China. Moreover, the Russo-Japanese War of 1904 and subsequent victory gave Japan an excellent opportunity to conquer, subjugate, and Japanize the Korean people.

It must be emphasized that the successive emperors of the Yi dynasty made profound reforms in social systems, including the family. As we shall see later in this chapter, many laws were enacted to govern broad marriage negotiations, property succession, inheritance, protection of rights and freedom, and methods of dissolving the marriage. During the Yi dynasty, society was rigidly stratified on the basis of clan groups and prestige, and authority and honors were assigned according to a clan-surname hierarchy (Chang, 1971b). In spite of a feudalistic outlook, the 500 years of the Yi dynasty initiated many significant steps towrd modernization.

Japan occupied Korea from 1910 to 1945 when Japan surrendered to the Free Allies, in August 1945. During the initial stages of the Japanese occupation of Korea, the Japanese applied military and police power and took over all local, provincial, and central governmental functions. Uprisings against Japanese domination were quickly suppressed. Economic exploitation, including labor mobilization, followed. The Japanese promulgated and applied their civil laws in Korea, thus affecting all of the existing Korean laws pertaining to marriage and the family. It was the first time in Korean history that the Korean people were forced to recognize the family, rather than the clan, as a unit of society. Vast social reforms were initiated during the Japanese domination of Korea. It must be recognized, moreover, that the Japanese did contribute toward broader modernization processes, including technology, education, urbanization, and politicization. Needless to say, the laws regarding marriage and the family were so profound that genuine social change was, in its broadest historical context, begun during this period.

The Japanese colonization of Korea officially ended on 15 August 1945, when Japan surrendered to the second world war Allies. Prior to the ending of the second world war, the United States did not have any concrete plans to occupy Korea when Japan surrendered. Since the Soviet Union had entered into the war against Japan a few days prior to the ending of the war, Russia was intensely interested in the Korean settlement; thus, two military governments, north of the 38th parallel under Soviet influence and South of it under American, were involved from the beginning. On 10 September 1945, the United States military government was established in southern Korea. Numerous US-USSR joint commission meetings were held but failed to unify Korea.

On 10 May 1948, a democratically based election was held in South Korea and on 31 May 1948, for the first time in her history, the national assembly convened and elected Syngman Rhee as its chairman. On 17 July 1948, the Korean constitution was promulgated. On the basis of a constitutional provision, the national assembly elected the new Republic of Korea's first president, Dr Syngman Rhee. This new republic was born separate from the northern half of Korea.

The Korean War broke out on 25 June 1950, in an attempt to unify Korea by military means. For the next three years many thousands of human lives were sacrificed on behalf of unification. Many sessions of the so-called armistice talks were held and, finally, on 27 July 1953, the armistice agreement was signed at Panmunjom, thus concluding the bloodiest fight between brothers on the Land of Morning Calm. The three-year war ended with 7,500,000 people either killed or wounded.

During the Rhee administration an active anti-Communist campaign was launched; the so-called Rhee-line, or peace line was established; anti-Communist prisoners of the Korean War were liberated; strong anti-Japanese policies were developed; etc. Rhee's government gradually acquired more dictatorial power by relying more heavily on the military and police. There was widespread corruption; foreign aid was channeled to exclusive government-backed large businesses. Inflation and mass starvation occurred. Police interference in local, provincial, and national elections was common. Rigging of elections and police violence were also prevalent. Student demonstrations were staged elsewhere in South Korea and lasted several months before President Rhee stepped down and a new cabinet, headed by John M. Chang as premier, was established. In spite of the premier's honest revitalization efforts, the government was unable to solve the nation's problems. On 16 May 1961, a *coup d'etat*, headed by General Chung Hee Park overthrew Chang's government; thus, the Third Republic was created and ultimately proclaimed.

In the past quarter of a century since the ending of the second world war, many remarkable changes have taken place in Korea. The country is striving for economic sufficiency. Korea is now entering a new era in which modernization is just around the corner. She is also striving for participatory democracy in which each individual should be given a maximum voice in determining his future, including his choice of mate and size of his family. Freedom, equality, liberty, and individual rights are words which cannot be separated from Korea's future development.

CONCEPT OF MARRIAGE AND THE FAMILY

The following passage may be cited to convey the basic concept of marriage and the family: "Marriage is the affectionate union of two persons bearing a different clan-name (surname) for the purpose of attending upon the ancestral temple on the one hand, and of continuing the genealogical line on the other." Marriage, then, was regarded chiefly as an agency through which to perpetuate the family tree and to render a service in the institution of ancestor worship. It was considered the duty of the living to maintain communication with the spirits through ancestor worship. Thus, the lineage of the family may be continuous everlastingly.

Traditionally, people were taught that family continuity was the basic objective of marriage. "By the united action of heaven and earth all things originate; the ceremony of marriage is the beginning of a line that shall last for a myriad of ages." Failure to produce offspring means not only the end of the family line but also of the ancestors. "There are three things which are unfilial, and to have no posterity is the greatest of them." Therefore, under the traditional family system, if a man died without leaving a son to perpetuate his line, it was considered the greatest misfortune that one could have on earth. Remaining single was regarded as the greatest crime one could possibly commit on this planet and everyone, regardless of his economic and physical status, had to get married. When it was physically impossible to obtain a male descendant to continue the family tree, traditionally adoption was encouraged. In view of the importance of children, it was a common practice to get married at a young age so that a "successor" could be safely obtained. Parental intervention was necessary because the marrying persons were not mature enough to select a mate.

Family continuity and childbirth were so important that when, for example, a pregnant woman was convicted of a crime, she usually was allowed to maintain a normal family life until the child was delivered, and the government allowed her to live with her child and husband. At times, the entire sentence was commuted if she produced a male heir to continue the family tree. When the eldest son was in prison and it was found that there was no one else to take care of his ailing parents, he was granted amnesty. An only heir to the family was exempted from military service and all other national emergency mobilization calls. Family continuity was indeed important for all family members. The family had to be preserved even if someone was sacrificed in the process.

Traditionally, people were taught that marriage was never designed to achieve or attain the husband's or wife's happiness alone, but to promote the family interests. Consequently, sexual gratification or sexual attraction never entered into matrimonial issues. As a matter of fact, traditionally, Koreans were taught that sex was nothing more than a "chain-of-pain," which was very different from the Western view that sex is something pleasant, desirable, and therefore good. Sex was instrumental in having offspring to perpetuate the family. Sexual gratification was sought

288 Family in Asia

outside the family—from female entertainers. Family sex was obligatory and therefore restricted to a specific purpose, while social sex was designed for enjoyment.

In short, the whole concept of marriage was centered around family continuity and ancestral worship. The Koreans regarded marriage as the highest virtue and the beginning of true harmony on earth. Because of the importance and solemnity of marriage, there were strict marriage regulations established and utilized for centuries. Their remnants are still felt in Korea today.

The concept of marriage and the family has been strongly influenced by the teachings of Confucianism. According to this system, the entire universe is viewed as one large family in which all things are interrelated and hierarchically ordered from the lowest man up to heaven. Heaven is viewed as the source of all and the ancestor of all things. All men are, therefore, subject to heaven and must conform to its natural ordering. Natural ordering is a theory covering all human existence, called "Oryun," which literally means the five fundamental socio-familial relationships. The first relationship, which is by far the most important and corresponds to the principle of heaven and earth, is that of male and female or husband and wife. The second relation, which is derived from the first, is that of father and son. The third specifies the relation between elder brother and younger brother. The fourth concerns relations of friend and friend. And, finally, there is the relationship between sovereign and subject (Kim, 1969:32).

Of these five relations, three pertain to the family and even the other two—sovereign and subject, and friend and friend—are interpreted in familial terms. Thus, the country or nation is described as "Kuk-ka," which means "nation-family." The emperor is called Kuk-bu, which mean "nation-father" and he is regarded as the head of the family; his subjects respect and obey him in the same manner that members of the individual family respect and obey the family head. True peace, harmony, and order exist automatically when every one observes the Oryun. To be specific, between father and son there should be affection; between sovereign ond subject, righteousness; between husband and wife, attention to their separate functions; between old and young, a proper order; and between friends, fidelity. As Confucius conceptualized them, these five relations are held to be as permanent as th universe.

KOREAN FAMILY IN OBSCURITY

How did the Korean family start? What were the modes of marriage in the past? Did Koreans practice group marriage or have polygamous or monogamous patterns? Who cared for the children? Was infanticide prevalent? What about the rule of residence? When and how were kinship terminologies established? Why was the incest taboo strictly enforced in Korea? Considerable speculation has been devoted to the early Korean marriage and family system, together with ancient societal behaviors, organizations, economics, and religious institutions. Every society, if it is to survive, must meet fundamental requirements, that is, biological, psychological, and social needs.

To this date, such diverse cultural traits as polygamy, promiscuity, infanticide, cannibalism, communism, etc. are still questioned but not clarified. However, it is assumed that, whatever the methods our forefathers applied to perpetuate their species, the devices must have been effective; otherwise their culture would have been terminated at a certain point in its historical development. Whatever devices they used, they are a testimonial to the ingenuity of man to respond to what he perceives as practical necessities or desirable goals.

Although it is difficult to ascertain what the family was like before civilization reached certain stages of evolution, this much is known:

1) The ties that bound the original human group, the family, were primarily organic. The bond between mother and child was definite and this obvious relationship was founded securely on physical compulsion. The idea of common blood, or pure organic nature, as the basis of kinship, is thus the typical organizing thread of most primitive societies. The organic dependence of the child upon the mother—matriarchal family—lays the groundwork for all the complex categories of societal experiences that have followed.

2) Diverse as the ways of man are, man is still the common denominator; all men everywhere try to provide for the same human needs. Patterns of culture first develop around the biological facts of man's structure and functioning: sex differences, birth, growth, aging, and death; the helplessness of

human infants; drives generated by hunger, thirst, and sex; the
need, in some environments, for clothing and shelter. Over the
centuries, as societies have grown larger and more complex, the
family has grown smaller and its functions have been reduced
to physiological and psychological essentials. To the individual
member of a primitive society, the family's property is the
source of livelihood—economics; its ancestors are his gods—
religion; its elders are his government; and its young men his
defense and his support in old age. In simpler cultures family
and society are actually conterminous.

A prerequisite for the establishment of the family is that of marriage itself, whether the form of marriage is promiscuous, communal,
plural ormonogamous. The problem of the origin of marriage has
been the subject of speculation from time immemorial, and practically every culture has embodied its own peculiar theory in some
myth or tradition. The generally accepted theory is that the original
family organization in Korea was nuclear. It is thought that our ancestors organized their family in a nuclear fashion, being composed of
one male, one female, and their offspring. It is also believed that
the nuclear family was the foundation of all other social units:
the extended family, clan, and tribe. Even the broader society is
an extension of the nuclear family itself.
    It is significant that there is not one scholar in Korea who
denies the existence of the matrilineal family during the earliest
stages of development. From the early Christian cra, the matriarchal family gradually evolved into the patrilineal form. Some
scholars in Korea support the thesis that the original human
marriage was communal, while others support the promiscuity
view. In fact, there is no common ground upon which to prove
either one or both. If we grant that our ancestors lived in a period
of unorganized gregarious life, then, just how did our original
ancestors manage to unite the family members? We now live in a
society within various organizations and communities and belong
to organizations with the object of attaining common ends. However, our primitive ancestors were ignorant of the advantages
resulting from cooperation and, furthermore, knowledge about how
to form the family was not yet developed because of the nomadic
life which used to prevail. Whatever the size of the family or its
place in society, as an institution, it invariably embodies norm

complexes regulating sex behavior and the care of children. Granting that the primitive Korean family system was matrilineal with a promiscuous or communal marriage as its basis, it was natural that children born of, and reared by, the same mother should live together. The natural basis for the beginning of man's social group is, then, the unity of blood between mother and children.

Questions as to how the matriarchal family developed into the patriarchal family, and what were the basic causes for such changes are equally uncertain. Although evidence is scattered and fragmented, many scholars mention various factors as the causes for change. These include marriage by capture, marriage by purchase, surplus of women over men, and, as a result of physical differences between males and females, psychological factors (e.g., males were more active and aggressive and thereby took over many of the women's rights). It is generally accepted that the Korean family was transformed from a matrilineal to a patrilineal system, probably during the Koguryo dynasty. The following passage will illustrate the transformation (Son, 1948:90):

It was common practice at that time [during the Koguryo, dynasty, 37 B.C.] that the matrilineal system prevailed. An abundance of evidence indicates that after the engagement was completed, the wife-to-be's parents customarily built a small hut behind the house. The son-in-law-to-be called on the house, knelt down on the ground, calling the wife-to-be's name, asking if he could stay with her. The parents granted the request. When children were born, and grew up to a certain age, the husband took the wife and children back to his home.

There is some evidence suggesting that since the Three Kingdom period, within the family the husband was the symbolic as well as the authoritative figure, and greater power was exercised by him to control other family members, including his wife. In fact, the father's authority was extended to selling, depositing, and exchanging his children and treating them as a piece of property. Beginning and during the period of Silla, the emphasis was placed more on the eldest male of the family and family properties were inherited by him. The marriage ceremony took place at the bride's home, who moved to her husband's family residence only after

the birth of her first child (Son, 1948:88-89). In order to consum-
mate the marriage, the husband had to pay a bride price. When
her husband died, a women became the wife of her husband's
brother. During the period of the Koryo dynasty (A.D. 918-1392),
more stable farming clan villages were established and the extended family was popular. Among commoners, it was ordered that
members of the same clan, or persons bearing the same surname,
were not allowed to intermarry. This practice is known as "Don-
sung Bulhon."

To maintain the stable traditional Korean family, it was necessary to adopt the Confucian teaching known as "filial piety," which
has carried into the 20th century with little modification. The
essential characteristics of filial piety are that: 1) it defines who is
superior-inferior; 2) it requires absolute subordination of sons to
their parents; 3) it requires obedience of young, women, and lower
status persons to the eldest male and to higher status persons; 4)
filial impiety is equal to crime and thus punishable. Moreover, filial
piety demands absolutely the following: 1) unconditional submission
to authority, including parents and grandparents; 2) provision of
psychological and physical comfort to the parents; 3) satisfaction
of material needs; 4) solemn performance of funeral services for
the parents; 5) daily ancestral worship; and 6) willingness to sacrifice oneself for one's parents, if needed. There are additional indirect filial piety practices that is, you should not exhibit affectionate feelings to your wife in front of your parents; do your best
to serve your friends and neighbors; never bring dishonor upon
yourself and your family name; be modest and courteous; do not
be idle; do not drink excessively or gamble; be brave in the war
front and ready for national emergencies; etc. Since the structural-
functional aspects of the family prior to 1392 are obscure, let us
move into the Yi dynasty. The writer has extensively utilized legal
codes in examining this society, as laws are often a reflection of
prevailing societal modes, or of what that society intends to be in
the future.

THE FAMILY SYSTEM DURING THE YI DYNASTY (1392-1910)

An examination of historic records reveals that the family system
of the Yi dynasty was clearly a consaguineous type, or an extended

family with patrilineal and patrilocal residence. During the Yi dynasty, successive emperors adopted Confucianism, rather than Buddhism, as its basis for social as well as political policies, and as a result, marriage and family rules were changed.

During the Yi dynasty, in order to legalize marriage, there were altogether six steps to be carefully followed. These were:

1) The parents or a go-between selected the prospect and inquired concerning the girl prospect's name and date of birth.

2) The horoscopic data of the two were examined by a fortuneteller or a diviner, in order to ascertain whether the proposed alliance would be happy.

3) The groom-to-be's family sent the girls's parents wedding presents of various kinds, including the bride's wedding dress.

4) The parents or go-between requested the bride-to-be's family to select a lucky day for the wedding.

5) The wedding ceremony took place mostly at the bride's house, in the presence of a witness, or witnesses. The witness had to be outside of the involved families.

6) After the wedding ceremony, the husband, with the consent of the parents, had to report, in written form, to the local registration office for the marriage registration.

There were some exceptions or limitations to the above rules. The laws specifically provided that "during the three years following the death of a parent no person shall be permitted to marry."[1] Moreover, since the emperor was regarded as the father of the nation-family, when an emperor's parents died, all subjects were "not allowed to marry, sing or slaughter animals for ten days in the capital city and five days outside the capital city." (April 1422). Another marriage regulation was that "no person shall remarry within three years of his wife's death; however, in case parents asked their son to remarry, or when a person at the

[1] The Yi dynasty's rules and regulations were taken originally from *Yicho Sillok (Annals of the Imperial Court of Korea)* by Kuksa Pyongcban Wiwon-hwe (Committee for the Compilation of the National History), which is published under the auspices of the Ministry of Education, Republic of Korea. The translated version of marriage and family rules appeared in Chang, 1967: 57-72. In this section, footnotes cite only the emperor's promulgation date, January 1399.

age of forty still had no sons, one was authorized to remarry one year after the date of his wife's death" (January 1440). A similar provision indicated that "during the three years from the date of the parents' death, no one could divorce" (April 1459).

During the Yi dynasty, rules stipulated that "no chunin" class should marry into the commoner class" (July 1401). The "chunin" class was the lowest social class in Korea for centuries (Chang, 1971b). During the King Saejong era (1419-50), the law prohibited monks from marrying. In almost all societies, when a marriage is contracted under legally recognized procedures, there is also the legal recognition of divorce. The records of the Yi dyansty reveal that divorce could be initiated by either the husband or the husband's parents, but not by the wife. Reasons for divorce were varied; however, the common ground was adultery. Next to adultery were communicable diseases. Mental illness was also a sufficient reason for divorce, as was a failure of the wife to support the family. A failure of the wife to produce children, especially a boy, was the most common and accepted ground for divorce. Misbehavior and cruelty were also reasons to effect legal divorce. On the other hand, if the wife had mourned her husband's parents for three years; if her husband's family had become wealthy; or if she had no family to take her in, the laws stipulated that the wife could not be sent away.

As has been previously stated, the family system of Korea was, and to a large extent still is consanguineous, patrilineal, and patrilocal. During the Yi dynasty great authority was vested by the laws in the father concerning family matters. The father had the right to assume the following responsibilities with regard to his children: 1) education; 2) protection, supervision and provision of food, clothing, shelter, and medical care; 3) disciplinary action or punishment; 4) determining place of residence prior to and after the marriage; 5) occupation; 6) management of finances; and 7) marriage and divorce. The mother could express her opinions only with regard to items 2), 3), and 7) (Chang, 1967: 37).

If the father died, all these responsibilities were carried out by the mother, with the guidance of a paternal uncle. When both the father and mother died, all matters were transferred to the eldest son. At the time of the father's death, if the eldest son was too young to administer the family's affairs, the paternal uncle assisted him; the uncle's responsibilities were then the same as the father's.

The traditional family may be defined as two or more nuclear or conjugal families, related by blood, marriage, or adoption, living under one roof: grandparents, parents, sons, their spouses (including children), their children and unmarried daughters (Lee, 1964: 152-153). The family jointly owns all properties—house, land, pond, etc., which are passed on to the eldest male member for the purpose of maintaining the livelihood of the family, observing the practice of ancestor worship, and safeguarding the ancestors' graveyards. The family inherits the "chokbo" or family registry. The administration of the family is usually exercised through the male line. Traditionally, in Korea, a married son rarely establishes a new residence but continues to live with his bride in his parents' or grandparents' house. Therefore, it is not uncommon to find a family with three or even four generations living under one roof. In Korea, this is called "taekajok."

In order to introduce the complex structure and function of the traditional Korean family, it may be useful to illustrate the gradual development of the Korean family through the use of a diagram. Let us, for the sake of clarification, assume that a married couple A) has two unmarried sons, B) and C), and one unmarried

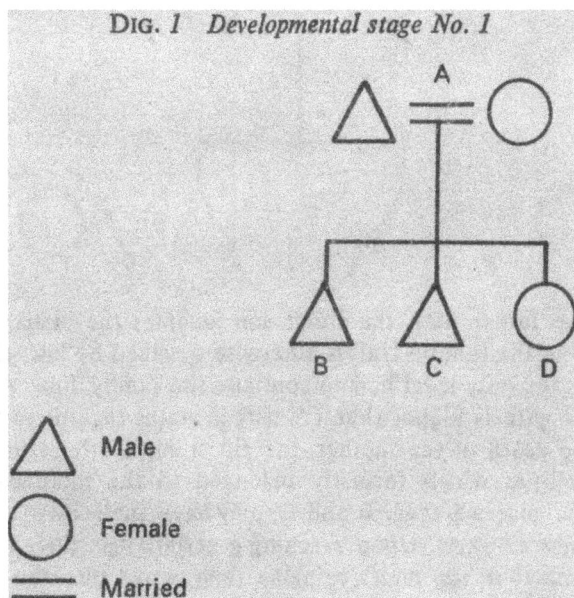

DIG. *1 Developmental stage No. 1*

daughter D). With this assumption, the reader will note that we are disregarding all earlier ancestors and tracing the extended family from this segment of the trunk. The first stage, the "sokajok," or conjugal family, is composed of parents and their unmarried children and is shown in Diagram (Dig. 1)

At this stage of development, the father is called "kajang," or family head. As long as the father lives, he is the central figure within the family. Respect and obedience (filial piety) are two essential duties of the children toward their parents. The essential characteristic of the traditional family is the fact that the sons continue to reside with the parents after marriage. For instance, after the two sons' (B and C) marriages, their wives will move into the house of their parents-in-law and all live together under the same roof. After her marriage, daughter (D) becomes a member of her husband's family. Therefore, after the children's marriage, the Diagram 2 (Dig. 2) would show the following relationship:

DIG. 2   *Developmental stage No. 2*

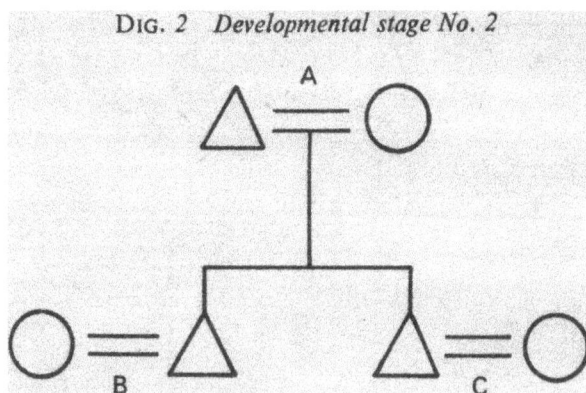

When the father dies, the eldest son assumes the "kajang," or headship of the family. Unless otherwise specified by law, the eldest son is the only legal heir to continue the family line. Accordingly, B's wife is higher than C's wife in status regardless of age. Upon the death of the mother, the eldest son's wife assumes the responsibilities which formerly belonged to the mother-in-law. Later, the married sons, B and C, may have their own children (grandchildren of A). Upon reaching a certain age, their children will get married, the males bringing their wives into the family, while the females will marry out of the family. These grandchildren

will still live with their parents, their grandparents, their uncles
and their aunts. At this stage, the famiiy consists of three generations and all the members still live under one roof. The third
developmental stage of the family may be depicted as follows in
Diagram 3 (Dig. 3).

DIG. 3 *Developmental stage, No. 3*

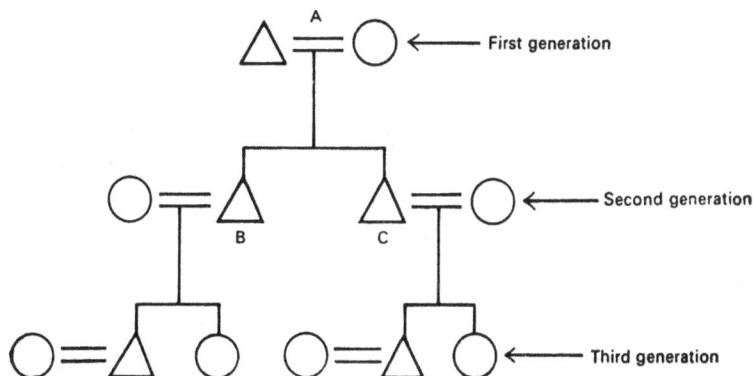

As we have observed at first, there is a simple family composed 'of
only parents and children, as in Diagram 1. This gradually grows
and reaches the second stage and then develops into a large group.
Such families often spread themselves and occupy a whole village,
which then is termed "dongsung burak," "dongnae," "dongni," or
clan village. Because of the patrilineal familism, all the clan members carry the same surname except for the married-in females.
When the family has grown into a very large group, it is difficult
for one house to accommodate all the members. Therefore,
the second or the third son and their wives often establish
separate households nearby, with the consent of the parents.
As time goes on, however, even a village may not be large enough
to retain all the members. Then a few households of the extended
family, with the arrangement of the clan council, emigrate into a
different locality. In time, a whole region may become occupied
and gradually formed into a tribe, and then may expand further
and become a separate state, nation, or society.

In its broadest sense, the traditional Korean family usually includes altogether eighty-one kinship positions. Below the extended family with blood relatives is described and one can follow the relationships step by step by starting at No. 9, ego. For each family member, a specific name and status are assigned.

TABLE 1.
Kinship terminology of the extended family and blood relatives

No.	Terminology in Korean	Kinship terms	Explanation
1)	Bu	Father	or step father
2)	Mo	Mother	or step mother
3)	Chobu	Grandfather	
4)	Chomo	Grandmother	
5)	Jingchobu	Great-grandfather	
6)	Jingchomo	Great-grandmother	
7)	Kochobu	Great-great-grandfather	
8)	Kochomo	Great-great grandmother	
9)	Boo (Nampyun)	Husband	Ego or I
10)	T'cho	Wife	
11)	Ja	Son	or adopted son
12)	Nyo	Daugther	or adopted daughter
13)	Jabu	Daughter-in-law	
14)	Sonja	Grandson	
15)	Sonnyo	Granddaughter	
16)	Sonbu	Granddaughter-in-law	
17)	Jingson	Great grandson	
18)	Jingsonnyo	Great granddaughter	
19)	Changjinsonbu	Wife of first great grandson	
20)	Hyonson	Great-great-grandson	
21)	Hyonsonnyo	Great-great-granddaughter	
22)	Changhyonsonnyo	First great-great-gandson's wife	
23)	Hoyngjae	Brothers	
24)	Maemae	Sisters	
25)	Jil	Nephew	
26)	Jilnyo	Niece	
27)	Jilbu	Nephew's wife	
28)	Jongson	Nephew's son	
29)	Jongsonnyo	Nephew's daughter	
30)	Jongsonbu	Nephew's son's wife	
31)	Jongjinson	Great-grandson's cousin	25's grandson
32)	Jongjinsonnyo	Great-granddaughter's cousin	25's grand-daughter

No.	Terminology in Korean	Kinship terms	Explanation
33)	Paiksookbu	Uncle	1's brother
34)	Paiksookmo	Aunt	1's brother's wife
35)	Ko	Father's sister	1's sister
36)	Jonghyongjae	Male cousin	33's son
37)	Jongmaemae	Female cousin	33's daughter
38)	Jongjil	Male cousin's son	33's grandson
39)	Jongjilnyo	Male cousin's daughter	33's grand-daughter
40)	Jongjilbu	Male cousin's son's wife	38's wife
41)	Chaejongson	Male cousin's grandson	33's great grandson
42)	Chaejongsonnyo	Male cousin's grand-daughter	33's great granddaughter
43)	Jongjobu	Grandfather's brother	
44)	Jongjomo	Grandfather's brother's wife	43's wife
45)	Daeko	Grandfather's sister	
46)	Jongpaiksookbu	Grandfather's brother's son	43's son
47)	Jongpaiksookmo	Grandson's nephew's wife	46's wife
48)	Jongko	Grandfather's brother's daughter	
49)	Chaejonghyongjae	Grandfather's brother's son's son	46's son
50)	Chaejongmaemae	Grandfather's brother's son's daughter	46's daughter
51)	Chaejongjil	Grandfather's nephew's son's son	49's son
52)	Chaejongjilnyo	Grandfather's nephew's daughter	49's daughter
53)	Jongjinjobu	Great-grandfather's brother	5's brother
54)	Jongjinjomo	Great-grandfather's bro-ther's wife	5's brother's wife
55)	Jindaeko	Great grandfather's sister	5's sister
56)	Chaejongjobu	Great-grandfather's nephew	53's son
57)	Chaejongjomo	Great-grandfather's nephew's wife	56's wife
58)	Chaejongdaeko	Great-grandfather's brother's daughter	53's daughter
59)	Chaejongpaiksookbu	Great-grandfather's nephew's son	56's son
60)	Chaejongpaiksookmo	Great-grandfather's nephew's son's wife	59's wife
61)	Chaejongko	Great-grandfather's nephew's daughter	56's daughter

No.	Terminology in Korean	Kinship terms	Explanation
62)	Samjonghyongjae	Great-grandfather's nephew's son's son	59's sons
63)	Samjongmaemae	Great-grandfather's nephew's sons's daughter	59's daughter
64)	Waejobu	Mother's father	
65)	Waejomo	Mother's mother	
		Mother's brother	
66)	Waesookbu	Mother's brother's wife	
67)	Waesookmo	Mother's sister	
68)	Eemo	Mother's brother's son	
69)	Waejonghyongjae	Mother's brother's daughter	
70)	Waejongmaemae	Mother's sister's son	
71)	Ijonghyongjae	Mother's sister's daughter	
72)	Ijongmaemae	Son-in-law	
73)	Yosu	Daughter's son	
74)	Waeson	Daughter's daughter	
75)	Waesonnyo	Daughter's son's wife	
76)	Waesonbu	Sister's son	
77)	Sengjil	Sister's daughter	
78)	Sengjilnyo	Sister's son's wife	
79)	Sengjilbu	Father's sister's son	
80)	Naejonghyongjae	Father's sister's daughter	
81)	Naejongmaemae		

During the Yi dynasty, "those who have the same surname shall not be permitted to marry." Although this rule suggests that the Korean traditional marriage is exogamous; in actual practice, it is endogamous. The royal family and the noble, or *yangban*, families married among themselves. Lower classes, that is, peasants and artisans, married freely among themselves. The "chunin," the lowest and most despised minority group in Korea, including the *paekchong* (butchers), could not cross the cultural barrier to intermarry with commoners, as they were physically segregated to special communities. An unborn child had a legal right to become engaged, by parental arrangement, and later married, provided the prediction of the sexes was correct.

Child marriage, that is, marriage at the age of less than fourteen, was popular during the Yi dynasty. Whenever a child marriage was involved, the bride's age was four to six years more than the

DIG. 4 *Extended Family and blood relatives*

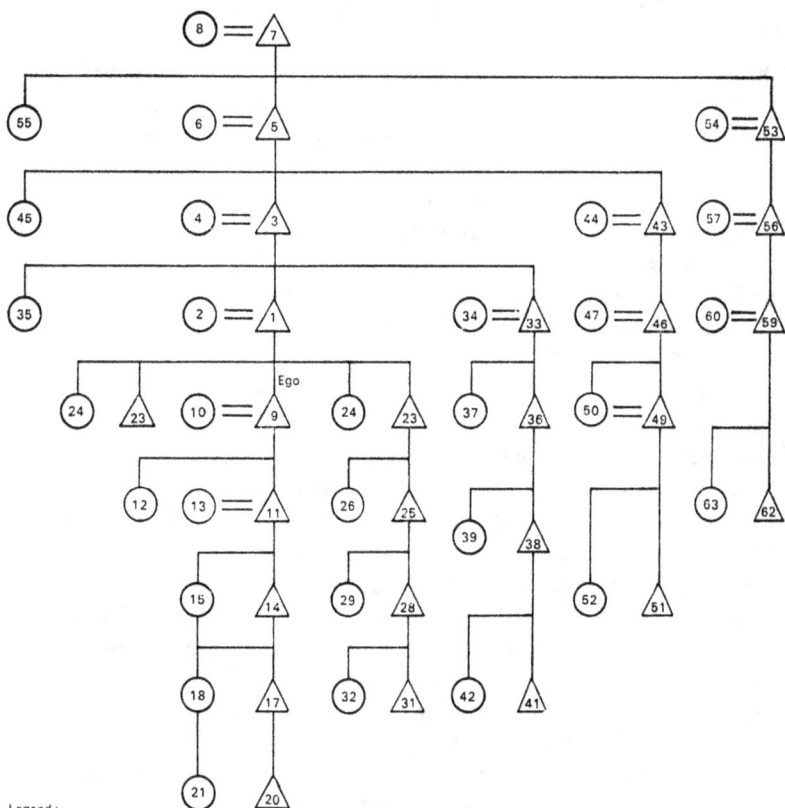

Legend :

△ Male

○ Female

═ Married

⊓ Relationships

groom's. Since females usually live somewhat longer than males, this scheme prevented one spouse from living alone. This scheme also provided an opportunity for well-to-do males to engage in polygyny, because by the time the groom reached the age of twenty-five with four or five children by his original wife, she was regarded by her husband as an old woman. It should also be cited that a woman's status was lower. By the time a girl was six years old, she was taught never to sit or talk with her own relatives, let alone with strangers, in the same room. She was taught to respect three lords, first, her parents, second, her husband upon marriage, and lastly, her own eldest son upon her husband's death. Prior to her marriage, she was taught all the virtues of her husband's family and was required to play, after marriage, the role of "three-year dumb," followed by "three-year deaf," and finally "three-year blind" (Kim, 1969:38).

For many centuries, the family was and still is known as "kajok," which was originally derived from Chinese characters. "Ka" means house and "jok," member, clan, or tribe. Therefore, the term "kajok" is rather broad and include all the paternal and maternal relatives who are related by blood, regardless of how close or how remote. In modern times, more and more people use Korea's own phonetic term, "jip," which means a small nuclear family. In its historical usage, "jip" means a patrilineal family succeeded continually from generation to generation. Historically, Koreans have viewed "jip" as a group, clan, or tribe, and at the same time "jip" has been regarded as an institution which provides for diverse human needs. In Korea, a person's last or family name comes first, followed by one's first name, which is the opposite of Western usage. This indicates the importance of the family, rather than the individual. In the West, due to emphasis placed upon an individual's position, one's first name is used more frequently than one's family name.

KOREAN FAMILY DURING THE JAPANESE OCCUPATION 1910-45

In the preceding sections, we have seen the gradual development of the Korean family prior to and during the Yi dynasty. Since 1910, the Japanese have modernized, and in some instances, disintegrated the traditional Korean family. Although formal annexation of Korea did not come into effect until 1910, the Japanese initiated their protectorate regime as early regime as 1905. Under the Japanese Imperial Ordinances, numbers 267, 268, and 275 of 20 December, 1905, the "Tokan-fu," which means supervisory office or office of the resident general, was set up under the control of the "Tokan" or resident-general. It specifically stipulated that no Koreans would be allowed to enact or amend a law, an ordinance, or an important administrative act without the prior full approval of the resident-general. In effect, the former Korean government machinery ceased to function, and this marked the beginning of Japanese supremacy in controlling the social, economic, and cultural spheres until Korea was liberated from Japan in 1945.

Civil law in Korea, based mainly on that of Japan, was instituted in March 1912; afterwards, regulations of matters relative to marriage, adoption, relationship, inheritance, etc. were also completed and put into effect under the name of "Chosun Minsa Ryung," or "Korean Civil Decree". In November 1921, the Governor's Decree on Civil Matters was revised and the Japanese Civil Code was made to apply in full in Korea with respect to individual capacity, parental power, and guardianship, irrespective of prior Korean customs. In July 1921, the intermarriage law of Japanese and Koreans was adjusted and its procedures simplified.

According to the Civil Law section on "The Family and Relative," the family was restricted to a small size, namely the family head, the spouse, relatives, and their own or adopted children. The stepfather and stepmother were also classified as legal family members (Civil Law, Articles 732, 733, 727, and 731). Thus, the family was restricted to married couples and relatives only, with or without their own or adopted children. All other members, whether they lived under the same roof or not, were not included in the family.

During the Yi dynasty, as we have already observed, regardless of the size of the family, the family included only one family or house head, the "ka-jang." However, according to the Civil Law, there could be several household heads, called "hoju" (Civil Law, Articles 729, 730, and 732). The fact that any married family member could establish a new branch family did not vitiate one of the basic concepts of the family—that the family shall last forever. In order to prevent family extinction, the law further provided that: "A person who has become the head

of a house by succession cannot abolish such a house, except
where permission to do so has been obtained from a court
of law for the purpose of succession to, or the reestablishment of,
the main house, or for any other just cause" (Civil Law, Article
762). In addition, "the legal presumptive heir to the headship of
a house is not permitted to enter another house, or establish a
new one, except where the necessity arises for succeeding to the
headship of the main house" (Civil Law, Article 744). In other
words, a legal presumptive heir, by law, could not become a member of another house by marriage, adoption, or in any other way,
nor could he establish a new house of his own. The civil law provided the means to reduce the size of the family and gave greater
freedom to the individual; however, the original thought behind
the family concept was still incorporated into the law.

In contrast to the Yi dynasty, with respect to parental authority
over children, there were a number of differences found in
Japanese Civil Law: 1) children under the age of twenty-one were
under the parent's strict supervision; 2) they were required to live
in the place which the parents provided; 3) children could not
volunteer for military service unless they first obtained permission
from their parents; 4) they could not establish a business unless
parental permission was given; and 5) children could not contract
marriage without prior consent from the parents. These laws were
equally applicable to adopted children (Civil Law, Articles 878,
729, 730, 880, 881, 772, and 727).

During the Yi dynasty, greater emphasis was placed upon the
eldest male heir of the family. This male was made the legal
perpetuator of the ancestral cult, and exclusive power was awarded to the family head to regulate, manage, and control both the
family members and the family property. During the Japanese era
however, the civil law recognized two types of succession, to family
headship and to property. Within the context of succession to
family headship, there were four kinds of heirs that were recognized; the legal heir, the appointed heir, the chosen heir, and the
ascendent heir.[2]

2*The legal heir:* The legal heir, who comes first in the order of succession
is the lineal descendant of a family head, who is at the same time a member of his house. Among lineal descendants, the nearest kinsman is preferred
to the remote, the male to the female, and the legitimate child to the ille-

Once a person succeeded to the family headship, he was prohibited from neglecting matters pertaining to the family. Laws were further established to prevent family discontinuation by the following provision: "The family head cannot bequeath away from him more than one half of the property, nor can he be disinherited, unless there exists one of the grounds mentioned in the civil law, article 975." Article 975 specifies the reasons as:

1) Ill-treatment or gross insult to the family head

2) Unfitness for family headship on account of bodily or mental infirmities

3) Being or having been sentenced to punishment for an offense of such a nature as to defy the name of the house

4) Interdiction of the court as a spendthrift. For these and any other just causes, a family head may, with the consent of the family council, bring an action against his legal presumptive heir with a view to depriving him of the right as succession.

Under both laws of succession, during the Yi dynasty and the Japanese era, it is apparent that every precaution was taken to prevent family discontinuation. The foundations of the law may be viewed as follows: the former period dealt exclusively with the clan or the consanguineous family as its basis for the perpetuation

gitimate, seniors in age being always accorded priority when they are equal in other respects. *The appointed heir:* In case there is no legal presumptive heir to a family head, the latter may "appoint" an heir, either in his life time or by his will. However, this appointment will not be effective, if he obtains a child in the course of nature or by adoption, for the latter will become his legal presumptive heir. *The chosen heir:* If at the time of the death of a family head, there is neither a legal nor an appointed heir, the father of the deceased, or, if there is no father, or, if he is unable to express his intention, the mother, or, if there are no parents or both are unable to express their intention, the family council "chooses" an heir from among the members of the house according to the following order: 1) the surviving wife, if she is a house-daughter; 2) the brothers; 3) sisters; 4) the surviving wife, who is not a house-daughter; and 5) the lineal descendants of brothers and sisters. *The ascendant heir:* If there is neither a legal, nor an appointed, nor a chosen, heir, then the nearest lineal ascendant of the last family head succeeds, the male being always preferred to the female in the case of persons standing in the same degree of relationship (Civil Law, Articles 964 through 991).

of the ancestral cult; the latter period emphasized the nuclear or conjugal family as the foundation for family continuity. Therefore, the application of the Japanese policies to Korean society was the first time in Koreas long history that the conjugal family began to form the legal unit of the state. Prior to 1910, an individual was merely the unit of the extended family or clan and functionally the clan was the unit of the state. Indeed, disintegration of the traditional family base, the clan, was initiated after 1910.

During the Yi dynasty, the legal marrige age was sixteen or over for the male and over fourteen for the female. According to the Civil Law applied in Korea , the legal marriage age was seventeen or over for the male and fifteen or over for the female (Civil Law, Article 765). The Civil Law provided that parental consent to marriage remained unchanged, but "if the man has completed his 30th year, or the woman her 25th year, no parental consent to marriage may be necessary" (Civil Law, Article 772). If a member of a house married with the consent of the head of the family, the latter could, within one year from the day of the marriage, exclude him or her from the household, or, if he or she entered another house by marriage, forbid his or her return to the original house in case of dissolution of the marriage (Civil Law, Article 750). The consequences of a marriage without the consent of the parents were that the parents could petition a court of law for the annulment of the marriage within a period of six months from the time they first became acquainted with the fact of the marriage, or within two years from the date of its registration (Civil Law, Article 784, Section 3).

Article 769 stipulated that "no one is permitted to marry amongst the third-degree blood relatives." Third-degree blood relatives included parents, grandparents, brothers, sisters, and sons and daughters of one's brothers and sisters. This meant that a marriage contract was legal even if the bride-to-be carried the same surname as the groom. During the Yi dynasty, "no one shall be permitted to intermarry within the same clan, or even if the parties are from different clans but are related by blood or through marriage alliances and adoption." Furthermore, during the Yi dynasty, the three years following the death of a parent, no person was permitted to marry. However, there was no such restriction in the Civil Law. In addition, there were no restrictions on marriage between different classes.

During the Yi dynasty, there were many plural marriages, particularly among the rich, noble, and ruling classes (Chang, 1971b).
With the introduction of the Japanese Civil Law and Criminal
Law in the Korean peninsula, monogamy became the established
rule (Civil Law, Article 766, and Criminal Law, Article 184).
Nonetheless, plurality of marriage continued, and to a certain
degree still exists in contemporary Korea. As mentioned earlier, a
wife could be repudiated by her husband on one of the following
"seven grounds of divorce" during the Yi dynasty: 1) disobedience to her husband and husband's parents; 2) barrenness; 3)
adultery; 4) jealousy; 5) repulsive disease; 6) talkativeness; and
7) larceny. An examination of the Civil Law during the Japanese
era reveals that the majority of the above seven items disappeared
except items 1), 3), and 7). Under the Yi dynasty's law, the divorce
suit was brought to the court by the husband or the husband's
parents; however, the Civil Law recognized that "either parties,
husband or wife, may initiate the divorce" (Civil Law, Article
808). The Civil Law recognized two kinds of legal procedures
through which a legal marriage could be terminated; the first one
is called "consensual" and the second "judicial." The former was
effected by the arrangement of the parties concerned, while the
latter was awarded by the court of law on the grounds specified
in the Civil Law, Article 813 Under the judicial divorce provisions, either side of the married couple could initiate a divorce
suit on the basis of one or more of the following grounds: 1)
being married twice or more without due process of law—bigamy;
2) adultery committed by the wife; 3) adultery committed by the
husband; 4) such offenses as forgery, bribery, corruption, theft,
robbery obtaining property under false pretenses, embezzlement,
receiving stolen goods, and sexual immorality: 5) desertion of
spouse or spouse's immediate family; 6) uncertainty of the spouse's
existence, or whereabouts, for a period of over three years (Civil
Law, Article 813).

Now that we have seen the marriage and family system during
the Japanese era, let us consider present trends in the Korean family.

KOREAN FAMILY SINCE 1945

The Republic of Korea was not formally established until 15
August 1948, in South Korea. Its constitution, which was pro-

mulgated on 17 July 1948, is based upon democratic principles; the government does not follow a particular established pattern of organization but draws upon a combination of American, European, and Oriental political systems which are designed to meet administrative problems peculiar to the Republic of Korea. The constitution stresses individual freedom, liberty, and equality regardless of sex, age, social status, political affiliation, and religion.

With the adoption of the new democratic constitution, society began to change. On 22 February 1958, the new Korean Civil Law was enacted by the national assembly; however, in general most of the provisions of the Japanese Civil Law remained the same with minor revisions. In the new Korean Civil Law, the family contains the "family head, his spouse, his parents and his own or adopted children" (Article 773). With regard to marriage, individual rights in the choice of a mate are fully respected by the new law as compared to the former Civil Law. As to the legal marriage age, the new provision is that "the male should be 18 or over and the female should be 16 or over to be of legal marriage age" (Civil Law, Article 801). No parental consent is required when the marrying party is over twenty years of age, for both the female and male. Furthermore, the new Civil Law stresses that marriage can be allowed only on the basis of agreement between the male and female. It means, then, whether a marriage is arranged by the parents, a go-between, friends, or by one's own choice, mutual agreement by both the marrying male and female is necessary in order to legalize the marriage. Concerning the dissolution of marriage, there are no critical changes in the new law. However, the individual rights of both parties involved are extended. Parental consent to the divorce is required only if the "child is under 20 years of age, either male or female" (Civil Law, Article 828).

According to the Civil Law, both marriage and divorce may be arranged without the parents' consent when one reaches the legal adult age of twenty. The contemporary Korean Civil Law, as well as the Criminal Law, clearly shows that both the Japanese and the Koreans took precautionary measures to prevent the extinction of the family. In other words, the basic philosophy underlying social legislation is to safeguard family continuity.

In spite of some changes that have been made in recent years to modernize the Korean family, this institution still portrays essential similarities to the structure and functions of the traditional family. The present Korean family is still viewed as a continuation of the ancestral family. It still recognizes only parental and consanguineous relatives as family members. People with the same surname still cannot marry each other, even though some relaxation has been introduced by the Civil Law. Property succession is still, to a large extent based on the parental line. Even a son adopted to continue the family name must come from parental relatives. In China and Japan, a son could be adopted from outside of one's own parental relatives. As a family responsibility, the right to ancestory worship is only given to the eldest son.

Even though family status or prestige should not enter into matrimonial considerations, the so-called "Kamun," meaning family honor, clan standing, or ancestors' achievement, still is the prevailing criterion for marriage. The traditional kinship terminologies are kept intact in the modern family and define the status and role of each family member. Traditional duties of sons to their dead parents—mourning and its associated rites—are still adhered to. Each clan is obliged to revive and update "chokbo," or the genealogical book of the clan, for future descendants. Established modes of marriage are still based on the principle of exogamy; however, intermarriage in rural communities is rare. Modern Civil Law does not permit marriage with the father's sisters' children or mother's sisters' children or mother's brothers' children, and such matrimonial union is still regarded as incestuous, in spite of the fact that in China and in Japan such marriages are legal and widely practiced.

The traditional large, extended, patriarchal family, which once was regarded as ideal and even necessary in the feudal society of the past is changing. In spite of some changes, there are still primordial traits that linger in Korea, particularly in rural communities. The traditional family is structurally bulky and complex and often discourages individual members from undertaking vigorous enterprises. From birth to death, a person is confined to the tasks of family procreation and continuity, individual while creativity is discouraged. Moreover, for a long time, Confucianism has overdomesticated Koreans and overemphasized filial piety discrimination against women, and illegitimacy. The prevailing economic system of serfdom, semislavery, domestic servants despised cul-

tural minority groups, and other formalities must change in order
to promote democracy.

It is recognized that some changes are necessary to adjust to the
new world scene. The traditional Korean family, even though containing some "undesirable" traits, has functional features worthy
of further development. It was the opinion of the legislature, at
the time of enacting the Civil Law, that some modification in the
family system was necessary in order to facilitate new adjustments.
However, radical and unplanned social change is always a cause
of social unrest.

CURRENT TRENDS AND THE FUTURE DIRECTIONS
OF THE KOREAN FAMILY

Korean society is undergoing a marked transformation from traditional to modern as a result of urbanization and industrialization. The
increased social mobility, the higher education among the masses,
the gradual increase in per capita income for each working family
member, a greater production and consumption of goods and
services, popular participation in the governing forces, and many
other factors have changed the structural and functional aspects of
the Korean family. In fact, many of the world's so-called developing nations are going through a similar process of modernization.

The most noteworthy changes have occurred in the composition
of the family itself. According to a survey conducted in 1955, the
average family size reached a low point of 4.8 persons in urban
areas and 5.3 in rural areas (Choi, 1970:3). The most recent
nationwide census was taken in October 1966. According to it, each
household contained an average of 5.49 persons throughout Korea
and 5.01 in the metropolitan city of Seoul. The rural-oriented provinces and communities seem to have an average of between 5.39
to 5.89 persons per family (Choe, 1970:56-57). In terms of family
composition, the two-generation family seems to be the predominant type as shown in Table 2.

The shifts from the large consanguineous to the conjugal family is
phenomenal in Korea. This also means that newly married couples,
regardless of their birth order, have been establishing separate
households and the trend is for newlyweds to live separately from
their parents. Another noteworthy development in modern Korea

TABLE 2. *Number of households by type and membership*

Categories	No. of households	No. of members
Nationwide (South Korea)	5,057,030	27,765,620
1) Related households	4,900,650	27,543,720
(i) One-generation household	277,880	627,680
(ii) Two-generation household	3,316,590	17,430,900
(iii) Three-generation household	1,178,700	8,654,660
(iv) Other	127,480	830,480
2) Nonrelated households	38,920	104,440
3) One-person households	117,460	117,460

Source. Statistical Yearbook of Korea, 1970, pp. 56-57. The population Census was taken in 1 October 1966.

is the eventual emancipation of family members from elders and the authoritarian father because of the shifts in the family structure. Male-female equality is not only the guiding principle, but is also widely practiced in politics, industries and factories, education, the family, and other social circles. It is the prevailing mood in Korea that marriage should be postponed until males and females are capable, economically, to sustain their own lives without depending upon their parents. Consequently, the age of marriage is gradually rising, the average male being twenty-five to thirty, and the female twenty to twenty-five.

It should also be indicated that young married couples, particularly those who are residing in urban regions, are not only conscious about the size of their future family, but also are concerned about Korea's future population growth. According to the latest press releases regarding population data by the Korean Family Planning Commission in Seoul, the rate of growth was maintained at 1.92 per cent per year during 1966-70, while this rate was 2.70 per cent and 2.88 per cent during the periods of 1960-66 and 1955-60, respectively. The government of Korea was planning to have the population stabilized at 1.5 per cent per annum by 1976 (Chung Ang Ilbo, 7 December 1971). The most favored number of children newlyweds in urban areas wish to have is two, one boy and one girl (70 per cent of the respondents). The next favored number is three, two boys and one girl (Han Guk Ilbo, 25 November 1971). In a recent survey conducted by the Korean Behavioral Science Research Institute of Korea and dealing with birth control and desired number of children, revealed that future mothers favored three children. Of the 1,883 fecund women, 53 per cent indicated that "I would prefer to have an unlimited number of children" (Seoul respondents 29 per cent, and rural 73 per cent). Another finding was that 50 per cent of the wives indicated that they would like their husband to obtain a concubine to have a boy rather than to adopt one from outsiders in the case where a wife is barren (Seoul respondents 25 per cent, rural 68 per cent (Chung Ang Ilbo, 18 November 1971). It is apparent then, that rural areas still cling to traditional family values and practices. Even though reliable studies are not available at this time, marriages through free choice of partners, particularly by young people in urban areas, are increasing. In a survey regarding the attitudes of parents toward mate selection among their children, Professor Kim remarked: "it could well be said that as far as the people of the urban middle class are concerned, those sticking to the traditional method of mate selection appear virtually to have vanished" (1969: 52).

The recent trend in Korea is to seek practicality in marriage and in funeral ceremonies rather than "face-saving" and formality, which have prevailed for over 500 years. Rituals among the young are becoming less important than personal problems. The marriage ceremony, which used to take over a week, has now been shortened to a day, and the honeymoon is kept minimal. Funeral services last several days rather than weeks, while mourning periods of three years are virtually disappearing. Due to the industry's increasing demand for female labor, more than half of urban women work prior to their marriage and the birth of the first child. Family planning has been encouraged and birth control techniques are widely available for people who desire to use them. (Abortion is illegal in Korea, but the law is seldom enforced.) For the past ten years, government propaganda efforts have been to limit families to two children.

A recent survey regarding marriage and the family has given the following results: family property will be inherited more equally among brothers, instead of a larger share going to the eldest son. Even though in urban communities more social welfare agencies are becoming active in supporting old parents, it is likely that the trend will be for all brothers to support them, rather than the eldest son alone. During the traditional era, when a son's wife was disliked by his parents, this was sufficient reason for a legal divorce. But now parental attitude is less influential in this respect. The predominant method of mate selection will be individual's choice, with or without the advise of parents. Even though the majority of males believe that girls should keep their chastity before marriage, premarital relations may be increasing and the traditonal role of husband-wife relations will be shifting more to the equalitarian principle. In the future, more women will attain prestige and freedom; and more women will participate in voting, run for office, work in factories, and attend colleges and universities. Women's voice will be heard in the family. At the present time, women can sue men and men can sue women. Women's criminality may also increase as they assume more social roles (Shin, 1965: 191-205).

For many centuries, women were regarded as daughters, wives, and mothers. But their higher status may now result in family disruption. Moreover, women may initiate more divorces. Remarriage, particularly by widows, was severely discouraged during the Yi dynasty and Japanese era, but it will become common. In the future, monogamy will prevail. Undoubtedly, the new feminist movement will be popularized by the nation's press. In time, it is predicted that the two-generation family—parents and their own or adopted children—will be common throughout Korea except, perhaps, in remote rural and fishing villages.

Since Korea is heading toward industrialization and urbanization, more and more people are engaging in geographic mobility. High crime and delinquency rates are predicted. Mental illness, suicide, and other forms of disorganization are also anticipated. Problems of the old, drug abuse, alcoholism, and prostitution are already recognized as key social problems. Juvenile runaways, from both home and school, are the concern of every politician. As such problems increase, the government may have to manage many family affairs. Functionally, the future Korean family will be more service-oriented rather than an economic production unit.

SUMMARY AND CONCLUSION

According to this study, the matriarchal family apparently prevailed prior to the Koguryo era (37 B.C. A.D. 668) and then gradually transformed itself into the patriarchal family system and, during the Yi dynasty (1392-1910), the patrilineal and patrilocal family system was well established and continued into this generation, with some modifications. At first, the nuclear family settled down in a certain locality and gradually formed a clan village. Since the clan village was an economic unit that produced goods for its own consumption and created rules to regulate the life of its members, it acted as the political subunit of the state during the Yi dynasty. In the traditional society, sharply differentiated social classes came into existence, these being a royal class, a nobility class, a commoners' class, and the lower and despised social classes. Polygamy was a common practice among landlords, and women were dependent upon and submissive to men. Social differentiation was largely based on the individual's sex, age, and order of birth. In fact, the status of the individual was mainly ascribed and special privileges were exclusively handed down, particularly to the oldest son. The traditional family system did not require establishing a new house for each marriage, as married sons brought their wives and lived with their parents and grandparents. Therefore, at least theoretically, the family never ceased to exist.

The traditional family was only a fraction of each clan and, to a large extent, the clan council was responsible for providing for intraclan activities, such as recreation, religion, education, welfare rehabilitation of criminals, marriage arrangements, funeral services, and village security. In terms of marriage, individual opinion was largely ignored and a divorce was considered disgraceful and was not widely practiced. Since the clan's livelihood was based on agriculture, the village needed large families. Moreover, child training was rigid, and children were taught to respect their parents and all authority from an early age.

The family traditionally included three generations, the past, present, and future. When Koreans spoke about the family (the "jip"), they meant both living members and those who had died. Through ancestor worship, they believed, they could strengthen the family as a group. There was no individual in the Western sense. Everything—property, house, ancestor's graveyards, livestock— belonged to the entire family. Everyone was taught to uphold the family name, known as "Kamun" and family honor for the sake of collective prosperity rather than for individual advancement. Shame and crime were also family matters and mechanisms were developed to preserve order within the family and the village community.

We can theorize here that the structural and functional aspects of the family were highly related to the prevailing economic activities. The rise of private enterprise—capitalism—that created the institution of the family was sanctioned by the largest and most powerful of all groups, the state, for the purpose of property succession. (A family with more property is historically more concerned with the legality of marriage because termination of marriage always includes a division of the property owned by the parties involved.) Legality and marriage ceremonies are not crucial among the poor. Under communal, primitive tribal settings, the legality of marriage did not exist and the family institution as we know it today was not developed. Group marriage, promiscuity, and marriage by capture were practiced because of necessity and were not due to cultural influence.

The Korean society has passed through at least three major stages since the Yi dynasty. These are, first, what the author designates as the "period of clan recognition," second, "period of family recognition," and lastly, "period of individual recognition." The first period covers the 500 years of the Yi dynasty, 1392-1910. The period between 1910-45 is that of "family recognition," and that between 1945 and the present, the "period of individual recognition." Each of these stays had its own concepts, rules, and regulations regarding marriage and the family.

In evaluating the aforementioned stages, we find that the government has gradually acquired more and more control, as evidenced by the increasing rigidity of the legislation system. During the Yi dynasty, an individual was recognized as a component of a family

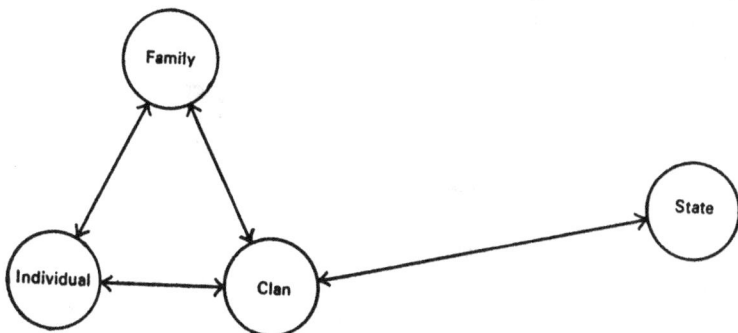

and clan, and there was no contact between the individual and the state.

During the Japanese era, the state did not recognize the clan, but only the family, as the unit of social control:

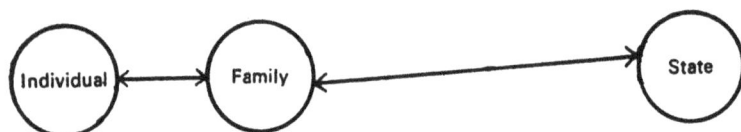

Since 1945, the state usually has bypassed the family entirely, when an individual has reached the adult legal age of twenty. The state's business is conducted on an individual basis, not the family as a whole:

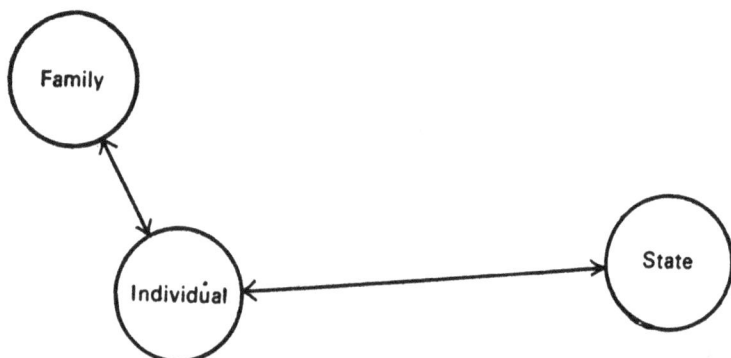

The above diagrams also indicate that the power or authority which was formally exercised by parents and clan council has been reduced or abolished and some of the family and clan functions have been taken over by the state, for the purpose of efficiency and effectiveness. The government has now focused its attention more on the individual in regard to his education, military service, health, welfare, and family life. Such trends may continue and the family may prove to be too weak to assume vital roles. In other words, today's Korea may be called an "institutional society" in that nonfamilial institutions are assuming and playing roles which formerly belonged to the family: the original clan council's responsibilities have been turned over to the state; ancestor worship has given way to the church; handicrafts by the clan village or by the family have been assumed by industries or factories; clan rules and regulations, including the punishment of offenders, are now handled by legislatures, courts, police, and prisons; the functions of the village clan school, known as "sontang," are now performed by public or private schools; village defense has been taken over by the police and the military; the sick are treated in hospitals; clan welfare has been replaced by social welfare agencies; the "chokbo," or family registry, has moved to government recording agencies, such as the city or country hall and the courts; clan festivals and recreation have been taken over by TV, radio, movies, public parks, recreational centers, and national holidays; etc. But one may ask: Can man live without a family? More broadly, can society become one large family in which individual families will vanish? Social research should throw some light on these questions.

The current trend seems to be that the Korean society is clearly heading for either a three-generation or a two-generation family, rather than the large extended family which, in the past, has been the predominant type. Emancipation of young from old, female from male, and despised minority groups from aristocratic classes is seen everywhere. Western influences are a fact of life in Korea, as more and more people are travelling abroad. The mass media, a higher living standard, and a higher education enable Koreans to seek individual freedom and chart their own future. On the other hand, it is anticipated that there will be new problems of social control as a result of periodic social dislocations.

Divorce, separation, and desertion rates may increase, along with the illegitimacy rate. A consequence of more divorces is that more children will be brought up under step-parent situations, or some portion of the child population will be reared in the absence of one or both natural parents. We are not certain whether boys are more adversely affected by parental divorce than girls, or *vice versa*. Are children that are reared in a large family more apt to achieve success in school and later in society? Does parental conflict cause young children to become more involved in delinquent acts? As of this date, no conclusive evidence has been found. Do upper class children perform better in school? If so, why? Traditionally, Korean mothers favored breast-freeding. In contrast, the modern bottle-feeding method provides the child with more nutrition and they are healthier. In terms of birth order, it was assumed in the past that the earlier the child, the brighter he will be. Is there any real difference in achivement and ability due to the order of birth? Modern parents wish to space their children two to three years apart. Do longer intervals produce more harmonious and stable intrafamilial relations? Working class parents apply more physical punishment than upper class parents, where reasoning and guilt seem to be the more predominant methods. What are the differences between these two forms of punishment? These and many other questions pertaining to family life should be answered through research. The future of any society hinges upon its children's aspirations, motivation, and perception, which that society determines.

In addition, questions as to how many of the traditional traits remain in Korea today, in spite of modernization efforts, are the subject of another study However, it is safely concluded here that the traditional Korean social structure, including that of the family, is disintegrating at least in urban communities.

All in all, it is clear that the factors of social change in Korea seem to be many, including wars, inventions, discoveries, the economy, technology, urbanization, education, Japanese colonization, new ideologies, Western influence, and the adaptive capacities of the Koreans themselves. In conclusion, it must be stated that unplanned and radical social change imposed upon the already burdened family is fraught with dangerous elements. Human habits ideas, ideologies, and values cannot change overnight. Some of the meritorious features of the traditional family should be honored and retained, and unworthy elements should be modified or rejected. Just how well Koreans can adjust themselves and reconstruct the basic social institutions to meet new challenges depends on themselves. Indeed, it is the Koreans' own ability, knowledge, skills, responsiveness, and above all, cooperativeness that will chart the course and mold the future of their family and society.

REFERENCES

Chang, Dae H.
   1967 "The Historical Development of the Korean Socio-Family System Since 1392—A Legalistic Interpretation." *Journal of East Asiatic Studies*, 11 (September). Pp. 1-124.
   1969 "Crime in Developing Societies: The Case of Korea." *Asian Forum*, 2 (April). Pp. 28-35.
   1971a "Intermarriage Practice in Traditional Korea." *International Journal of Sociology of the Family*, 1 (May). Pp. 137-146.

1971b "Traditional Stratification System in Korea: With a Particular Emphasis on the Packchong." *International Review of History and Political Science*, 2 (May). Pp. 56-74.

Choe, Sun Ray
1970 *Hanguk Tongke Yongkam (Statistical Yearbook)*. Seoul, Korea: Bureau of Statistics, Economic Planning Board, Republic of Korea.

Choi, Jae Suk
1970 *Hanguk Kajok Yonggu (A Study of Korean Family)*. Seoul, Korea: Minjung Sokwan.

Chung Ang Ilbo (Daily newspaper in Seoul, Korea). 18 November and December 1971.

Fujita, Tozo
1941 *Richo Jitsuroku: Chosen Konin-ko* (Ye Dynasty's Marriage Custom: An Official Record). Tokyo, Japan: Taido Insatsukan.

Ginsburg, Norton
1961 *The Pattern of Asia*. Englewood Cliffs, N.J.: Prentice-Hall.

Han Guk Ilbo (Daily newspaper in Seoul, Korea) 25 November 1971.

Kim, C.I. Eugene
1969 *Aspects of Social Change in Korea*. Kalamazoo, Mich: The Korean Research and Publications.

Kim, Doo Hyun
1949 *Chosun Kajok Jaedo Yonggu* (The Study of Korean Family). Seoul, Korea: Eul-Yoo Munwha-sa.

Kim, Ick Dal
1970 *Korea: Its People and Culture*. Seoul, Korea: Hakwon-sa.

Lee, Hang Nyung.
1964 *Minpuphak Kaeron* (Principles of Civil Law). Seoul, Korea: Bakyong-sa.

McCune, George M.
1950 *Korea Today*. Cambridge: Harvard University Press.

Oh, Chae Kyung.
1958 *Handbook of Korea*. New York: Pageant Press.

Reischauer, Edwin O. and John K. Pairbank.
1960 *East Asia: The Great Tradition*. Boston: Houghton Mifflin.

Shin, Shik Soo
1965 *Bomjae Baekso* (Whitepaper on Crime). Seoul, Korea: Dae Kumchal Chong.

Son, Jin Tae.
1948 *Chosun Minjok Munwha Ui Yonggu* (The Study of Korean Cultural History). Seoul, Korea: Eul-yoo Munwha-sa.

II. MODERNIZATION AND BIRTH CONTROL—AN INTERNATIONAL SURVEY OF ATTITUDES TOWARDS ORAL CONTRACEPTION*—
Panos D. Bardis

A "pill scale" and two stratified samples of American and Korean university students are employed to test the hypothesis that "the modernization of a given nation is accompanied by increasingly liberal attitudes toward birth control." The study includes a summary of the major features of the American family with main emphasis on birth control. The section on the Korean family system is more detailed and discusses both historical and present-day characteristics, as well as the development, nature, and effects of family planning programs in South Korea. The data, secured through interviews involving the "pill scale" and a personal data questionnaire, are analyzed by means of various statistical tests. The findings tend to support the hypothesis and lead to the follwing additional conclusions: first, a cross-cultural survey of attitudes toward the pill seems feasible; second, the Korean respondents appear to be overpopulation-conscious and highly interested in scientific studies dealing with birth control; third, females tend to be significantly more conservative in Korea, while in the USA the pill scores of the males and females differ insignificantly; fourth, agriculture majors in Korea are highly liberal; fifth in the United States, the mother's gainful employment does not appear to affect her college child's attitudes toward oral contraception; sixth, in both countries, the relationship between the subject's own pill attitudes and the following factors is insignificant: age, number of siblings, birth order, parents' education, and father's occupation; seventh, although, in Korea, the pill-education associatian is insignificant, in the USA, the respondents' education appears to liberalize their birth control attitudes; eighth, the pill-religiosity relationship is inversely proportionate among American students; ninth, American parents are significantly more conservative with reference to the pill than their college children; and tenth, in Korea, family size and maternal education level are significantly and inversely proportional.

*This paper was presented at the 7th World Congress of the International Sociological Association, VARNA, BULGARIA, 14-19 September, 1970. Reprinted with permission from INTERNATIONAL JOURNAL OF SOCIOLOGY OF THE FAMILY, MARCH 1971: Vol. I, No. 1, pp. 21-35.

INTRODUCTION

Is it possible to employ attitudes toward oral contraception as a partial index of modernization?

As an answer to this question, the present paper offers some of the findings of an international study of such attitudes involving both developing and developed countries.

Modernization

A social scientist has asserted that "modernization is the current term for an old process—the process of social change whereby less developed societies acquire characteristics common to more developed societies" (Lerner, 1968:386). Diminishing provincialism has accompanied this process. In early imperialistic times, for example, the colonial spirit could be detected in phrases such as "The 'Anglicization' of India." Late imperialism, however, witnessed what was known as "Europeanization," in view of the similarities among the various imperialistic nations. The dominant term during the third stage, the second world war, was "Westernization," whereas after the war "modernization" referred to the entire planet.

In 1955, Lewis mentioned economic development as an exceedingly important component of modernization. A better analysis has been presented by Lerner (1968:387), who has listed the following constituents: first, self-sustaining economic growth; second, public participation in the polity; third, a diffusion of secular-rational norms; fourth, increasing physical, psychic, and social mobility; and fifth, corresponding personality changes to facilitate adjustment to the new social system.

Although Lerner's list seems adequate, his definition of modernization appears to be slightly narrow. Indeed, "Modernization may refer to one and the same highly developed society—even the most modern one—when various forces generate a social system which is more developed than the one that it succeeded, and which has never existed in any other society. This dimension makes the study of social change more inclusive and fruitful. Needless to add, such change involves all major social institutions—the family, the church, the economy, and so on" (Bardis, 1969c; 1971).

Hypothesis

The specific hypothesis tested in this survey is that "the modernization of a given nation is accompanied by increasingly liberal attitudes towards birth control."

METHODOLOGY

To test this hypothesis, the author compared the attitudes of two sets of subjects representing two different cultures, one developing and the other developed.

The Samples

The first sample consisted of forty South Korean students attending a large university in Seoul. The characteristics of this group, which was stratified by sex and amount of education, were as follows:

Sex: 20 males and 20 females
Age: an average of 20.95 years
Number of additional siblings: an average of 4.80
Birth order: an average of 2.78
Marital status: all single
Religion: none, 31; Buddhism, 6; Protestantism, 3
Amount of own education: 5 males and 5 females from each university
    class, namely, first through fourth years
Major field of study: social sciences and humanities, 25; agriculture, 15
Parents' education: fathers, an average of 11.92 years; mothers, 8.00
Father's occupation: an average of 3.68 on the Alba Edwards scale[1]
Mother's occupation: housewives, 35; gainfully employed, 5.

The members of the second sample were forty American-born, white, Protestant students attending a large state university in an American metropolis, and coming from various parts of the United States, primarily from the Midwest. The characteristics of this

---

[1]Occupation was quantified as follows: unskilled workers, 0; semiskilled workers, 1; skilled workers and foremen, 2; clerks and kindred workers, 3; proprietors, managers, officials, 4; professionals, 5 (Edwards, 1943: 181-186).

sample, which was also stratified by sex and education, were as follows:

Sex: 20 males and 20 females
Age: an average of 20.05 years
Number of additional siblings: an average of 2.52
Birth order: an average of 2.80
Marital status: single, 28; engaged, 7; married, 5
Religious services attended per month: an average of 1.82
Amount of own education: 5 males and 5 females from each university class, that is, first through fourth years
Major field of study: social sciences; and humanities, 31; natural sciences, 9
Parents' education: fathers, an average of 12.72 years; mothers, 12.85
Father's occupation: an average of 2.80 on the Edwards scale
Mother's occupation: housewives, 26; gainfully employed, 14.

The "Pill Scale"

The subjects' attitudes toward birth control were quantified by means of the writer's "pill scale" the construction, validity, and reliability of which have been described in detail elsewhere (Bardis, 1969b).[2] Needless to add, the scale, which emphasizes oral contraception, deals with an issue whose timeliness and controversial nature render research of this type both interesting and useful. The theoretical range of scores on this device is 0-100, the latter representing the highest possible degree of liberalism.

In the present study, a split-half reliability test (scale item 1 was omitted) involving thirty South Korean cases gave a raw Pearson *r* of 0.89. When the Spearman-Brown prophecy formula (Garrett, 1955: 338-341) was employed, the corrected reliability coefficient proved to be 0.94, that is, significant much beyond 0.001 (degrees of freedom, 28).

A coefficient which was similarly obtained from thirty of the American subjects was 0.91, namely, significant much beyond 0.001.

The pill data, like those involved in a personal information questionnaire (sex, age, religion, and other independent variables),

[2]Copies of the scale may be obtained upon request from the author. Incidentally, the scale excludes all medical matters completely, dealing only with the economic, moral, psychological, religious, and social aspects of attitudes toward oral contraception regardless of any possible physically harmful side effects.

were secured by means of personal interview.[3] Various statistical
tests were employed for the analysis of the data thus obtained.

THE AMERICAN AND KOREAN FAMILY SYSTEMS

An analysis of attitudes regarding contraception and modernization should be preceded by a brief account dealing with the
respective family systems within which these attitudes developed.
Since there are countless studies of the American family, the
description of this familiar system will be much shorter.

The American family

Here emphasis is placed on the various forces which have led
to the modern birth control movement in the United States.
These forces may be outlined as follows (Bardis, 1964; 1969a:
Section K):

1) The emancipation of women, which has rendered them much
less reproduction minded.
2) The economic insecurity generated by industrialization.
3) The often exorbitant expenses involved in child-rearing.
The passing of the frontier and the adoption of laws against
child labor have changed the pre adolescent and, to some extent,
the adolescent into liabilities. Even childbirth itself has become
more expensive, since it now usually takes place in a hospital.
4) The prevailing budgeting complex, because of which even
children must be budgeted through planned parenthood.
5) The educational and other advantages enjoyed by children
coming from small families.
6) The vertical social mobility which parents ordinarily emphasize at the expense of having children.
7) The decline of religiosity and the corresponding prevalence
of secularism, due to which a child's birth is no longer regarded
as an act of God. In 1931, even the Federal Council of Churches
expressed its approval of birth control.

[3]The author is very grateful to Dr Seong Hi Yim, a south Korean Scholar,
who collected the Korean data for this study.

8) Recognition of birth control by the medical profession—the American Medical Association recognized this practice officially in 1937.

9) The increase in the number of birth control clinics.

10) The legal approval of medical advice concerning contraception for reasons of health.

11) More extensive education, which tends to liberalize the population in many respects, including acceptance of birth control.

12) The philosophy of individualism.

The Korean Family

Korea's old civilization is revealed by many spectacular achievements, including the fact that "the casting of type and the printing of books" goes back to the first half of A.D. 13th century (McMurtrie, 1967:97).

The southern part of the country, which is officially known as the Republic of Korea, and unofficially as South Korea, was inaugurated as a republic on 15 August 1948. The nation's capital is Seoul, a city whose population was 3,805,261 in 1966 (Reader's Digest Association, 1968: 518).

"Agriculture, forestry, and fishing account for over one-third of the gross national product and manufacturing and construction account for 22 per cent. Only 23 per cent of the land is arable. Rice is the major crop and most valuable export; barley ranks second. Livestock and poultry are increasing in importance" (Reader's Digest Association, 1968:519). Thus, the sphere of agriculture encompasses 70 per cent of the population, the average farm having "about two acres to support the average rural family of six persons" (Cha, 1966:21). Moreover, out "of a total labor force of 10.5 million (age group 14-60), 2.75 million are unemployed or underemployed" (Cha, 1966:21), the per capita national income being $88 (USA, $2,893 *circa* 1968) (Petersen, 1969:330). In addition, in 1966, the net supply of food per person was 2,390 calories per day (USA, 3,200 in 1967), while the annual number of pounds was 447 for cereals, 171 for potatoes and the like, and 8 for meat [(USA, in 1967, 142, 107, and 237, respectively (Bureau of the Census, 1969:833)].

Because of "a lowering of the death rate by the introduction of modern medicines and health improvements," the growth of population has been quite high (T.I. Kim, 1969:26). Indeed, such growth was 2.8 per cent *circa* 1968 (USA, 1.1) (Petersen, 1969:330). At that time, the population of the country whose area is 38,022 square miles (98,476.98 square kilometres), was 30.7 (USA, 201.3), the density being 785 per square mile (Petersen, 1969:330; Bureau of the Census, 1969:829). The relative success of the national family planning program partly explains why the birth rate per 1,000 population per year, which was 42 in 1960, fell to 33 in 1968 (USA, 18.5) (Petersen, 1969:330). In 1955, the sex ratio, that is, the number of males per 100 females, was 100 (Mayer, 1968:363). Three years earlier, the percentage distribution of the population by age was as follows: 0-14 years, 41.1; 15-64, 55.2; and 65 and over, 3.7 (Mayer, 1968:365). *Circa* 1968, expectancy of life from birth was 55-60 (USA, 71), the death rate per 1,000 population per year being 10-14 (USA, 9.5) (Petersen, 1969:330).

As for housing, there are "five or six persons to the average dwelling of two rooms" (Cha, 1966:21). Moreover, in 1960, the percentage of private housing units with piped water was 21.4 (USA,94), and that of dwellings with electricity, 28.4 (Bureau of the Census, 1969:857).

In 1966 South Korea had 156 hospitals with 23,330 beds, the number of physicians (registered personnel) being 11,456 (USA, 288,671 in 1965). Thus, the number of persons per physician was 2,500 *(USA, 700).* In the same year, there were 1,810 dentists (registered personnel) in the country (USA, 93,400 in 1965) (Bureau of the Census, 1969:857).

In 1967, the system of communications included 344,000 public and private telephones (USA, 104,074,000). At about the same time, the number of receiving radio sets was 2,632,000 (USA, 285,000,000), and that of receiving television sets 78,000 (USA, 78,000,000) (Bureau of the Census, 1969:855).

Also related to the concept of modernization and to the family system of Korea are the various religious forces. Here, Buddhism became a state religion in A.D. 500 and under "its influence Korea attained a high state of prosperity and culture," while Confucianism was adopted as the official faith 1,000 years later (Humphreys, 1963:110). The *Mahayana* (great vehicle), a more pantheistic and spiritual Buddhism stressing mutual aid, universal salvation, ritualism, and an altruistic code of ethics, was instituted by the poet

Asvaghosa in the A.D. first century or by Kanishka in the second century B.C. (Hardon, 1965: 104-105; Thiollier, 1966:38-42). By now, the great vehicle comprises the largest number of sacred works in the entire world. The *Mahayana Bodhisativa* (Sanskrit: *bodhi*, englightenment; *sattva*,being), which emphasizes compassion and wisdom, constitutes one of the greatest concepts of all time. Another school of Buddhism, the Korean *Won*, which was founded by So-Tal-San in 1916, has been concerned with social welfare and social reform (Humphreys, 1963:217). Today, although Korea still has many Buddhist monastries, the social status of the monks is gradually declining. Also declining is ancestor worship, which is indicative of a diminishing familism. At the present time, the Korean population is 16 per cent Buddhist and 5 per cent Christian—primarily Protestant (Reader's Digest Association, 1968:519).

In old Korea, the main purpose of formal education "was political office. Society had but two classes, the *yangban* (civil and military), office seekers and holders, and the masses or commoners, given up to ignorance and superstition, there being virtually no middle class" (Griffs, 1968:527). A major pedagogical reform occurred in 1909 when "the regulations for establishing industrial schools and increasing the curriculum of agriculture, commerce, and industry in the higher schools already in operation, were issued" (Griffs, 1968:528). In the previous year, "to encourage female education, a girls' high school was established...to serve as a model, while girls in separate classes were admitted to the public schools" (Griffs, 1968:528). "By 1962, over 86 per cent of South Korea's children between the ages of 6 and 11 were attending elementary school....The public school system is financed largely from various fees paid by students; government support covers little more than payment of teacher salaries" (Thompson, 1967: 106; Wood, 1959:99-106). Thus, in 1966, the public expenditure for education was 3.5 per cent of the national income (USA, 6.5 in 1965), and in 1960, the illiteracy rate among those aged 15 years or more was 29.4 per cent (USA, 2.2 in 1959) (Bureau of the Census, 1969:859-860).

Recent studies dealing with student values and attitudes in South Korea cover chiefly four areas (these overlap to some extent):

First, the family. For instance, a survey involving mainly social science students was made at Seoul's Korea University (Hong, 1962:1-11). Such studies have revealed a less wide generation gap in Korea than in the United States (Yim, 1969:6).

Second, moral values. Rettig and Pasamanick (1962:73-84), for example, employed factorial analysis to investigate American and Korean university students' attitudes toward morality, especially of the puritanical and religious types. Rettig and Lee (1963:3-9) also explored the influence of the Korean Revolution of 1961 on the attitudes of Korean university students toward morals, stressing economic, religious, and general areas. Their sample, consisted of males and females at the freshman and sophomore levels, among whom they distributed a device of fifty items with a ten-point scale for each of them. In another article, Rettig and Pasamanick (1959:65-73) compared the moral values of American and Korean students and reported that the later, because of their Buddhist and Confucian convictions, as well as their family training, were somewhat more conservative, adding that many Korean Christians were not truly religious converts, since they merely identified with the Western world. Indeed, the mean of the Korean males was 7.67, and that of the females 8.53, the corresponding American values being 6.59 and 7.07 (Rettig and Pasamanick, 1959:69).

Third, political attitudes. For instance, a survey of values was done to explain political instability in South Korea and to predict the country's political future (Hong, 1967:329-340); a study among university students in Seoul (Hyo-chai, 1962:12-19); and an examination of the student movement of April 1960, involving a sample of young people attending Seoul's Konkuk University (Kim and Kim, 1964:83-92).

Fourth, ethnocentrism among young Koreans (Simos, 1956: 181-185).

Some marriage and family customs. Three of the criteria emphasized in mate choice in old Korea were the family name, the tabus pertaining to families that had the same surname and genealogy, and astrological considerations (Song, 1958:4-12; Yu, 1962:29-31). In other words, romantic dating was absent, marriage being of the arranged typed, as the following Korean poverb partly indicates: "Love does not always lead to marriage, but marriage often leads to love." Ordinarily, such arrangement was the function of a professional broker, the *chung-mai*—usually a widow—who collected a fee from both families. Child "engagements" were not exactly uncommon, and the services of a chaperon—something like the Spanish *duena*—were more than desirable. Moreover, during the early decades of the 20th century, youthful marriages were prevalent, "the brides being usually older than the grooms" (Griffs, 1968:528).

Although dynastic incest was often practiced in the past, its approval was not common, as is revealed by the sister's changing of her family name, upon marrying her brother, in order to "conceal" her identity (Weems, 1962: Volume 1, 144-145).

When engaged, a young woman prepared her trousseau which was rather expensive. This explains the Korean proverb which states: "No thief attempts to rob the house of a man who has three daughters." The wedding ceremony used to be virtually the most important celebration in old Korea. Due to Western influences, however, the spectacular, colorful, and highly symbolic weddings of the past have disappeared almost completely.

Similarly, patriarchy has been declining even in rural areas. This explains why somewhat less emphasis is now placed on having male children, for in old days, a son, who had a much higher status than his sister, continued the family line and facilitated the practice of ancestor worship. Thus, the father-son relationship constituted the strongest bond within the family. Still, respect for the father, and not friendship, was stressed, and discipline was considered desirable. In addition, the father was not highly demonstrative as far as his affection for his son was concerned (Song, 1958:4-12; but see Hakwon-Sa, 1963:627).

When a wife was barren, therefore, her husband was permitted to take a concubine, the legal reason being "the lack of an heir." Kings were further allowed to practice polygyny. Regarding concubinage, we are told that, in 1583 and 1625, "the king promulgated a most important law, sweeping away the disabilities of sons by concubines and giving them the right to become officials." (Weems, 1962: Volume 1, 144, 221, 340; Volume 2, 80-81). Of course, concubinage is no longer practiced in south Korea—at least not in its traditional form.

The low status of women is also indicated by the fact that, in the 15th century, the king "ordered that widows should not be allowed to re-marry" (Weems, 1962: Volume 1, 321). Besides, a wife was expected to respect her husband, while her social freedoms were exceedingly limited; a man, for instance, never took his wife to a place where a *kisaeng*, or female entertainer, performed. Moreover, men were not required to help in the kitchen, domestic tasks being assigned almost exclusively to the females. After the Korean War (25 June 1950-27 July 1953), however, women's occupational emancipation became necessary. It is also interesting to add that the tradition has been for a married woman to retain her maiden surname, although one might address her as, for example, "Mr. Han's wife."

It has further been traditional for the two spouses not to employ their respective first names in addressing each other. Using the word *yobo*, a term of endearment, could be sufficient. Other appellations in the husband-wife relationship were *anhai* (wife), *aigi omoni* (mother of the child), *uri chuin* (my master), *aigi aboji* (father of the child), and so on. In addition, this relationship did not include a public demonstration of affection, while kissing was practically absent in the past.

Such traditionalism party explains why the divorce rate has been relatively low. Of course, the well-defined sex roles of the two spouses have usually tended to diminish marital conflict. Also, the limited individualism that has characterized Korean society has not rendered the social stigma attached to divorce less painful.

According to a Korean proverb, "A man is good when he is old, a thing is good when it is new," which recalls the German, *"Der Bart macht den Mann,"* "The beard makes the man." Indeed, respect for the older members of society has been exceedingly high. This has manifested itself in various ways, including the practice of living with one's old parents—even after one's marriage—in order to support them, which constitutes a form of filial piety. It is no wonder, then, that in old Korea, having children was regarded as the best source of security in one's later years. Obviously, education, secularization, urbanization, industrialization, and the like have altered many of these traditional features of the Korean family, at least to a certain degree. As for the number of marriages in South Korea, it has recently been reported that, in 1965, there were "some 3.6 million married couples in the 20-40 year age group" (Hartman, 1966:345).

Family planning. After the revolution of May 1961, the government adopted an impressive five-year plan for economic development, which included a national family planning program. A law that prohibited the importation and manufacture of various contraceptives was also repealed. In June 1963, the Ministry of Health and Social Affairs further established a family planning department. About one year later, a ten-year plan was formulated, which was aimed at lowering the population growth rates. As time went on, many Korean, American, and Swedish mobile units began to circulate in Korea's rural areas, where they provided contraceptive information and clinical services.

In 1965, a national survey (Ministry of Health and Social Affairs, 1966) which evaluated this vast program already indicated the following: of the relatively few people who opposed family planning, a mere 8 per cent did so for moral and religious reasons, the rural and urban sections not differing much in this respect. In general, only about 1 per cent of the entire population objected to the program because of religious convictions. Then, of the husbands, 79 per cent approved, while 89 per cent of the wives did so. Birth control was particularly popular among women aged thirty to thirty-nine years and having four or more children, at least two of whom were male. Korean studies reveal that the most desirable number of offspring is four. Furthermore, if they were given the means, 65 per cent of the rural males stated, they would practice family planning, the percentage of the females who gave the same answer being 71; the corresponding values for city dwellers were 71 and 77.

Another finding was that approval and family size were directly proportionate. The highest approval characterized couples that were twenty-five to forty years old—obviously, younger people, who did not have the desired number of children as yet, and older ones, who would soon become infertile, were less enthusiastic about family planning. The influence of illiteracy was virtually nonexistent. Indeed, 81 per cent of the illiterate population favored birth control, 51 per cent were familiar with at least one contraceptive technique, and 10 per cent of all illiterate couples were practicing family planning. On the other hand, familiarity with the pill was slightly higher in the cities. The survey also indicated that 21 per cent of all urban couples and 14 per cent of rural ones were employing various birth control methods, although three years earlier practically none of them were doing so. The percentages for these methods were (for rural and urban areas, respectively): condom, 61 and 51; foam tablet 42 and 34; IUD, 27 and 18; and pill, 4 and 8. As for personnel, the study found that the Planned Parenthood Federation of Korea, a private organization, had field workers in all provinces, while, by April 1965, the national family planning service had 2,207 such workers.

More specially, the situation has been as follows:

First of all, the so-called National Englightenment Campaign was organized for the purpose of informing and educating the public about the family planning program of the revolutionary government. Two of the successful approaches have been movies dealing with birth control and the "Family Planning Month" program of May 1964. So far, urban groups have been harder than rural residents to reach by means of this campaign, apparently because the work schedule of the lower class husbands and wives precludes easy contacts with the family planning workers, while the upper classes believe that such education is below their intellectual level. Nevertheless, those involved in this ambitious program have continued their activities indefatigably, and there are now many reports on how to introduce birth into a province (Yang *et al.*, 1965:237-250) and the results of family planning education (Bang, 1966:5-12).

As for the training of the personnel needed for such work, we are told that the lectures and seminars organized for family planning workers last three weeks, while physicians study vasectomy and the IUD for one day each (Yang, 1966:310).

Consequently, there "are some 2,220 field workers in the Korean program... the program has 1,100 IUD clinics, 700 sterilization clinics, and 11 mobile family-planning teams" (Merrill, 1969:280). All of the field workers are high school graduates, almost 20 per cent of them have also college degrees, and 35 per cent are nurse midwives.

Regarding the birth control methods employed, Cha (1966:26) informs us that the "practice is to distribute a one month's supply: one vial of 16 foam tablets, one package of 6 condoms, or 15 grams of spermicidal jelly packed in three plastic containers." The specific data pertaining to this matter are as follows:

i) The rhythm method has been abandoned, as it was quite unsuccessful.

ii) The Koreans disapprove of *coitus interruptus*.

iii) The condom (one of the three traditional methods, the other two being spermicidal foam tablets and jelly) has been distributed free of charge.

iv) Spermicidal jelly has been popular among many couples.

v) "After 1964, the advisory council set the proportion of the supplies of usual contraceptives at about 80% condoms, 15% *foam tablets* (italics not in original), 5% jelly" (Yang, 1966:317).

vi) The diaphragm is not acceptable in Korea.

vii) The insertion of IUDs, which are "the best method at present in most developing countries" (Yang, 1966:320), is regarded as part of medical practice in Korea "and therefore only a qualified physician can receive the instruction and authority to insert them. By mid-1967, over 1,600 physicians had been trained and authorized to work in the program, either to insert loops, or to perform vasectomies, or both" (T.I. Kim, 1969:30; but see Guttmacher, 1968:47). A small polyethyline device known as the Lippes loop, which was introduced into the country in September 1962, has been emphasized by the national program so much that, in December 1967, more women were using it in Korea than in any other nation in the world, except India and Pakistan. Some women, however, have discontinued this method because of pregnancy, expulsion, or removal due mainly to bleeding, infection, leukorrhea, or pain.

viii) As for the pill, for "those who can afford them, the use of oral contraceptives is encouraged. The women who use these, however, do not get ony subsidy. The government allows the importation of oral contraceptives" (Yang, 1966:316-317). Accordingly, in January 1965, there were 6,000 pill users in Korea (4,000,000 in the USA) and 10,000 in January 1966 (5,000,000 in the USA) (Lewin, 1966:488).

ix) Although sterilization was discouraged at first, "from 1963 it was actively promoted among those who had had three or more children. Government subsidy is limited to male sterilization" (Yang, 1966:317). So, by "the end of 1968 over one million first insertions of loops have been made, over 150,000 couples were receiving traditional contraceptives monthly, and 115,000 vasectomies have been performed" (T.N. Kim, 1969:29). In 1964, the percentages of the complications resulting from such surgery were: minimal, 3; and severe, 0.5 (the corresponding figures for the IUDs were 15 and 0.5) (Yang, 1966:313).

These services involve no charge as far as the poor are concerned. Others, however, are expected to pay, for instance $1.20 for an IUD insertion and $2.00 for a vasectomy. In general, the entire program has cost approximately $2,000,000 in 10 years, or 6.5 cents per year per person (T.I. Kim, 1969:33). The latter figure was 1.2 in 1962 and 4.8 in 1964 (Ross, 1965:760), while more recently "the per capita cost to the government is about 7 cents a year" (Keeny, 1969:225). Moreover, "in 1967, for about $2,250,000 the following services were provided free: 330,000 loops were inserted; 150,000 couples were using condoms; and 20,000 sterilizations were performed" (Keeny, 1969:224).

It is no wonder, then, than South Korea's impressive plan is "one of the most effective programs in the world" (Keeny, 1969:224), or that "the observed, and quite marked, fall in the birth rates . . .has been significantly contributed to by the family-planning programs" (Deverell, 1969 : 259). Induced abortion, for example, is emphasized much less now and, due to the family planning program, 89 per cent of south Korea's women are familiar with the term "family planning," 86 per cent approve of it, and 30 per cent are using or have used it, and 30 per cent are using or have used contraception (T.I. Kim, 1969 : 32; but see Hong and Yoon, 1962 : 443-452). Of course, in the developing areas of the world, countries with a similar success, "are relatively small," and in "size, in complexity, in receptivity to any modernizing influence, Taiwan is not India, Puerto Rico is not Brazil" (Petersen, 1969 : 613). In any event, South Korea's spectacular success may be attributed to at least eight specific factors:

i) The assistance provided by other nations, such as Sweden and the USA.

ii) Coordination and hard work from the highest level—the president and the legislators—to the lowest—the field workers and the participating couples themselves. Indeed, the "classical example of a fruitful combined effort must surely be Korea, where the government, the Population Council, and the family planning association combine so effectively that if something has to be done, one or the other agency will find the means to do it" (Deverell, 1966:792).

iii) Extensive education and information. The Sungdong Gu program, for instance, which began in July 1964, used leaflets, pamphlets, posters, newspapers, radio and television stations, home visits, and meetings. As a result, within fifteen months, about 20 per cent of all wives aged twenty to forty-four displayed some interest in the plan, and virtually all of them adopted at least one birth control technique (School of Public Health, 1966).

iv) The interdisciplinary approach—the program involves experts in many related fields.

v) Continuity in personnel—incidentally, South Korea is practically unique in such emphasis.

vi) Stressing more than one birth control method for each couple.

vii) Publication of frequent progress reports.

viii) Research and evaluation studies by Seoul and Yonsei Universities, as well as other institutions, initiated by the Ministry of Health and other organizations.

In brief, to return to the theoretical aspect of the present study, namely, the relationship between birth control and modernization, the above accounts of the American and South Korean family systems would lead to the conclusion that Korean students should make somewhat (that is, not very significantly) lower scores on the "pill scale."

FINDINGS

The main findings of the present survey may be summarized as follows:

Koreans

The arithmetic mean of the South Koreans' oral contraception scores was 63.52.

The males made an average of 66.65, while the females were represented by a value of 60.40. These means differed significantly between 0.01 and 0.02 (t, 2.49; degrees of freedom, 38) (Miller, 1964 : 79-81); Arkin and Colton, 1964: 13-14; 121).

The mean of those majoring in the social sciences and humanities was 61.76, while those studying agriculture gave an average of 66.46, the difference between these figures being significant just below 0.10 (t, 1.75; degrees of freedom, 38).

The Pearsonian coefficients of correlation (Szulc, 1965:495-497) Arkin and Colton, 1964:24, 155) for pill score and each of the following independent variables were statistically insignificant (degrees of freedom, 38): age, 0.00; number of siblings, 0.01; birth order, —0.08; amount or own education, 0.18; father's education, 0.07; mother's education—0.08; and father's occupational level, 0.17.

Some of the significant coefficients were: number of siblings and mother's education,—0.45 (degrees of freedom, 38; significant almost at 0.001); father's education and mother's education, 0.62 (degrees of freedom, 38; significant much beyond 0.001); and father's education and occupation, 0.58 (degrees of freedom, 38; significant much beyond 0.001).

Americans

The total mean of the American subjects was 67.88. The males made an average of 69.40, and the females 66.35, the difference between the two being insignificant almost at 0.50 (t, 0.72; degrees of freedom, 38).

The mean of those whose mothers were gainfully employed was 68.92, while that representing the nonworking mothers' children was 67.30. The t value for this comparison was 0.36, namely, insignificant slightly above 0.70 (degrees of freedom, 38).

The Pearsonian coefficients for oral contraception and each of the following characteristics were (degrees of freedom, 38): age, 0.16; number of siblings,—0.03; birth order,—0.11; number of religious services attended,—0.32 (significant slightly below 0.05); amount of own education, 0.30 (significant slightly above 0.05); father's education, 0.08; mother's education, 0.21 (significant above 0.10); and father's occupation,—0.07.

Two of the additional significant r's were (degrees of freedom, 38); number of siblings and father's occupation,—0.28 (significant slightly below 0.10); and father's education and mother's education, 0.41 (significant at 0.01).

American-Korean Comparisons and Conclusions

Finally, on the basis of the above data, as well as those secured previously by means of the same "pill scale," the following conclusions may be drawn:

1) Since the Korean subjects' average was 63.52 and that of the Americans 67.88 (t, 1.74; degrees of freedom, 78; somewhat significant between 0.05 and 0.01), the hypothesis that attitudes toward irth control constitute a partial index of modernization must be

accepted. Undoubtedly, the fact that this difference was not highly significant must be attributed to the much higher than average education of the Korean group. Also influential must have been Korea's recent family planning program. On the other hand, the liberalism of the typically Protestant sample in modernized and developed America does not have to be explained. The mass media discuss this subject daily. Here are a few pertinent comments: "Goddard college...made birth-control pills available upon request to any coed....More and more universities are adopting a similar policy....Some physicians in the community have been dispensing the pill without getting a medical history or giving a pelvic exam (precautions most doctors take), so we thought it would be better to handle it on the campus. Spokesmen for other colleges describe similar policies as an integral part of a comprehensive university health service....A 1966 survey of 330 university health clinics by the American College Health Association found that 141 did prescribe the pill" (Weinstein, 1970:1). The oral contraception means of three other groups of American college students are also revealing: Protestants, 73.50; religiously mixed, 65.95; and another religiously mixed sample, 68.35 (Bardis, 1969b: 38-39).

2) A cross-cultural survey of attitudes toward the pill seems feasible. The subjects of the present study at least did not indicate in any way that similar investigations are highly problematical.

3) The Korean respondents appeared to be overpopulation-conscious and highly interested in scientific studies dealing with birth control. One of them stated: "This is a useful survey and it will help with the overpopulation problem." Five more Koreans made analogous remarks. Similarly, "whether or not they now use contraceptives," most Berkeley, California, girl students in the United States support the establishment of birth control clinics "for two reasons: The need they see for the service on campus and their growing concern about world overpopulation" (Weinstein, 1970: 5). The Korean subjects further suggested that more studies of the present type be conducted. A senior female, for instance, whose pill score was 71, wrote: "You must also give your questionnaire to a group of married women in Korea."

4) Such surveys, a Korean third-year girl concluded, may enable us to discover and define now hidden problems and thus facilitate their solution; her oral contraception score was 68.

5) Another female respondent in Korea indicated that men should adopt a higher degree of liberalism regarding contraception. In revealing the effect of a double standard, this young lady was not particularly unusual; for the mean of the females was significantly lower than that of the males in that country. In the United States, however, the author has, so far, consistently found that women tend to be about as liberal as men in this respect. Perhaps, then, since the pill involves the female directly, she desires a substantial degree of autonomy in this area, although she typically is more conservative in general than the male. In other words, the modernizing forces which have liberated the American woman to a high degree are sufficiently limited in Korea not to diminish or terminate the traditional gap that separates the sexes even in college.

6) In South Korea, the study of agriculture appears to generate a somewhat higher degree of birth control liberalism. This is difficult to explain, unless, of course, we assume that a certain amount of transfer occurs from the manipulatory nature of agricultural techniques to the philosophy and ideology involving human groups.

7) In the United States, the mother's gainful employment does not seem to affect her college child's attitudes toward oral contraception. Apparently, other forces neutralize the influence of this important variable.

8) In both countries, the relationship between the subjects' own pill attitudes and the following factors is insignificant: age, number of siblings, birth order, parents' education, and father's occupation.

9) Although, in Korea, the pill-education association is insignificant, in the United States the respondents', education appears to liberalize their birth control attitudes at least to a limited extent. If this difference is real, perhaps its explanation may be found in the two different pedagogical systems. It must be emphasized, however, that the pill data collected so far suggest that education is a definitely liberalizing influence, although this effect is partly concealed by the relative educational homogeneity of certain samples.

10) In the United States, the pill-religiosity relationship is inversely proportionate. As for Korea, in a letter to the present author, Seoul's Dr Seong Hi Yim wrote the following on 2 September 1969: "Somehow, being culturally different from you in the West, we do not face the strong religious resistance to the use of contraceptive

pills which Catholics and conservative Protestants present in the United States."

11) In view of the controversy concerning the possible physically harmful side effects of the pill, it is interesting to add that, in both countries, students constantly compartmentalize the physical and social aspects of oral contraception, thus preventing the former from affecting their attitudes in the latter sphere. Here are a few randomly selected comments by subjects who made extremely high scores, although they were concerned about the potentially abortifacient, carcinogenic, mutagenic, and teratogenic nature of the pill: Korean male sophomore: "If the pill is going to be harmful in health, I will say that use of the pill should be forbidden" (score, 78); American male senior: "The only objection to the pill I have is the possibility of cancer mentioned in some studies" (score, 74); American male senior: "On questions dealing with giving the pill without restriction, I assume the doctor gives an OK sign as to the health of the women and to any effects that may come from taking it" (score, 86); and American female sophomore: "I have used the pill for four and a half years. Besides, 1 am Rh-negative and my husband is Rh-positive, and we don't want any further children, to avoid the risk of having one retarded, deformed, or stillborn" (score, 76). (Although emphasis is here placed on a factor other than the pill, a personal interview suggested that this liberal young woman was exceedingly sensitive about organic consequences in general.)

12) American parents are significantly more conservative with reference to the pill than their college children, and even than the Korean subjects. Indeed, the means of two parental samples in the United States were only 51.05 and 51.29 (Bardis, 1969b:38-39 .

13) In the United States, family size and maternal occupational level are somewhat signincantly and negatively related, which may suggest that one of the ways of combating overpopulation is more modern forms of occupational training.

14) Especially helpful may be additional education for women, since, in Korea, family size and maternal educational level were significantly and inversely propoitional.

15) As far as the subjects of the present study indicate, in both countries, educational homogamy is prevalent.

16) Finally, in Korea, paternal educational and occupational levels are positively and significantly related.

SUMMARY

In brief, a study of attitudes toward oral contraception among college students in South Korea and the United States has revealed that crosscultural investigations of this type are possible, and that such attitudes may be fruitfully employed as a partial index of modernization.
Needless to add, these investigations will be more significant and valuable if the same, plus additional, variables are explored more extensively and intensively.

REFERENCES

Arkin, Herbert, and Raymond R. Colton.
    1964 *Tables for Statisticians*, second edition. New York: Barnes and Noble.
Bang, S.
    1966 "The Koyang study: results of two action programs." *Studies in Family Planning*. Pp. 5-12.
Bardis, Panos D.
    1964 "Family forms and variations historically considered" in Harold T. Christensen (ed.), *Handbook of Marriage and the Family*. Chicago: Rand McNally. Pp. 403-461.
    1969a The Family in Changing Civilizations, second edition. New York: Simon and Schuster, Associated Educational Services Corporation.
    1969b "A pill scale: a technique for the measurement of attitudes toward oral contraception," *Social Science*, 44 (January). Pp. 35-42.
    1969c "The principle of instrumental parsimony." *Revue Internationale de Sociologie*, 5 (December). Pp. 92-101.
    1971 "Counselling and the evolution of the concept of sin" in Hirsch Lazaar Silverman (ed.), *Moral Issues in Marriage Counselling*. Springfield, Illinois: Thomas. In press.
Bureau of the Census.
    1969 Statistical Abstract of the United States: 1969. Washington: United States Government Printing Office.
Cha, Y.K.
    1966 "South Korea" in Bernard Berelson *et al.* (eds.), *Family Planning and Population Programs*. Chicago: Universtty of Chicago Press. Pp. 21-30.
Deverell, C.
    1966 "From the planned parenthood community" in Bernard Berelson *et al.* (eds.), *Family Planning and Population Programs*. Chicago: University of Chicago Press. Pp. 791-794.

1969 "International Planned Parenthood Federation: a world pioneer" in Bernard Berelson (ed.), *Family-Planning Programs*. New York: Basic Books. Pp. 252-261.

Edwards, Alba M.
1943 *Comparative Occupational Statistics for the United States, 1870-1940*. Washington: United States Government Printing Office.

Garrett, Henry E.
1955 *Statistics in Psychology and Education*, fourth edition. New York: Longmans, Green.

Griffis, W.E.
1968 "Education in Korea" in Paul Monroe (ed.), *A Cyclopedia of Education*. Volume 3. Detroit: Gale. Pp. 526 529.

Guttmacher, Alan F.
1968 *The Complete Book of Birth Control*, revised edition. New York: Ballantine Books.

Hakwon-Sa
1963 *Korea: Its Land, People and Culture of All Ages*, second edition. Seoul.

Hardon, John A.
1965 *Religions of the World*. Westminster, Maryland: Newman.

Hartman, Paul
1966 "Informational and Educational Programs" in Bernard Berelson et al. (eds.), *Family Planning and Population Programs*. Chicago: University of Chicago Press. Pp. 345-351.

Hong, S.C.
1962 "A pilot survey of the Korean students." *Korean Affairs*. Pp. 1-11.
1967 "A Political diagnosis of Korean society: a survey of military and civilian values." *Asian Survey*, 7(May). Pp. 329-340.

Hong, S., and J. Yoon
1962 "Male attitudes toward family planning on the Islands of Kangwha-Gun, Korea." *Milbank Memorial Fund Quarterly*, 40 (October). Pp. 443-452.

Humphreys, Christmas
1963 *A Popular Dictionary of Buddhism*. New York: Citadel.

Huo-chai, L.
1962 "The Korean's understanding of democracy." *Korean Affairs*. Pp. 12-19.

Keeny, S.M.
1969 "Family-Planning programs: what they cost and how they work" in Bernard Berelson (ed.), *Family-Planning Programs*. New York: Basic Books. Pp. 215-225.

Kim, C.I.E., and K. Kim
1964 "The April 1960 Korean student movement." *Western Political Quarterly*, 17 (March). Pp. 83-92.

Kim, T.I.
  1969 "South Korea: enlightened leadership and enlightened parents" in
        Bernard Berelson (ed.), *Family-Planning Programs*, New York:
        Basic Books. Pp. 26-34.
Lerner, D.
  1968 "Modernization: social aspects" in David L. Sills (ed.), *Inter-
        national Encyclopedia of the Social Sciences*. Volume 10. New York:
        Macmillan. Pp. 386-395.
Levin, H.L.
  1966 "Distribution of contraceptive supplies through commercial
        channels" in Bernard Berelson *et al*. (eds.), *Family Planning and
        Population Programs*. Chicago: University of Chicago Press. Pp.
        487-494.
Lewsi, W. Arthur
  1955 *The Theory of Economic Growth*. Homewood, Illinois: Irwin.
Mayer, K.B.
  1968 "Population composition" in David L. Sills (ed.), *International
        Encyclopedia of the Social Sciences*. Volume 12. New York:
        Macmillan. Pp. 362-370.
McMurtrie, Douglas C.
  1967 *The Book*. New York: Oxford University Press.
Merrill, M.H.
  1969 "The United States Government: a new and important factor" in
        Bernard Berelson (ed.), *Family-Planning Programs*. New York:
        Basic Books. Pp. 277-287.
Miller, Delbert C.
  1964 *Handbook of Research Design and Social Measurement*. New York:
        McKay.
Ministry of Health and Social Affairs
  1966 *The Findings of the National Survey on Family Planning*. Seoul:
        Planned Parenthood Federation of Korea.
Petersen, William.
  1969 *Population*, second edition. New York: Macmillan.
Reader's Digest Association.
  1968 *1969 Reader's Digest Almanac and Year-book*. Pleasantville, New
        York.
Retting, S., and J. Lee
  1963 "Differences in normal judgments of South Korean students before
        and after the Korean Revolution." *Journal of Social Psychology*,
        59 (February). Pp. 3-9.
Rettig, S., and B. Pasamanick
  1959 "Moral codes of American and Korean college students." *Journal
        of Social Psychology*, 50 (August). Pp. 65-73.
  1962 "Invariance in factor structure of moral value judgments from
        American and Korean college students." *Sociometry*, 25 (March).
        Pp. 73-84.

Ross, J.A.
1966 "Cost of family planning programs" in Bernard Berelson *et al.* (eds.), *Family Planning and Population Programs*. Chicago: University of Chicago Press. Pp. 759-778.

School of Public Health,
1966 *Sungdong Gu action-research project on family planning*. Seoul: Seoul National University.

Simos, I.
1956 "Ethnocentrism and Attitudes toward the Rosenberg case and the Republic of Korea." *Journal of Social Psychology*, 43 (February). Pp. 181-185.

Song, U.S.
1958 "Marriage and the Family in Korea." *Korean Survey*, 7 (April). Pp. 4-12.

Szulc, Stefan
1965 *Statistical Methods*. London: Pergamon.

Thiollier, Marguerite-Marie
1966 *Dictionnaire des Religions*. Paris: Larousse.

Thompson, Elizabeth M.
1967 *Other Lands, Other Peoples*, fourth edition. Washington: National Education Association of the United States.

Weems, Clarence N. (ed.)
1962 *Hulbert's History of Korea*. New York: Hillary House.

Weinstein, H.
1970 "The pill on campus." *The Wall Street Journal*, 50 (19 January). Pp. 1, 15.

Wood, C.W.
1959 "Secondary education in South Korea." *The Educational Forum*, 24 (November). Pp. 99-106.

Yang, J.M.
1966 "Planning the program" in Bernard Berelson *et al.* (eds.), *Family Planning and Population Programs*. Chicago: University of Chicago Press. Pp. 305-320.

Yang, J.M., *et al.*
1965 "Fertility and family planning in rural Korea." *Population Studies*, 18 (March). Pp. 237-250.

Yim, Seong Hi
1961 *Die Grundlage und die Entwicklung der Familie in Korea*. Klön: Universitöt zu Köln.
1969 "The generation gap." Seoul: Korea University. Mimeographed.

Yu, C.
1962 "Korea's marriage." *Korean Report*, 2 (November-December). Pp. 29-31.

CHAPTER IX

The Filipino Family

GLORIA V. JAVILLONAR

INTRODUCTION

Many students of Philippine society (Fox, 1966, 1963, 1959; Jocano, 1969, 1968, 1966; Donoghue, AHOP, I; Guthrie and Jacobs, 1966; Hollnsteiner, 1963; Corpuz, 1957) have argued, explicitly or implicitly, that to understand Philippine society one must study the Filipino family and kinship system. The Filipino extended family exerts a ubiquitous influence on all other aspects of Philippine social organization—political, economic, social, educational, religious. It also lays an exclusive claim on the individual's loyalty and sense of identity, resulting in the stunting of participatory skills and interest in extrafamilial collective endeavors, such as in civic voluntary associations. The familistic orientation, moreover, inhibits the development of a sense of loyalty and identification with any higher level of social organization much so that some authors (probably overstating the case) describe the Philippine society as "fragmented" (Donoghue, AHOP, I), or as an "anarchy of families" (Fox, 1959). Indeed, the widely noted corruption in politics and government service is probably more a function of the Filipino kinship system than of individual avarice and greed.

This chapter focuses on the structural characteristics of the Filipino family and kinship; on its impact on various aspects of Philippine social organization and on the individual; and on the societal changes impinging on the extended family system. It is a summary and review of researches on the Filipino family and kinship conducted by students of Philippine society over the past three decades. Sources on the Filipino family covering an earlier time span are also noted. The bulk of these studies are anthropological investigations of both the non-Christian and mountain peoples who are largely outside the mainstream of Philippine society (Jocano, 1968; Oracion, 1952; Eggan, 1954) and the lowland Christian Filipinos who constitute about 90 per cent of the population (Jocano, 1970, 1969; Fox, 1966, 1963, 1959; Stoodley, 1957). Sociological (Hollnsteiner, 1963; Pal, 1966, 1960, 1954; Castillo and Pua, 1963; Liu, Rubel, and Yu, 1969; Santos-Cuyugan, 1961) and psychological (Bulatao, 1964; Guthrie and Jacobs, 1966) investigations also are becoming increasingly important sources of careful documentation of various aspects of the Filipino family and kinship.

A caveat must be mentioned at the outset. The chapter may give a much more homogenous picture of the Philippine society in general and of the Filipino family in particular than may actually be the case. The Filipinos are a highly heterogenous people in items of their racial-ethnic, linguistic, and religious backgrounds. Such differences may reasonably be expected to be reflected, at least to some degree, on the structural characteristics of the family and on its impact on individual orientations, as well as on other aspects of the social organization. Unfortunately, while the family has been the most researched unit of Philippine social organization, there has been no systematic effort at establishing structural similarities and differences across ethnic-linguistic groups.

A brief description of the Philippines and its people would give the reader an idea of the heterogeneity and complexity of Philippine society.

THE PHILIPPINES AND THE FILIPINOS

The Philippines, which consists of 7,100 islands, lies 900 miles (1,440 kilometres) east of Saigon across the South China Sea. The southernmost island, Sibutu, lies less than five degrees above the equator, while the northernmost island, Y'ami, is located at about 21 degrees North Latitude. The total land area of the Philippines is 115,600 square miles (2,378,404 kilometres), of which 70 per cent is found on two islands, Luzon and Mindanao. About 95 per cent

of the total land area is located in its twelve largest islands—
Luzon, Mindanao, Samar, Leyte, Mindoro, Negros, Panay, Palawan,
Cebu, Bohol, Masbate, and Marinduque ("The Land," Human
Relations Area Files, I, II; Carroll, 1968). Philippine topography is
characterized by

> rugged and irregular coasts providing numerous harbors of all
> sizes; hilly and mountainous terrain, with ranges generally
> parallel and in close proximity to the coast lines, a characteristic
> island-form being the mountainous spine, few large rivers, but
> many streams which are short and swift; a relatively small num-
> ber of lakes, with those formed by lavadams probably constituting
> a majority; heavily forested mountain ranges; comparatively
> narrow coastal plains; and broad and flat alluvial plains found
> between mountains though not strictly inter-montane in charac-
> ter "(The Land," Human Relations Area Files, I, II; Carroll,
> 1968).

The Philippines is a society of racial-ethnic diversity. Cordero and
Panopio (1969:227-228) identify four racial-ethnic groups in terms
of their distinctive physical characteristics: 1) the Negritos, a black
pygmy group, who are the original inhabitants of the Philippines;
2) those of Indonesian-Malayan stock, who constitute the dominant Filipino physical type; 3) Filipinos of Chinese ancestry, who
make up about 10 per cent of the total Filipino population; and 4)
a much smaller number of "mestizos" and "mesticillos," who are
offsprings of Filipino-European (largely Spanish) marriages, and
who vary in degree of Caucasian physical characteristic but are
primarily Spanish in cultural orientation.

Culturally, the Indonesian-Malayan group, the largest racial-
ethnic group, may be divided into three major categories: 1) more
than thirty pagan, mountain tribes, which are linguistically different
from one another; 2) the Muslims or Mohammedans, also popu-
larly known as "Moros" who are concentrated in Mindanao; and
3) the Christian Filipinos, who constitute nearly 90 per cent of the
total Philippine population (Fox, 1966:1).

The Christian Filipinos are further divided into eight major linguistic groups—the Tagalog, Iloko, Pampangan, Pangasinam, Bikol,
Cebuano, Hiligaynon, and Samar-Leyte. Although systematic data
are not available, Fox (1966:1) argues that these eight groups exhibit

significant variations in their social organization due to a number of factors, particularly differences in subsistence base, ecology, settlement patterns, and historical origins and influences. However, as Fox (1966:1) further notes:

> When the similarities between the eight major Christian groups are abstracted and analyzed, a "model" of social organization becomes apparent which may be called "Filipino." Thus, Filipino educators and sociologists speak of "Filipino society," of the "Filipino family," and of "Filipino courtship," reflecting a belief in, as well as an awareness of, basic likenesses.

The literature on Philippine social organization in general and of the Filipino family in particular implicitly treats the eight major Christian groups as homogenous and as highly distinguishable from the pagan mountain tribes and the Muslims. For purpose of this discussion such an assumption is considered defensible and of practical necessity. Thus, research findings on the eight major Christian Filipino linguistic groups will be treated cumulatively to give an overall view of the structural characteristics of the family in the Philippines. References will be made to non-Christian family types when data are available.

STRUCTURAL FEATURES OF THE FILIPINO FAMILY AND KINSHIP

The Filipino family has remained remarkably stable despite some marked and drastic social, political, economic, and religious changes the country has gone through over the past several centuries. Thus, despite more than 300 years of Spanish political and cultural subjugation, 44 years of American colonization, and four years of Japanese conquest, the Filipino family has retained its predominantly Malay characteristics (Fox, 1966; Guthrie and Jacobs, 1966: 42). Carroll (1968:139), in an outline survey of changing patterns of social structure in the Philippines, reports on the stability of the Filipino family over the past seven decades of post-Spanish Philippines. Using 1896 (immediately before the Philippine revolution against Spanish rule) and 1963 as points of comparison, Carroll notes that there has been no significant change in the bilaterally extended kinship structure, in parental and sibling roles, and in the interaction patterns between parents and children. He reports, however, that 1963 children seem to be more assertive of their independence, particularly in mate selection, than their 1896 counterparts. The data, it may be noted, are at best sketchy (particularly for the earlier period) and are far from adequate in supporting such claim regarding the stability of the Filipino family. Due to lack of evidence to the contrary, however, this paper will assume tentatively the validity of this assertion.

The Filipino family has the following structural characteristic: it has a bilaterally extended kinship system; it has an age-based hierarcy of authority; the relationship between husband and wife is highly egalitarian; Christian marriages are monogamous, while non-Christians are polygamons; legal separation but not divorce is allowed among the Christians, while both are permitted among the non-Christians; mate selection is based mostly on the romantic love principle plus parental approval; endogamy based on locality, class, linguistic-ethnic, and religious grouping is generally practiced, but there are no rigid normative rules defining the field of eligibles; and finally, there are no set rules of residence for the young married couple.

These structural features of the Filipino family and kinship are discussed in some detail in the next several pages.

The Filipino Family has a Bilaterally Extended Kinship System

There are three ways by which a Filipino may acquire kins—by the principle of consanguinity, by affinity, and by ritual.

Consanguinity. Although surnames are traced through the male line, the Filipino family is bilateral in terms of recognizing descent, in allocating inheritance, and in degree and type of kin involvements. Thus, to a Filipino child, his or her mother's kins are as important sources of support and security and agents of social control as are his or her father's relatives. Indeed, it is the birth of the child which gives formal structure to the family, since the child shares equal relationships with the maternal and paternal kin groups, unlike his or her own parents (Fox, 1963:348).

Consanguineal ties are taken very seriously. Theoretically at least, the emphasis on blood ties could extend the kin group a long way. In practice, however, recognition of consanguineal kinship ties rarely extends beyond third cousins. As noted by Jocano (1969:83), "there are relatives whom the individual considers important and others, unimportant, irrespective of whether they are structurally close or distant." Thus, the boundaries of kinship are sometimes vague and interactional patterns which involve reciprocal duties and obligations are determined by such factors as physical proximity, personal compatibility and preferences, the social positions of the parties concerned or a combination of these and other factors (Fox, 1963:348; Carroll, 1968:134; Hollnsteiner, 1964:345).

Once recognized, however, the relationship carries far-reaching mutual obligations and responsibilities, as well as rights and privileges. The individual depends mostly on his consanguineal kin group for assistance in carrying out his numerous social, economic, and religious commitments (Jocano, 1969:83). Kins expect and get mutual support and assistance, particularly in coping with crisis situations and, generally, in meeting the exigencies of daily life. Even relatives far removed may be taken into the household as members of the family when circumstances require it (Hunt *et al.*, 1963:158), such as when rural relatives migrate to the city in search of jobs or better educational opportunities. And, as Cordero and Panopio (1969:270) point out, the consanguineal family arrangement places the responsibility of caring for the children not only on the parents but also on the grandparents, aunts and uncles, older siblings, and cousins.

Early in the child's life, he or she is made aware of who his or her relatives are and who are not, and accordingly socialized into the norms governing interpersonal relationships among kinsmen. Thus, as Jocano (1969:83) notes, if the child quarrels with his relatives, he is scolded by the older folks as follows:

Do not fight with your relatives. These are the people from whom you can ask help in time of need. Do you think other people will help you? No—but your relatives will. So be nice to them.

By Affinity. When a man and a woman marry, each acquires the other's set of consanguineal as well as affinal and ritual kins. Each partner, thus, doubles his or her circle of relatives at marriage. The same norms of reciprocal obligations and rights theoretically apply between the individual and his or her in-laws as apply to one's consanguineal relatives. Each spouse is expected to give as much importance to the other's relatives' claims on the family's attention, time, deference, and support or assistance as he or she does to his or her own family of orientation. Ordinarily, however, the husband or the wife would turn to his or her blood relatives first for assistance. To do so otherwise would "shame" or show up one's kin group as being incapable of taking care of their own flesh and blood. Conversely, one is expected to feel a stronger sense of responsibility for one's family of origin than one's adopted family, in recognition of the care and support accorded to the individual by his or her kins from both until the marriage. Kin support and protection, as a matter of fact, continue through the marriage. The wife, for example, could count on her kins' intervention and protection in case of abuse by her husband.

It is not only the individual who acquires a new set of kins at marriage. Marriage is usually seen as an alliance of two families and their kindred, not just of two individuals. It is an alliance which frequently results in the formation of a "highly central unit demanding interests and loyalties of its members to the exclusion of the broader units of society" (Fox, 1959:6). Indeed, marrying into a large, well-to-do family may be an avenue to social mobility for an ambitious young man or woman. For, as Hunt *et al.* (1963:159), note:

> A large family is respected, and perhaps, also feared in the community. The tradition of unity can make it very powerful and influential.

On the other hand, to many a young man and woman and their kins, marriage may mean the acquisition of a number of poor relations with whom one has to share one's limited resources. The characterization of the strongly cohesive extended family applies more frequently to the upper and, to a much less extent, to the middle classes than to the lower classes. Liu, Rubel, and Yu (1969: 395), in a study of urban families in Cebu, for instance, report of the lack of kin cohesiveness among lower-class Cebuanos, "particularly with respect to mutual help and social control." As the authors note, economic factors play a major part in determining degree of kin solidarity. The subsistence standard of living of the lower class family precludes extending financial and material assistance to kins. The authors, thus, argue that the lower class family system in Cebu is nuclear "by default." That is, economic reasons rather than socio-emotional preference family arrangement account for the predominance of the nuclear family type (60 per cent of a random sample from 1,200 households studied). As evidence, they observe that nucleation is not characterized by strong emotional involvement between husband and wife. On the other hand, a high degree of socio-emotional interaction does take place among Kins. The normative expectation of mutual help and support among kins remains strong despite limited actual helping relationships. The authors further note that to the middle class family, particularly a mobility-oriented one, the extended family system of reciprocal obligations and rights becomes problematic, since receiving assistance from some kins implies in return a willingness to share resources needed for social mobility with less affluent relatives. Further research evidence provided by Pal and Arquiza (1957:4) indicates that, at least within the immediate family, the normative expectation of helping kins is strongest among persons from low socio-economic backgrounds and lowest among those who come from the upper classes.

Ritual kinship. The Filipino family is further extended by the *kumpadre (compadrazgo)* system or ritual coparenthood. Usually, the best friend or friends of the mother or the father are invited to stand as sponsors for the child on the latter's baptism or confirmation. The ritual confers on the sponsors the status of coguardians of the child. In a sense, the sponsors become "family" and are expected to take an active interest in the child's welfare, even to the extent of assuming parental responsibilities for the child should the parents die. Ordinarily, however, the child's paternal or maternal kins take over the child's care and support in such an instance. If the godparents are wealthy or childless, they may assume the financial responsibility for the education of the child, even if the parents are alive. Usually, however, the godparents' obligations to the child are gift-giving on special occasions, particularly Christmas day and the child's birthday. In return, the child is expected to accord his or her godparents the deference, respect, and obedience as he does his real parents, and to treat his godparents' children as his own siblings. In some cultural-linguistic groups, the relationship between ritual siblings is viewed as a spiritual bond and marriage between them is frowned upon. In others, particularly the Tagalogs, marriage between ritual siblings is permissible (Fox, 1966).

Although ostensibly the important relationship that is developed in the *kumpadre* system is that between godparents and godchild, the basic orientation of the system is horizontal. That is, the rela-

tionship established between the parents of the child and the godparents supersedes the vertical relationship between the child and
the godparents (Fox, 1966). The *kumpadre* system serves to strengthen the friendship ties between the adults by bringing the primary
relationship within the framework of the extended family system.
Or it may serve to reaffirm close ties with a favorite kin. Thus, not
infrequently, a relative is chosen as sponsor for the child's baptism
or confirmation. Seldom, however, is choice confined to relatives in
both occasions, since acquiring ritual kins is generally considered
desirable. In some cases, the main criterion in the selection of the
godparents may be purely utilitarian (Fox, 1966). A tenant farmer,
for example, may invite the landlord to stand as sponsor for his
child's baptism or confirmation in an effort to stabilize the relationship with the landlord, probably even strengthen his bargaining
power with the latter. Or a lower level employee in a Chinese firm
may select his employer as a godparent for his child in order to
gain some status in the firm or to get handsome gifts after the ritual
and on important feast days from the godparent. Politicians, other
prominent public figures, businessmen, employers, and landlords
usually have scores of their subordinates' children as godchildren.
In these instances, the godparents do not become "family" nor does
the *kumpadre* relationship change the vertical relationship between
the parents of the child and the godparents. Moreover, while in
some instances a wealthy godparent may finance the godchild's
schooling or even assume full financial responsibility for the child,
ordinarily, interclass coparenthood does not entail the assumption
of any parental surrogate role on the part of the godparents.

When the child reaches adulthood and marries, he or she acquires
another set of godparents, the wedding sponsors. The sponsors may
be chosen by the couple's respective families (the woman's family
(choosing the female sponsor, and the man's family the male sponsor) or by the couple themselves. The important criterion in the
choice of wedding sponsors is the social prominence of the sponsors
or their gift-giving capacity. The vertical and the horizontal relationships established by the ritual may be much more superficial than
those involved in the baptismal or confirmation sponsorship.

Ritual Kinship in a Non-Christian Filipino Group

An equivalent of the Christian ritual kinship system is found in a mountain people, called the Sulod, in Panay, Bisayan Islands, studied by Jocano (1968). In this society, kinship is extended either by blood brotherhood or through a food-feeding ceremony. In the first, two men go through a ritual where they cut each other's index finger and draw seven drops of blood from each finger, mix the blood in rice wine and drink it. The ceremony is witnessed by the relatives of both parties who each become linked in a kinship bond to the blood brother of their kinsman and to each other. In the food-feeding ceremony (called *higara*), the respective families of the two men (it appears that women cannot initiate the ceremony) participate in the ritual which consists of members of one family feeding the members of the other's family. The participants in this ceremony become each other's *kahigara*. The two ceremonies carry the same kinship significance and involve reciprocal obligations and responsibilities which far outweigh those involved in the *kumpadre* system. The blood brother, for instance, is obligated to support and take over the responsibility for his blood brother's household in case of the latter's death. This practice, according to Jocano (1968:94), "appears to be an extension of the levirate system obtaining between real siblings." Jocano reports of an actual case where a man took over his blood brother's widow and child in fulfillment of the latter's deathbed request. In no case could a ritual kin refuse his blood brother's, or *kahigara's*, wish or request for assistance, regardless of the nature or magnitude of the sacrifice involved. Jocano (1968:98) reports of one instance where a man took advantage of the *kahigara* relationship by asking for his *kahigara's* wife. Despite the husband's consternation and vigorous resistance to the request, he was eventually forced to give up his wife, for he did promise to grant his *kahigara* the latter's every wish. It was a matter of honor (reinforced by strong pressure from the community elders) that he go by his word. This instance, however, was an unusual case of abuse of the relationship which was not repeated, since provision was made in subsequent rituals in the village that wife giving would not be a part of the system of reciprocal obligations and rights in the relationship.

The Non-nuclear Family Household is a Frequent Arrangement

The typical Filipino household is an extended family arrangement, although not necessarily in the classical three-generational sense of the term. A typology of households has been developed by

Eslao (1966:199-208) to represent developmental cycles of urban households. The typology revolves around the lineal relationship of the household members and their marital status. Six household types are described (Eslao, 1966:200):

1) Nuclear-family household consisting of husband and wife, with or without unmarried children.

2) Nuclear-lateral household consisting of a nuclear core plus a relative or relatives who are not lineally related to either of the spouses and whose own parents are not in the household. Unmarried siblings, children of siblings, siblings of parents or their children constitute the most common type of lateral extensions.

3) Nuclear-joint household which is simliar in composition to the nuclear-lineal type except that at least one of the lateral extensions is currently married or has had conjugal experience in the past.

4) Nuclear-lineal household consisting of a nuclear core plus one or more of the following sets of relatives: married children, their spouses or both, with or without children; grandchildren whose parents are not in the household; parents of one or both of the spouses; parents and siblings (with or without spouses and children) of one or both of the spouses.

5) Less-than-nuclear household consisting of only one spouse, with or without children.

6) Single-person household consisting of an individual who has never married.

A study of 194 households in a Manila district (Malate), from which Eslao developed the typology above, shows that 50.5 per cent of the households had non-nuclear members (Eslao, 1966:202). The nuclear-lateral household type was found to be as frequent (22.7 per cent) as the nuclear-family type (23 per cent), while 15.4 and 12.4 per cent, respectively, were nuclear-lineal and nuclear-joint households. However, Liu, Rubel, and Yu (1969:397), using the Eslao typology to describe household types in another urban setting (Cebu), report the preponderance of the nuclear-family household. Cross tabulating by social class, the authors give the following frequencies of the nuclear-family household (N=1,521),68.3 per cent of the upper class, 62.6 per cent for the middle class, and 66.3 per cent for the lower class.

Some investigators have suggested that, contrary to research expectations, the non-nuclear household type is more prevalent in the urban and non-farm than in the rural and farm areas. In a study of 95 households in rural Canaman, Camarines Sur, Eslao (1966:204), for example, found one out of two households to be nuclear, compared to about one out of five among the Manila households reported on above. Similarly, Castillo and Pua (1963) note that only 21 per cent of 1,653 heads of households in four *barrios* (villages) they studied reported having extended family households. Moreover, the authors state that the proportion of nuclear over extended family households was greater in the more rural than in the more urban *barrios*. Along the same trend of findings, Polson and Pal (1952:61-62), in a study of another rural areas, note that non-farm households had a higher average number of non-nuclear household members (1.00) than the farm households (0.87).

In addition to being more frequently found in more urban settings, the non-nuclear household is also found in greater proportion in "more economically secure settings" (Carroll, 1968:135). He cites as evidence the findings of two studies. The first was by Castillo and Pua, cited above—a relatively smaller number of skilled and unskilled workers (15 per cent) living in extended family households compared to white-collar, farming, and proprietor-manager groups (22 per cent) in similar arrangements. The second evidence came from a comparison of findings of household surveys in the Tondo and Malate districts of Manila conducted by Ateneo de Manila in 1962 and 1964-66, respectively (Carroll, 1968:135). The analysis shows that Malate, which "has a larger representation of families in the middle-and upper-income ranges," had a proportionately higher number of extended family households. Further confirming evidence is provided by Rivera and McMillan (1954) in an economic and social survey of rural households in central Luzon. They found that 54 per cent of business proprietors had non-nuclear households compared to 30 per cent of the professionals and 18.8 per cent of the farm laborers. It may be noted, however, that Liu, Rubel, and Yu in the study cited above reported no clear-cut relationship between social class and household type.

While empirical data on rural-urban as well as class differences in household types are barely supportive, the argument that non-nuclear household types would be more frequently found in more economically secure urban areas than in subsistence rural settings has an intuitive and commonsensical ring to it. A plausible explanation for class differences in kin group cohesiveness (of which providing shelter for kins is one operational definition) has been given by Liu, Rubel, and Yu (1969:395), as noted in another section of this paper. The rural-urban differences may be explained in terms of the steady and increasing influx of rural migrants to the urban areas either in search of work or to study. Like migrants everywhere, they seek out relatives and people from the same village in order not to be totally lost in a strange, new environment. Moreover, the urban extended family household is probably a natural response to the inadequate and relatively expensive housing facilities in the city and town. As Eslao (1966:206) notes:

> ...the family and kinship system has certain built-in mechanisms for accommodating some of the strains and stresses of urban living. The extended household furnishes evidence of the organized way in which the system deals with such problems of urbanization as the difficulty of obtaining shelter and, in the case of new arrivals from the rural areas, the uncertainty of living in an unfamiliar environment.

An aspect of the extended-family household that needs systematic study is the degree of fluidity of its membership, particularly in the urban areas. The use of the urban extended family household as a "way station" by rural migrants suggests a relatively high turn over rate in household composition as the migrants become economically stable or finish school and new ones come in. Relatives, moreover, may move from one kin household to another as the circumstances demand. The mother, an aunt, sister, or cousin, for example, may stay with a married kinswoman's household, while the latter is convalescing from an illness or from the birth of a child. Or a married son or daughter may stay with his or her family of orientation for a period of time after marriage.

The Filipino Family has an Age-based Hierarchy of Authority

Within the family as well as in the larger society, interpersonal relationships are characterized by strict observance of generational respect which involves difference and obedience to all individuals of both sexes who are older than oneself. Children are expected to obey, not only their parents, but also their grandparents, aunts, uncles, other adult kinsmen, older siblings and cousins, and to show respect for them by proper forms of kinship address and behavior at all times. The norms of respect and obedience are extended to nonkins as well. Even the family servant, for example, may request the child to run errands for her and expect obedience (Guthrie and Jacobs, 1966: 102). The behavioral norms governing a child's interaction with an adult are aptly summarized in a grandfather's admonition to a grandchild, as described by Jocano (1969: 93) below:

> In passing between two older people talking, ask their permission before you pass; show signs of respect by bowing your head a little and by walking slowly. In speaking to those who are older than you, lower the tone of your voice. Remember that all the time.

Infractions of such norms of conduct by the child may bring immediate punishment from any of the adults present, particularly if they are kins. A child's misbehavior and lack of manners are seen as a reflection on the whole family and kin group. Thus, theoretically at least, all adult kins have the right and the responsibility to punish the child for such misconduct. Ordinarily, however, the right and responsibility to discipline the child are assumed mainly by the parents. Older siblings and adult kins assume the role of punishers only when they have the explicit or implicit authority from the child's parents to do so (Guthrie and Jacobs, 1966: 111).

The traditional respect for age among Filipinos insures a highly valued status for the aged and their integration in the family and society. The aged continue to wield considerable power and influence, despite their economic dependence, in the extended family household. Their power and influence are due in part to their widely acknowledged wisdom accumulated over the years and partly to their past social roles. The latter is discussed in some detail below.

Parent-child interactions. Parents, particularly the mothers claim an inherent right to the child's unquestioning obedience as an expression of the child's gratitude for having been given life by the parents. From early in the child's life through adulthood, he or she is always reminded:

You would not have been [here] if something had happened
to your parents before you were born. You owe the fact of your
existence to your parents (Guthrie and Jacobs, 1966:101).

Disobedience of parental advice or demands is viewed as ingratitude on the part of the child. Ingratitude is a "cardinal sin" in Philippine society and severe collective action is imposed on the ingrate.
Moreover, the collective sanction is strongly reinforced by the
belief that misfortune and hardship will plague a disrespectful and
disobedient child throughout his or her life. This belief is incul-
cated into the child's mind early in the socialization process and
repeatedly brought into his consciousness whenever an occasion
of disrespect or disobedience arises. It is this belief, together with
the sense of gratitude and fear of collective sanction, that keeps
many an adult under parental control even after he or she has
married and left the parental household. For having been given
life (and particularly for the mother risking her own life during childbirth), as well as for being reaved from a helpless infant, the child
owes the parents a lifetime of indebtedness which could never be
repaid. Thus, the Filipino child is obligated to respect and uncon-
ditionally obey his parents and serve them and take care of them
during their old age. Hollnsteiner (1964: 344) describes the parent-
child relationship as complementary rather than reciprocal, since
the parents are not expected to feel a sense of gratitude toward the child. They take the child's services and assistance
during their old age or any other time of need as being rightfully
due them.
    Another basis of the parental, as well as kin, claim on the child's
obedience is that the child's behavior reflects on the parents and
the whole kin group. The child, regardless of his or her age, is
viewed by both kins and nonkins alike not as an individual in his or
her own right but as an integral part of his or her kin group. Thus,
his or her actions will have repercussions on the whole family and
kin group, whether he, she, or they like it or not. As Guthrie and
Jacobs (1966: 195) note:

They control him because he can quite literally get them into
trouble. In a land where vengeance patterns are still strong, a
wrongdoing involving one member involves all members; dishonor to one is disgrace to all.

To enforce obedience and respect, Filipino parents, particulary mothers, frequently resort to physical punishment, such as spanking, pinching, or ear-pulling. This the child is expected to accept stoically and without resentment. Guthrie and Jacobs (1966: 115), in a study of child-rearing practices of 279 mothers in five Tagalog-speaking provinces, report that 73 per cent used physical punishment from fairly to very frequently, compared to 24 per cent who resorted to "scolding and haranguing" and 3 per cent who withheld privileges. As the authors further note, threat of loss of love, a frequently used technique among American mothers (48 per cent of those studied by Sears, Maccoby, and Levin, 1957), would not be an effective sanction among Filipino children, since they could always turn to another member of the usually large nuclear or extended family for nurturance and love.

The father generally maintains an aloofness from the daily operations of the house, including the discipline of the children. However, he is generally feared a great deal more than the mother. Although he seldom punishes the child, when he does, it is usually an experience the child does not forget readily. In contrast to the mother's pinching, ear-pulling, or scolding, the father may give the child, especially a boy, a beating which may leave the seat of his pants sore for several days. The father, however, assumes the punisher role only for major infractions of behavioral norms by the child.

Sibling interaction. A ladderlike structure of authority governs interaction patterns among siblings. An older brother or sister has authority over a younger one, including the authority to punish him or her. The degree of an older sibling's authority over a younger one is directly related to the magnitude of the age differrence between them, as well as parental sanction of such an assertion of authority by the older sibling. Thus, while theoretically a younger sibling is expected to show deference and obedience to every sibling older than himself or herself, the closer the two siblings in age, the less likely is the younger one to acknowledge the authority of the older sibling over him or her. The older sibling will then need parental support of his or her claim to obedience from the younger brother or sister. Guthrie and Jacobs (1966: 101), for instance, report that in 61 per cent of the families they studied, the older siblings were obeyed because the parents demanded it of the younger ones.

The eldest sibling generally assumes the authority of a second parent and is expected to assume the parental surrogate role in case of the absence, incapacitation, or death of the parents. Jocano (1969: 78) writes of the story of Leonardo who became a father surrogate to his siblings at the age of twelve.

When Leonardo's father died, his mother became an invalid. There were seven of them in the family, and he suddenly found himself its head. He was only twelve years old. Neighbors came to help them from time to time, but Leonardo shouldered most of the hard work in keeping the family intact and alive. Early in the morning he would bring the younger siblings to the neighbors' house and then proceed to his work in the field. He would pick them up after he was through with his work. The younger siblings, in turn, respected and obeyed Leonardo as though he was their "parent."

Siblings are socialized early in life into the norms of mutual protection and respect. At the age of seven or younger a boy or a girl is given charge as caretaker of a younger sibling (Minturn *et al.*, 1964: 212). The older sibling usually has the younger one in tow as he or she plays with his or her own peer group or runs errands for the mother or an adult kin. Responsibility for the younger sibling's safety and wellbeing is taken very seriously by the older child. Any dereliction of duty, especially if it leads to the younger child's being hurt, will surely bring severe punishment from the parents.

The normative expectation that the older sibling should take care of the younger ones is carried over to adulthood. Thus, the older sibling is expected to help finance the younger ones' education, a very highly valued goal in Philippine society. In a study of familism among college students, for instance, Pal and Arquiza (1957: 2) report that 74 per cent (N=236) agreed with the following statement:

You should not marry immediately after your graduation so that you can help your parents educate younger brothers and/or sisters.

The authors further note that interviews with a number of the students showed their awareness of parental disappointment if they married within a year after graduation. Only a few of the students expressed some resentment of the parental expectation.

It is not infrequent that the older sibling is called upon to make personal sacrifices for the younger ones, sometimes to the extent of giving up his or her own schooling or postpone marriage in order to support a younger brother or sister through a vocation or a profession.

The siblings' deep concern for each other's welfare extends through adulthood and old age, although quarrels, bickerings, and latent or overt resentment, for example, over a younger one's ingratitude or an older sibling's undue assertion of authority, may characterize their day-to-day interactions. The strong cohension of the sibling group comes into full force when one of them needs the assistance of the others, such as in providing shelter or financial support for a widowed sister, in protecting a sister from an abusive husband, in sharing expenses for the marriage of a brother or in supporting each other in conflicts with nonkins.

The Relationship between Husband and Wife is Highly Egalitarian

Although the father does occupy a dominant position in the family, the typical Filipino family is not patriarchal (Carroll, 1968; Fox, 1956, 1963, 1966). Nor was it ever patriarchal in the past, as claimed by some students of Philippine society (e.g., Macaraig, 1948). Despite more than 300 years of Spanish influence which institutionalized the legal and social dominance of the male, the Filipino family has retained its predominantly Malay characteristic of equality between husband and wife in the allocation of authority within the household and in decision-making on matters affecting the family (Cordero and Panopio, 1969: 270; Fox, 1966). Kroeber (1928: 151), an early student of Philippine society, has noted the highly egalitarian relationship between males and females in the family and in the large society.

. . . the inevitable physiological differences are recognized, but they are not used as a starting point from which social distinctions or restrictions are developed as by so many other nations. The Filipino may well be described as an unconscious and thorough going feminist,

Research evidence provided by Liu, Rubel, and Yu (1969:400), as
a matter of fact, suggests that the wife may be the more dominant
and influential figure in the household. Using Herbst's (1952)
method in getting at the decision and activity style in the household, the authors analyzed family role constellations in seven areas
representing samples of common household activities selected from
the total parameter of family activities. These were: children's
schooling; family health care; household money spending and
budgeting; leisure time social activities; food preparation and
serving; family economic security; and child-rearing and control.
The authors report that, regardless of social class, the following
four household activities were autonomous regions of the wife;
family health, money control, food preparation, and child control.
Economic planning was the autonomous region of 25 per cent
of the lower-class and 20 per cent of the middle class wife. And,
although husbands entered into the decision regarding the children's education and family leisure time utilization, in both cases
either the decision or the activity was shared by the wife.

The Filipino woman's customary rights taken away from her
by the Spaniards were restored to her by the post-independence
system of laws. She now can legally transact business without the
prior consent of the husband, dispose of her paraphernal property,
and enjoy the same educational, occupational, and voting rights
and privileges as the male.

There are several factors which contribute to the egalitarianism
between husband and wife. Firstly, egalitarianism is inherent in the
bilateral nature of the kinship system which provides for the
continuing support and protection to the woman by her kin group
(Fox, 1966: 4). A husband who mistreats his wife will have her
father, brothers, uncles, and male cousins to contend with. A quarrel
between the couple, as a matter of fact, may easily expand to
involve their kins. Secondly, the age-based structure of hierarchy
in the family, allocating authority and respect on the basis of age
and not sex, gives siblings of both sexes equal status. This provides
an experiential basis for egalitarianism at marriage. Moreover,
equal inheritance among male and female siblings and the woman's
control of property inherited or acquired before or after marriage
further strengthen her negotiating position in the conjugal power
relations. Furthermore, the Filipino woman of the past and of
modern times has always been socially, politically, and economic-

ally active. Carroll (1965), in a study of Filipino entrepreneurs, reports that mothers or wives of a number of these enterpreneurs were actively engaged in the family business. Almost invariably, the wife's or mother's role as controller of the family purse strings is extended to that of treasurer of the family business. Among the lower classes, both in the urban and rural settings, the wife helps supplement the family income by setting up a *sari-sari* (tiny grocery) store in front of the house or in the marketplace; by engaging in household crafts and cottage industries, for example mat-weaving or basket-making, embroideries, etc.; and by keeping a vegetable garden or poultry, even piggery, in the backyard for home consumption or for sale. The middle class housewife may set up a dress or beauty shop at home. In the farm, the wife helps in the planting, harvesting, and marketing of crops. The 1962 Philippine Statistical Survey of Households reports that 36.4 per cent of the labor force were women (Guerrero, 1965: 275). The prominent and influential position that Filipino women occupy in society is aptly summarized by Fox (1963: 353) below:

In the mid-twentieth century Philippines, there are few occupations, no professions, in which women do not participate, and they dominate many, such as pharmacy, teaching, nursing, chemistry, certain phases of commerce, merchandizing, and others. In the Christian areas women have been elected to every office of the land but that of president and vice-president. They are respected as behind-the-scene leaders of industry. Women's organizations form powerful and feared pressure groups.

Despite the above characterization of the Filipino woman, she is by no means close to the women's liberation movement's ideal. Her relatively dominant position at home as noted, for example, by Liu, Rubel and Yu above, is partly by default on the husband's part. The husband generally maintains an aloofness from the daily household decisions and activities since to do otherwise would be "unmasculine." However, he has the final word on any family activity or decision, including the disciplining of children. He has veto power over the wife's desire to pursue a profession or an occupation (Cordero and Panopio, 1969: 273). And, as noted by Guerreoro (1965: 278) in a study of husband and wife roles among a group of Filipino professionals, a full-time job outside the house does not lead to the reallocation of household roles between husband and wife. "To the husbands, wives have to hurry home after office hours to assume their other role—that of wife and mother." Husbands still expect their employed wives to wait on them—for example, put out their clothes for work in the morning and pick up after them; prepare or at least supervise the preparation of meals, and perform any number of chores to insure the comfort and relaxation of their husbands at the end of a hard day in the office, regardless of how badly their own workday went. As Fox (1963: 353) has noted, Filipino family, as well as society, is largely patricentric, in the past and in the present.

The Christian Filipino Marriage is Monogamous: Polygyny is Legally Permitted for the Muslims and Tribal Groups

Philippine marriage laws allow only monogamous marriages among the Christian Filipinos, but respect the polygamous marriage customs, rites, and practices of the non-Christian groups—the Negritos, the Muslims, and the more than thirty pagan mountain tribes. Generally speaking, the non-Christian Filipinos are polygamous, although there are some groups which are monogamous in practice if not in theory. The Negritos of Island studied by Oracion (1963), for example, are generally monogamous, although allowed by law and tradition to enter into polygamous marriages. The cost of supporting several wives and maintaining a large household makes most of the Negrito marriages monogamous by default. A similar situation applies to the Muslims who are allowed by the Islam religion to take as many as four wives. The majority, especially the educated Muslims, practice monogamy (Arce, 1963). Polygamous marriages are also very infrequent among the various mountain tribes (Jocano, 1968; Wood, 1957).

On the other hand, although Christian marriages are theoretically strictly monogamous, an arrangement resembling polygyny, called the *querida* system, is widely practiced and implicitly accepted by the larger society (Jocano, 1969; Hunt *et al.*, 1963). Thus, a married man who can financially afford to do so may maintain a *querida* or mistress and have children by her. The liaison may be a more or less permanent arrangement especially when children result from it. The wife usually accepts the situation stoically, although she may make sporadic efforts at retribution by "raiding" the other woman's household to call her names and probably pull her hair. She also may try to embarrass the *querida* in public whenever the opportunity arises.

There are, indeed, very few alternative courses of action open to the wife. Cultural norms operate in favor of the husband in matters related to the sexual aspects of a male-female relationship. There is, for example, the cultural belief that man is a sexual animal and will enter into sexual liaisons with other women whenever the opportunity arises. Thus, the betrayed wife's relatives and friends may try to placate her by reminding her that "a man is a man." Moreover, there is the cultural expectation that it is the woman's duty to keep the man satisfied and contended at home and it is a sign of her failure as a wife if the husband takes a *querida*. Furthermore, the husband's ability to maintain one or more mistresses is a symbol not only of his virility but also of his socio-economic status.

While these cultural expectations largely absolve the man of blame for his infidelity, they do not do so for the *querida*. The *querida* is culturally defined as the wife's moral and social inferior. By being able to assume a stance of moral and social superiority over the *querida*, the wife is able to "save face" and does not feel impelled to make the husband choose between her and the other woman. To do so would be putting herself in the same category as the *querida* and risking the complete break-up of her marriage, an unhappy prospect especially if there are children involved. In addition to the culturally sanctioned face-saving device to a psychological blow, the wife also has the extended family system to provide her with moral support and an opportunity to ventilate her feelings. The wife's kin who would readily intervene on her behalf in case of physical abuse by the husband, however, would rarely, if ever, negatively sanction the husband for his infidelity.

Divorce is not Allowed for the Christian Filipinos, but Permitted Among the Non-Christians

The Philippine Civil Code views marriage among Christian Filipinos as a permanent contract and as an "inviolable social institution" (Fox, 1966:3). This legal prescription is strongly reinforced by the Catholic Church to which the great majority (83.8 per cent) of the Filipinos belong (de los Angeles, 1965:234).

Marriage customs in pre-Hispanic Philippines permitted divorce. Spain instituted anti-divorce legislation during its more than 300 years of colonial rule in the Philippines. Divorce was legalized during the next half century which spanned the American colonial rule and the Japanese occupation. The ban on divorce for Christian Filipinos was restored when the country became independent in 1946. As Hunt *et al.* (1963: 150) point out, the Catholic religion and the "feeling that divorce was so evil in its effect on both children and parents" were the major reasons for abolishing divorce. Legal separation, however, is allowed on either of two grounds: adultery or an attempt of one spouse to take the life of the other. Some couples do make informal arrangements to separate when the reason for the marital break-up is other than those legally acceptable, for example, incompatibility, erosion of affection, etc. (Cordero and Panopio, 1969: 281). Moreover, although legal separation does not sever the marriage tie, some couples do informally agree to permit each other to enter into consensual unions with other partners or get a Mexican or American divorce and remarry without threat of legal prosecution by each other.

As noted earlier, the marriage customs, rites, and practices of the non-Christian Filipinos are accepted as legally valid by the Philippine system of laws. Thus, a Muslim may divorce his wife on the ground of incompatibility, infidelity, or desertion (Arce, 1963: 248-251). And while the legal system recognizes equal rights between the male and the female in initiating legal separation, it respects the Muslim tradition which grants the male the sole prerogative of seeking divorce. Among Negritos, infidelity, laziness on the part of the wife, and cruelty are sufficient grounds for divorce (Oracion, 1963: 61-64). Among some mountain tribal groups, for example, Bontoc highlanders (Hunt *et al.*, 19 63: 150) and the Sulod people of Panay (Jocano, 1968: 190), sterility on the part of either spouse is a ground for divorce.

Marriage has been remarkably stable among both the Christian and the non-Christian Filipinos. The extended family system, which defines marriage as an alliance of families, as well as of individuals, and the active interest and involvement (e.g., as mediators) of kins in keeping the marriage intact (Lynch, 1960) provide a solid structural base for the stability of Christian, as well as non-Christian Filipino marriages. Thus, according to the 1960 Census of the Philippines, only 0.4 per cent (81,175) of all Filipinos ten years or older reported their civil status as separated or divorced. This figure, however, may not reflect the actual cases of separation or divorce. Some persons who are separated or divorced from their original spouses but living in consensual unions with other partners may report their status as "married," while separated or divorced persons who do not take in new partners may claim to be widowed (Cordero and Panopio, 1969: 281).

Mate Selection is Based on Romantic Love, as well as Parental Approval

Filipino parents and older relatives traditionally have exerted strong influence on mate selection among children of marriageable age. In the pre-Spanish times, parents arranged the marriage of their children who were often pledged at a very young age. In some contemporary non-Christian tribal groups, arranged marriages, including child marriages, are still common (Jocano, 1968: 154; Fox, 1966: 2). And in some Christian rural groups, vestiges of the traditional arranged marriage are found. Here marriage negotiations are conducted by the parents of the young couple through the mediation of an influential person known to both parties. An important aspect of the negotiations is the payment of a dowry by the young man and his parents to the parents of the girl. The dowry is a symbol of the alignment of the two families and of the reciprocal obligations incurred by marriage (Fox, 1966: 2). It also represents some form of compensation for the expenses involved in rearing the daughter (Cordero and Panopio, 1969: 275). The amount and form of the dowry (e.g., land, work animals, money, household items) depend on the man's socio-economic status. If the man cannot afford to give a dowry, he may render services in the girl's household or farm from a few weeks to several months. He may cut timber for firewood, build a fence, repair the house, or do any number of things to prove his industry and other qualities deemed desirable by the girl's parents.

Among the Tagalogs, this personal service to the girl's parents (called *manlulusong*) forms part of the courtship and is not a substitute for a dowry. It is intended to give the girl's parents an opportunity to observe the man's "real character." The suitor is allowed to pursue his courtship of the girl or is asked to terminate it on the basis of how he comes out in the parents' estimation during the period of *manlulusong* (Fox, 1966: 3).

The degree of parental influence on mate selection in the past and in the present time may have been overstated by some students of the Filipino family (e.g., Lynch, 1960: 48-51; Fox, 1959: 2-11; Carroll, 1968: 213; Cordero and Panopio, 1969: 276; Santos-Cuyugan, 1961:21; Reynolds, 1966: 213). Parents do advise their children on important qualities to look for in a mate; they may show a preference for one suitor over another, or object strongly to a daughter's or a son's choice. Forcing their choice on the child, however, very rarely, if ever, happens. As Arceo-Ortega (1963: 372) notes, "A marriage arranged exclusively by parents has never been the Filipino way." Moreover, a son or daughter may countermand the parents' objections to his or her choice by eloping. The parents generally give their blessing to the couple when the latter comes back to the *barrio* after the wedding.

Romantic love and freedom of choice may have been more prevalent as operating principles of mate selection in the past and are not recent American-introduced innovations, as some authors suggest. Individual freedom of choice governs mate selection among some non-Christian tribal groups who are largely untouched by Western influence (Jocano, 1968: 154-160; Arce, 1963: 267; Reynolds, 1968: 191-92). Arceo-Ortega (1963: 372) suggests that the difference between traditional and modern Filipino mate selection practices

> ... must be in the degree of outspokenness of the children in explaining their side of the matter. Certainly today's youngster is more candid and frank—sometimes to the point of being aggressive and (sad but true) disrespectful.

Parental and kin guidance in mate selection and active involvement in the marriage preparations may be viewed more as expressions of the mutual concern and effectivity characteristic of the close-knit extended family system than deliberate attempts of the parents and kinship group to control the young people's choice of mates. Parental involvement in the child's marriage is probably as much sought by the child as offered by the parents. In a study of expectations in mate selection and marriage among college students Reynolds (1966: 215), for example, reports that the students equally favored marriage arranged jointly by parents, but according to student's desire and free choice with or without approval of parents.

Belief in fate or *swerte* not infrequently also governs mate selection (Medina, 1971). Young people and old believe that fate would bring the couple together if they are destined for each other or intervene to separate them if they are not. Such a belief cushions the psychological blow of unrequited love or break-up of an engagement among Filipino couples.

Endogamy is generally Practiced, but there are no Rigid rules Defining the field of Eligibles

Filipinos are generally inclined to be endogamous, although the norms governing mate selection tend to be flexible (Tangco, 1951; Medina, 1971; Reynolds, 1966; Jocano, 1968, 1969). Social class, regional-linguistic, as well as religious backgrounds define the field of eligibles. Moreover, some students of Philippine society have noted the relatively high degree of intermarriage among cousins, both affinal and consanguineal. As Quisumbing (1965: 282) has pointed out:

One often hears it said that all the inhabitants in a Philippine barrio are related to each other. While one takes this statement broadly to refer to the proverbial Filipino trait of hospitality, of treating every guest like a member of the family, actual contact with barrio folks may reveal this fact to be literally true.

In a *barrio* studied by Jocano (1969), first-cousin marriages were considered highly desirable because they were believed to have greater stability than nonkin marriages. Among the upper classes, cousin marriages might be entered into to keep the wealth within the extended family (Espiritu and Hunt, 1964: 148). Among a non-Christian tribal group studied by Reynolds (1968: 191), marriages among second and third cousins were fairly common due to the limited field of nonrelative eligibles in the community. It was for the same reason that cousin marriages were allowed among a mountain people studied by Jocano (1968). Among some regional-linguistic groups, however, cousin marriages, especially between first cousins, are proscribed (Quisumbing, 1965: 282).

Intermarriages across regional-linguistic lines have been considerable (Corpuz, 1954). A recent study by Medina (1971) of marriage patterns among couples (N=362) in the Greater Manila area showed the trend toward intermarriage to be on the increase. The researcher found that 43.6 per cent of the couples studied had married outside of their regional-linguistic groups, compared to 16.1 per cent and 26.4 per cent of the husbands' and wives' parents, respectively, who themselves had intermarried. Furthermore, the majority of the couples (65 per cent of the husbands and 51.5 per cent of the wives) expressed favorable attitudes toward intermarriage, while the overwhelming majority (98.2 and 93.8 per cent, respectively) indicated that they would allow their children to intermarry. Reynolds (1966) in a study of mate selection attitudes of college students (N=52) reported that the majority were willing to marry across regional-linguistic, as well as racial-ethnic lines.

Urban Filipinos are more likely than their rural counterparts to intermarry with individuals of different regional-linguistic backgrounds. In the Medina study mentioned above, for example, intermarriage among the male respondents who lived in Manila prior to marriage was 36.6 per cent compared to 17.5 per cent for those who were rural residents before marriage. Intermarriage rates among the female respondents were 36.8 and 23.8 per cent, respectively. The high degree of rural migration to the urban area, particularly Manila, leads to greater interactional opportunities among people of different regional-linguistic backgrounds and greater attitudinal receptivity to, and opportunity for, intermarriage than is possible in the rural areas.

There are no systematic data on the degree to which class endogamy is practiced. Class endogamy seems to be more prevalent among the wealthy than among the middle or lower classes (Espiritu and Hunt, 1964).

Research evidence on the importance of religion in mate selection is similarly scarce. It probably may be reasonably assumed that intermarriage of Christian Filipinos with the Muslim or the tribal "atheistic" minorities is very minimal. The relative isolation of these non-Christian groups from the largely Christian society severely limits opportunities for meaningful social contacts which may lead to intermarriage. Among the Christian groups, Catholics are more favorably disposed than Protestants toward intermarriage with other Christians (Reynolds, 1966).

There are no Rigid Rules of Residence for the Newly Married Couple

There are no rigidly defined norms governing location of residence of the newly married couple. Some students of Philippine society (e.g., Rivera and McMillan, 1954; Fox, 1966) suggest that patri-locality is held as an ideal and that empirical evidence tends to show a patrilocal tendency. Jocano (1969), however, in a study of a fairly typical Bisayan *barrio* has found an initial matrilocal pattern, followed by neolocal residence after the birth of the first child. In the Philippines, particularly in the rural areas where geographical mobility is very limited, the terms describing the rules of residence—patrilocal, matrilocal. and neolocal—may be more meaningfully used, respectively, to refer to the couple setting up residence in the parental household of the husband or the wife, or in a separate household in the·same village. Not infrequently, the newly married couple may stay in the parental household of the husband or the wife for a period of time, usually until they are economically secure enough to maintain a separate household. Liu, Rubel, and Yu (1969: 398), for instance, report that couples in one-fourth of 100 sample households, studied from a larger sample of 1,200 households, had lived with either set of parents at some time in their marriage. The length of stay in the parental households ranged from less than a month to fourteen years. Pal (1956), in a study of a Bisayan village, found that 64 per cent of the married sons in his sample and 63 per cent of their fathers had lived in the parental household for varying periods of time after marriage. As noted earlier, Jocano (1969) in a study of another Bisayan village, reports that newly married couples frequently lived in the wife's parental household until after the birth of the first child.

A variety of factors may determine the location of the newly married couple's residence. The parents' socio-economic status, the number of siblings each of the couple has, compatibility with either set of parents, and other variables influence choice of residence. Thus, the couple may live in the wife's parental household if the maternal kins are more economically well off than the husband's parents. They may reside with the husband's parents if he is an only son or with the wife's parents if she is an only daughter. In either case, the couple may be responding to the strong behest of either set of parents to stay with them after marriage. In some cases, the couple may live with each set of parents alternately in order to placate the parents for the "loss" of their child or to equalize the financial burden if the couple is economically dependent. As a general rule, the location of the new couple's residence is determined by the needs and capabilities of both the couple and their respective families of orientation.

The Future of the Filipino Family and Kinship

The stability of the Filipino family and kinship system in the context of rapid and sometimes revolutionary social change has been noted by students of Philippine society. Instead of breaking up in the face of urbanization and industrialization, as has been the Western experience, the extended kinship system provides a viable organization for facilitating the adaptation of its individual members to the problems of urban living. It is a built-in mechanism for facilitating geographical and social mobility for its members by providing shelter and other material assistance to kins who aspire to improve their socio-economic status by entering the non-agricultural labor market or by going to college in the town or city. It is a major source of manpower and financial assistance in a country where access to such aid from institutional sources is highly limited. The extended family or kinship also is the sole or major source of insurance against crisis situations and old age, since public welfare and public or private insurance systems are not yet fully institutionalized.

Thus, the stability of the Filipino family and kinship may be due in part to the relative inability of other aspects of Philippine social organization to take over its functions as a production unit or as a social service agency. Forced to its own devices in meeting the needs of daily living, as well as in times of crisis, the family forms a systematic and cohesive network of mutual protection and assistance. As such, it demands the exclusive loyalty of its members and the subordination of their individual interests to the common, collective good. Whether recent political developments which call for loyalty to the larger national identity, as well as gradually increasing availability of public social services, would substantially detract from the centrality of the family and kinship in Philippine social organization is too soon to predict.

In no small measure is the stability of the Filipino family and kinship probably attributable to the flexibility of the norms governing interaction and individual actions of its members. Such flexibility enables the family to adapt to changing social conditions and absorb the strains and stresses concomitant with social change.

REFERENCES

Afable, Lourdes
1960 "The Muslims as an ethnic minority in the Philippines." *Philippine Sociological Review*, 8 (1-2). Pp. 16-33.

Angeles, Noli de los
1965 "Marriage and fertility patterns in the Philippines." *Philippine Sociological Review*, 13 (4). Pp. 232-248.

Arbues Lilia
1960 "The Negritos as a minority group in the Philippines." *Philippine Sociological Review*, 8 (1-2). Pp. 39-46.

Arce, Wilfredo F.
1963 "Societal organization of the Muslim people of Sulu." *Philippine Studies*, 11 (2). Pp. 248-251.

Arceo-Ortega, Angelina
1963 "A career-housewife in the Philippines" in Barbara E. Ward (ed.), *Women in the New Asia*. Paris: UNESCO.

Asuncion, Ampro L. (ed.)
1960 "The family—its concept, its structure and its functions." Manila: The First National Training Institute of Family Life.

Bulatao, Jaime C.
1964 "The Manileno's mainsprings" in Frank Lynch (Ed.), *Four Readings on Philippine Values*. Quezon City: Ateneo de Manila University Press.

Carroll, John
1965 *The Filipino Manufacturing Entrepreneur: Agent and Product of Change*. Ithaca, New York: Cornell University Press.

1968 *Changing Patterns of Social Structure in the Philippines: 1896-1963*, Quezon City: Ateneo de Manila University Press.

Castillo, Gelia T., and Juanita F. Pua
1963 "Research notes on the contemporary Filipino family: Findings in a Tagalog area." *Philippine Journal of Home Economics*, 14 (3). Pp. 4-35.

Castillo, Gelia, Felicidad Cordero and Manuel Tanco
1967 "A scale to measure family level of living in four barrios of Los Banos." *Philippine Sociological Review*, 15 (March-April). Pp. 67-87.

Castillo, Gelia, Abraham Weiselat and Felicidad Villareal
   1968   "The concepts of nuclear and extended family: An exploration of empirical referents." *International Journal of Comparative Sociology*, 9 (1). Pp. 1-40.

Espiritu, Socorro C. and Chester L. Hunt
   1964   *Social Foundations of Community Development*. Manila: R.M. Garcia Publishing House.

Eufemio, Flora
   1967   "Foster mothers: Their responses on the parent attitude research instrument (PARI) in relation to their role performance." *Philippine Sociolgical Review*, 15 (3-4). Pp. 94-105.

Ewing, W.F.
   1958   "Some rights of passage among the Tawsug of the Philippines." *Anthropological Quarterly*, 3 (2). Pp. 33-41.

Fox, Robert B.
   1956   "Social organizations" in *Area Handbook on Philippines*, I. New Haven: Human Relations Area Files, Inc. Pp. 413-470.
   1959   "The study of Filipino society and its significance to progress of economic and social development." *Philippine Sociological Review*, 7 (Jan-April). Pp. 2-16.
   1963   "Men and women in the Philippines" in Barbara E. Ward (ed.), *Women in the New Asia*. Paris: UNESCO. Pp. 342-364.
   1966   "The family and society in the rural Philippines." Filipino Cultural Heritage Lecture Series, The Philippine Women's University. Mimeographed.

Goduco-Agular, C., and R. Wintrob
   1964   "Folie a famille in the Philippines." *Psychiatric Quarterly*, 38 (2). Pp. 278-291.

Gonzalez, Mary
   1965   "The Ilongo kinship system and terminology." *Philippine Sociological Review*, 13 (1). Pp. 23-31.

Guerrero, Sylvia H.
   1965   "An analysis of husband-wife roles among Filipino professionals at UP Los Banos Campus." *Philippine Sociological Review*, 13, (October). Pp. 275-281.

Guthrie, George M.
   1961   *The Filipino Child and Philippine Society*. Manila: Philippine Normal College Press.
   1966   "Structure of maternal attitudes in two cultures." *Journal of Psychology*, 62 (2). Pp. 155-165.

Guthrie, George M., and Pepita Jimenez Jacobs
   1966   *Child Rearing and Personality Development in the Philippines*. College Parks: Pennsylvania State University Press.

Coller, Richard W.
   1954   "A sample of courtship and marriage attitudes held by UP students." *Philippine Sociological Review*, 2 (4). Pp. 31-45.

1960 "Changing family patterns in the Philippines and minimizing family tensions." *Philippines Journal of Home Economics*, 11(3). Pp. 6-8, 10, 23.

Concepcion, Mercedes
1964 "Some socio-economic correlates of completed family size, 1960." *Philippine Sociological Review*, 12 (1-2). Pp. 16-26.

Concepcion, Mercedes and Wilhelm Flieger
1968a "Family building patterns of young Manila couples." *Philippine Sociological Review*, 16 (3-4). Pp. 162-183.
1968b "Studies of fertility and fertility planning in the Philippines." *Demography*, 5(2). Pp. 714-731.

Cordero, Felicidad and Isabel Panopio
1969 *General Sociology: Focus on the Philippines*. Manila: College Professions Publishing Corporation.

Corpuz, Onofre D.
1957 *The Bureaucracy in the Philippines*. Manila: Institute of Public Administration, University of the Philippines.

Critchfield, Richard
1972 "Macros—Philippines' savior or South Seas dictator?" *The Kansas City Times*, (21 December 1972).

Diaz, Ralph, Judith von Oppenfeld and Horst von Oppenfeld
1962 *Case Studies of Farm Families, Laguna Province, Philippines.* Laguna: College of Agriculture, University of the Philippines.

Eggan, Fred and William Henry Scott
1965 "Ritual life of the Igorots of Sagada: Courtship and marriage." *Ethnology*, 4(1). Pp. 77-111.

Elkins, Richard
1964 "A matrix display of Western Bukidnon Manobo kinship." *Philippine Sociological Review*, 12 (1-2). Pp. 122-129.

Eslao, Nena
1962 "Child-rearing among the Samal of Manubul, Siasi, Sulu." *Philippine Sociological Review*, 10 (3-4). Pp. 80-107.
1965 "The learning situation in the home and in the school." *Contemporary Studies*, 2 (2-3). Pp. 107-115.
1966 "The developmental cycle of the Philippine household in an urban setting." *Philippine Sociological Review*, 14 (4). Pp. 199-208.

Gutierrez-Gonzales, Elizabeth
1968 "Duration of marriage and perceptual behavior of spouses." *Philippine Journal of Psychology*, 1 (1). Pp. 53-61.

Hart, Donn
1965 "From pregnancy thru birth in a Bisayan Filipino village" in Donn Hart, *Phya Anuman Rajadhon* and Richard Coughlin (eds.), *Southeast Asian Birth Customs: Three Studies in Human Reproduction.* New Haven, Conn.: Human Relations Area Files. Pp. 1-113.

Herbst, P.G.
    1952   "The measurement of family relationships." *Human Relations*,
           5. Pp. 3-35.
Himes, Ronald
    1964   "The Bontok kinship system." *Philippine Sociological Review*, 12
           (3-4). Pp. 159-172.
Hollnsteiner, Mary R.
    1963a *The Dynamics of Power in Philippine Municipality*. Quezon City:
           Community Development Research Council, University of Philip-
           pines.
    1963b "Social control and the Filipino personality." *Philippine Sociologi-
           cal Review*, 11 (July-October). Pp. 39-42.
    1964   "Reciprocity in the lowland Philippines" in Frank Lynch (ed.),
           Four Readings on Philippines Values, revised edition. Quezon City:
           Ateneo de Manila University Press.
    1965   "Modernization and the change to the Filipino family" in *The
           Filipino Christian Family in a Changing Society*. Manila: Christian
           Family Movement. Pp. 10-20.
Hunt, Chester
    1963   "The family" in Chester Hunt *et al.*, *Sociology in the Philippine
           Setting*, revised edition. Quezon City: Phoenix Publishing House.
Hunt, Chester and R.W. Coller
    1957   "Intermarriage and cultural change: A study of Philippine-Ameri-
           can marriages." *Social Forces*, 35 (3). Pp. 223-230.
Jimenez, Ramon
    1965   "The Filipino working mother and the children she sends to school."
           Contemporary Studies, 2(2-3). Pp. 126-135.
Jocano, Felipe Landa
    1966a *Filipino Cultural Heritage*. Lecture series No. 2. Manila: The
           Philippine Women's University, Gems Publications.
    1966b "Filipino social structure and value system" in F.L. Jocano (ed.),
           Filipino Cultural Heritage. Lecture series No. 2. Manila: The
           Philippine Women's University, Gems Publications.
    1968   *Sulod Society: A Study in the Kinship System and Social
           Organization of a Mountain People of Central Panay*. Quezon City:
           University of Philippines Press.
Jocano, Felipe Landa (continued)
    1969   *Growing up in a Philippine Barrio*. Holt, Rinehart and Winston.
    1970   "Maternal and child care among the Tagalogs in Bay, Laugna,
           Philippines." *Asian Studies*, 8 (December). Pp. 277-300.
Juco, Jorge
    1966   "Fault, consent and breakdown: The sociology of divorce legisla-
           tion in the Philippines." *Philippine Sociological Review*, 14 (2).
           Pp. 67-76.
Kroeber, A.L.
    1928   *Peoples of the Philippines*. New York: Anthropological Handbook.

Liu, William T. and Siok-Hue Yu
1968 "The lower class Cebuano family: A preliminary analysis profile."
Philippine Socioligical Review, 16 (July-Obtober). Pp. 114-123.

Liu, William, Arthur J. Rubel and Elena Yu
1969 "The urban family of Cebu: A profile analysis." *Journal of marriage and the family*, 31 (2). Pp. 393-402.

Lynch, Frank
1960 "The conjugal bond where the Philippines changes." *Philippine Sociological Review*, 8 (3-4). Pp. 48-51.

Lynch, Frank (ed.)
1964 *Four Readings on Philippine Values*. Quezon City: Ateneo de Manila University Press.

Macaranas, Eduarda
1968 "Perceived parental attitudes and scholastic achievement in a group of adolescent boys." *Philippine Journal of Psychology*, 1 (1). Pp. 11-15.

Madigan, Francis C.
1962 "Population pressures in the Philippines and some ethical aspects of government planning." *The Philippine Statistician*, 11 (June).
1965 "Estimated trends of fertility, mortality, and natural increase in the North Mindanao regions of the Philippine Islands, 1960-1970." *Philippine Sociological Review*, 13 (4). Pp. 260-267.

Manalili, Alfredo Lusi Cura
1966 "The family planning movement and the Protestant view." *Unitas*, 39 (3). Pp. 383-399.

Manuel, E. Arsenio
1963 "Manuvu marriage." *U.P. Anthropology Bulletin*, 1 (1). Pp. 8-9, 12.

Medina, Belen Tan-gatue
1958 "A study in non-European migration: Chinese-Filipino intermarriage." *Migration News*, (July-August). Pp. 13-15.
1971 "Urban marriage patterns." Diliman, Quezon City: University of the Philippines. Mimeographed.

Mendes, Baz
1968 "The home in the making of the Filipino." *Contributions to Education Science, Culture*, 19. Pp. 1-10.

Minturn, Leigh and William Lambert (Eds.)
1964 *Mothers of Six Cultures: Antecedents of Child Rearing*. New York: Wiley.

Nazaret, Francisco and Chaves Hidalgo
1964 "Fertility survey of 1963 in the Philippines." *Philippine Sociologica Review*, 12 (1-2). Pp. 5-16.

Nurge, Ethel
1956 "Economic functions of the child in the rural Philippines." *Philippine Sociological Review*, 4 (1). Pp. 7-11.

1965   *Life in a Leyte Village.* Seattle, Washington: University of Washington Press.

1968   "Factors operative in mate selection in a Philippine village." *Eugenics Quarterly,* 5. Pp. 163-168.

Nydegger, William and Corrine Nydegger

1963   "Tarong: An Ilocos barrio in the Philippines" in Beatrice Whiting (ed.), *Six Cultures: Studies of Child Rearing.* New York: Wiley. Pp. 693-867.

1964   "The mothers of Tarong, Philippines" in Leigh Minturn and William Lambert (eds.), *Mothers of Six Cultures· Antecedents of Child Rearing.* New York: Wiley. Pp. 209-221.

Oracion, Timoteo S.

1963   "Notes on the social structure and social change of the Negritos of Negros Island." *Philippine Sociological Review,* 11 (1-2). Pp. 61-64.

1964   "Magahat marriage procedures." *Philippine Sociological Review,* 12 (1-2). Pp. 101-108.

1965   "Magahat pregnancy and birth practices." *Philippine Sociological Review* 13 (4). Pp. 268-274.

Pacheco, Antonio aud Trinidad Osteria

1966   "Some findings of the attitudes toward family size preferences and family limitation." *Statistical Reporter,* 10 (3). Pp. 1-15.

Pacyaya, Alfredo

1961   "Changing customs of marriage, death, and burial among the Sagada." *Practical Anthropology,* 8 (3). Pp. 125-133.

Pagsibigan, Gloria

1968   "Attitudes toward working mothers of children in six selected public elementary schools in Manila." *Contributions to Education, Science, Culture,* 19. Pp. 71-85.

Pal, Agaton

1966a   "Aspects of lowland Philippine social structure." *Philippine Sociological Review,* 14 (1). P. 36.

1966b   "Socio-psychological correlates of family size." *Philippine Journal of Home Economics,* 7 (1). Pp. 1-11.

Pal, Agaton P. and Lino Q. Arquiza

1957   "Deviations and adherences in Philippine familism." *Silliman Journal.* 4 (1). Pp. 1-7.

Perez, Bernardino

1962   *Family Living Surveys.* Manila: University of Philippines Statistical Center.

Pido, Antonio

1963   "Differential fertility patterns in Cagayan de Oro City." *Philippine Sociological Review,* 11 (1-2). Pp. 91-98.

Polson, Robert and Agaton Pal

1956   *Status of Rural Life in the Dumaguete City Trade Area, Philippines,*

1952. Ithaca: Southeast Asia Program, Department of Far Eastern Studies, Cornell University.

Pratt, William
1967 "Family size and expectations in Manila." *Saint Louis Quarterly,* 5 (1-2). Pp. 153-184.

Quisumbing, Lourdes
1963 "Characteristic features of Cebuano family life amidst a changing society." *Philippine Sociological Review,* 11 (1-2). Pp 135-141.
1964 "Child rearing practices in the Cebuano extended family." *Philippine Sociological Review,* 12 (1-2). Pp. 109-114.
1965a *Marriage Customs in Rural Cebu.* Cebu City: University of San Carlos Publications, Ser. A, Humanities No. 3.
1965b "Interlocking relationships in a Cebuano mountain sitio and their implication for child rearing." *Philippine Sociological Review,* 13 (4). Pp. 281-284.
1968 "An introduction to the study of child rearing practices in the rural environs of Cebu City" in *Miscellaneous Contribution to the Humanities,* No. 1. Cebu City: University of San Carlos Publications, Ser. E. Pp. 78-85.

Reynolds, Harriet
1962 "The Filipino family in its cultural setting." *Practical Anthropology* 9 (5). Pp. 223-234.

Reynolds, Harriet (continued)
1966 "Evaluation and expectations toward mate selection and marriage of Filipino college students." *Philippine Sociological Review,* 14 (4). Pp. 212-226.
1968 "Modern marriage and courtship among the Isneg,, Apayao." (Abstract) *Philippine Sociological Review,* 16 (3-4). Pp. 191-192.

Rivera, Generoso and Robert T. McMillan
1954 *An Economic and Social Survey of Rural Households in Central Luzon.* Philippine Council for U.S. Aid and United States Operations to the Philippines, Manila.

Santos-Cuyugan, Ruben
1961a "The changing Philippines: A problem of cultural identity." *The Chronicle Yearbook.*
1961b "Socio-cultural change and the Filipino family." *Science Review* 2 (3). Pp. 9-13.

Sanvictores, Lourdes
1965 "Is there an economic need for family limitation in the Philippines?" *Unitas,* 38 (3). Pp. 439-447.

Sarreal, Roberto A.
1954 "Pattern of age at marriage in Manila, 1952." *Philippine Sociological Review,* 2 (4). Pp. 27-31.

Scheans, Daniel
1965 "The Ilocano: Marriage and the land." *Philippine Sociological Review,* 13 (1). Pp. 57-62.

1968   "Patterns of kin-term usage among young Ilocanos and a method for determining them." *Philippine Sociological Review*, 16 (1-2). Pp. 17-29.

Scott, William Henry
1958   "Boyhood in Sagada." *Anthropological Quarterly*, 31 (3). Pp. 61-72.
1960   "Social and religious culture of the Kalingas of Madulayan." *Scuthwestern Journal of Anthropology*, 16 (2). Pp. 174-190.

Smith, Peter
1968   "Age at marriage: Recent trends and prospects." *Philippine Sociological Review*, 16 (1-2). Pp. 1-16.

Smith, Robert, Charles Ramsey and Gelia Castillo
1963   "Parental authority and job choice: Sex differences in three cultures." *American Journal of Sociology*, 69 (2). Pp. 143-149.

Stoodley, Bartlett
1957a   "Some aspects of Tagalog family structure." *American Anthropologist*, 54 (2). Pp. 236-249.
1957b   "Normative attitudes of Filipino youth." *American Sociological Review*, 21, (5). Pp. 553-561.

Tangco, Marcelo
1951   "The Christian peoples of the Philippines." *Natural and Applied Science Bulletin*, 11 (1). Pp. 110.

Wood, Grace L.
1957   "The Tiruray." *Philippine Sociological Review*, 5 (2). Pp. 12-29.

CHAPTER X

The Japanese Family

MINAKO KUROKAWA MAYKOVICH

INTRODUCTION

This paper presents 1) the profile of Japanese society; 2) the traditional family system, including type, marriage and divorce, and child-rearing practices; 3) the changing Japanese family, consisting of causes, direction, and consequences of change; 4) family planning; 5) intermarriage; and 6) the future of the family.

Japan presents an interesting combination of both Eastern and Western culture, the traditional and the modern, the agrarian, and the industrial. She was the first industrialized country in Asia and has adopted Western culture rapidly since the late 19th century.

The feudal era ended in 1868 when the Meiji government centralized the political power through the Meiji Restoration. When the Japanese opened the door to Western influence, they realized the necessity of catching up with the Western countries, particularly for military purposes. An industrial revolution was undertaken by the central government together with the introduction of Western culture. However, the traditional elements remained deeply in the social structure and the value system of the Japanese.

Another epoch-making event in Japanese history toward Westernization was Japan's defeat in the second world war. American influence was remarkable after 1945 in democratizing the traditional Japanese society. The recovery from war damage has been extremely rapid and now Japan is competing with the U.S., USSR, and other nations in the international economic arena.

As far as the national income is concerned, the Japanese figure of $920,000,000,000 in 1967 exceeds the American figure of $658,000,000,000 (Nihon Tokei Nenkan, 1968). Of course, the national income alone is not a perfect indicator of the general socio-economic status of a society. The living standard of the general public in Japan is considerably lower than that in America. Agriculture supplied 12 per cent of the gross domestic product in Japan against 3 per cent in the United States, while industrial activity provided 29 per cent in Japan and 33 per cent in the United States in 1966. Twenty-seven per cent of the economically active population in Japan against 5.5 per cent in the United States are engaged in agriculture. This means that despite rapid industralization, Japan is still heavily dependent on agriculture, although 66 per cent of the total population are living in urban areas (*ibid.*).

Politically, Japan is a democratic country, although socialism is strong and the Communist Party is legal. According to the 1968 election, 278 out of 486 in the House of Representatives were Liberal Democrats, 137 Socialists, 31 Democratic Socialists, and four Communists. In the House of Councillors, 169 out of 250 seats were taken by Liberal Democrats, 64 by Socialists, 10 by Democratic Socialists, and 7 by Communists (*ibid.*).

As for the religious climate in Japan, the ranks of Christianity are numerically small. In 1967 there were about 766,000 Christians registered against 80,922,000 shinfoists and 81,492,000 Buddhists (*ibid.*)

If culture is divided into a material, tangible part and a non-material aspect, or instrumental and integrative parts, Japan has gone far in the direction of Westernization in the material and instrumental part, while retaining traditional Eastern elements in the non-material sphere of her culture. Religious orientations and family values are some of the most deeply seated factors in Japanese culture, hence most resistant to change.

The major objectives of this paper are to report the extent of change in the family system and values, and to delineate the borderline where traditional and modern family values coexist in the contemporary Japanese society. The paper consists of two major parts: the traditional Japanese family system and the contemporary family since 1945. Concerning the traditional family, historically dominant family types, marriage types, mate selection procedures, divorce procedures, and child-rearing patterns will be described. In the second part, changes in the family since 1945 are examined in terms of the causes of change, directions of change, and the consequences of these changes in society. Finally, attitudes and practices of family planning, and future implications of the family will be discussed.

The statistics used in this paper cover the period from 1920 to 1965 and were taken from the Japanese Census and from data collected by other authors. Data on attitudinal changes in contemporary Japan were gathered by the author in 1969 from three types of areas: rural, semirural and urban. Approximately 500 families in each area were contacted through the junior high schools, and children and their parents were interviewed. Although the data were gathered for a different research project, pertinent information was derived to describe contemporary family relations. In addition to this primary source, the secondary source of opinion polls taken by national opinion survey organization are utilized.

TRADITIONAL FAMILY SYSTEM

1. Family type

Structure and human relations in a family are governed by the dominant value a orientation in a given society In defining man's relation to man, Kluckhohn (1965) introduces a conceptual framework based on three relational orientations: the lineal, the collateral, and the individualistic. Where the lineal principle is most heavily stressed, it is group goals that are of primary concern to individuals, but there is an additional factor—continuity through time. Both continuity and ordered positional succession are of great importance when lineality dominates the relational system. Japanese society has been one with a relatively strong lineal stress (Kurokawa, 1968).

The institutional family of Japanese society is a lineal family, that is, a complex family with a singular principle of inheritance and residence. The lineal family extends its membership indefinitely to all the relatives along a direct line of descent. It is characterized by its clearly defined patterns of succession and residence, which incline toward patrilocality and patrilineality (Ariga, 1953;

Tamaki, 1953). The lineal family may include, in addition to the regular members of a nuclear family, grandparents or the parents of either the husband or the wife. Ideally, the parents and one of the offspring (usually the eldest son) are not separated upon the latter's marriage.

The oldest document in which there is information on the structure of the Japanese family goes back to A.D. 702. It is the *Koseki*, or register of households for Mino Province (Toda, 1953). In this and similar documents of this early period, the following types of households are distinguished: *Goko*—a regular household, recognized as an official, full-fledged and independent unit of society; and *Boko*—a dependent household, subordinate to *Goko*. There was a wide range in the size of a *Goko*—five to thirty members. That the nuclear family enjoyed little recognition as such is shown by the lack of any term for its designation and by the manner in which the members are groups, that is, the eldest son's nuclear family did not act as a unit, but was involved also with directive concern from the sister (Sano, 1958).

Before the war, there were some cases in the villages of collateral families. However, they were not based on the idea of the joint family but of the stem family. The stem family has historically been the typical family type in Japan in spite of fluctuations from time to time and from social class to social class. During the Tokugawa era (17-19C), the stem family was idealized among the warrior and upper classes but not among the farmers and the lower class. It was rather through the establishment of the Meiji Civil Code (1898), the emphasis on Confucian ideals, and the spread of the familistic nationalism based on the emperor that the ideal of the stem family was imposed over all the social classes (Koyama, 1962a; Ohashi, 1968).

During the Meiji restoration, however, the idea of the nuclear family was introduced from Western countries and gradually permeated Japanese society along with industrialization. It was in 1947 that the nuclear family was legally supported by the new Constitution and the new Civil Code. At present, the traditional stem family and the new nuclear family coexist. The process of nuclearization was slow between 1920 and 1960, but seems to be faster after 1960. As expected, the percentage of nuclear families varies according to occupation. In 1960, 70 per cent of non-agrarian families, 43 per cent of agrarian families, and 38 per cent of half-

agrarian families assumed the nuclear family type. It is noteworthy
that even among the farmers over 40 per cent reported nuclear
family types (Koyama, 1962b; Murai, 1965).

TABLE 1. *Family type (in percentages)*

Family type	1920	1930	1964
Nuclear family	60.0	65.1	69.0
Stem family	30.0	27.9	25.2
Collateral family	9.8	7.0	5.8

Sources. Takashi, Koyama, "Kazoku kosei no henka" ("Change in family
Composition"), Jinbum Gaku-ho. Tokyo Municipal University, 1962,
1961 No. 29.
Takashige Murai, "shotai no bunseki—Showa thirty-nine nen no shotai
kosei (Analysis of Household Composition, 1964)," Kosei no Shihyo, 1965,
12:15.

As far as the number of people per family is concerned, family size
did not change significantly between 1920 and 1955. A change began
to appear only after 1960 (Matsubara, 1964).

TABLE 2. *Family size*

Year	Number of People per Family
1920	4.89
1930	4.98
1940	5.00
1950	4.97
1955	4.97
1960	4.56
1965	4.08

Source. Japanese Census.

If we look at the change in the family composition over time, we
note a decrease of lineal descendants and the collateral members
in 1964.

TABLE 3. *Family composition (average number of people per family)*

Family member	1920	1950	1960	1964
Family head	1.00	1.00	1.00	1.00
Family head's spouse	0.80	0.78	0.78	0.79
Lineal descendant	2.14	2.54	2.21	1.91
Lineal descendant's spouse	0.13	0.12	0.14	0.12
Lineal ascendant	0.28	0.25	0.21	0.19
Other family member (collateral)	0.17	0.19	0.11	0.08
Servants etc.	—	0.07	0.02	0.02
Total	4.52	4.92	4.47	4.11

Sources. See *Supra*, Table 1.

2. Marriage and Divorce

In the premodern period, marriage patterns differed in various regions of the country. Before the Edo period (1600), the visiting marriage pattern was practiced among some people, according to which the husband visited his wife at her house in the evenings only and their children became members of the wife's family. The idea was that a woman belonged to a house and could not be separated. A man could visit more than one wife (polygyny), but the predominant marriage type was that of monogamy (Kikuchi, 1967; Yamamuro, 1970).

During the Edo period the patriarchal stem family was reinforced, which ascribed low status to women. Marriage meant that a woman would be given to the family of the man whom she was to marry. The purpose of marriage was to continue the family line by gividg birth to an heir. For men, polygyny was publicly recognized. For a man, it was accepted to have more than one wife or concubine, but chastity for women was emphasized. A woman lived with her husband's family. If she was not liked by her parents-in-law or could not give birth to an heir, she could be divorced even if the man and woman loved each other. If a wife could not give birth to a son, the husband sometimes took a concubine to have a son who would continue his family line.

In 1898 the Meiji Civil Code recognized monogamy as a rule, but the status of women remained low.

The number of marriages recorded per 1,000 total population changed little in Japan from the beginning of the 20th century to the beginning of the war of 1937-45. There were episodic fluctuations but no long-term trends. Divorce rates, in contrast, revealed a generally consistent downward trend (Taeuber, 1958). However, the rates alone do not reveal specific conditions under which divorces have taken place. In the prewar days, divorce was initiated by the man or by his family arbitrarily and mainly for the sake of family continuity. On the other hand, postwar divorce is increasingly becoming a mutual matter. According to the new Civil Code, women have equal rights concerning divorce, and as women gain economic independence they are less likely to avoid divorce when marriage is not working out to their satisfaction.

The codified laws of the Great Reform of the serenth and later centuries until the Civil Code of the 19th century prescribed family domination and individual submission in the selection of marriage partners, as well as the behavior of wives and the dissolution of marriages. The regulations of legal marriage were reasoned specifications rather than simple assertions of male prerogatives. If the head of the house was to be responsible for the veneration of ancestors, the continuity of the house, and the preservation of property, he had to control the marital selection of the son who was the heir and to guard against the dissipation of property or the disgrace of his name by his other children. Thus, marriages were arranged between families. The families concerned followed the procedure of requesting the go-between to assume the chief role in negotiations and the responsibility for the proper ceremonies. The intermediary's negotiations were considered by the heads of the families concerned. If interest was expressed on either side, arrangements were made for one or more opportunities to meet. Individual wishes were ignored for the interest of the family.

3. Child-rearing Practices

Lineal relations emphasize superior and subordinate positions in the exercise of authority. The family is considered important as a unit rather than as a system of interrelationships, and the family head is considered to be the symbol of the family as an integrated whole. Confucianism, with its instance upon absolute obedience of the children to their parents, as well as the complexities of family

TABLE 4. *Rates of marriage and divorce among Japanese in Japan, 1900-55 (per 1,000 total population)*

Period	Marriage	Divorce
1900-1904[a]	8.2	1.4
1905-1909	8.4	1.2
1910-1914	8.4	1.1
1915-1919	8.3	1.0
1920-1924	9.0	0.9
1925-1929	8.2	0.8
1930-1934	7.6	0.8
1935-1939	8.1	0.6
1940	9.2	0.7
1941	10.8	0.7
1942	9.1	0.6
1943	10.0	0.7
1947[b]	12.0	1.0
1948	11.9	1.0
1949	10.3	1.0
1950	8.6	1.0
1951	7.9	1.0
1952	7.9	0.9
1953	7.8	0.9
1954	7.9	0.9
1955	8.0	0.8
1956	7.9	0.8
1957	8.5	0.8
1958	9.0	0.8
1959	9.1	0.8
1960	9.3	0.7
1961	9.4	0.7
1962	9.8	0.8
1963	9.7	0.7
1964	9.9	0.7
1965	9.7	0.8
1966	9.5	0.8
1967	9.5	0.8

[a]Japan, including Okinawa, 1900-43.   [b]Area of the period.

Sources. 1912-42: *Jinko Dotai Takei*, Tokyo: Naikaku. Tokei-kyoku.

1943-49 and 1956-67: *Nihon Tokei Nenkan*, Tokyo: Sori-fu, Tokei-kyoku.

1950-54: *Kokumin Eisei no Koko. Kosei No Shihyo.* Tokyo: Kosei Tokei Kyokai.

1955: *Jinko Dotai Tokei Maigetsu Gaisu.* Tokyo: Kosei-sho, Eisei Tokei-bu, composition and the prevalent political system, affirmed the concentration of authority in the family head. Greater importance was attached to the parent-child relationship than to the conjugal relation. The latter was a matter of contractual relationship, which could be dissolved by the decision of the husband or of the families concerned, while the preant-child relationship, being a natural tie, could not be annulled. Until the birth of her first son, a wife was, in a sense, an outsider to the family group, since ties of blood, common ancestry, and shared childhood experience were thought to have stronger force than those generated by sexual relations (Morioka, 1968).

While children were young, they were well protected and supervised by parents, grandparents, brothers, and sisters. They were rarely left alone and were discouraged from engaging in venturesome activities. Children were considered helpless and immature by parents who fostered dependency needs in their offspring.

Absolute obedience to the parents was demanded of the children, who were supposed to be seen but not heard, and were not allowed to explain their behavior when disapproved by parents.

Patrilineal relations placed the status of women low and emphasized sex role differentiation. Thus, boys were expected to play a masculine role and to prepare themselves to be good providers by going to school and learning trades. On the other hand, education was not considered to be very important for girls, who were expected to learn domestic chores.

Collateral relations of the Japanese family system had two major consequences. Suppression of self-interest and or self-expression was vital to the harmonious operation of the family collectivity. Social systems in which individuals live in a complex hierarchical interdependence tend to inhibit personal expression of emotion. Any considerable personal range of affective spontaneity would tend to impinge on the status and interests of others and disturb the system as a whole. Thus, children were reared under psychological handicaps, at least if viewed from the present day doctrine of opportunity for full personality development.

The othre result of collateral relations on child-rearing practices is seen in the method of disciplining children. Ridicule and shame were used to compare unduly a misbehaving child with children of other families so that the former would feel ashamed of himself for having brought shame to his family. Any misconduct of an indivi-

dual brought shame to his family and he had to be punished for
that purpose. (Kurokawa, 1968).

THE CHANGING JAPANESE FAMILY

1. Causes of Change

Through contact with Western culture, traditional Japanese
society has undergone structural changes such as rapid industrialization and urbanization. Even in prewar Japan (about the late
1930s), before the so-called thought-control measures were tighten-
ed, such family-centered legislation was exposed to attacks from the
more liberal intellectuals. However, the Civil Code enacted in 1898
reflected accepted ideas of feudalism, and it was only after the
second world war that a change was evidenced. The Constitution
of 1948 liberated the family members from the authority of the
family, established equality between husband and wife, and assured
higher regard for the offspring than before (Matsumoto, 1960;
Sano, 1958).

Japan's defeat in the second world war had external and internal influences on the Japanese family. As an immediate consequence of the last war, American occupation effected a series of
legal changes relating to the family. A dominant value in the
traditional agrarian society was the biological perpetuation of the
patrilineal system. It was the duty of the eldest son rather than any
of the younger sons to perpetuate the family collectivity, and
hence he inherited the entire family property. The revised Civil
Code of 1948 under occupation guidance now stipulated equality in
inheritance for all children in the family. Such elimination of
primogeniture and legal equality, if it became widespread, would
increase individual rights and weaken family collectivety orientations.

Of the many social and economic reforms instigated by the
occupation to de-emphasize the traditional collectivity orientations
and to give greater importance to the individual, land reform in
rural Japan, dissolution of the financial monopoly (*zaibatsu*), and
the institution of a democratic educational system probably caused
the most basic changes. The fundamental principle of familistic
social structure of traditional Japan with the emperor as the head

of the family nation was replaced by equalitarian, individualistic orientations.

Along with these strucutural changes, was a more internal change. Immediately after the second world war, ideological change was most noticeable. There was widespread popular reaction against traditional values, and these values were replaced by emphasis on individualism. Writers repeatedly expressed the belief that the old values were outmoded, and that the country was moving toward individualism. In more recent years, however, there have been a number of attempts to describe the blending or clashing of traditional and modern value; and behavior patterns rather than a unilinear change from the traditional to the individual (Matsumoto, 1960).

2. Direction of Change

Caudill and Scarr (1962) data on family life in Japan do not support the view that the revolt against the traditional values has materialized. They found that Japanese prefer collaterality, lineality, and then individuality in the family work relations; they prefer collaterality, individuality, and lineality in wage-work relations. Their data indicate that the youths prefer collateral orientation to individuality orientation. The children rejected lineality when it was presented to them in a blatant form and instead chose collaterality. But in so doing, a certain fondness for lineal value orientation accompanied the dominant collaterality.

Family types. In May 1950, 7,056 married persons in a national sample were interviewed by the Mainichi Newspaper and asked their opinions as to dependency on their children in old age (Matsumoto, 18). Most of the respondents were planning to live in their old age as dependents with one of their children. A minority, one out of ten persons, stated explicitly that they planned to be independent of their offspring. A similar proportion who planned to live with their children pointed out their personal financial independence. At least one-fourth of the parents were concerned over the continuity of the family business, and said they would be dependent upon whichever child carried on the home enterprise. Cleavages in parent-child relations seemed slight as indicated by the relatively small number of respondents who aspired to follow the traditional pattern but felt that such dependency would not be realized.

TABLE 5. *"Do you plan to be dependent upon your children when you grow old?"* (*in percentages*)

	1950	1969			
		Total	Rural	Semi-rural	Urban
N	7,056	1,400	440	460	500
Will not be dependent	11.1	20	7	15	36
Will be dependent	29.1 ⎫				
	⎬ 45		73	43	20
Will be dependent on who-ever continues the family enterprise	25.6 ⎭				
Will live together but be financially independent	10.2	20	18	22	20
Would like to be dependent but unlikely	2.7				
Others	21.3	15	2	20	24

Source. 1950: Mainichi Newspaper opinion poll.
1969: Data gathered by the author.

By 1969 the proportion of those who reported their plan of independence from their children's support increased from 11 per cent to 20 per cent. Particularly among the urbanites the proportion is greater. More than a third of the respondents would rather be independent. Likewise, the percentage reporting their intentions to be dependent on their children in old age has decreased since 1950 and is considerably lower among the urban respondents.

In a 1954 survey of 2,000 persons, 20 to 25 years of age throughout Japan, 79 per cent expressed the opinion that the husband-wife relationship should be more important than the parent-child relationship (*Shukan Asahi*, 1954). Only 21 per cent gave the parent-child ties greater importance. The tendency in modern Japan appears to be the Western emphasis on husband-wife relations, at least verbally, and especially by the young, the urbanites, and the intellectuals. However, actual practices confirm traditional orientations. In the same survey, 500 persons over 60 years of age were interviewed and it was found that 82 per per cent of these aged people lived with one or more of their children, whereas only 15 per cent lived apart although their children were still alive.

One serious consideration is that of economic necessity for two married generations to live together. It is very expensive to establish a separate household for the newlyweds in an overcrowded country such as Japan. In 1960 Sori-Koho Shitsu surveyed a national sample of 3,067 people over 60 years of age concerning their old age (Sori-Koho Shitsu, 1960). As many as 82 per cent reported that they were living with their children, 3 per cent living with other relatives, 10 per cent living with their spouses alone, and 4 per cent living alone. Among those who were living with their children, only 5 per cent wished to live separately and 74 per cent expressed their desire to live with their children even if they could live separately. Only 9 per cent mentioned the possibility of rest homes, while 81 per cent said that they did not like to enter rest homes even if they were well accommodated there. Thus the older generations in contemporary Japan dislike rest homes and prefer to live with their children, but by the time the contemporary younger people reach old age they are likely to have different views from those of their parents.

Marriage. In February 1949, the National Public Opinion Research Institute (Toda and Fukutake, 1955) conducted a survey on the attitude of the Japanese males toward the traditionally arranged marriage. The data are based on a national stratified sample of 2,500 respondents with 2,229 returns. Despite legal abolition of the family head system, the majority of the respondents felt that the individual should consult with the family before taking final decisions concerning marriage. Although 33 per cent of the respondents felt that the individual should personally decide the selection of his marriage partner, 20 per cent of the respondents would leave the final decision entirely to the parents. The youngest age group, twenty to twenty-two years of age, felt most strongly that the individual should have most say concerning his marriage. The individual-oriented tended to be younger, urban, never married, and better educated; conversely, the family-oriented tended to be older, rural, already married, and less educated.

In the 1969 study of parents between the ages of thirty and fifty the tendency toward individual mate selection is seen in comparison to the data of 1949. Among the urbanites only 8 per cent mentioned parental choice and as many as 44 per cent preferred individual choice. Since the question was phrased as "How should one choose a mate for marriage?," the answers were given in a general form instead of reporting their own mate selection experience. Many modern Japanese emphasize the importance and desire of individual choice in the selection of a mate, but marriage to a great extent still seems to involve the consideration if not the final decision of the family collectively (Baber, 1958).

TABLE 6. *Mate selection* (*How should one choose a mate for marriage?*) (*in percentages*)

	1949	1969			
		Total	Rural	Semi-rural	Urban
	2,229	1,400	440	460	500
Individual choice	20	30	10	30	44
Discussion by both	40	50	45	56	48
Parental decision	33	15	40	9	8
Don't know	7	5	5	5	—

Sources. 1949: National Public Opinion Research Institute, reported in Toda and Fukutake, 1955.
1969: Data gathered by the author.

TABLE 7. *Reasons for divorce* (*in percentages*)

	1960					1949	
	Total	Love marriage	Arranged marriage	Friend marriage	Other	Tokyo	Saga
N	1,032	293	600	124	15	362	102
Husband has a girl friend	29	41	24	25	33	30	34
Wife has a boy friend	1	3	1	1	—		
Husband's physical cruelty	12	12	11	15	7		
Cannot get along with husband's family member(s)	13	14	14	11	7		
Cannot fit into husband's family life style	9	6	11	9	—	30	44
Personality incompatibility	35	28	39	33	47	24	22
Husband's illness	8	7	9	5	—		
Wife's illness	9	7	10	7	—		
Economic reasons	38	40	36	36	53	34	18
Other	21	20	22	24	7		

Some subjects marked more than one reason, hence the percentages do not add up to 100.
Source : 1949 : Ohama, 1953.
Ohashi, 1960.

An examination of the reasons given for divorce requests helps disclose the decreasing importance attached to the parent-child relationship between the married couple and the parents in the household. In 1949 a common reason for divorce was the incompatibility of the bride with the parent-in-law, usually the mother-in-law. The relationship of the husband and wife was secondary. Ohama (1953) presented figures on the reasons for divorces granted in 362 cases in the Tokyo Domestic Court in 1948, and 102 divorce cases in the Saga Domestic Court in Kyushu in 1949. Thirty per cent of the cases in Tokyo concerned unfavorable relations of either a husband or wife with the parents. In the less urbanized area of Saga Prefecture the proportion rose to 40 per cent.

According to Ohashi's (1968) study in 1960 the incompatibility with parents-in-law and their family life style was mentioned by only 22 per cent as the cause for divorce. The percentage of those giving this reason did not vary very much whether marriage was arranged or for love. The proportion of those who reported personality incompatibility increased between 1949 and 1960. Particularly those whose marriage was arranged by parents were likely to refer to incompatibility with the spouse (39 per cent) as the cause for divorce. The extent of the husband's infidelity contributing to marital dissolution remained similar between 1949 and 1960. It is interesting to note, however, that in the case of love marriage the proportion (41 per cent) of the said cause is greater than that in the arranged marriage (24 per cent). This seems to imply that if a woman marries for love, she is less tolerant of her husband's infidelity and more ready to dissolve the marriage than if she marries through family arrangement. Or, it may be that a love marriage is less stable than an arranged marriage as far as a man's emotional loyalty is concerned.

As the reasons for divorce indicate, the proportion of cases of the wife's infidelity is much smaller than that of the husband's infidelity. However, the 1955 study by Ohashi (1968) in Kobe concerning the authority relation between husband and wife indicates that out of 274 nuclear families and 190 stem families interviewed, 70 per cent were the autonomic type. In both nuclear and stem families the percentage of husband-dominant type was less than 5 per cent. It is interesting to note that the proportion of syncratic types with a high degree of shared, though equal authority is rela-

tively small. Liberated from the traditional patriarchal family relation, the Japanese in this sample seem to have gone to the other
extreme of the automatic type (Herbst, 1954; Koyama, 1967).

In the traditional Japanese family there was a clear sex role
differentiation, and the husband was not supposed to do household
chores. According to our 1969 study, in rural areas almost two-
thirds of the husbands did not participate in any household chores,
while in the urban area 39 per cent reported no participation. In
major and minor house cleaning which requires a certain amount
of physical strength, husbands are more likely to participate than
in cooking, doing dishes or laundry. Even in the city, laundry is
still predominantly a female chore.

TABLE 8. *Husband's participation in household chores*
(in percentages)

| Household chores | | 1969 | | |
| | | Rural | Semi-rural | Urban |
	No	440	460	500
None		62	44	39
Major cleaning		29	47	53
Cleaning		22	38	41
Cooking, dishes		15	12	17
Laundry		8	10	7

Source Data gathered by the author.

Parent-child relation. Since the war there have been many studies
of parent-child relations both by interviweing and by participant
observation. Dora (1958) and Vogel (1963) observed the differences
between the common patterns in the American middle class family
and in the modern Japanese family in which the husband is part of
the new bureaucratic organization. Although, in comparison to
other families, salaried-man families are in the forefront in breaking down the traditional system, the degree of breakdown has been
infinitesimal. The unique features of the salaried-man family are
the insulation of the family from the firm, the lack of participation
of husbands in households tasks, the narrow range of the wife's
social participation, and her close relationship with the children.

A pattern of actual behavior in the urban Japanese family that
seems congruent with the expression of collateral value orientation

was observed in a study of sleeping arrangements among 300 families. Caudill (1966) found that sleeping arrangements in Japanese families tend to blur the distinctions between generations and between the sexes, to emphasize the interdependence of individuals, and to underplay the potentiality for the growth of conjugal intimacy between husband and wife in favor of a more general familial cohesion. Caudill argues that the apparent over-crowding in the bedroom is only in part a function of lack of space—it derives more directly from the need for family bonds.

Caudill and Weinstein's (1966) observational study of mothers and infants in their homes in Japan and the United States indicates cultural differences still persistent at present. The American baby is more alone, more vocal, and more active in manipulation of his body and in the use of objects. The American mother talks to her baby more and seems to encourage more response and activity from him. In contrast, the Japanese mother rocks her baby more and talks to him less. Her actions seem directed toward soothing and quieting the baby rather than encouraging response and activity.

Vogel (1963) notes encouragement of a child's dependence in Japanese middle class families. Close physical contact of mother and child is seen in such practices as breast feeding, bathing, and sleeping arrangements. It is assumed that the child is afraid to be alone. The mother agrees that the outside world is frightening and that her presence can protect the child from the outside dangers. Although the mother is not consciously aware of her techniques, her attitudes and approach tend to arouse in the child a fear of making independent decisions and to create an anxiety about being isolated from family or friends. Goodman (1962) also observed that Japanese children are more responsive to adults' wishes and less concerned in determining their adult occupations and roles.

Decision-making processes between parents and children in various areas where studied by the author in 1969 comparing rural semi-rural, and urban samples on the degree of parental permissiveness in letting their children make decisions. As Table 9 indicates, urban parents are more lenient than rural parents in pressuring their children's study behavior. Urban parents are more strict with boys' study behavior than girls'. Because of the young age of the studied children, parents are in general strict about their children's working to earn money. In helping around the house, urban parents are lenient, although rural parents are fairly strict. In determining future plans, urban and semi-rural parents are considerably more lenient than rural parents. In the selection of friends, about two-thirds of the parents give freedom to their children. In matters of pocket money, urban parents are more lenient than rural or semi-rural parents.

TABLE 9. *Parental permissivensss in child's decision-making (in percentages)*

	1969					
	Rural		Semi-rural		Urban	
	Male	*Female*	*Male*	*Female*	*Male*	*Female*
Study	45	44	48	45	50	63
Work	33	40	41	38	42	32
Selection of friends	65	64	66	67	68	67
Pocket money	34	36	43	42	68	69
Help around house	35	40	42	43	64	65
Further plan	54	53	82	80	90	80

Source. Data gathered by the author.

Percentage permissive is measured by five-point scale of authoritarianism, permissive consisting of the top two points for permissiveness.

In short, the data indicate an increasing amount of permissiveness in parental control over the child's decision-making processes.

3. Consequences of Family Change in Society

In American society the loss of functions which used to be performed by the traditional extended family, due to increased division of labor and role specialization, has been deplored by many family sociologists. The nuclear family has lost the religious function because the church plays the religious role better than the family, has given up the educational function to schools, and the welfare role to the welfare organizations. In Japan the situation is slightly different. Industrialization did not destroy the extended family system but rather was supported by household labor contracted by large firms. In spite of industrialization and urbanization, the family had maintained various traditional functions, such as education and welfare. A sudden change of the family after the war was met by unprepared social institutions. Welfare organizations are not equipped to take care of old people or children of divorced parents. Public recreation organizations are not prepared to take care of many children who are squeezed out of the home because of their working mothers.

Thus, the immediate effect of family changes upon society is the development of various other institutions which are to take care of roles played by the traditional family. For instance, the change from the stem family to the nuclear family produced many old people who need protection outside the home of their children. The rise of women's status leading to the employment of females and a higher divorce rate has driven many children from the care of parents and requires the development of proper welfare, recreational, and educational organizations.

The most fundamental consequence of the changing Japanese family involves social structure and social values in general. Japanese traditional society was a familistic one, permeated by familistic collateral and lineal orientation (Kawashima, 1968). Everywhere, whether in occupational, educational or recreational situations, hierarchical pseudo-parents-child relations controlled social interaction. Disappearance of the familistic nature of social relations has positive and negative effects on individuals. On the one hand, the individual can determine his own life independently of his sense of obligation to his family. On the other hand, he has lost the shelter of collectivity behind which he could protect himself against hazards.

FAMILY PLANNING

After the surrender in August 1945, a baby boom followed as soldiers were demobilized and overseas civilians were repatriated to Japan. The extension of public health activities lowered the death rate. The high fertility rate and the reduced mortality rate made for a rate of natural increase of over 2 per cent a year. In the postwar period population problems have continued to be a major concern of the Japanese.

The Diet approved the Eugenics Protection Law which legalized abortion, contraception, and sterilization on 10 September 1948, and subsequently revised and liberalized the law three times. Child bearing which might result in injury to the health of the mother because of physical or economic reasons could be legally prevented by one or another means under the liberal Eugenics Law. The government sanctioned measures designed to prevent undue economic stress upon the family or injury to the health of mothers from repeated pregnancies.

Throughout Japan, the means of family limitation became available at the health centers to all the people. The use of contraception increased somewhat, but it was the number of abortions which increased tremendously. In 1933-37, the crude birth rate was 31 per 1,000; in 1954, it was below 20. This decline in fertility in postwar Japan has been the most rapid in the history of any modern nation (Amamo, 1955).

Approximately two-thirds of respondents interviewed in two national polls in 1949 (Asahi Nenkan, 1949a) on eontrol of pregnancy thought that birth control in general terms was a good thing. Fifteen per cent were opposed. However, when it came to the actual practice of contraception as a means of controlling fertility, the relationship was reversed. Although two-thirds of the national samples felt that birth control was desirable, from one-half to two-thirds of the married respondents never practiced any form of contraceptive techniques. According to the 1964 national opinion poll of married women of ages twenty to thirty-nine, the percentage of those using birth control has risen sharply. Only 25 per cent answered that they had never practiced it, while the rest has practiced some form of birth control during some time of their married life.

Although the production and distribution of contraceptives have greatly increased since the passage of the Pharmaceutical Affairs Low in 1948, abortions have been the more important aspect of population control in Japan. From 246,000 reported abortions in 1949, the total increased to over 1,000,000 induced abortions in 1954 (Amamo, 1955). Since the number of unreported abortions is great actual abortions are probably grossly understated.

In the 1949 Asahi survey (Asahi Nenkan, 1949b), a national sample of 3,500, of whom 87 per cent replied, was about abortion as a method for limitation of population increase. Nine per cent verbally expressed support for abortion as a means of controlling the number of children born. A third of the respondents stated their belief that abortion should not be permitted. An equal proportion, however, felt that such channels should be left open for cases of special circumstances, including elimination of hereditary illness, danger to mother's general health, etc. A similar trend was indicated in the poll conducted by the National Public Opinion Research Institute in 1951 (Sori-fu Koho-shitsu, 1951). Thirty-two per cent of the total respondents maintained that abortion was morally wrong even if the birth of the baby meant additional hardship for the family. In this same survey of married respondents in 1951, an effort was made to measure the extent of abortions. Twelve per cent of the married respondents admitted abortions, the great majority denied the practice, and about one-fourth refused or gave no answer. In the 1964 national survey of married women, as many as 41 per cent reported the practice of abortion and 58 per cent denied it. Resort to abortion is common in countries where strong motivations to limit fertility exists without a wide knowledge and availability of acceptable and effective techniques of contraception. In the 1964 survey 38 per cent of those who practiced contraception reported failure leading to pregnancy.

INTERMARRIAGE

For the most part, Japan does not face the dilemma of race, nor has she had a long history of admission of foreign elements in which to develop a melting pot tradition. Minority phenomena are regarded only as transitory or as problems to be obliterated as rapidly as, possible for the health of the society, ideally without residue. Therefore, the statistics and the problems of intermarriage in Japan, like those of low social classes generally, are poorly documented. Since racial minorities are ideological outside normal society, they have either been systematically ignored or information concerning them has been distorted.

Although racially homogeneous, Japan has had a problem of an "invisible race," *Burakumin* or *Eta* (Wagatsuma and De Vos, 1966). who are segregated at least in the critical respects of residence. marriage, and frequently occupation. They originated as an occupational group engaging in the slaughter of animals. which was considered to be most degrading in Buddhist philosophy. Unlike racial groups, *Burakumin* is not physically distinguishable but is an outcast in Japan. During the Tokugawa period outcasts were often not listed in census tabulations, and when they were, they were often entered separately from "people." It is only recently that the status of *Eta* began to be examined by social scientists and no systematic data are yet available. However, secession of *Eta* from the larger society has been such that few intermarriages could have taken place.

The first time in the history of Japan when a sizable foreign element was admitted to the country was after the defeat in the second world war. U.S. occupation soldiers were stationed in Japan and many of them married Japanese women. There were many precipitating factors to this intermarriage. First, the sex ratio in Japan after the war was unbalanced. Because of the loss of young marriageable men and married men, Japanese women in certain age brackets were left without eligible Japanese males. In addition to such a demographic factor, American soldiers presented attractive conditions to Japanese females. Economically, Americans stationed in Japan could maintain an upper class status. Culturally, American men's feminism was gratifying to the Japanese female. In turn, Japanese women's femininity was comforting to American soldiers away from home.

However, there are no official statistics (Office of Prime Minister, 1972) available documenting the extent of this intermarriage. For one thing, the legality of many of these marriages was questionable, as some American men had wives at home. There must have been many common law marriages. In addition to this ambiguity in the definition of intermarriage, there was another factor which could have impeded rigorous statistical investigation by the officials. The general sentiment toward such a union was so negative that there could have been reluctance to register these cases into the official records, which will remain forever. This is an author's speculation based on the previous example that *Eta* was not entered in the census.

War brides were viewed by Japanese as prostitutes who had sold their body and their Japanese spirit for the wealth and power of the winning nation. It was much later that intermarriage began to be recognized independent of the war. During the past two decades there appeared some, although still scanty, empirical data concerning attitudes toward intermarriage.

According to Suzuki's study (1969), based on a rural sample in 1943, social distance was least to Americans and Nisei (second generation Japanese Americans) and greatest to Negroes and Russians. Germans were fairly well liked, while the British and the Koreans were viewed as neutral, and the Chinese and the Filipinos were rated as unfavorable. The general tendency was the preference of Western Caucasians for fellow Asians. As marriage partners or close relatives, Americans were favored most, followed by the Chinese, the Koreans, and the Russians. Male and younger respondents were more likely to show tolerant attitudes toward intermarriage.

Wagatsuma's study (1967), based on an urban and predominantly middle class sample, showed a basic similarity to Suzuki's data on Caucasian preference. But preference was given to Caucasians in the order of British, French, Germans, Americans and Italians. The Koreans, Negroes and mixed Negroes were rated lowest.

TABLE 10. *Selection of marriage partner (Would you agree to allow your family member or close relative to marry_____?)*

	Disagree	Agree	Neither	No answer
British	34.4	13.4	49.3	2.9
French	34.8	11.1	50.8	3.3
German	34.8	11.8	47.4	6.0
American	36.3	11.1	48.1	4.5
Italian	36.7	8.2	51.8	3.3
Indian	50.8	7.0	40.0	2.2
Russian	48.9	5.6	44.0	1.5
Thai	43.7	11.1	37.1	8.1
Chinese	45.9	8.9	39.3	5.9
Indonesian	47.4	4.8	41.0	6.8
Filipino	37.1	5.1	40.7	17.1
Korean	62.2	4.4	29.6	3.8
Black	61.1	3.3	30.7	5.2
White mixed blood	40.7	10.4	38.9	10.0
Black mixed blood	61.9	6.7	28.9	2.5

Source. Hiroshi Wagatsuma and T. Yoneyama, *Henken no Kozo (Structure of Prejudice)*, Tokyo: NHK Books, 1967.

Long before any sustained contact with either Caucasoid Europeans or dark-skinned Africans or Indians, the Japanese valued white skin as beautiful and deprecated black skin as ugly (Wagatsuma,

1968). During the initial encounter with Caucasians, the Japanese felt alien to the whiteness of the Caucasian skin. However, the ambivalence toward the Western civilization was gradually focalized in the admiration, envy, sense of being overwhelmed or threatened, fear or disgust that were evoked in the Japanese mind by the image of a hairy giant with vigor and sexuality.

Thus, conceptually, the Japanese would prefer to marry Europeans or Americans to Asians, who have similar skin color and physical characteristics. In reality, however, Table 11 indicates the reverse fact. Between 1965 and 1969 approximately 80 per cent of the Japanese male intermarriage cases involved Korean females and only a low percentage included American women. Of course, the major problem is availability. Because of geographical proximity, there are many Koreans but few Americans and even fewer Europeans residing in Japan.

TABLE 11. *Number of marriages*

	1965	1966	1967	1968	1969
Total	954,852	940,120	951,748	956,312	984,142
Both Japanese	950,696	936,144	948,611	951,528	979,063
Husband Japanese	1,067	1,056	1,348	1,460	1,719
Wife: Korean	843	846	1,097	1,124	1,284
Chinese	121	115	139	176	206
European	19	30	40	—	—
American	64	43	53	53	80
Other	20	22	19	107	149
Wife-Japanese	3,089	2,920	3,137	3,324	3,360
Husband: Korean	1,128	1,108	1,157	1,258	1,168
Chinese	158	166	175	208	194
European	103	110	115	—	—
American	1,592	1,433	1,555	1,600	1,734
Other	108	103	135	258	264

Source. Ministry of Welfare, *Vital Statistics*, Tokyo.

However, in the case of Japanese women, a half of the intermarriage partners are U.S. males and a third Korean males. Apart from the demographic fact that there are more U.S. males than females residing in Japan, a psychological factor should be considered. Japanese males, who are socialized to play a dominant role, will find it difficult to marry a Caucasian female whom they admire but who feels inferior. On the other hand, Japanese females with a submissive role will rather be dependent on a Caucasian male whom they admire than on an Asian man.

The latter may even be a Japanese. In other words, some Japanese females may prefer Caucasian males to Japanese men. Indeed, the female exogamous rate is higher than male exogamy by two-to-one or three-to-one.

In general, intermarriage constitutes a very small percentage of Japanese marriages, namely, less than 0.5. The overall trend has remained constant during the recent five years. Thus, we can say that the Japanese are predominantly homogamous in terms of race and ethnicity. Although they may prefer Whites to Blacks, their adherence to their own race is still very strong.

FUTURE IMPLICATIONS FOR THE FAMILY

The future direction of the Japanese family appears to be toward the nuclear family with one or two children. On the basis of previous census data and the prevailing socio-economic conditions, Koseisho Jinko Mondai Kenkyu-jo (Ministry of Welfare, Population Research Institute) has predicted family size as follows (Morioka, 1968):

TABLE 12. *Anticipated family size*

Year	Family size
1970	3.78
1975	3.53
1980	3.33
1985	3.21
1990	3.11

Source. Koseisho Jinko Mondai Kenkyu-jo (Ministry of Welfare, Population Research Institute), quoted in Morioka, 1968, p. 32.

By the turn of the century, today's young people with modern views will reach old age and will practice ideas such as going to rest homes rather than depending on their children. At present, old people prefer to live with their children, who in turn feel protective of their aged parents. However, the younger people nowadays express the desire to be independent of their own children.

The birth rate has been declining since the widespread adoption of birth control. The idea that children are assets in an agrarian economy or during the war has been replaced by the desire for a higher living standard and a higher educational level for a smaller number of children. Thus, the stem family with several children will be rare by the end of the century.

Mate selection will be more and more an individual choice. At present, most young people consult with their parents and frequently honor their final decision. This consultation pattern will not disappear in one generation, but emphasis will be placed on the opinion of the individuals to be married rather than on parental advice. In conjugal relations the status of women will be raised and the traditional sex role differentiation will be minimal. The husband's participation in household chores and the wife's employment outside the home will lead to relative individual autonomy. The number of divorces based on personality incompatibility and husband's or wife's infidelity will be increased as romantic love becomes more important than the continuity of the family line.

In parent-child relations filial piety and emotional interdependence will be replaced by individualistic orientations. Children will no longer be considered to belong to the house but will be regarded as independent individuals. In short, lineal and bilateral orientations will be replaced by individualistic attitudes in family relations by the time today's young people reach old age.

The above predictions are based on the historical trends in Japanese society. Under the Tokugawa regime during the 17th through 19th centuries the familistic structure of the society and the patriarchal stem family system based on Confucian doctrines were reinforced by the warrior class, which has had a lasting impact on the Japanese family. During the Meiji Restoration (1868), political power moved from feudal lords to the emperor government. The Meiji government realized the necessity of catching up with the Western material culture, and hence encouraged the introduction of Western ideas, supported industrialization, and promulgated the new constitution and new civil code. However, the contents of the new laws merely reinforced traditional familistic ideas. Westernization, industrialization, and urbanization affected only the external, material aspects of the Japanese culture and left family values almost intact.

The real change took place as a result of Japan's defeat in the second world war. The psychological effects of the loss took the form of distrust of traditional values. The American occupation imposed a structural change in Japanese society. Immediately after the end of the war (1945), there was a reaction by the Japanese against traditional values expressed verbally through the mass media, writings, and opinion polls. However, by 1960 (Matsumoto, 1960), the postwar trend toward individualization subsided and the traditional collectivity orientation was observed as a predominant feature of the Japanese family.

It was after 1960 that significant changes in family structure and values began to appear, such as the decline in family size; the increase in the divorce rate due to personality incompatibility, including conflict with in-laws; and individualistic orientations in conjugal as well as parent-child relations. The changes since 1960 are not the result of drastic measures such as the new political regime or foreign occupation, but rather a gradual process along with the global changes of urbanization, industrialization, and individualization. Therefore, it is possible to predict that the changes taking place at present will continue for another generation. For the first time in Japanese history, the family is going through an evolutionary change instead of a revolutionary one.

SUMMARY AND CONCLUSION

Traditionally, Japanese society has been a familistic one with lineal and bilateral orientation. The individual was subject to the interests of the family collectivity, which took the form of a patriarchal stem family. It was this familistic nature of the society that facilitated the industrialization of the Asiatic agrarian economy within a generation and the adoption of the Western material culture in the 19th century.

The fundamental change in family values was imposed by the defeat in the second world war (1945) and the American occupation. The new constitution and civil code stressed the importance of individual rights at the expense of the family collectivity. Although older people still adhere to traditional values, the younger urbanites are being individualized. Even after the immediate shock and reaction as a result of the loss of the war, the tendency toward the individualistic, nuclear family was persistent and even intensified.

Now it has become the force of evolution, not of revolution, and is expected to endure for some time. By the turn of the century, the Japanese family will assume a small nuclear form consisting of individuals with equal rights.

REFERENCES

Amano, Fujiko
  1955 "Family planning movement in Japan." *Contemporary Japan*, 23 (October-December). Pp. 760-780.
Ariga, Kizaemon
  1953 "Nippon Kodai Kazoku" (Japanese Ancient Family) in K. Tanabe (ed.), Kazoku (Family). Tokyo: Sekisen-sha.
Baber, Ray E.
  1958 *Youth Looks at Marriage and the Family: A Study of Changing Japanese Attitudes.* Tokyo: International Christian University Press.
Caudill, William, and David W. Plath
  1966 "Who sleeps by whom? Parent-child involvement in urban Japanese families." *Psychiatry*, (November). Pp. 344-366.
Caudill, William, and Harry A. Scarr
  1962 "Japanese value orientations and culture change." *Ethnology*, (January). Pp. 53-91.
Caudill, William, and Helen Weinstein
  1966 "Maternal care and infant behavior in Japanese and American urban middle class families." *Yearbook of the International Sociological Association.*
De Vos, George, and H. Wagatsuma
  1966 Japan's Invisible Race. Berkeley: University of California Press.
Dore, R.P.
  1958 *City Life in Japan.* Berkeley: University of California Press.
Goodman, Mary Ellen
  1962 "Values, attitudes, and social concepts of Japanese and American children" in Bernard B. Silberman (ed.), *Japanese Character and Culture.* Tucson: University of Arizona Press.
Herbst, P.G.
  1954 "Conceptual framework for studying the family" in Oeser, O.A., and S.B. Hammond (eds.), *Social Structure and Personality in a City.* New York: Macmillan.
Kawashima, Takeshi
  1968 "Nihon Shakai no Kozoku-teki Kosei (Familistic Structure of Japanese Society). Tokyo: Nihon Hyoron-sha.
Kikuchi, Sachiko
  1967 Kazoku Kankei no Shakaigaku (Family Sociology). Tokyo: Sekai Shoin.

Kluckhohn Florence R.
   1965 "Dominant and variant value orientations" in *Clyde* Kluckhohn and Henry A. Murray (eds.), *Personality in Nature, Society and Culture*. New York: Alfred A. Knopf. Pp. 342-360.

Koyama, Takashi
   1962a *Gendai Kazoku no Kenkyu* (Study of Modern Family). Tokyo: Kobundo.
   1962b "*Kazoku kosei no henka* (Change in family composition)." *Jimbun Gaku-ho*, Tokyo Municipal University, 29.
   1967 *Gendai Kazoku no Yakuwari Kozo* (Role Structure in Modern Family). Tokyo: Baibu-kan.

Kurokawa, Minako
   1968 "Lineal orientation in child rearing among Japanese." *Journal of Marriage and the Family*, 30 (February). Pp. 129-136.

Motsumoto, Yoshiharu S.
   1960 "Contemporary Japan: The individual and the group." *Transactions of the American Philosophical Society*, 50 (January). Pp. 1-75.

Matsubara, Haruo
   1964 *Gendai no Kazoku* (Modern Family). Tokyo: Nihon Keizai Shimbunsha.

Morioka, Kiyomi
   1968 *Kazoku Shakai-gaku* (Family Sociology). Tokyo: Yuhikaku.

Murai, Takashige
   1965 "*Shotai no bunseki-Showa 39 nehn no shotai kosei*" (Analysis of household, 1964). *Kosei no Shihyo*, 12. P. 15.

Office of Prime Minister
   1972 Official letter notifying the author the absence of data.

Ohama, Kideko
   1953 "*Kaji jiken kara mita tazoku no tenshon*" (Family tension as viewed from domestic cases) in *Nihon Jimbun Kagaku-kai, Shakaiteki kincho no Kenkyu* (Studies in social tensions), Yuhikaku 62. P. 75.

Ohashi, Kaoru and Kokichi Masuda
   1968 *Kazoku Shakaigaku* (Family Sociology). Tokyo: Kawashima Shoten.

Sano, Chiye
   1958 "Changing values of the Japanese family." *Anthropological Series*, 18. Washington, D.C.: The Catholic University of America.

Suzuki, Saburo
   1969 *Jinshu no Henken* (Racial Prejudice). Tokyo: Kinokuniya.

Taeubar, Irene B.
   1958 *The Population of Japan*. New Jersey: Princeton University Press.

Tamaki, Hajime
   1953 *Nihon Kazoku Seido-ron* (A Theory on the Japanese Family System). Kyoto: Horitsu Bunka-sha.

Family in Asia

410

Toda, Teizo
1953 *Kazoku Kosei* (Structural Organization of Families). Tokyo: Kobundo.

Toda, Teizo, and Tadashi Fukutake
1955 *Kazoku-kekkon* (Family-marriage). Tokyo: Matsuo shoten.

Vogel, Ezra F.
1963 *Japan's New Middle Class*. Berkeley: University of California Press.

Wagatsuma, Hiroshi
1968 "The social perception of skin color in Japan" in John H. Franklin, *Race and Color*. Boston: Beacon Press.

Wagatsuma, Hiroshi and T. Yoneyama
1967 *Henken no Kozo* (Structure of Prejudice). Tokyo: NHK Books.

Yamamuro, Shuhei, and T. Himeoka
1970 *Gendai Kazoku no Shakai-gaku* (Sociology of Modern Family). Tokyo: Baihu-kan.

Statistics and National Opinion Survey

Asahi Shimbun
1949b "Sanji seigen o do miru?" (Views on birth limitation) *Asahi Nenkan* (Asahi Yearbook).

Japanese Census
Jinko Dotai Tokei (Demographic Statistics). Tokyo: Nihon Naikaku Tokei-kyoku.

Jinko Dotai Tokei Maigetsu Gaisu. Showa-30-nen (Demographic Statistics Monthly), 1956. Nihon Kosei-sho. Eisei Eokei-bu, No. 117.

Kosei no Shihyo (Welfare Index)
1954 "*Kokumin Eisei no Kokyo, Showa 28-nen*" (National Welfare Statistics, 1954) 1. P. 7.

Mainichi Newspaper Opinion Poll, 1950.

Nihon Tokei Nenkan (Japanese Statistical Yearbook). Tokyo: Nihon Sori-fu, Tokei-kyoku.

Shimbun Yoron Chosa Renmei
1949 "*Sanji chosetsu* (Birth control)" Asahi Nenkan (Asahi Yearbook)
Shukah Asahi (Asahi Weekly), 25 July 1954.

Sori-fu Koho-shitsu
1951, 1968, 1966-Office of Prime Minister, General Information. Public Opinion Survey.

CHAPTER XI

Summary and Conclusions

MAN SINGH DAS and PANOS D. BARDIS

In this brief concluding chapter the editors will attempt to summarize some of the important points made in the preceding chapters on the various Asian family systems. The purpose here is to tie together the characteristics of these systems by providing the reader with a short summary of the changes that have taken place within each individual family structure. The material presented in simplified form can then be used for comparative purposes.

THAILAND

A large percentage of families in this nation live a peasantlike existence in rural agricultural areas. Smith reports that the nuclear family is the dominant family form, although limited extended and traditional extended families are also quite common. The kindred, a grouping of kinsmen other than the dominant small family unit, provides social ties and reciprocal economic aid through mutual help with the rice crops. The kindred takes parts in rites of passage, marriage ceremonies, or any communal work. Mate selection is carried out by the young people themselves, although the couple must secure the approval of their parents before the marriage occurs. Young married couples are often found to live with their parents until they are able to achieve economic stability and learn thoroughly the business of rice farming. There is an unusual tendency toward equality of the sexes in rural Thai subcultures, with men and women performing many tasks interchangeably. But the male still retains ritual superiority, based primarily on Buddhist religious beliefs. A great deal of respect is accorded to older persons. Almost all socialization and education of children take place within the family unit. In contrast to the peasant orientation in the rural areas, the urban population in the nation's capital displays a life style similar to that of the American middle class. Education in formal institutions is greatly valued, and occupations are distinctly separated from the family. Family planning and birth control programs have been established by the government and seem to be gaining acceptance within the general populace. Smith believes that relative to Western societies, the tempo of social change in rural Thailand is very gradual. The population has grown rapidly in the rural areas, which has led to a situation where many families are now landless and must work as laborers for those who own the land. This has had an effect on the kindred units, because mutual exchange and reciprocity are not possible when many do not have anything to exchange. Childbearing patterns may be modified by an increasing number of women joining the labor force. In general, nearly all aspects of Thai rural life are contained within the family structure.

AFGHANISTAN

Afghan society, according to Hanifi, is overwhelmingly rural-agricultural. A very small proportion of the people live in cities. The fundamental unit of Afghan society is the extended family. The Islamic cultural tradition emphasizes complete loyalty to the family, and gives the family unit a vital role in social, economic, and political matters. Family elders are respected and the well-being of the family is placed above individual goals. The extended family in Afghanistan is patrilocal, with the sons customarily bringing their wives into the father's house. Although the full extended family is the ideal, short life spans tend to preclude its occurrence in many instances. The difference between men and women is emphasized in every conceivable way, particularly by the strict division or labor. Women are expected to follow the dictates of their fathers and husbands unquestioningly. This is a truly sexist society. A successful marriage is not measured in terms of good personal relationships, but instead on the basis of procreation of healthy sons. Wives who are infertile or bear only daughters are not valued in this society. The relationship between brothers is often much closer than that between husbands and wives. The wife's relationship with her mother-in-law is of crucial importance for the stability of her marriage. As an event, marriage is the most expensive, elaborate ceremony in rural and urban life. It is quite common for a man to marry his patrilineal and matrilineal cross-cousins. Parents of the boy, especially the father, theoretically control selection of the bride, although in reality the boy has a great deal to say about his perspective mate. The girl's "honor" is of utmost importance. She should have no previous interest in, or contact with, the opposite sex. Divorce does occur and is acceptable in Afghan society.

INDIA

The subcontinent of India is located in the southwestern region of Asia and has a population of about 600,000,000. Approximately 60 per cent to 75 per cent of the people live in rural villages, the Indian economy being predominantly agrarian. The Indian people are highly heterogeneous in terms of their racial-ethnic, linguistic, and religious backgrounds. The Indian family, which is predominantly joint or extended, has remained remarkably stable despite some marked and drastic social, political, economic, and religious changes the country has gone through over the last thirty years. The family has retained its primarily joint or extended characteristics. In general, the Indian family has the following structural features: In the cyclical family pattern, that is, joint family—nuclear family—joint family, landowners maintain the multicouple life style for a longer time while noncultivating landowners retain this family pattern for a shorter period; landless laborers tend to adhere to the extended family system for at least a while, despite the hindrances of early mortality and independent wives. The socialization process is composed of a series of ceremonies beginning with the bathing and naming of the infant.

Marriages are highly endogamous and arranged by parents or other relations. But the importance of intercaste and interreligious marriage is increasing, and the general attitude of the members of the castes and religious groups conceived in such unions is one of non-opposition, tolerance, or indifference. Those who oppose inter-caste and interreligious marriages do so out of their ignorance, pre-judice, or ethnocentrism.

The implication is that, as intercaste and interreligious marriages increase in number, they would help to wipe away caste and reli-gious distinctions, discrimination, and segregation. As India gra-dually moves toward industrialization and urbanization, the traditional caste system will gradually become unstable with secular norms opposing and replacing older Hindu religious precepts. This social change will alter the rigid attitude of people toward intercaste and interreligious marriages.

Some of the changes which have recently taken place in the joint family are: The freedom of children is greater than in the past; parental authority clashes are increasing and are likely to become much more common; the Indian family is now failing as a "social security system," and this family function is being transferred over to other social groups and institutions; the Indian family is also failing as an "emotional security system"; mate selection by romantic love and by the partners concerned is more prevalent; the dowry system is declining; residential and geographical mobility is becoming more dominant; there is much change in household types; and young people are becoming better educated than their parents.

Indian women are changing their traditional roles in society. They are no longer thinking of themselves as childbearing agents. They are moving out of their homes and choosing careers in lieu of marriage, thus becoming working members of society.

PAKISTAN

Here again there is a rigidly defined sexual division of labor. The extended family is the ideal, but perhaps more important is *biraderi*, or large kinship group. Members of the *biraderi* will gather to celebrate events such as births and marriages, and to assist in the mourning of the dead at a funeral. There is an intricate system of favors and obligations which includes a system of gift-giving. The Muslim who succeeds in business may be expected to provide for his less fortunate relatives. As modernization and urbanization increase in Pakistan, Korsin feels that the *biraderi* will weaken and there will be a trend toward individualism. This has already hap-

pened to some extent on account of extensive male migration that
has taken place in the past few years. The highly institutionalized
sexual segregation in Pakistan known as *purdah* will also begin to
break down as urbanization takes place. As it stands now, some
women still wear veils and are totally segregated from any type of
contact with any males outside of their immediate families. It is
felt (in Islamic philosophy) that women must be fully and constantly protected from the sexual advances of males. Girls are taught
to be docile and obedient and to defer to male members of the
family. They are socialized to depend on the male and not to
develop any self-reliance. An increasing number of women in the
labor force in urban areas may serve to hasten the demise of the
purdah. Endogamous marriage is still a common practice, with
many of the Muslims marrying their first or second cousins. Most
marriages are still arranged by the parents. The government in
Pakistan has sought to implement programs in family planning,
although some conservative religions have objected. Korsin reports
that Pakistan has one of the lowest divorce rates in the world.

IRAN

Traditionally, mate selection has been kept within the family unit,
with first cousin marriage preferred. Arranged marriages are also
fairly common. Individual selection of mates is found only in the
large cities, and parental approval is still obtained even in these
cases. There are several types of marriage in Iran, including a temporary union which is somewhat similar to Western concubinage
or prostitution. The permanent forms of marriage include both
monogamy and polygyny, although the former is more prevalent.
A large age gap is often found between spouses, with the husband
being anywhere from fifteen to twenty years older than the wife.
Girls often marry quite young, with the legal age for females to
marry now set at fifteen. Couples may live with their in-laws during
the first year of marriage, patrilocal residence being more common
than matrilocal. Although Iran is another sex-segregated Islamic
society, changes brought on by industrialization have improved the
status of women and will affect the Iranian family. Women are
being educated in the urban areas, and some are finding white-
collar jobs, thus securing a certain amount of economic indepen-

dence. National family planning has been instituted. Widowhood is a big problem in Iran, due to the large age gap between husbands and wives. Widows are often left destitute or must rely on their extended families for support.

CHINA

A great many changes have taken place in the Chinese family, particularly since the communist take over in 1949. In traditional Chinese society the family was the chief economic unit and family interests came before the individual or the nation. Now the nation is seen as a "big socialist family," and the interests of the Communist Party take precedence over those of the family. The small nuclear family has replaced the large extended family. Marriages were formerly consummated at an early age, arranged by parents, and romantic love was disfavored, but now the individual has freedom of marital choice, late marriage is more common, and compatibility of personalities and ideological beliefs is the major criterion for mate selection. The old family structure was patriarchal, patrilineal, and patrilocal, women being subjugated to men and the clan having authority over the individual. Now the family is ideally democratic, bilateral, and sexually equalitarian, and the clan has no claims over the family or the individual. In modern China the family lineage, ancestor worship, and status ascription have been deemphasized, and the family is now secularized, with the stress being on individual achievement. The individual's social and cultural life is now mainly outside of the family. Birth control is also strongly advocated. Child brides and prostitution are prohibited by law, and monogamy is the approved marital form. Woman is free to divorce and remarry. The husband-wife relationship has replaced the father-son relationship in modern patterns of family interaction. The parent-child relationship is further viewed as one of comradeship, although it was formerly regarded as one of complete obedience on the part of the child.

KOREA

Traditionally, the patrilineal and patrilocal nuclear family units formed clan villages that were the primary economic units. There were sharply differentiated social classes. Polygyny was commonly practiced in the upper classes, and women were dependent upon, and submissive to, men. Married sons brought their wives into the households of their parents and grandparents. The traditional family was only a part of the clan, and the clan council was responsible for recreation, religion, education, welfare, punishment, marriage arrangements, funeral services, and village security. Marriages were arranged and divorce was considered disgraceful. Large families were desirable to supplement the village labor force, and child training was rigid. Ancestor worship was common, and the family itself was valued above any one individual. In modern times, the state has assumed a great deal of power, and it deals directly with the individual and bypasses the family altogether. Non-familial institutions are assuming roles that were formerly the sole province of the family. Big industry has replaced the clan village handicrafts; government schools have replaced the clan schools; and village defense and law enforcement have been taken over by the police and the military, respectively. The old extended family structure is rapidly crumbling. Problems may develop on account of there rapid changes, including an increase in the rate of divorce, dissension, and separation. Chang feels that too rapid a change in the family structure may have a deleterious effect on Korean society.

PHILIPPINES

The Filipinos are a highly heterogeneous people in terms of their racial-ethnic, linguistic, and religious backgrounds. The Filipino family has remained remarkably stable despite some major and radical social political, economic, and religious changes that the country has undergone during the past several centuries. The family has retained its predominantly Malayan characteristics. Its main structural features are as follows:

It has a bilaterally extended kinship system and an age-based hierarchy of authority; relationships between husband and wife are highly egalitarian; Christian marriages are monogamous while non-Christians are polygamous; legal separation, but not divorce, is allowed among Christians, while both are permitted among non-Christians; mate selection is based mostly on the romantic love

418 *Family in Asia*

principle, plus parental approval; endogamy stressing locality, class, linguistic—ethnic and religious characteristic is generally practised, but there are no rigid norms defining the field of eligibles; and finally, there are no set rules of residence for the young married couple.

The Filipino extended family is viewed as a built-in mechanism for facilitating geographical and social mobility for its members by providing shelter and other material assistance to relatives who aspire to improve their socio-economic status by entering the non-agricultural labor market by going to college in the town or city.

JAPAN

Of all the countries discussed in this book, Japan is the most highly industrialized and urbanized. The traditional Japanese society was family-centered with lineal and collateral orientation. The major family form was the patriarchal stem family. The individual was not so important as the overall family reputation and honor. The fundamental change in family values was imposed following the defeat of Japan in the second world war. It was then that the Japanese people accepted the Western industrial model and began to approximate the Western nuclear family life style. Maykovich predicts that the future direction of the family in Japan appears to be toward a nuclear family with one or two children. She also feels that there will be a trend away from old people's living with their children, placing the care of the elderly in the hands of the state. The birth rate is declining as birth control methods are becoming common. Mate selection will be more and more by individual choice, although at present most couples still consult with their parents. In parent-child relationships, emotional interdependence will be replaced by individualistic orientations. The divorce rate in Japan is increasing as the family structure changes. It should be noted that the Japanese have succeeded more than many other Asian nations in incoporating some of their traditional values into the framework of the modern nuclear family.

CONCLUSIONS

Having reviewed the basic characteristics and changes taking place in the family structures of a diverse group of Asian nations, we can now summarize some of the general trends that have resulted and will continue to emerge as industrialization, urbanization, and modernization proceed. A brief list might include trends toward a greater degree of: 1) equalitarian family relations, with less sexual segregation and limited subjugation of women to an inferior status; 2) emphasis on individualism and independence; 3) greater differentiation and specialized functioning of social institutions; 4) life in an urban setting; 5) birth control and family planning; 6) social mobility; 7) marital disruption and divorce; 8) neglect and improper care for the elderly; 9) formal education for children; and 10) governmental influence on family activities.

INDEX

Abortion in India, discussion on, 159-164; findings of, 156-164; laws in relation to, 152-153; methodology for, 152, 155-156; problems of, 153-154

Afghan family, analysis of, 412-413; attitude towards sex, 63; birth of a daughter and father's reaction to, 53; brother-brother relations, 51; brother-sister bond, 51, 54-55, 66; brothers' wives relations, 51; child-rearing among Pushtuns, 60-68; denial of masturbation in, 63; divorce in, 59-60; ecological factors, 48; economic factor, 49-50; enculturation and socialization in, 51; extended family, 48-49; proportion of, 50; father-son relations, 51,53; father-daughter relations, 51; generational distinctions of, 51; girls' marriage system in, 53; husband legitimate authority, 51-55; husband-wife relations, 51-52; mother-daughter relations, 51; mother-son relations, 51; patricentic, 51; portrait of, 47; resources of, 50; sister-sister relations, 51; social structure of, 48-49; Westernization, impact of, 47-48; women's relationship with mother-in-law, 55

Afghan marriage, 48, 51; age of, 58; and bride role, 55; and sex roles, 55-59; choice of, 57; cost of wedding, 56; mate selection, 57; wedding ceremony, 56-59

Afghan mother, suggestion and advice to young people, 57-58

Afghan society, characteristics of, 47

Afghan women, their role after marriage, 56; household activities of, 51; divorce rights, 56; inheritance rights, 56; rate of infertility and miscarriage among, 50; role of, 51

Afghanistan, background of, 47-50; cultural differences among, 47; geographical position of, 47; infant mortality rate in, 50; population of, 47; socio-cultural diversity in, 47

Age of Consent Act of 1881 (India), abolition of, 113

All-China Democratic Women's Federation (1949), formation and membership of, 263

All India Women's Conference, role of, 114

All Pakistan Women's Associations (APWA), aim of, 192-194; membership of, 192; interim constitution of, 193-194

American family and Korean family, compared, 335-340; modern birth control movement in, 324-325

Asian, definition of, 2

Asian family, convention diversion of, 3; stages of, 3

Asian societies, theory of, 3
Asian theology vs western, 5-6

Bang Chang Study (Thailand), suggestions on family conflict and dissolution, 37-38
Bangkok University, role in family planning, 39-40
Biraderi (Pakistan), definition of, 174; role of, 174-177; *see also* Pakistan
Birth control movement in American and Korean family, 324-340

Caste system in India, modernization effect of, 85; political reforms, 85
Child Marriage Abolition Act of 1860 (India), 112
Chia concept (China), 247-248, 248n, 273
China's collectivization Program (1956), beginning of, 262
China's textile industry, impact of, 245
Chinese civil code (1931), 258
Chinese Communist Party, and social reform in marriage law, 258-262; revolutionary changes by, 246
Chinese Cultural Revolution, 272; aim of, 246; starting of, 265; turmoil of, 266
Chinese family, analysis of, 416; abolition cases, 267; and family relations, 251-252; and marriage reforms, 258-262; and Western nuclear family compared, 246; birth control campaign, 268-269; change in the economic conditions, 245; *Chia* concept in, 247-248; child marriage, prohibition of, 259; Ch'ing code, 255; clan functions in, 251; condition of life in rural, 248, 248n; Confucian model, 247; concubine footbinding and prostitution practice, 254;

concubinage disappearance of, 266; Cultural Revolution impact on, 265-266; divorce, 259, 266; divorce reasons, 261; during Ch'ing regime, 245; educational campaign for modernizing of, 246; end of footbinding system in, 257; extended, 249; father-son identification in, 252; female infanticide practice in, 252; form and size of, 248-250; functions of, 250-251; 271-272; husband-wife relationship, 269-270; industrialization impact on, 245; internal structure of, 251-252; interplay between ideology and pragmatism, 246; joint-fraternal, 249; marital disputes statistics, 260-261; mother-in-law and daughter-in-law relations, 270-271; no place of love in, 255, 266; nuclear, 249; past, present and future of, 272-275; *pater familias*, 249; people's communes, impact on, 262-264; prostitution, common among, 248n; remarriage of widows, 259; revolution, background impact on, 245-247; sex-equality, 259, 269; socialization of children, 264, 272; socialization of domestic work in, 264; structure of, 270-271; traditional, 247-248; wedding celebration, 270; Western cultural impact on, 245
Chinese female education, co-education setting up of, 258
Chinese feminist movement, 250
Chinese intellectuals, impact of, 245
Chinese kinship structure, 251
Chinese marriage, analysis of, 267-268; age of, 268; bride price practice prohibition of, 259; sex equality, 259; under the new civil code, 258
Chinese Marriage Law of 1950, 258-262; 273; passing of, 246; promulgation of, 259; social reforms,

258-262; social and political implications of, 259-262; spirit of, 263

Chinese Marriage Law movement 261, 266

Chinese Nationalist Civil Code (1931), 246

Chinese Natianalist movements, female students participation in, 258

Chinese people's communes, 262-265; advantages of, 263; failure of, 265; formation of, 264; launching of, 262; objectives of, 262-263; number of women worked in, 263; slogan of, 263; women membership of, 264

Chinese women, active participation in nationalist movements, 258; agricultural occupation of, 253; and marriage reforms, 258-262; constitutional rights to, 257-258; divorce rate in, 256, 258, 269; economic and educational facilities for, 245, 258; emancipation, and the communes, 262-264; footbinding practice, 245-253; infanticide practice, 252-252n; industrial force statistics, 263, 263n; low status of, 253-254; political status of, 258; position in the husband s family, 253-254; primary duty after marriage, 253; relationship between wife and mother-in-law, 253; sexual liberation, 258; status of, 252-254

Chinese women's organization, abide by the *Wu-Lao*, 263; peasants, 263; trade unions, 263

Christian and non-Christian inter-religious marriages in India, 98-107; age differential factors, 100-101; analysis of, 105-107; educational differences in, 101-102; field of specialization, 101-103; findings of, 100; limitations of, 107; nature of, 99; number of children born, 104-105; places of

origin, 102-103; religions participation of, 104-105; statistics of, 99

Christian Filipino marriage, 364-365; norms of, 365; divorce not allowed, 366

Christian Filipino population, 345, 346

Civil Marriage Act of 1872 (India), 112

Confucian teaching, 208, 246, 292, 257, 309, 387

Congress session, Indian women's role in, 115

Developing economies, concept of, 170

Developing societies, concept of, 170

Development, concept of, 170

Dowry Bill of 1960 (India), 117

Education Commission, setting up of, 113-114

Employed mothers in India, study of, 129; and husband-wife relationship, 129

Endogamy, study in Iran, 210

Esfahan *Shahrestan* in Iran, 227

Europeanization, meaning of, 321

Extended family, definition of, 173

Family, definition of, 1-2, 219

Family classification, 221-222

Family protection Law (1960), (Iran), 214, 225

Family-society relationship, dimensions of, 3-4, 13

Filipino Child, interactions of norms of conduct, 356, 358

Filipino-European marriages, 346

Filipino Family and kinship system, affinity principle, 349-350; American colonization, 347; an age-based hierarchy of authority, 356-359; analysis of, 417-418;

child-rearing practices, 359; Christian ritual system in, 352-353; Christian and non-Christian marriages, 348; class differences, 355-356; consanguinity principle, 348-359; divorce, 366-367; economic and social survey of, 355; endogamy practice among non-Christian groups, 369-370; factors which determine the location of newly married couples' residence, 371-372; food feeding ceremony, 353; future of, 372-373; husband-wife relationship, 361-364; Japanese occupation of, 347; Manila district survey of, 354; mate selection, 367-369; non-Christian and Muslim marriage, 364-365; non-nuclear family, 353-356; norms governing a child's interaction, 357; norms of respect and obedience, 356-)57; parent-child interaction, 357-358; ritual system, 351-352; rural-urban differences, 356; sibbling interaction, 359-360; sources of documentation of various aspects of, 345; Spanish political and cultural subjugation on, 347; structural features of, 347-348; study of, 344-345, 356; study on the lower class in Cebu, 350-351; traditional respect for age, 357; types of, 354; urban settings, 355

Filipino marriage, 350; age of, 367; dowry, 367-369; customs of, 364-367; divorce among, 367-368; endogamy among non-Christian groups, 360-370; inter-marriages, 369; patterns of, 369-370

Filipino Muslim marriage, 364-365; divorce, 366

Filipino women, characteristics of, 363-364; rights of 362; study of, 362-363

Filipinos, heterogenous people, 345

Footbinding, (China) practice of,

245, 253, 253n; legislation against and end of, 257

Great Leap Forward (China), 262, 268

Hindu Adoption and Maintenance Bill of 1956 (India), 117

Hindu Law, 70

Hindu Marriage Act of 1955 (India), 117

Hindu Marriage Disabilities Removal Act of 1946 (India), 113

Hindu Succession Act of 1956 (India), 117

Hsiao-tao, doctrine of, 257

India, agriculture in, 71; area of, 70; average diet of, 148; background of, 70; birth rate, 148; Buddhism and Zorastrianism, population of, 71; death rate, 148; fertility rate, 134-135, 148; location of, 70; population of, 148; political sphere of, 71; racial differences, 71; religions in, 71; social place in the world, 71; social structure of, 71

Indian educated women, change in the attitude of, 119; two roles of, 120

Indian family, analysis of, 413-414; birth rate decline of, 133-135; divorce causes, 110, 130; effects of modernization on, 80-84; example of Rajput family and socialization process of, 75-76; father-child relations, 75; factors of mate selection, 78-80; father's role, 75; male control over, 133; mixture of tradition and modernity in, 137-141; mother-child relations, 75-76; myths about, 81; norms of relationship, 133-134; pattern of husband-wife relatinship, 127-

129; preference for nuclear family, 132-133; Rajput child-rearing process, 75-76; sex relations in, 129; size of, 134-135; structural changes in, 141; types of, 131-132

Indian family planning programme, 134, 148-149; birth control methods, 151-152; annual national budget for, 149; motorized clinics, introduction of, 149; number of IUD insertions, 151; philosophical aspects of, 149-150; schools for auxiliary nurse midwives, 150; vasectomy campaign, 151; *v.* economic development, 162-163

Indian female education, efforts for, 113; neglect of, 110-111

Indian joint family, caste and, 73-74; change in, 132; difficulties experienced by women in, 133; eldest male control over, 70; factors conducive to the decline of, 83; modern women attitude towards, 139-140; nature of, 70-74; opposition to, 132-133; pattern, 70; socio-economic differences, 73; socialization process of, 74-75

Indian marriage, concept of, 121-122; age of, 125-126, 135; and mate selection, 123-125; arranged, 76, 79-80, 124; child marriage, practice of, 78; expectations from, 122-123; factors of mate selection, 78-80; group marriage, 138-139; love marriage, 125; necessity of and motivation for, 122; style of ceremony, 127; trial marriage, 139; type of, 123

Indian married woman, changing role of, 129; fertility rate declines among, 135

Indian Muslims, and abortion issue, 161; and attitude towards family planning, 149

Indian nuclear families, married women, role in, 129

Indian widows, ill-treatment with, 111; status of, 110

Indin women, arranged marriage, 110; as legislators, 115; attitude towards mate selection, 138; attitude towards monogamy, 138-139; attitude towards sex, 136-137; attitude towards family pattern, 139; attitude towards divorce, 139; attitude towards group marriage and trial marriage, 138-139; attitude towards marriage, 136-137; changes in, 120-121; changing roles of, 84-85; co-existence of tradition and modernity, 137-141; education of, 110; employment statistics, 118-119; gap between theory and reality with regard to the status of, 135-137; decision-making power and interspouse communication among, 134-135; empirical view on the role and status of, 111-112; improved status of, 134; in education field, 116-117; in the legal sphere, 117-118; in political sphere, 116; in public life, 110; legal status of, 112-113, 131; political awakening among, 135; preference for marriage celebrated, 138; perspective of, 111, 136; political awakening and privileges to, 114-115; post-independence era, 115-116; position in the ancient times, 109-112; position in the 19th century, 112, 115; principle of emancipation, 112; equal rights, 135; reformative measures for, 112-115; right to divorce, 130; role in national movement, 110, 115; tendency towards neo-arranged marriage, 138

Indian women's employment, 113-114

Indian Women's Organizations, role of, 114-115

Individualism, concept of, 174

Industrial Revolution, rapid social change through, 2

Industrialization, impact of, 245, 278.

313, 390; universal phenomenon of, 246
Inheritance, problem of, 5
Institute of Social Studies and Research, Theran and family planning, survey, 227
Intercaste marriage in India, 88-89, 127; findings of, 88-91; age differentials in, 92; condemnation of, 112; professional and non-professional levels of, 91; rural-urban background of, 91-92, 94; importance and increase of, 95-96; analysis of, 96; limitations of, 97
Intermarriage in India, 96-97
Interprovince marriage in India, 127
Inter-racial marriages in India, 127
Inter-religious marriages in India, 127
Iran, development corps in, 225; economic and social development of, 209; educational and health programmes, 209; electoral law, 225; establishment of Literacy Corps and health corps, 225; family protection law of 1968, 228-229; geographical position of, 208; migration data of, 210; nationalization of forests, in, 225; per capita income of, 241; political stabilization in, 209; population growth of, 208-209, 227; private investment in, 209; Shism, 209; sources, of 208
Iranian census of 1966 and family planning survey, 227
Iranian family, analysis of, 240, 242, 415-416; authority patterns, 222-223; care of children and care of the elderly in, 239; ceremonies in, 236; changes in the mate selection, 22; changes and projections for the future of, 224-226; classification of rural, 221-222; diminishing of traditional function, 239; disintegration of, divorce causes, 228-237, 230-231; divorce laws, 217, 238, 241; divorce rates in, 228-229;

divorced males and females in the Ostans and Farmandarikols 232; future of, 237-242; laws of inheritance in, 236-237; management of joint income, 239; marital status of rural/urban areas by sex, 228-233; *mashateh* role and function, 210-211; mate selection through *khastegari*, 211-212, 238; *mehr*, 238; norms related to mate selection, 212-213; nuclear groups and kinship groups in, 221-222; polygamy practice and disappearance of, 214-241; power elite impact on, 225; sex age characteristics, 217; *Shirbaha* custom, 212; socialization of, 223-224; structure of, 218; study of endogamy, 210; types of housing unity, 218-219; types of mate selection, 210-212; types of private households, 219-220; typology of, 210-211; women's role, 224-225
Iranian family planning, 227-228, 239
Iranian marriage, arusi ceremony, 215-216; changes in, 225; intermarriages in, 216; legal age for, 217; *mahreih* role, 215; monogamy and polygamy, 214; new laws on, 214-215; norms of, 215-218; patterns of, 241; trend in, 238; wedding ceremony in, 215; types of, 213-215; differences between *Sigheh* and permanent, 213-214
Iranian power elite and intelligentia, impact of, 225
Iranian women, cultural position of, 241; divorce right to, 225, 228-230; education, emphasis on, 224; increase of, 226; in educational field, 238; in labour force, 238; in political sphere, 225; inheritance rights, 236-237; new divorce laws for, 226; power of, 238; rights of, 241; rights during the pre-Islamic period, 222; role of, 224; socialization patterns, study of, 223

Iranian womanhood, 232-235
Iranian youth, role of, 226

Japan, contribution of both Eastern and Western cultures on, 387; cultural climate of, 382; first industrialized country in Asia, 381; gross domestic product in, 382; history of, 381; industrial activity compared with USA, 382; Meiji Restoration in, 381; national income of, 382; political profile of, 382; population engaged in agriculture, 382; religious climate of, 382; standard of living, 382; trade unionism in, 10; youth movement, 12
Japanese civil law, 304, 307-308
Japanese family, agrarian and non-agrarian data on, 384-385; analysis of, 407-408, 418-419; anticipated size of, 405; causes of changes, 390-399; child-rearing practices, 387-390; collateral relations of, 389-390; composition of, 386; consequences of change in a society, 398-399; direction of change, 391; further indications of, 405-406; husband's participation, 396; lineal, 383-384; mate selection, 393-394; nuclear family process of, 384-385; parent-child ties, 392-393, 396-398; parental permissiveness in child's decision making, 398; reasons for divorce, 394-396; size of, 385; stem family, 384; types of 383-385, 391
Japanese family planning, analysis of 399-401
Japanese marriage and divorce, 386-388; attitude of males towards arranged marriage survey of, 393-394; intermarriages, 401-403; number of intermarriages, 404; selection of partner statistics, 403
Japanese society, profile of, 381

Japanese women, role and status of, 389
Jati system in India, multitude of, 71; social norms, 71; rituals of, 71; temple visit restrictions, 71
Joint family, definition of, 173

Ka, meaning of, 302
Kajok, term as, 302
Khanevadesh (Iran), term, 218
Khastegari (Iran), meaning and mate selection through, 211
Korea, changes in, 278; *coupd'etat* in 1961, 286; crime rate in, 313; cultural heritage of, 277; drug and alcohol usage, 279; elections in, 285; geography and history of, 281-286; geographic, economic and strategic importance of, 277; industrialization and urbanization impact on, 278, 313; Japanese colonization of, 284-285, and end of, 285; juvenile runaways, 313; Koryo dynasty rule in, 283; less developed in terms of industrialization, 277-278; per capita income of, 325; population of, 281, 311-312, 325; Republic of, 307; contribution of, 307-308; Rhee administration, 285-286; Yi dynasty in, 283-284; Western education's contribution to, 278
Korean Behavioral Science Research Institute of Korea and birth control, 311-312
Korean civil law, 303, 306, 308
Korean family, analysis of, 313-318, 416-417; and American family, compared, 335-340; attitudes regarding contraception and modernization, 325-335; attitude towards morality, 327-328; birth control system in, 310-312; child-rearing methods, 280; clan role, 280-281; collective suicide, 279; Confucian techings, impact on, 288, 292; continuity and child birth

importance in, 286-288; current trends and the future directions of, 310-313; customs, 328-329; divorce, 279, 308, 330; during the Japanese occupation of, 1910-45, 302-307; during Koryo dynasty, 292; during Yi dynasty, 292-298, 303-305; development stages of, 295-298; expectancy of life, 326; father's responsibility with regard to children, 294-295; findings of, 335-336; historical background of, 278-279; housing, 326; illiteracy rate among, 327; in obscurity, 289-292; juvenile delinquency and crime rates, 279; marital issue in, 279; mate selection system, 279; modern, 280; monogamy in, 279; number of households old by type and membership, 310-311; patriarchal principle, 278; political, attitudes, 328; population data, 311; property succession, 309; religious forces in, 326-327; rituals, 312; sections of, 281; semi-communal family-clan system, 278; since 1945, 307-310; size of, 310; structure of, 297-281; western culture impact on, 280

Korean family kinship, terminology of 298-300

Korean family planning, analysis of 330-335, 351-352

Koranic law, 239

Korean marriage, 330; and the new democratic constitution, 308; ceremony of, 329; child marriage age, 300-302; concept of love, 278-279, 286-288; inter-marriage practice, 278; law in relation to dissolution of, 308; legal age during Yi dynasty, 306; plural during Yi dynasty, 307; survey of, 312-313

Korean women, status of, 313; low status of, 329-330

Kindred, account of, 24-27; definition of, 25; *see also* Thai rural family

Kumpadre system in Filipino, 351-352; *see also* Filipino family.

Land reforms, in China, 260
Local Fund Committee 1870, establishment of, 113

Mahrieh, custom in Iran, 212-213; *see also* Iran family

Mao Tse-tung and Cultural Revolution in China, 266

Mashateh (Iran), replacement of, 210-211; role of, 210

Masturbation in Afghanistan, denial of, 63

Matrimonial cases disputes in China, statistics of, 260-261

Medical Termination of Pregnancy Act of 1971 (India), 117, 152

Medical Termination of Pregnancy Bill (India), 152-153

Mitakshara, and common ownership property in India, 70

Modern Asian family, child-rearing practices in, 11; division of labour in, 10; economic concept in, 9-10; economic opportunities, 11; level of personal income, increase of, 11; low birth and death rates in, 11; model of, 9; mother-child interaction, 11; principle of romantic love in, 14; political system of, 11-12; power of youth enhancing of, 12-13; value of systems, 13; youth discontent in, 12

Modern Asian society, economy of, 9-10; model of, 9; principle of inheritance in, 10; principle of elite rule, 14; system of value, 13; young people's role, 12-13

Modern society, definition of, 2; *v.* traditional, 2

Modernization, concept of, 169-170; definition of, 321-322; Lerner's analysis on, 321-322; social aspect

of, 321; vs religion, 171-172; *v.* traditional, 204
Muslim societies, and purdah system,
178-180; divorce in, 201-202; low
rate of participation of women in
labour forces, 184; polygamous
marriages in, 201; role of *dai* in,
181-182

National Council of Women, role of,
114
National Enlightenment Campaign
(Korea) and family planning
program, 332
National Sample Survey and fertility
rate in India, 134-135
North China, survey of, 249-250

Ostan and Farmandarikols of Iran,
divorced males and famales, 232
Overpopulation, problem of, 163

Pakistan educational system, role of
182-183; expenditure on, 183
Pakistani family, agents for change,
190-192; analysis of, 202-204, 414-
415; *biraderi*, role of, 173-177;
change in purdah system, 202;
extended family in, 173; formation
of, 194-200; labour force, 177, 202;
modernization and social change
in, 189-190, 201; purdah practice
of, 178-180, 196; role of *dai* in,
181-182; sex ratio 177; social
structure of, 172-177; socialization
process in, 178
Pakistan family planning, 200-201
Pakistani marriage system, age of,
200; *mehr* system in, 197-199
Pakistani women, franchise rights,
182; role in elections, 182; in the
labour force, 184; role in education,
182-183; status of, 202-203;
Pakistan women's Voluntary service,
192

Pativrata, ideal of, 128
Perpetual tutelage for women, theory
of, 110
Philippine marriage laws, analysis of,
364-365
Philippine Civil Code, 365-366
Philippine society, study of, 344
Philippines, area of, 346; geographical
position of, 345-346; Indonesian-
Malayan group in, 346; literature
on social organization, 347; racial-
ethnic diversity, 346; topography
of, 346; *see also* Filipino family
Pill scale, attitude towards, 323
Politicization, impact of, 278
Population Council in the United
States, aid to Iran, 227; role of,
40
Property Act of 1874 (India), 112
Purdah, 111; changes in 202; demand
for the removal of, 180-181; literal
interpretation of, 178-179; problem of, 178; practice of, 179;
social change in, 180; status of
women in, 178; *see also* Pakistan
family
Pushtan society, manifestations of
modernization in, 61-62; peace of
family in, 62; study of, 61

Red Guards of China, role of, 12
Regulations governing marriage
registration (China), passing of,
259
Remarrige in India, 131; approval
of, 131; change in the attitude
towards, 131; position in the traditional family, 131; widening of,
130
Roman Catholic, member-nations,
role of, 150

Sati Abolition Act of 1829 (India),
112
Sati practice in India, 112; decline
of, 110-111

Sattapadi, formula in India, 128
Shah of Iran, and family planning programmes, 227; influence of, 241
Shanghai, survey of, 249-250; sample of class families in, 250
Shirbaha (Iran), meaning of, 212; prevalance of, 212; *see also* Dowry and Iran family
Sigheh (Iran), concept of, 213-214; *see also* Iranian marriage
Special Marriage Act of 1954 (India), 117
Socialization, issues related to, 13-14
Streedhana, scope of, 112
Suppression of Immoral Traffic in Women and Girls Act of 1956, 117

Thai child, changes in, 42; characteristics of idea daughters, 34; compensation to, 36; compulsory education to, 36; effects of, 36; ideal sons characteristics of, 33-34; minimal teaching about sexuality, 35-36; physical punishment to, 35-36; socialization of, 33-36, 44; teaching life on farm to, 36
Thai culture, 31-32, 38; social change in, 40-41
Thai family planning, expenditure on, 40; factor in the rapid progress of, 40; government policy on, 39-40; progress in, 44
Thai kinship, structure of, 30
Thai landless rural families, increase of, 41-42; pattern of, 42
Thai marriages, 20-21; and mate selection, 27-29; causes of separations and dissolutions of, 36-37; pattern of, 37; pattern of, 43-44; registered, 37; registration of, 29
Thai physicians and role in family planning, 40
Thai polygamy, phenomenon of, 24-25, 43
Thai rural family, account of Kindred,

25-26, 42, 44; abult roles, 31-32, 43-44; analysis of, 411-412; causes of separation and marriage dissolution, 36-37; changes in child-rearing practices, 42; extended family analysis of, 24, 43; English language use in, 38; husband-wife relationship, 31; income, consumption and size of, 22-23; male-female equality, 44; male-famale distinction in religious affairs, 31; modernization of, 40-41; nuclear, 23, 43; newly married couples life pattern, 29-30; other family systems, 24; out-migration of villagers, 41; parent-child relations, 33, 44; respect to older persons, 32-33; rice farming and village labour exchange, 20-21; rural social organization of, 19-20; social change in, 40; socialization of child in, 33-36; types of systems, 21-25; typology of, 43; westernization impact on, 38, 43
Thai rural population, growth of, 41
Thai society, characteristics of, 18-19; social kinder group, 43; organization of, 19-20
Thai universities, European and North American college degrees, compared, 138; study by, 18
Thai village school, role of, 36
Thai villages, administration of, 19; types of, 19; vary in size, 19
Thai youth and marriage pattern, 43-44
Thai women, role of, 31-32
Thailand, absentee ownership in, 20, 41; background of, 16-18; commercialization of agriculture in, 41; *coupd'etat* in, 17; ethnic background and local dialect, 17; economy of, 17; expansion of urban job market, 41; history of political independence of, 17; increased reliance on money as medium of exchange, 41; landless

in, 20; location of, 16; modernization process in, 17; population of,
16; religion of, 17-18; rural
population of, 17
Thailand's married women, use of
contraceptive by, 39-40
Third World countries and overpopulation problem, 163
Traditional and modern Asian family
compared, 13; child-socialization
practices, 7; control of adults over
young people in, 8; ecological
dimension of, 7; division of labour
within, 6-7; limitation of, 6; meaning, of 7; restriction of young
people in, 8
Traditional society, definition of, 2;
discussion on, 4-6; *v.* modern, 2;
political system of, 7
Transportation and communication,
impact of, 41

Underdeveloped, concept of, 169
University of Teheran, and family
planning survey, 227; and mate
selection survey, 212
USA, average diet in, 148; death
rate in, 148; fertility rate in, 148;
gross domestic product of, 382;

industrial activity in, 382; national income of, 382
US Agency for International
Development and family planning
program in Thailand, 40
Urbanization, impact of, 60, 226,
278, 313, 390; process of, 246

Western culture, impact of, 245
Western educated women study of
marriage, 124
Western nuclear families, process of
industrialization and urbanization
in, 246
Westernization, impact of, 278
Widow Remarriage Act of 1856
(India), 112
Woods despatch of 1854 on education,
113
Women's Indian Association, role
of, 114
World Health Organization, role of,
150

Young Women's Christian Association, role of, 114
Youth movement in politics, 12-13

For Product Safety Concerns and Information please contact our EU
representative GPSR@taylorandfrancis.com
Taylor & Francis Verlag GmbH, Kaufingerstraße 24, 80331 München, Germany

www.ingramcontent.com/pod-product-compliance
Lightning Source LLC
Chambersburg PA
CBHW050557270326
41926CB00012B/2085

9 7 8 1 0 3 2 5 3 9 4 6 1